New Releases from IRM Press

- **Multimedia and Interactive Digital TV: Managing the Opportunities Created by Digital Convergence**/Margherita Pagani
  ISBN: 1-931777-38-1; eISBN: 1-931777-54-3 / US$59.95 / © 2003
- **Virtual Education: Cases in Learning & Teaching Technologies**/ Fawzi Albalooshi (Ed.), ISBN: 1-931777-39-X; eISBN: 1-931777-55-1 / US$59.95 / © 2003
- **Managing IT in Government, Business & Communities**/Gerry Gingrich (Ed.)
  ISBN: 1-931777-40-3; eISBN: 1-931777-56-X / US$59.95 / © 2003
- **Information Management: Support Systems & Multimedia Technology**/ George Ditsa (Ed.), ISBN: 1-931777-41-1; eISBN: 1-931777-57-8 / US$59.95 / © 2003
- **Managing Globally with Information Technology**/Sherif Kamel (Ed.)
  ISBN: 42-X; eISBN: 1-931777-58-6 / US$59.95 / © 2003
- **Current Security Management & Ethical Issues of Information Technology**/Rasool Azari (Ed.), ISBN: 1-931777-43-8; eISBN: 1-931777-59-4 / US$59.95 / © 2003
- **UML and the Unified Process**/Liliana Favre (Ed.)
  ISBN: 1-931777-44-6; eISBN: 1-931777-60-8 / US$59.95 / © 2003
- **Business Strategies for Information Technology Management**/Kalle Kangas (Ed.)
  ISBN: 1-931777-45-4; eISBN: 1-931777-61-6 / US$59.95 / © 2003
- **Managing E-Commerce and Mobile Computing Technologies**/Julie Mariga (Ed.)
  ISBN: 1-931777-46-2; eISBN: 1-931777-62-4 / US$59.95 / © 2003
- **Effective Databases for Text & Document Management**/Shirley A. Becker (Ed.)
  ISBN: 1-931777-47-0; eISBN: 1-931777-63-2 / US$59.95 / © 2003
- **Technologies & Methodologies for Evaluating Information Technology in Business**/ Charles K. Davis (Ed.), ISBN: 1-931777-48-9; eISBN: 1-931777-64-0 / US$59.95 / © 2003
- **ERP & Data Warehousing in Organizations: Issues and Challenges**/Gerald Grant (Ed.), ISBN: 1-931777-49-7; eISBN: 1-931777-65-9 / US$59.95 / © 2003
- **Practicing Software Engineering in the 21st Century**/Joan Peckham (Ed.)
  ISBN: 1-931777-50-0; eISBN: 1-931777-66-7 / US$59.95 / © 2003
- **Knowledge Management: Current Issues and Challenges**/Elayne Coakes (Ed.)
  ISBN: 1-931777-51-9; eISBN: 1-931777-67-5 / US$59.95 / © 2003
- **Computing Information Technology: The Human Side**/Steven Gordon (Ed.)
  ISBN: 1-931777-52-7; eISBN: 1-931777-68-3 / US$59.95 / © 2003
- **Current Issues in IT Education**/Tanya McGill (Ed.)
  ISBN: 1-931777-53-5; eISBN: 1-931777-69-1 / US$59.95 / © 2003

Excellent additions to your institution's library!
Recommend these titles to your Librarian!

To receive a copy of the IRM Press catalog, please contact
(toll free) 1/800-345-4332, fax 1/717-533-8661,
or visit the IRM Press Online Bookstore at: [http://www.irm-press.com]!

Note: All IRM Press books are also available as ebooks on netlibrary.com as well as other ebook sources. Contact Ms. Carrie Stull Skovrinskie at [cstull@idea-group.com] to receive a complete list of sources where you can obtain ebook information or IRM Press titles.

Managing Globally with Information Technology

Table of Contents

Preface

Organizations around the world are increasingly focusing on managing their organizational and business transactions using advanced information and communication technology (Haeckel and Nolan, 1999). With the advent of the Internet and the World Wide Web, such transactions have extended beyond the constraints of time and distance to reach all corners of the globe. Respectively, to succeed in the global marketplace, organizations must reposition themselves to tap the sources of sustainable growth and to exploit the vast new opportunities enabled. Information is one of the primary tools that are becoming a vital focus. Information is the way people in business express, represent, communicate and share their knowledge with others to accomplish their activities and achieved business objectives (Marchand, 2000). The world is changing fast and the role of information and communication technology is increasingly having more of an impact on every sector as well as on the society at large. Such technologies are creating business value with information with its related tools and techniques (Marchand, 2000). There is no doubt that information is currently used as a very effective and rewarding competitive tool. Information technology helps creating new reality, adding value to customers, reducing costs and minimizing risks. Therefore, management across different organizational levels should be capable to turnaround their strategies to adapt the role of information and information technology in building an organizational competitive advantage. It is the era of the new organization (Drucker, 1998). As today's businesses undergo change, information and communication technology will be the critical foundation during the evolution of such new form of organization and this will be reflected in the structure, size, skills, and operating performance of every organization among other elements. It will be up to management levels to adapt their organizations and bring them to the age of the information-based organization of the 21st century.

The future of the new organization, to be able to adapt to the themes of globalization, will be affected by a number of factors. It will also be reshaped by fierce global competition, changing markets and technological breakthroughs leading to the emergence of distinct characteristics including an information and knowledge-based environment that is decentralized though densely linked through information and communication technology. The environment is also rapidly adaptable and extremely agile, creative, and collaborative with an environment — based on a team structure, staffed with a variety of knowledge workers and based on self-controlling and strong and shared operating principles (Champy and Nohria, 1998). The management of the organization will require the professional development and management of information networks to be able to globally compete and penetrate new markets and adapt to changing needs across the globe (Charan, 1998).

This book, through its 20 different chapters, provides a variety of issues and concepts that relate to the changing nature of the organization and how this is affecting competition and management practices when it comes to handling innovative and changing information and communication technology on a global scale. The book contributes with a number of case studies and an analysis of a variety of projects and practices in different parts of the world in an attempt to learn from a set of experiences how societies and organizations are managing globally with information and communication technology (Kamel, 2001a).

The book includes a variety of vital issues to the world of management and the application of information and communication technology in managing organizations, resources and businesses in a global marketplace. This includes information infrastructure requirements, their role and implications on the development of organizations in specific and on the society at large and the re-engineering process required to adopt and adapt the organization to survive, grow and compete in the global economy, the role of information systems as a strategic resource that could be used for the improvement of management practices and the need to adapt the organizational culture to fit the needs of the proper information systems implementation, the changing nature of information systems development in the age of the digital economy and the variances in the structure and form of the information technology industry across different parts of the world, as well as the growing trends of the digital divide and its implications on the development of the information technology industry as well as its contribution in the development of many societies across the world and the possible challenges and opportunities especially in developing nations where the usage of information and communication technology varies according to information dissemination and knowledge acquisition and management and finally the migration to the digital economy and the trends of the electronic business environment with its different components, needs and requirements and the power that can enable small- and medium-sized enterprises as well as developing countries to grow and compete on equal grounds with multinationals and developed nations in the global marketplace and the role of information technology managers on the changing role of organizations and the different innovative roles of information and communication technology and their implications on the development of individuals, organizations, industries, societies and nations. One of the building blocks in that domain is the development of human resources capable to compete and adapt to the changing nature of the environment (Kamel, 2001b).

With the developments of information and communication technology taking place worldwide and affecting different organizational, managerial and industrial levels, the interfaces between corporations and markets, the clear separation between the internal and external disappear (Wigand et al., 1997a). Reflecting the fact to being able to manage on a global scale and at the same time localize such management style to fit the needs and the purpose of the business and that of the organization. This is creating new forms of coordination such as network organizations, cooperative ventures, virtual organizations that are all becoming increasingly popular. Such developments and change in the organizational form and structure represent the reactions to new market and competitive situations and of new information and communication technologies (Wigand et al., 1997a).

It is fair to say that for years to come, innovative information and communication technologies will lead to a fundamental change in the exogenous and endogenous parameters of entrepreneurial decisions at various organizational levels and across different sectors and industries (Wigand et al., 1997a). Technology and its innovations will also bring more knowledge and comprehension about the market, not just the local market and the local forces, but also at regional and international levels. Managing globally, using information and communication technology is a newcomer that contributes to globalization and its potentials to enable information distribution across national boundaries irrespective of time or distance (Wigand et al., 1997b). Mobility, expansion, diversity, cross-border business development, real-time and online digital transactions are a few terms and directions that represent part of the new digital economy that information and communication technology are very much helping to build and to make it the way to manage, compete and grow as we embark on the 21st century with the motto to succeed is speed, knowledge and the ability to adapt to change.

ORGANIZATION OF THE BOOK

The book is organized into 20 chapters. A brief description of each of the chapters follows:

Chapter 1 explores information technology issues with respect to an organization's transition towards globalization with a focus on the main transitional elements, such as global information technology infrastructure, global business applications, global telecommunication network, and data/information systems improvement as well as a proposition of future research directions to incorporate organizational scopes in the global information technology transition framework.

Chapter 2 explains the need for a new dimension in the evaluation of the benefits of information technology where technology has impact on the broader society rather than just on the organization that implements it. The chapter demonstrates the peculiarities and constraints on public sector use of e-marketplaces through the provision of an evaluation framework that can be used by public sector organizations when examining the adoption and evaluation of e-marketplace procurement that emphasizes the experimental nature of many e-commerce related projects.

Chapter 3 focuses on the development of information systems as strategic resources in the Western world and how the transfer of such management practice to a different cultural environment generates new challenges such as the experience of a Pacific Basin public institution. The chapter explains that the value of the investment in information resources is judged not only on technical merits, but also on the ability of the organization to properly address the cultural and organizational issues related to information usage.

Chapter 4 demonstrates the interaction between new technologies and the process of cultural adoption resulting in convergence with cultures becoming more similar as a result, or divergence when cultures adopt technology in different ways that maintain or even further accentuate their differences. The chapter provides an analysis of several countries' full-service national web portals that offer a variety of services and show evidence of both trends.

Chapter 5 reflects on the results of a comprehensive study of women in the South African information technology industry, while demonstrating the factors affecting the retention of women in the industry and providing valuable insights that can be used by companies world-wide to enhance employment policies as well as recruitment and retention strategies aimed at women in information technology.

Chapter 6 focuses on software systems that tend to be virtual "peer-to-peer" networks of permanent autonomous services called networks' software confederation (SWC), which is orthogonal to the paradigm of the object-oriented methodology. It describes their architecture in global and very large information systems providing many software engineering advantages like incremental development, openness, modifiability, and maintainability. The chapter demonstrates how SWC supports the trend of large enterprises or modern states to be decentralized, dynamic, and adapt to the needs of globalization especially in supporting decentralization.

Chapter 7 investigates the issues related to the global transition of an enterprise through the application of information technology and information systems. The chapter starts with discussing the issues that are critical to successful transition of an enterprise towards trans-border business operations using information systems leading to the expected outcome that is a global organization that would not be limited to geographical and time zone barriers and would not be restricted by cultural differences. The global transition issues covered include embracing business information systems management, information technology management, people management, end user management, and culture.

Chapter 8 presents the concept of the digital divide being a vital issue in today's development efforts of international and non-governmental organizations and developing countries. The chapter shows that the digital divide do not only include access to new information and communication technology such as the Internet, but also access to the knowledge of how to use such technologies for economic development. The chapter outlines the business model framework and the business model handbook that can help develop a knowledgeable class of e-entrepreneurs that are able to use ICT and to detect the opportunities of the Internet era.

Chapter 9 focuses on knowledge management defined as the ability to create and retain greater value from core business competencies and the role played by information technology as an enabler of knowledge management in regions such as sub-Saharan Africa. The chapter demonstrates how information technology outsourcing could be a better approach to information technology management for an organization considering knowledge management. The chapter presents the outcome of an empirical research of a case organization where information technology outsourcing seems to contribute to a high performance in knowledge management efforts.

Chapter 10 covers the issue of the needs of developing countries with special needs for information and communication so that they are not left behind with the waves of globalization and the need to close the gap between the information rich and information poor. The chapter gives an account of some development problems and current initiatives. It also describes ways that advancing technology can be manipulated by the developing world to gain social advantage through the introduction of the term *leapfrog effect*. This term is used to explain how advancement can be made in a revolutionary fashion and not incrementally, while focusing on experiences in Papua, New Guinea and its possible applicability to many other developing nations.

Chapter 11 proposes that all business strategies should be harmonized into a single strategy rather than attempting to align information technology strategy with business strategy. It focuses on two hypotheses: firstly, that information technology strategy is not widely aligned with business strategy; and secondly, that information technology is still thought of as something different in businesses.

Chapter 12 demonstrates how developing countries were using information and communication technologies in the management of their business and administrative affairs to improve efficiency and effectiveness and how they innovated the establishment of information services sectors. Some developing countries that have moved from the initial provision of data entry services, as participants in the global software outsourcing movement, have also embarked on the development of software for export. These countries were faced with many challenges ranging from a lack of skilled personnel to competition in a fierce market-place. The chapter examines the participation of two small Caribbean countries and describes their education and training initiatives and other policy approaches.

Chapter 13 demonstrates how small- to medium-sized enterprises contribute significantly to the national economies and to the employment levels of different countries and represent a viable source for inventions and innovations especially with the emergence of electronic commerce that can provide different opportunities to the small business sector to overcome its inadequacies. The chapter attempts to depict an agenda for electronic commerce success in small- and medium-sized enterprises made up of 10 influencing factors and trying to better understand the factors influencing electronic commerce success in small- and medium-sized enterprises.

Chapter 14 presents the key factors affecting electronic business such as the law, infrastructure, tax, payment processes, consumers, suppliers, education and business culture. The chapter reveals the outcome of a survey of Thai business executives. It confirms that culture, society, organizational infrastructure and English literacy were found to be internal and external barriers to providing a foundation for future research on developing a holistic framework to guide business in Thailand and other countries; to successfully implement the new generation of e-business activities.

Chapter 15 focuses on the power and challenges of e-business in enhancing competitive advantage in developing countries' industries and reports some results of a survey in the Asian auto-industry. The chapter demonstrates that as many web-based businesses are learning, the real value of e-business comes not in the form of sales but in removing inefficiencies in traditional business models. That is reflected in the fact that most auto manufacturers in Asia use e-business only for internal administration; companies need a clearly planned vision, starting with basic solutions. From there, the strategy will evolve to solutions in wider marketplaces.

Chapter 16 shows that information and communication technology is a growing worldwide industry, penetrating all sectors, and services. Therefore, organizations are formulating different formulas and mechanisms to provide a competitive and challenging working environment to attract the best human resources around the globe to join their infrastructure build-up in terms of humanware. The chapter focuses on Egypt, which has been heavily investing in building its information and communication technology infrastructure with a focus on human resources. However, many organizations are continuously challenged to keep their key human resources due to emerging opportunities at local, regional and international levels. This chapter presents findings of research conducted to understand the overall level of job satisfaction among employees in the ICT sector in Egypt, at identifying major factors that affect their satisfaction and highlighting the driving forces leading to the brain drain of skilled ICT professionals to jobs overseas.

Chapter 17 draws on a survey of CEO and IT managers in local authorities in Egypt to explain the key factors affecting their use of DSS in making strategic decisions. The chapter proposes and tests a Structural Equation Model (SEM) that extends the generally accepted Technology Acceptance Model to assess relationships between an extensive range of constructs and their relation with DSS usage via Perceived Ease of Use and Perceived Usefulness. The SEM approach has enabled the development of a framework that will support a sustainable approach towards the adoption and use of DSS in developing Middle Eastern countries.

Chapter 18 analyzes the perception of managers on the efficiency, access importance, and use as a communication tool, benefits and difficulties of Internet use in Brazilian hotels and showing significant difference on the perception of managers on the impact of Internet use in hotels, depending on variables such as age, experience and hotel standards.

Chapter 19 focuses on applying the best practices in information technology project management in Brazil using the Capability Maturity Model, the Project Management Maturity Model, the Project Management Body of Knowledge and Quality Systems for software. The chapter presents information technology project cases in Brazilian companies based on multiple cases financial services, telecommunications and building materials companies.

Chapter 20 covers Enterprise Resource Planning systems designed to integrate various functions and processes; they are used by organizations as the first-level transaction processing systems in their information architecture. They focus on Asian companies and the developing world, which confront issues that are significantly different from those in the developed world because of differences in the sophistication of information technology use and the cultural and social contexts.

REFERENCES

Champy, J. & Nohria, N. (eds.)(1998). *Introduction in Fast Forward.* Boston, MA: Harvard Business School Press.

Charan, R. (1998). *How Networks Reshape Organizations – For Results in Fast Forward.* J. Champy & N. Nohria (Eds.), Boston, MA: Harvard Business School Press.

Drucker, P. (1998). *The Coming of the New Organization in Fast Forward. J.* Champy & N. Nohria (Eds.), Boston, MA: Harvard Business School Press.

Kamel, S. (2001a). The information society in Egypt. In G. Nulens, N. Hafkin, L. Van Audehove & B. Cammaerts (Eds.), *The digital divide in developing countries: Towards an information society in Africa.* Brussels: Brussels University Press, (pp. 299-313).

Kamel, S. (2001b). Virtual learning networks in higher education: The case of Egypt's regional IT institute. *Journal of Global Information Management, 8*, 3, (July-September) Special Issue on Global Knowledge Management in e-Economy.

Marchand, D. (ed.)(2000). *Creating Business Value with Information in Competing with Information.* Chichester, UK: John Wiley and Sons.

Marchand, D. (ed.)(2000). *Why Information is the Responsibility of Every Manager in Competing with Information.* Chichester, UK: John Wiley and Sons.

Nolan, R.L. & Haeckel, S.H. (1999). Managing by wire. *Harvard Business Review on the Business Value of IT.* Boston, MA: Harvard Business School Publishing.

Wigand, R., Picot, A. & Reichwald, R. (1997a). Market dynamics and competition: The Fundamental Role of Information. *Information, Organization and Management. Expanding Markets and Corporate Boundaries.* Chichester, MA: John Wiley and Sons.

Wigand, R., Picot, A. & Reichwald, R. (1997b). The potential of information technology in developing the market-driven organization. *Information, Organization and Management. Expanding Markets and Corporate Boundaries.* Chichester, UK: John Wiley and Sons.

Acknowledgments

The editor would like to acknowledge the help of all involved in the collaboration and review process of the book, without whose support and assistance this project could not have been satisfactorily completed. Putting together a book of this magnitude requires a tremendous cooperation and assistance by everyone involved. Respectively, I would like to express my sincere gratitude to all the contributors of the book. A further special note of thanks goes also to all the staff at IRM Press whose contributions throughout the whole process from inception of the initial idea to final publication have been invaluable. In particular, I would like to thank Amanda Appicello who kept the project on schedule and to Mehdi Khosrow-Pour whose enthusiasm motivated me to initially accept his invitation to take on this project. I would also like to acknowledge most of the authors of the book chapters included in this book who also served as subject matter experts for chapters written by other authors. Thanks go to all those who provided constructive and comprehensive reviews. In closing, I wish to thank my family for their love and support throughout this project.

Sherif Kamel, PhD
Cairo, Egypt
September 2002

Chapter I

A Framework for an Organization's Transition to Globalization – Investigation of IT Issues

Yi-chen Lan
University of Western Sydney, Australia

ABSTRACT

This chapter explores information technology (IT) issues in regard to an organization's transition towards globalization. The challenges of IT dealing with transforming enterprises to globalized organizations require the identification, consolidation, and resolution of issues to support the organizations towards globalization. The chapter begins with identifying and classifying four major IT transition issues: global IT infrastructure, global business applications, global telecommunication network, and data/information systems improvement. It is then followed by detailed discussion of each issue with regards to its importance and relevance in global transformation. The chapter concludes by indicating a future research direction to incorporate organizational scopes (inter-organizational and intra-organizational) in the global IT transition framework.

INTRODUCTION

Rapid development of information technology (IT) has the capability of providing most organizations to conduct their business operations efficiently. It is even more significant for multinational corporations (MNCs). Undoubtedly, a well-designed global information system is a critical success factor for managing and operating the MNCs smoothly and effectively. In the past decade, researchers have identified a number of IT issues that relate to an organization's transition to globalization (Burn et al., 1993; Edberg et al., 2001; Nelson, 1996; Palvia et al., 1992; Sankar & Prabhakar, 1992; Watson et al., 1997). However, the challenges of information technology dealing with transforming enterprises to globalized organizations are not just identifying the IT issues, but consolidating and resolving these issues to support the organizations towards globalization. The intent of this chapter is to identify and classify the IT issues in globalization process, and develop a global transition framework based on these IT issues.

GLOBAL IT TRANSITION FRAMEWORK

Based on the review of the global IT literature and its issues, an organization's IT structure can be divided into four classes (Sankar & Prabhakar, 1992; Lan, 2002), and they are:
1.   *Global IT infrastructure*–refers to system hardware
2.   *Global business applications*–refers to systems software
3.   *Global telecommunication network*–refers to communication
4.   *Data/information systems improvement*–refers to data and information

In order to obtain in depth understanding of the global IT management issues, the following sections investigate each of these classes and explore the corresponding issues for the conceptual direction of global IT transition.

Global Information Technology Infrastructure

Global information technology infrastructure is made up of the equipment and facilities that support the global information systems. It can be classified in four categories:
1.   *Computer hardware*—includes workstations (desktop computers, terminals), mainframes, servers, digital cameras, printers, and scanners.
2.   *Network related facilities*—includes cables, modems, gateways, routers, adapters, bridges, converters, hubs, concentrators, repeaters, switches, transceivers, and multiplexers.
3.   *Backup equipment*—includes storage facilities such as tape and disk, and uninterrupted power supply (UPS) devices.
4.   *Mobile equipment*—includes notebook computers, personal digital assistants (PDAs), mobile phones and wireless facilities.

Global Business Applications

Global business applications refer to the agents, or instruments that make the business operation. These agents are principally business functional and personal software applications in the global business environment. Hence, effective management and utilization of these applications is critical to the construction and operation of global information systems. Furthermore, issues such as handling systems integration, maintaining software application availability, and applying systems standards are imperative to the successful implementation and management of global information systems. Thus they are further explored in the following sections.

Systems Integration

Systems do not operate in isolation. They are always interconnected to each other. When developing new global information systems, the organization must ensure that the designs and structures of the new systems are flexible enough to connect and integrate with the existing systems. The compelling reason to integrate the systems is that organizations need to continue to flourish in the constantly changing competitive business environment. The need for systems integration is also driven by new forms of businesses, such as transition of the organization's business from domestic context to global perspective. Systems integration allows organizations to expand their business operations and services.

In planning for systems integration, the scope and objectives should be clearly identified to ensure that new systems and equipment are able to work with the existing components. This can be achieved by applying Mische's (1998) four states of systems integration strategy, which are:

1. *Interconnectivity*—is the initial and the fundamental state in the systems integration. It requires all new and existing information system components and equipment to connect and work together. This includes the sharing of peripherals such as printers, scanners, and backup devices through network communications, the creation of gateways that allow different components to interact each other, and the development of interfaces that permit separate applications to communicate and even integrate into a single system.

2. *Interoperability*—means that all interconnected information system components and equipment should be able to function and interact with each other. For example, a new deployment of global inventory system should be designed to function and interoperate with the current regional or domestic inventory systems. The implementation of interoperability is carried out through the interconnected information technology facilities that are the information infrastructure of the organization. For most organizations, interoperability is considered as the key state of systems integration.

3. *Semantic consistency*—refers to the concern of consistency at data level. Once the information system components and equipment are interconnected and operational, organizational users are able to access systems and manipulate data (create, retrieve, modify, and delete) across business units around the world. For this reason, the implementation of global databases management is essential to prevent data duplication, redundancy, and instability.

4. *Convergent integration*—systems integration involves a lot more than the integration of the information system components, technology, and global database management. Convergent integration involves the amalgamation of components and technology with business processes, people, skills, and knowledge. In Ginige et al.'s (2001) "e-business transformation roadmap," convergence is also an imperative stage which involves the integration of information technology with both internal and external business processes. In addition to the above requirements in the convergent integration state, the convergence in global organization also incorporates the organizational structure and other business factors (Mische, 1998). Thus, the proposed convergence model for information systems in a global organization involves the consideration of eight components, namely organizational structure, information system components, data and database management, knowledge, skills, people, external business processes, and internal business processes. This is illustrated in Figure 1 and described on the following page.

Figure 1. Convergence model for information systems in the global organization

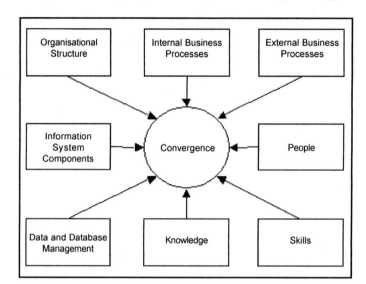

The proposed convergence model aims to provide global organizations with an overview of the integration of planning systems during the development of global information systems. Development of global information systems does not merely involve design and construction of software applications; it requires consideration of business factors and operations from a global perspective. The factors are business components that need to be identified and linked through a process towards the convergence state. To succeed in the development of integrated global information systems, it is imperative to recognize how these components are related and incorporated into information systems. By adopting the model, organizations are expected to develop an effective global information system that would carry out the global business operations as well as enhance the interconnection of dispersed business units around the world. The following points provide detailed descriptions of each component in the convergence model.

a) *Organizational structure*—refers to the management and strategic hierarchy of the business. Four types of multinational corporations include multinational, international, global, and transnational organizational structures (Bartlett & Ghoshal, 1998).

b) *Information system components*—include parts, modules, and components that are involved in the enterprise's global information systems such as IT infrastructure, business applications, and telecommunication networks mentioned in the earlier section.

c) *Data and database management*—data can be seen as one of the most valuable assets in any firms, and it is even more critical in global enterprises. By applying appropriate database management systems, enterprises are able to effective by manipulate and mange data from diverse business units globally.

d) *Knowledge*—through effective management of global database systems the collection of information from various sources can be transformed into invaluable knowledge that would provide senior executives rigorous supports in decision-making situations.

e)   *Skills*—refer to the competence and capability that employees are required to have to accomplish daily business operations.

f)   *People*—refer to staff members regardless of location.

g)   *External business processes*—contains business functions linking different enterprises. For example, supply chain management, customer relationship management, and supplier relationship management.

h)   *Internal business processes*—comprise high-level business functions within the enterprise such as management, finance, accounting, inventory, production, sales, and marketing.

Software Applications Availability

Software applications either can be purchased off-the-shelf, or can be written in-house. Many enterprises have adopted off-the-shelf software applications as the business tools that enable employees to carry out their business operations. For example, some of these applications include general office automation software such as word processors, spreadsheets, and project plan; special purpose applications like engineering and designing softwares. In a global organization, the availability of software applications in each business unit and subsidiary has a direct influence on the effectiveness of cross-border information sharing and communication, efficient performance of business operations and collaborative teamwork. For instance, if the organization has decided to use AutoCAD as the designing tool for their products, then it should be made available for all business units and subsidiaries that require to view, modify, and create designs.

Additionally, an alternative is provided by "component-based" technologies, wherein ready-made components are put together to form an application. These applications, when made available on the Internet, are able to provide information to employees, enabling them to become knowledge workers. Under certain conditions, and for some functionality, even potential clients can use software applications (for example, calculators for home loan or home content insurances).

Systems Standards

Systems standards are an important issue when dealing with the global information systems in terms of the development, operation, communication, and maintenance. Three levels of systems standards should be considered including at project level, organizational level, and industrial level.

1.   *Project level standards*—it is mainly dealing with the analysis, design and development of the new global information systems. In the analysis and design stage, business functions and operations are often presented in models. These models should be standardized to provide the convenience of communications between development teams, users, and managers. The solution is to introduce a unique modeling technique that is well presented and accepted by most of developers, business and industrial users. For example, the Unified Modeling Language (UML) is a modeling technique that fulfils the requirement. In the development phase as well, the development teams should focus on few standard programming languages. This would facilitate the tasks for the purposes of future integration and maintenance.

2.   *Organizational level*—the focus of standards at the organizational level is the business process. For a global organization to be efficient, one would expect that

multiple, dispersed business units carry out business processes in a similar manner. It would be very difficult to develop global information systems when a business process is implemented in different ways by different business units. Consequently, the organization must make sure each business process has a unique and standard procedure for any required business unit. In addition to the business processes, the systems operation and maintenance procedures should be standardized throughout the organization. These standards then apply to all projects within the organization.

3. *Industrial level*—this is based on quality evaluation of the organization's products and services. The implementation of global information systems should be incorporated into the organization's quality assurance policy and procedures to ensure the products and services are in a constant quality level. ISO (International Organization for Standardization) assurance system, for instance, is one of the well-known standards to enable organizations to consistently produce products and services that will meet the customer and regulatory requirements, and address customer satisfaction.

Global Telecommunication Network

The current telecommunication and networking infrastructure serves as the global organization's nervous system that interconnects the information systems of dispersed business units through the telecommunication and internetworking protocol called TCP/IP (see Figure 2). To maintain continuous and quality services of the networking systems, the global organization should be concerned about the availability of network bandwidth, national telecommunication services, and networking facilities and equipment as well as essential security strategies for both collection and distribution of business information.

Network Bandwidth

The network bandwidth continuous to be an issue for a global organization because of its limitation and delay of transmitting large-sized high-volume files across business units. Although the speed of data transmission has reached a certain degree of satisfaction such as instant e-mail delivery, the capability of delivering large-sized files in real-time mode is still unreliable.

Furthermore, the network bandwidth may also rely on the telecommunication services of individual nations. Depending on the level of ICT (information and communication technology) adoption, some nations have advanced telecommunication infrastructure and services (such as the availability of cable, ADSL or mobile communications) while others may provide elementary supports only (dial-up connection). For this reason, the network bandwidth issue should be taken into account when planning the global information systems development strategy.

Figure 2. Internetworking through TCP/IP protocol

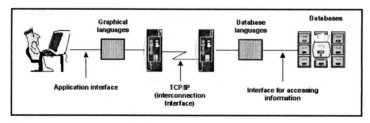

Telecommunication Availability

To make the effective use of information technology, the availability of connecting between business units in a global organization seems to be prominent than other domestic companies. Hence, all types of connection methods should be considered to provide the best performance of a global organization's information systems. Furthermore, availability of connections in today's world is imperative to the success of global business operations, particularly in electronic business. Although most of the developed and developing countries have cutting edge technology, organizations still have to realize the available telecommunication services provided by each proposed country in terms of the availability, flexibility and feasibility.

Network Infrastructure

Network infrastructure is the communication backbone for flow of data and information in any enterprises. As business units are required to interconnect each other, the network infrastructure is even imperative for the global organizations. An appropriate network infrastructure is crucial as it enhances the intra-organizational communication services for global business operations in a number of perspectives, such as real-time communications within or cross-regional borders, ability to reach out each end-node within the organization, to be used as fundamental architecture for organization-wide application deployment base, and full utilization in terms of bandwidth and costs.

In addition to the network infrastructure itself, network maintenance is also an important task that requires a well-defined strategy. A well-defined network maintenance strategy will include the control of users on the network, implementation of various security levels on accessing facilities and applications, maintenance of the software license agreements across the network, agreement of standard application setup and upgrade procedures to a single source, implementation of efficient backup procedures, maintenance of virus protection strategy, and implementation of constant network transmission speed (bandwidth) to meet certain business requirements.

Data and Information Systems Improvement

In the modern digital world, it is believed that data and information is the imperative asset of any organization and it should be made available whenever needed. Furthermore, efficient organization and utilization of data and information would result in the creation of new knowledge that may provide organizations with critical information in decision-making. On the other hand, the sensitivity of data and information requires carefully planned mainte- nance, security and recovery strategies. Issues in relation to data and information improve- ment include data resources utilization, security, and systems recovery, as described below.

Data Resources Utilization

In the global business environment, more data resources are available than local business environment. Data can be collected from a variety of sources such as customers, suppliers, employees, managers, as well as for business processes, business units, and subsidiaries and so forth. One way of utilizing business data is through the creation of data warehouses with the ability to drill down deep inside the data and ascertain new and innovative correlationships between various data items. Therefore, understanding and utilizing data is not merely creation of information systems, but creation and sharing of knowledge. Good utilization of data deals with capturing, storing and retrieving unique relationships between pieces of information that are known as "knowledge." Usually, this knowledge remains in the minds of people. Good data utilization means good "electronification" of knowledge. Examples of data utilization include sales forecast, prediction of market demands, support of decision-making, allocation of human resources, and business negotiation.

In addition to the way that we use data, it is also important to "manage" this data. Effective data management is crucial as it facilitates the data to be transformed into information and knowledge for maximum use in the organization. This requires regular backups, offsite storage of databases, as well as regular cleanups of databases so that they are not riddled with redundant and archaic data items. Finally in addition to backing up data, respective versions of software that specifically deal with the data should also be backed up to facilitate retrieval.

Security

As more and more business operations are transformed into global arena and cyberspace, organizations have to face an increasing number of security related threats than before. It is crucial that the organization constructs a realistic security strategy early in the global transition process. Various elements should be considered in the development of the security strategy, including the connection with business strategy, the organization's security and privacy policy, authentication, authorization, administration, recovery, and enabling technology and issues. These are discussed in detail below.

1. *Connection with business strategy*—The security plan must be linked with the organization business strategy. All decisions must be passed through the filter of the organizational structure and business models. In global organization structure, the security plan should cover the headquarters as well as foreign business units and subsidiaries.
2. *Policy*—All of the organization's security and privacy policies and procedures must be codified, communicated, and updated on a regular basis. The security policy needs to be specific enough to reduce ambiguity. All levels of employees should be aware of the policy and the training programs may be conducted where needed. Some essential items that may be included in the organization's security are data access, applications access, network access, software, privacy, business resumption planning, systems design and development, and risk assessments.
3. *Authentication*—Authentication is commonly done through the use of logon passwords. In the networked global information systems, password policies should be well developed to efficiently control the use of applications or systems, and minimize complicated administrative tasks. Firewall is another import aspect an organization should focus on when planning its authentication strategy.
4. *Authorization*—Once users are authenticated, they need to be monitored according to a pre-defined authorization schema. Access to networks, applications, and databases needs to be defined, and individual and classes of users need to know where they can go and what they can do once they get there.
5. *Administration*—All security and privacy policy, authentication, authorization, and recovery requires administration. Organizations need to ensure the consideration of methods, tools, techniques, and processes as main part of the administrative procedures.

6. *Recovery*—It is as essential to security as authentication. Organizations need to make sure the investments in systems recovery are equal value as any prevention tasks.

7. *Enabling technology*—Technologies enable the implementation of security strategy including firewall technology, anti-virus technology, certificate authority technology, biometric technology, encryption technology, and privacy compliance technology.

After the September 11 tragedy, many organizations realized a complete backup strategy should also include a multi-backup plan at various remote sites. A single backup plan in one location (either remote or local site) does not guarantee the security of organizations' data and information. Global organizations have the advantage of planning multiple backups at transborder sites. Ideally, each business unit in the global organization should have a multi-backup plan of its own data locally as well as remotely. A number of factors should be taken into account when deciding a remote backup site. They are technological capability, level of data sensitivity, and level of national security. When a system failure occurs in a business unit, the data can be easily restored through the remote backup site; and if the business unit is also a remote backup site of another, it will request the original site to replicate the data for remote backup purpose. As Figure 3 illustrates, Business Unit 1 backs up its own data as well as data from Business Unit 2 (remote site). Business Unit 1's data is also transferred to Business unit 3 for remote backup. Thus if Business Unit 1 is destroyed, it can easily to reinstate it own data through a restoring request from Business Unit 3. In the meantime, Business Unit 1 can also request data from Business Unit 2 for remote backup.

Systems Recovery

A systems recovery plan is culmination of the details on how to recover an organization's entire operations, especially the mission critical processes. The recovery plan also identifies the recovery resource to effect recovery operations. The main objective of the recovery plan is to prepare the emergency business operations strategy for the situations caused by

Figure 3. Multi-backup model for global organizations

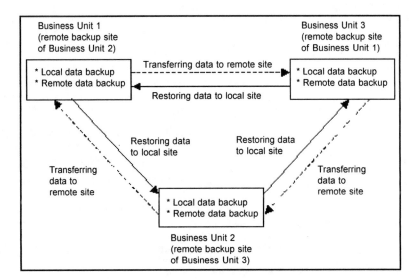

disasters resulting in inoperability and inaccessibility of any information systems. As global information systems require more complex and sophisticated procedures in system recovery, global organizations need to pay more attention on developing the system recovery plan.

The impact of a disaster can be tremendous. It includes temporary and permanent loss of revenues (customers, business opportunity, market share, competitive edge, or customer confidence), violation of regulatory requirements, legal liabilities, personnel safety, damages to personnel morale, expense of personnel downtime, embarrassment of not being prepared, and so forth. There are numerous events that can cause a disaster such as fire, flood, earthquake, power outage, and terrorism.

Due to high level of complication in recovering global business operations, the business continuity and disaster recovery planning is essential to every global organization. As multiple business units operate all over the world, many business rules such as the auditing compliance, insurance requirements, and legislation and regulatory requirements are varying from country to country. Hence, global organizations should have multiple business recovery plans that cover all business operations across the world.

CONCLUSION AND FUTURE DIRECTION

Information technology has become one of the core components of many enterprises. It is even more essential for organizations engaged in the transition to globalization. Prior to incorporating information technology in business operations, identification of IT related issues and development of IT transition solutions are considered to be the preliminary tasks in enterprise global transition process.

This chapter discusses the development of global IT transition framework through the categorization of global IT transition classes:
1.   Global IT infrastructure
2.   Global business applications
3.   Global telecommunication network
4.   Data and information improvement and detailed investigation of related issues

The identification of global IT transition classes, together with their corresponding issues provide enterprises a conceptual vision of global IT architecture taxonomy and suggestions that might be considered in the development of global information systems.

To enhance the completeness of global IT transition process, the author suggests a future research direction in regard to the relationship between global IT transition classes and organizational transition scopes. The organizational transition scopes refer to intra-organizational scope and inter-organizational scope. Indeed an enterprise's global transition process involves business operations within the organization as well as external business parties. Hence, there is a need to incorporate both internal and external scopes in the process of globalization. Furthermore, components and requirement of each organizational scope in relation to global IT transition classes are needed to be identified in the future study.

REFERENCES

Bartlett, C. A. & Ghoshal, S. (1998). *Managing Across Borders: The Transnational Solution*, (2nd ed.). Harvard Business School Press, 55-61.

Burn, J. et al. (1993). Critical issues of IS management in Hong Kong: A cultural comparison. *Journal of Global Information Management*, 1(4), 28-37.

Edberg, D., Grupe, F.H. & Kuechler, W. (2001). Practical issues in global IT management. *Information Systems Management*, 18(1), 34-46.

Ginige, A., Murugesan, S. & Kazanis, P. (2001). A road map for successfully transforming SMEs into e-businesses. *Cutter IT Journal*, 14(5), 43.

Lan, Y. (2002). Development of a global IT transition framework. *Proceedings of Information Resources Management Association International Conference*, (May, pp. 1024-1025) Hershey, PA: Idea Group Publishing.

Mische, M.A. (1998). Defining systems integration. In M.A. Mische (Ed.), *Reengineering Systems Integration Success*, Florida: CRC Press LLC.

Nelson, G.K. (1996). Global information systems quality: Key issues and challenges. *Journal of Global Information Management*, 4(4), 4-14.

Palvia, S., Palvia, P.C. & Zigli, R.M. (1992). Global information technology environment: Key MIS issues in advanced and less-developed nations. In S. Palvia, P. Palvia & R. Zigli (Eds.), *The Global Issues of Information Technology Management*. Hershey, PA: Idea Group Publishing.

Sankar, C. S. & Prabhakar, P. K. (1992). Key technological components and issues of global information systems. In S. Palvia, P. Palvia, & R. Zigli (Eds.), *The Global Issues of Information Technology Management*. Hershey, PA: Idea Group Publishing.

Watson, R. T. et al. (1997). Key issues in information systems management: An international perspective. *Journal of Management Information Systems*, 13(4), 91-115.

Chapter II

Impact on Society: The Missing Dimension in Evaluating the Benefits of IT in the Public Sector

Ian M. Sims
Edith Cowan University, Western Australia

Craig Standing
Edith Cowan University, Westen Australia

ABSTRACT

This chapter explains the need for a new dimension in the evaluation of the benefits of information technology where the technology has impact is on the broader society rather than just on the organization that implements it.

In the early 1990s, when DeLone and McLean (1992) developed their framework, the benefits described were intra-organizational. A decade later, many major IT systems directly impact on the society within which they function. This is the especially true of systems designed to provide the interface between government and the private sector. Additionally, the procurement environment is increasingly becoming more complex for practitioners with new e-marketplace developments.

This case illustrates specific peculiarities and constraints on public sector use of e-marketplaces. It provides an evaluation framework that can be used by public sector organizations when examining the adoption and evaluation of e-marketplace procurement that emphasizes the experimental nature of many e-commerce related projects.

INTRODUCTION

Procurement historically was "the activities which ensure the availability of material in the desired quality, quantity, place and time to the requesting unit" (European Logistics Association, 1994). The intervening years have seen subtle change; in particular today "procurement" encompasses both materials and services, particularly with the emphasis moving from service delivery to purchaser provider models in the public sector around the globe.

This chapter covers the main issues in relation to the procurement environment and benefits evaluation of IT projects in the public sector. These issues are by no means limited to the public sector however, as corporate social responsibility Web sites such as the "Business in the Community" site demonstrate (Business in the Community, 2002). The details of the case study are described together with the research method. The usefulness and validity of the various benefits frameworks are then discussed and conclusions are drawn on ways that they can be improved.

PROCUREMENT ENVIRONMENT AND THE RISE OF E-MARKETPLACES

There is ample evidence that in the private sector procurement environment benefits, risks and opportunities may accrue to both purchasers and suppliers (Greenstein & Vasarhelyi, 2002). When e-marketplaces are established as an independent business, this may bring a third party into the benefits equation. Even in this situation, the assessment of benefits and costs is relatively straightforward. However, public sector procurement can be a far more complex environment with its potential to impact on a variety of other policy issues of interest to stakeholders, particularly the government of the day and the bureaucracy. For example, in Western Australia, the state government has a "Buy Local" policy that is expressly designed to further the government aims of regional development, rather than to achieve the most cost-effective procurement for the purchasing agency.

There has been a plethora of e-marketplaces developed in the last decade. These marketplaces come in many forms.

- The development of traditional markets into electronic marketplaces, for example, the conversion from floor trading to electronic trading at most major world stock exchanges.
- Some markets have been established as vertical markets to service specific industry sectors, including motor vehicle manufacture, mining, plastics and the pharmaceutical industry.
- Some markets appear to have been established simply on the basis that integrated software solutions enable them to be effective, for example www.Mysap.com.

On another dimension, markets have been established by:
- Buyers (typically where the buyers are in a position of power in the market)
- Sellers (typically where they have the power)
- Intermediaries (typically where there is threat of disintermediation in the market)

E-marketplaces may be seen to facilitate the stages in the life cycle of trade which cover *negotiation, execution* and *settlement* (Bytheway, 1995a).

Nokkentved (2000) provided a continuum of functionality for the development of marketplaces. He suggests four major categories of function can be provided by e-marketplaces, from the provision of information to facilitation, then transaction and finally, integration.

In this chapter, we consider e-markets as they relate to e-procurement, therefore we concentrate on markets which reflect different structures according to the demand for products and services rather than their supply. The characteristic "configurations of demand" (Edquist & Hommen, 1998) in which buyers operate are known as monopsony, oligopsony, and polypsony. These configurations relate directly to the more common categories of supply: monopoly, oligopoly and open competition.

In a geographically isolated location such as Western Australia, it is apparent that the government, if it exercises a central influence on agencies in their selection of suppliers, has the capacity to create an oligopsonistic market for some classes of goods and services. This market configuration leads to a "buyer's market," therefore, given our previous discussion; it is no surprise that it has embarked upon its own e-marketplace.

EVALUATION OF BENEFITS CONCEPTS

The benefits evaluation literature has three main themes or sets of issues. The first is the benefits evaluation classification as defined by DeLone and McLean (1992) and subsequently extended by other researchers. This framework has been in place for some time and referred to extensively by IS researchers. The extent to which this framework is useful as a way of classifying benefits, especially for electronic commerce systems such as e-marketplaces, is worthy of examination since the classification was developed as a tool for use with information systems in the 80's and early 90's and has mainly a technical focus.

The second issue related to e-commerce benefits evaluation is the process of evaluation. A growing body of literature highlights that benefits evaluation cannot be disentangled from the method of evaluation. In particular, whether a quantitative (rationally constructed) or qualitative analysis (socially constructed) is taken (Hirschheim & Smithson, 1988) and (Serafeimidis & Smithson, 1994).

The third, and often overlooked, aspect of evaluation of benefits is that their perception of significance can change significantly through time. Only a relatively small percentage of studies take a longitudinal approach. There may even be a cycle of benefits that can be derived from e-marketplaces that cannot be brought out by one of data collection or a case study over a short period of analysis.

Bytheway's (Bytheway, 1995b) taxonomy of the strategic benefits of the application of IT to the supply chain may alternatively be described as a taxonomy of motivation. It is suggested that there are three core benefits provided:
- Efficiency: doing things right
- Effectiveness: doing the right thing
- Evolution: doing something else

In addition, he proposed two other "extreme reasons" for implementing innovation in technology. These are:

- Defensive: reacting to moves made by competitors
- Experimental: trying to understand your opportunities

While these reasons may have seemed extreme when they were proposed in 1995, in the addition to the expected returns in the core categories, we think that it serves as a useful framework for analyzing adoption and support for the introduction of e-marketplaces.

RESEARCH METHODOLOGY

In this section of the chapter, we explain the research questions, the research approach, the data gathering and data analysis methods. Based on our analysis of the literature on evaluation of benefits we argue that there are several issues worthy of investigation. For our main question, we would like to determine the levels and types of benefits derived from engaging in e-marketplaces. There may be, for instance, new types of benefits not previously identified or certain types of benefits may or may not be significant.

The study is shaped by existing benefits evaluation theory and so we also wish to determine the extent to which the evaluation frameworks developed in the past with information systems are relevant and appropriate for electronic commerce applications and in particular e-marketplaces.

The project involves an in-depth case study of a government department. The information-gathering component of the research has involved face-to-face discussions and interviews, and e-mail and telephone communication, access to company documentation, and attending company meetings. Information has also been gathered from strategic plans, job descriptions, company reports, and the Web site.

An interpretive approach was used to analyze the data. The main research themes are shaped by the research literature and questions and the transcripts were analyzed, classified according to these, and validated using a second researcher. However, the research interpretation is influenced by a number of research traditions and these are briefly explained. Several research approaches advocate the examination of the macro and micro forces related to any particular organizational situation. A dialectic hermeneutic approach suggests that the wider environment is an important issue for explaining organizational decisions. However, it provides few, if any, methods or techniques for identifying the wider issues. Hermeneutics is primarily concerned with the meaning of a text or text analogue (Myers, 1995). The data, which are interview transcripts, are analyzed in terms of themes, motifs, and key words in the same way, as a literary text is (Bronsema & Keen, 1983). One of the main differences between pure and dialectical hermeneutics is that, in the latter, the researcher does not just accept the opinions of the participants, but tries to evaluate the totality of understandings in a given situation. The role and understanding of the participants are interpreted historically, and in terms of social and political structures and includes the contribution of the researcher in the analysis process.

CASE STUDY DESCRIPTION

The Western Australian Government currently spends approximately $A5 billion on goods and services and estimates of average transaction cost are estimated at an average for simple purchases of $100 (DoIT, 2001b).

Early in 2000, the West Australian government agency responsible for management of government purchasing, the Department of Contract and Management Services (CAMS), embarked on the development of major project known as the Government Electronic Marketplace (GEM)(DoIT, 2001a). On July 1, 2001, because of Ministry of Government changes, the responsibility for the project moved to the replacement for CAMS, the Department of Industry and Technology (DoIT). This case study traces the development GEM from inception to pilot implementation within one major government agency. This process illustrates several of the major issues associated with marketplaces in general and highlights some special difficulties in implementing such a marketplace within the public sector.

The published objectives and benefits of the system listed on the DoIT Web site (DoIT, 2001b) are:

Project Objectives

1. To provide an end-to-end online buying solution using Web browser technology.
2. To enable supplier created and maintained catalogues.
3. To enable distributed requisitioning and workflows.
4. To satisfy Government buying and policy compliance. *
5. To enable buyer-to-buyer (sic) procurement efficiencies.
6. To integrate Financial Management Information Systems (FMIS) with Gem.
7. To support the Open Buying on the Internet (OBI) standard and Australian Procurement and Construction Council (APCC) Guidelines. *
8. To provide a confidential and secure infrastructure.
9. To provide a vehicle for procurement reform. *

Expected Benefits

a. Reduced time to perform searches, secure approvals, place orders, make payments and acknowledge receipts.
b. Reduced 'real' cost of procurement and processing times.
c. Reduced duplicate payments.
d. Minimized data entry and streamlined data collection.
e. Improved data quality for management reporting.
f. Open trading model for transacting on a many-to-many basis.
g. Added value to supply chain management.
h. Supplier maintained catalogues.

The items marked with an asterisk are those that differentiate this e-marketplace from those in the private sector. Note that on further discussion with the Project Sponsor, we established that Objective 5 should read "project-to-buyer procurement efficiencies." The establishment of GEM is not just a tool for implementing market efficiencies, but also for implementing a variety of policies as discussed above.

As addressed earlier, there are many stakeholders in any marketplace; typically, all markets must have both buyers and sellers in order to exist. Additionally, the market may be owned controlled by third party whose business is the delivery from effective and efficient market to the both buyers and sellers. In the case of GEM, the government owns most of the buyers, some of the sellers *and* the operator of the market. To further complicate matters, it also owns the policy-making body that sets the rules for open and effective competition for all government purchasers. This separate body is known as the State Supply Commission.

In identifying potential leading-edge buyers for the market, the selected agency was selected for a variety of reasons. It had already commenced the process of reviewing supply chain management with a view to outsourcing the management its supply chain. The Chief Executive had been the chief executive officer of CAMS in his previous position and was known to be a strong supporter of the implementation of strategic procurement initiatives. A solution value assessment conducted as part of the process of implementation of a new financial system (Oracle 11) had indicated in the transaction costs within the supply chain could be significantly reduced by the application of current information technology.

In early 2000, CAMS held a series of briefings for agencies. Initial proposals established that GEM was more than simply an e-marketplace. It was in fact a front-end procurement system and marketplace combined. GEM was designed to provide a complete service from the time a need was identified (purchase requisition) through purchasing to the receipt of goods.

As mentioned earlier, the agency was, at this time, in the process of re-implementing its Financial Management Information System (FMIS) and upgrading the application software to and ERP system (Oracle Financials, Version 11). A significant feature of this implementation was the implementation of the procurement module of Oracle Financials that included provision for self-service purchasing (SSP).

At these meetings, it was established that there was considerable overlap between the proposed functions for GEM and the functionality of the ERP solution *in situ*. As GEM was at the time, an unproven concept, it was decided to run parallel implementation of GEM and SSP, with the split along functional lines:
- Main function procurement: GEM
- Rest of ministry: SSP

It was considered that within the agency the introduction of e-procurement systems was in its infancy and that the organization would be prudent to "hedge its bets" by this method.

The GEM solution proposed at this stage addressed only the negotiation and execution phases of the trade life cycle and did not address the settlement (and costing) requirements of the agency. The concept had been conceived from the procurement perspective, rather than from an integrated accounting information systems perspective, thus, the issues associated with payment and distribution of costs had not been addressed.

To address this problem, the first step was to decide on the point of integration between the FMIS and GEM. This was particularly difficult as the project was of a scale that would require a phased implementation over an extended period. The need to run two systems in parallel also influenced the decision.

It is important to note that many state government agencies in Western Australia have implemented Enterprise Resource Planning (ERP) systems. Each agency has selected the system that it considers most appropriate for itself resulting in a heterogeneous collection of Oracle, SAP, Peoplesoft and other systems across the sector. It is clear that Western Australia has chosen to consider the agency as the "enterprise" for these systems, rather than take a whole of government approach such as that adopted in the state of Victoria. This results in some difficulties for the integration of GEM into the FMIS of buyer agencies.

After due consideration of many integration points, it was agreed that the most feasible point at which to integrate would be after the settlement (payment) phase of the transaction had been completed. These issues were crucial to the success of the implementation from the point of view of the agency. DoIT agreed to modify the system to handle the complete cycle from Procurement to Payment, in order to meet the needs of the agency.

With the widened scope, GEM was implemented at a single pilot site in July 2001. At October 2001, GEM is operational at limited purchasing sites with several hundred suppliers actively participating in the market. It will be progressively rolled out to further sites, other agencies and suppliers.

DISCUSSION

The evolution of GEM from a procurement system to a market that fulfils almost all of the criteria presented by both Bytheway and Nokkentved is of some significance in providing a degree of support for the validity of these models. It became clear early in the project that to achieve a real benefit from the implementation of the e-marketplace at the integration level, the transaction level must be satisfied first.

In this section of the chapter, we examine and classify the declared project objectives and benefits listed earlier by DoIT in using e-marketplaces in the government sector.

The established benefits evaluation frameworks are used to structure the examination of benefits. We also highlight a number of issues that are still to be resolved because of the strategy adopted in relation to e-marketplaces with some suggestions for organizations on how to deal with these.

Analysis Within the DeLone and McLean Framework

We did not find it surprising that most of the declared objectives and benefits fit this well accepted model, nor did we find it unusual that many of the benefits postulated by the model were not enunciated in the statement. The list obviously was not intended to be an exhaustive model of the benefits to be gained by the introduction of the GEM system, but specifically to address the perceived benefits from procurement perspective. We believe that each of the aspects of the DeLone and McLean model should be included in the evaluation of the benefits of GEM. The measurement of these constructs from each perspective (supplier, seller and policy maker) could be incorporated into a balanced score card for the long-term evaluation of the project.

What we consider of most interest are the perceived objectives and benefits that do not fit the model, viz:

Objectives
4.   To satisfy government buying and policy compliance.
7.   To support the Open Buying on the Internet (OBI) standard and Australian Procurement and Construction Council (APCC) Guidelines. *
9.   To provide a vehicle for procurement reform. *

Benefits
F.   Open trading model for transacting on a many-to-many basis.

Table 1. Objectives and benefits of electronic marketplaces categorized under MIS success measures (DeLone & McLean, 1992)

System quality	Information quality	Information use
Ease of use, Convenience of access System flexibility, Usefulness of features and functions, response time, Integration of systems *Objectives:* 6. Integration with FMIS 8. Confidential and secure infrastructure *Benefits:* None recorded	Current, Timely, Reliable, Useable Complete, Accurate, Free from bias *Objectives:* None recorded *Benefits:* A. Reduced time C. Reduced duplicate payments E. Improved mgt. reporting	Purpose of use Recurring use Motivation to use *Objectives:* 1. End-to-end buying solution *Benefits:* None recorded

User satisfaction	Individual impact	Organizational impact
Overall satisfaction Information satisfaction Full information required Enjoyment Decision-making satisfaction *Objectives:* None recorded *Benefits:* E. Improved mgt. reporting	Problem identification, information awareness and decision effectiveness through provision i. Analytical capabilities for business analysis ii. Market intelligence iii. Forecasting iv. Greater visibility of supply chain v. Project management collaboration vi. Information sharing vii. Interorganization connections viii. Instant communications ix. Mediated business processes *Objectives:* 2. Supplier maintained catalogues 5. Buyer-to-supplier efficiencies (through automated communication technologies) *Benefits:* G. Added value to supply chain management H. Supplier maintained catalogues	Operating cost reductions. *Objectives:* 6. Integration with FMIS *Benefits:* A. Reduced time B. Reduced real cost Overall productivity gains. Staff reductions *Benefits* D. Minimize data collection H. Supplier maintained catalogues Contribution to achieving goals through improved management of data and 'near perfect' information flow. *Objectives:* 3. Work flow management 5. Buyer-to-supplier efficiencies

Conceptually, these items may be grouped as extra-organizational impact (within the public sector, we would suggest the title of *impact on society*). This reflects the significant swing in emphasis from the internal focus of information technology in the early 1990s to a much wider approach a decade later as the introduction of technology and the consequent changes in process cross organizational boundaries. This seventh dimension may be particularly important for the evaluation and measurement of large IT projects in the public sector as they impact on the society which they serve in a way which may be separate from the public sector outcomes which they are initially designed to support.

It is interesting to see that Objective 4: "To satisfy government buying and policy compliance," might be the subject some considerable debate in terms of its impact on society. On the one hand, it may be argued that compliance with government policy is of benefit to society, allowing suppliers equal access to the public purse. However, as we have described earlier, this could also be interpreted as ensuring strict compliance with central purchasing contracts negotiated with a select few suppliers, excluding others form the market.

Analysis Within the Bytheway Evaluation Framework

In this case we have been able to categorize all of the published, perceived objectives and benefits within the framework. One category, the "defensive" is hardly used and this can be attributed to the dominant role of the government within the market of Western Australia. The framework is not as detailed as that proposed by DeLone and McLean and is not a substitute, yet they appear to be complementary, allowing for the categorization along different important dimensions.

- Efficiency: doing things right
  - Objectives:
    1. End-to-end buying solution,
    2. Supplier maintained catalogues.
    5. Buyer-to-supplier efficiencies
  - Benefits:
    A. Reduced time
    B. Reduced real cost
    D. Minimize data collection
    H. Supplier Maintained Catalogues

- Effectiveness: doing the right thing
  - Objectives:
    6. Integration with FMIS
    8. Confidential and Secure
  - Benefits: A, C & G
    A. Reduced time
    C. Reduced Duplicate payments
    G. Added value to supply chain management

- Evolution: doing things different
  - Objectives:
    3. Work flow management
    7. OBI/APCC
  - Benefits:
    E. Improved mgt. reporting
  - Defensive: reacting to moves made by competitors
  - Objectives:
    7. OBI/APCC (possibly)
  - Benefits:
    - None recorded

- Experimental: trying to understand you opportunities
  - Objectives:
    4. Policy compliance
    7. OBI/APCC
    9. Procurement reform
  - Benefits:
    F. Open trading model

Limitations of Benefits Evaluation Frameworks

This study shows that the DeLone and McLean framework is robust from an internal perspective, but is incomplete in that this internal focus is a limitation where the effect of the introduction of a new IT system is such that it is designed to have an impact on the whole society in which it operates. This can be addressed by the extra dimension proposed as "impact on society," with the development of measurable constructs to reflect this dimension required as a matter of urgency.

The extended Bytheway framework proved robust within its limitations, and the case study provides evidence to support a significant investment by the Western Australian government on an experimental basis. It must be noted that as this framework addresses mainly organizational benefits, it does not stand alone as well as the extended DeLone and McLean framework. It assumes the realization of other benefits such as the technical integration in order to obtain the organizational benefits.

The Bytheway framework is organizational and should be used with a traditional framework such as DeLone and Mclean's, hence the constructs are sufficiently broad to be applied to benefits accruing to the community in general as well as the parties to the transaction.

Again, the Bytheway framework does not address the issues of measurement and evaluation of benefit when it has a community focus. These too, require urgent attention.

This case study and analysis highlights several issues of importance:

Accounting Information Systems texts generally (Bodnar & Hopwood, 1998; Gelinas Jr., Sutton, & Oram, 1999; Hall, 1998; Hollander, Denna, & Cherrington, 2000; Romney & Steinbart, 2000; Wilkinson & Cerullo, 1997) and established frameworks for e-marketplaces address the corporate AIS needs in the context of the major business cycles:

*   Revenue and collection
*   Acquisition and payment

This case study clearly shows that the implementation of a system to achieve only a portion of a cycle was not acceptable to the users of the system and that the proponents of the system modified the scope to meet this requirement. In planning IT initiatives, proponents need to address integration issues early in the process.

The case also provides strong evidence that the implementation of e-marketplaces by the Western Australian government has objectives and perceived benefits which fall outside of the traditional, internally focussed IT benefits framework dating from the early 1990s. A seventh dimension to the DeLone and Mclean framework "Impact on Society" is proposed to address this issue.

It is clear from the case that the implementation of e-procurement systems is still largely at an experimental stage and that the concept of running parallel systems within different organizational units is still a useful tool when technology is either unproven or immature.

FUTURE TRENDS

The case illustrates that the measurement of benefits from major IT projects such as an e-marketplace (GEM) is a complex task. There is a need to design valid and reliable measures for each perceived benefit, measure their achievement and rank their importance in order to develop an appropriate "balanced scorecard" by which to measure the project. It is important that we do not always assume that the introduction of technology such as this with always have a positive impact on society. Increased concentration of market power on both supply and demand sides may have unforeseen deleterious impacts on the society in which they are introduced.

We have noted that the development of measurable constructs to reflect the "impact on society" is required as a matter of urgency. Further investigation of the use and sponsorship of e-marketplaces by other public sector jurisdictions would be useful in order to further refine this dimension.

This in turn begs the wider question of the "impact on society" of e-marketplaces in the private sector, and of the implications and application of extra-territoriality for the regulatory environment.

REFERENCES

Bodnar, G. H. & Hopwood, W. S. (1998). *Accounting Information Systems* (7th ed.). New Jersey: Prentice Hall.

Bronsema, G. S. & Keen, P. W. G. (1983). Education intervention and implementation in MIS. *Sloan Management Review, 24*(4), 35-44.

Business in the Community. (2002). *Corporate Impact Reporting*. Retrieved July 27, 2002, from the World Wide Web: http://www.iosreporting.org/

Bytheway, A. (1995a). *Electronic Markets: A Framework for the analysis of trade and its potential for development.* MCB University Press. Retrieved December 16, 1996, from the World Wide Web.

Bytheway, A. (1995b). *Information in the Supply Chain: Measuring Supply Chain Performance.* Cranfield: Cranfield School of Management, Cranfield University.

DeLone, W. H. & McLean, E. R. (1992). Information systems success: The quest for the dependant variable. *Information Systems Research, 3*(1), 60-95.

DoIT. (2001a). *GEM*. Retrieved September 24, 2001, from the World Wide Web: http://www.gem.wa.gov.au/default.jsp

DoIT. (2002b). *What Is Gem*. Retrieved July 27, 2002, from the World Wide Web: http://opal.gem.wa.gov.au/aboutgem/what_is_gem.jsp

Edquist, C. & Hommen, L. (1998). *Government Technology Procurement and Innovation Theory.* Linköping: Linköping University.

European Logistics Association. (1994). Terminology in Logistics.

Gelinas Jr., U. J., Sutton, S. G., & Oram, A. E. (1999). *Accounting Information Systems* (4th ed.). Cincinnati, OH: South-Western College Publishing.

Greenstein, M. & Vasarhelyi, M. (2002). *Electronic Commerce: Security, Risk Management, and Control* (2nd ed.). New York: McGraw-Hill Irwin.

Hall, J. A. (1998). *Accounting Information Systems* (2nd ed.). Cincinnati, OH: South-Western College Publishing.

Hirschheim, R. & Smithson, S. (1988). A critical analysis of information systems evaluation. In N. Bjorn-Andersen & G. B. Davis (Eds.), *Information Systems Assessment: Issues and Challenges* (17-37). Amsterdam: Elsevier Sciences.

Hollander, A. S., Denna, E. L., & Cherrington, J. O. (2000). *Accounting Information Technology and Business Solutions* (2nd ed.). Boston, MA: Irwin McGraw Hill.

Myers, M. D. (1995). Dialectical hermeneutics: a theoretical framework for the interpretation for the implementation of information systems. *Information Systems Journal*, 5, 51-70.

Nokkentved, C. (2000). Collaborative planning in e-supply networks, Business Briefing: Global Purchasing and Supply Chain Strategies: World Markets Research Centre.

Romney, M. B.& Steinbart, P. J. (2000). *Accounting Information Systems* (8th ed.). New Jersey: Prentice-Hall.

Serafeimidis, V. & Smithson, S. (1994, September). Evaluation of IS/IT investments: Understanding and Support. Paper presented at the First European Conference on Information Technology Investment Evaluation, Henley on Thames, UK.

Wilkinson, J. W. & Cerullo, M. J. (1997). *Accounting Information Systems: Essential Concepts and Applications* (3rd ed.). New York: John Wiley & Sons, Inc.

Chapter III

Information Resources Development Challenges in a Cross-Cultural Environment

Wai K. Law
University of Guam, Guam

ABSTRACT

Organizations in the Western world devote much attention to the development of information systems as strategic resources. The transfer of this management practice to a different cultural environment generates new challenges as reported in the experience of a Pacific Basin public institution with Western affiliation, while under strong influence of local cultures and practices. The value of the investment in information resources is judged not only on technical merits, but also on the ability of the organization to properly address the cultural and organizational issues related to information usage.

INTRODUCTION

Information Resources Development is a new frontier for organizations in Asia Pacific countries. In many cases, the expectation for information reports from external funding agencies and investor groups has been the primary driving force for the construction of information systems. While justification for capital investment in information technology remained the major challenge, management must overcome organizational inertia and the general deficiency in information literacy. The mingling of Western management approaches with regional administrative styles creates new dynamics for the management of information resources (Shea and Lewis, 1996; Raman and Watson, 1997). Western management theory considers information the lifeblood of organization. The sharing of information lubricates the interlocking divisions within the organization, promoting the effective achievement of organizational goals. Externally, information exchanges strengthen business relationships in a value chain, improving the competitive positions of business partners. In many regions of the world, information represents power; managers often try to accumulate as much of it as they can while denying access to others (Oz, 2002). The disclosure of information is considered a threat to the span of management control (Rocheleau, 1999). The strategic manipulation of information flow is frequently valued over the potential knowledge gain from the objective evaluation of organizational data. This chapter examines organizational dynamics and possible management solutions in the deployment of information system in a cross-cultural environment. User actions and their interpretation of data reports create challenges that demand the attention of information system managers and designers.

BACKGROUND

The information system literature provided thorough coverage on designs, features and implementation methods for computer-based information systems. Numerous studies examined broad varieties of systems-solutions for organization needs (Applegate, 1995; McLeod, 1998; O' Brien, 2002). Much attention has been on the development of information systems since the lack of them can impede an enterprise in its competitive success. The projected value of information technology has been formulated based on a rough assessment of the possibilities without full appreciation of the limitations due to resistance to organizational and social changes (Osterman, 1991). Lesser known was guidelines for information system managers to ensure a positive contribution to business performance. Well-managed information systems may not guarantee any business value. The information system function must create the conditions that enhance user effectiveness and efficiency in using the information to improve value delivery for the organization (Parker, 1996).

Increasingly, management has realized that massive deployment of information systems on a global basis is not producing the desirable outcomes of value generation. Recent studies confirmed the significant role of cultures towards the success of transferring information technology beyond the Western world. National culture, organization culture, and MIS cultures induced influence over the successful development and management of information resources (Hofstede, 1980; Raman and Watson, 1997). Shea and Lewis (1996) suggested the desirability of placing close attention to user absorptive rate in the transfer of new technology into a different cultural environment. It became apparent that adaptation of information system designs to new cultural environment was insufficient to guarantee successful implementation. User selection of technological features, driven by cultural preferences, could be a key factor for designing information systems in multi-cultural environment.

New challenges emerged as non-technical issues clouded the measurement of information system performance. Since computer information systems were often promoted for the increased speed of data processing, users became conditioned to evaluate the performance of information systems based on the speed of data report delivery. However, the timely delivery of information is only one of several factors for quality information. Data reports must contain all the required information with accurate representation of events. The reports needed to be generated in a timely fashion and in a format usable by the users (McLeod, 1998). To complicate matters, a typical information system was designed to provide information to users with common needs, in the form of standard reports. Information systems were seldom designed to meet the individual needs of users in specific circumstances. However, information users tended to value information systems for their abilities to generate custom reports (Heeks, 1999). The initial excitement of users seeking data reports would be ultimately transformed to total frustration in the flood of data in unusable report formats. The confidence in the information system would be further eroded with inconsistent information reports, representing shifts in data points through time. Damaging criticisms surfaced from questionable data quality, due to lack of attention to the data acquisition and processing activities.

Organizations, especially those in the public sector, faced the challenge of maintaining a delicate balance as they attempted to fulfill their responsibilities for both confidentiality and access to data (Osterman, 1991; Duncan, 1999). The department that owned the information system controlled the data and became obligated to provide information to other units (Oz, 2002). Under uncertainty in liability and severe budget constraints, some department heads shifted the data reporting responsibilities to other divisions, creating a bureaucratic nightmare for the data users. Some data managers ignored data requests, and others manipulated the data flows with respect to organizational politics (Oz, 2002; Rocheleau, 1999).

Makeshift management decision generated new dynamics in several ways. In the spirit of promoting the free exchange of information, some organizations instructed the custodian of valuable information to provide it to others. However, the new responsibility seldom came with additional resources. The appointed information owner became reluctant to supply information; doing so would take away resource from other regular tasks (Davenport, 1997). Some information owners would release a data sample, fulfilling their obligation, but had the least concern about the data quality. Other managers would shift the data responsibilities to other divisions (Oz, 2002). The ability to locate information reports through internal alliances became a new dynamic in organizational politics.

Cultural backgrounds shaped the preference Information System model. In a multicultural setting, some managers would be intuitive, and feelings based, and had vague expectation for the performance of information system. Other managers would be more interesting in simple information system providing operational information for task performance. The controlling manager would be interested in complex and broad information system providing qualitative data (Kluckhohn and Strodtbeck, 1961; Lane and DiStefano, 1992; Shea and Lewis, 1996). It became obvious that a single system design may not satisfy all users in a cross-cultural environment.

A PUBLIC INSTITUTION AT THE CROSSCURRENT OF EAST AND WEST

The University of Guam is a fully accredited four-year U.S. university; it is about a four-hour flight from major Asian cities. The university must comply with standards of Western universities and United States federal funding agencies, while simultaneously expected to be culturally sensitive to a multi-ethnic mix of student body and a multi-cultural workforce.

Guam emerged recently as an international Internet traffic hub in the Pacific, with investment interests from the top global telecommunication firms. This promoted the interests in the aggressive installation of advanced technological infrastructure in the region and the university. However, grants and federal agencies funded much of the technical progresses. The local community has been slow to support the ongoing deployment and development of the information systems.

The university invested on a campus-wide information system in early 1990. The purchase of a Data Management System (COLLEAGUE) for higher educational institute initiated the computerization of many internal operations. A computer center was established to handle the general system maintenance and technology acquisition. The registrar's office, business office, and financial aid office were among the first to computerize their operations. Some of the initial benefits include a telephone registration system, electronic payroll deposit, a text-based email system and the availability of many standardized management reports. In the mid-1990s, the installation of a campus-wide fiber optics communication backbone positioned the university as a major Internet Hub in the Western Pacific, and stimulated various data communication developments including Intranet capability, and distance education. In 1994, the Computer Center of the University took pride in obtaining a class B domain, establishing Guam as one of the first 100 countries in the Internet world. At the same time, the university continued its development on state-of-the-art information technology, while the campus faced great difficulties in finding data to evaluate its internal operations. Recently, the university was strongly criticized for the lack of planning data to support strategic planning in an increasing competitive higher educational industry.

THE DILEMMA OF DUAL PROCESSES

The university implemented a telephone registration system with the intention to speed up the registration process, and to reduce the confusion from the manual processing and verification of documents. Telephone registration has been successfully implemented in many universities. However, a local culture of hospitality translated to great personal attention to special needs of individual students. A staff-assisted registration process was retained to allow overriding of the telephone registration system. Under a friendly and accommodative culture, the administration deactivated many data input verification mechanisms of the telephone registration system to ensure user-friendliness of the registration process, and the verification of eligibility of students was substantially relaxed. Students were allowed to register for courses in satellite registration locations, and it became difficult to verify the authenticity of the approval signatures of academic advisors. Although students were required to consult an academic advisor, many did not. The implementation of the dual registration process created many problems, and severely affected the quality of the registration process and associated information. A sample of the problems include:

- Students accustomed to special administrative attention ignored rules and procedures of the telephone registration system, demanding human assistance throughout the registration process.
- Student enrollment exceeded class cap due to the simultaneous access to the registration system by telephone, and by staff from satellite terminals. However, the administration was lax in enforcing capacity limits.

- A great portion of the population were blood relatives, and "sympathetic" staff members would allow students to enroll in special project classes without the permission of instructor, and register in courses without proper prerequisites.
- Students signed up for courses to reserve seats for friends, and greatly inflated the perceived demand for courses. The distorted information eventually prompted the opening of new sections with extremely low enrollment.
- Students encountered problems in graduation due to the omission of academic requirements because many students were able to bypass academic advisement through the new system.

The telephone registration system was blamed for many of these problems even the system design was capable of handling many of these problems. The coexistence of a staff-assisted registration process allowed the bypass of registration restrictions, and ill-trained staffs allowed ineligible students to register for courses. The continuation of the paralleled staff-assisted registration option restricted the telephone registration system to a supportive role for data entry, rather than being used as an intelligent data processing system. The lesson learned is that excessive human intervention can destroy the credibility of an automated data processing system. This is an old lesson that organizations repeatedly fail to learn. It is also an important lesson for the implementation of information system in cross-cultural organizations, where cultural considerations supersede information technology deployment. An information resource manager should evaluate the role of information system according to its ability to generate value for specific culture, beside technical integrity. Special attention should be given to examine the cultural acceptance of assumptions and restrictions adopted in the system design.

Challenge One: The design objectives of transaction procession system must shift from efficiency orientation to adaptive accommodation of cultural habits. It becomes desirable to allow and track dynamic modification of data processing procedures according to shifting organizational and cultural influences.

THE RELUCTANT DATA OWNERS

The implementation of a campus-wide Data Management System created a new demand for data reports. Top management assigned the functional units the responsibilities to collect data at the points of transaction, and the functional managers became responsible for the proper release of the data for approved usage. The new responsibility was added without additional resources, and most functional units delegated the tasks to the lowest level staff members. The functional units continued to use paper-based data collection instruments and relied on low-cost staff for data entry. There were minimal guidelines for data quality assurance and the accuracy of the resulting database was questionable.

The new responsibility as owners of functional data took managers by surprise. Many managers hesitated to release data for the fear of giving out inaccurate data and the possible violation of information privacy when the data ended up in the wrong hands. Managers would release data only with the explicit instructions from top management. As a result, only a privileged few were able to have access to the database.

After years and the assertive effort of a budget planner, functional managers finally agreed to certify a version of the database as "official data," but there was no mechanism to ensure the credibility of the database in the long-term. Different versions of "official data" existed under various circumstances, and there was a lack of interest within the organization to ensure data integrity.

Challenge Two: There is a need for the clear definitions of data ownership, and responsibilities for data acquisition, data quality control, and data distribution. This is especially challenging in cultural environment where the political attributes of information interfere with the communicative value of information.

THE RACE FOR DATA REPORTS

The existence of an information system allowed the development of the Management Database. At best, the Management Database was an electronic collection of selected operational data for auditing reports and compliance reports, with little consideration for data needs for academic program planning and evaluation. For example, the enrollment database dynamically recorded the latest changes to the enrollment figures. There were no information system components designed to track historical trends, transient enrollment patterns, policy effects, or schedule changes. The result was multiple sets of enrollment figures depending on the time the data reports were generated from the Management Database.

For compliance with external expectation, as well as potential improvement in internal control, management began to expect data reports as required support for internal reports. This became a major challenge throughout the organization in the absence of a data collection and data distribution scheme to support the new management mandate.

Senior managers assumed that standardized data reports prepared by the Computer Center would be sufficient for all data needs, and special data report could be researched and generated by the Institutional Research Office. The reality was that while the Computer Center prepared standardized reports, it was not designated as a data distribution center. The reluctant functional managers avoided their assigned roles in data distribution, triggering a mad race for data reports. When available, the functional data reports provided very low value for other applications.

On the other hand, the Institutional Research Office became overwhelmed with requests for data requests. There were long delays in preparing customized data reports as the Institutional Researcher juggled requests among deadlines for other institutional reports. In many instances, the Institutional Researcher would produce different data reports to users for similar needs because the users have stated their needs differently. The mad race for data reports ended in meetings where participants arrived with different versions of data reports, with a variety of formats in data presentations, and the hottest issue during the meetings became the accuracy of conflicting data from the various data reports. Evidentially, there was more interest in obtaining data reports, than quality data through the reports.

Challenge Three: Management must meticulously plan data acquisition, data preparation, data distribution, and data usage, and fully understanding the required organizational incentive and associated costs for maintaining information flow within the organization. This is especially important in cultural environment where data-driven decision-making is a new practice.

THE BATTLE OF DATA DEFINITIONS

Although the Data Management System provided standard data reports, users soon found out that these reports could not satisfy the evolving needs for information. For example, a user requesting a historical breakdown of graduates by majors could be given a printed list of 5,000 names. Users who were unfamiliar with data analysis techniques would be overwhelmed by the data report. An additional complication was the coexistence of multiple versions of data files, each tailored to a specific data query. Conflicting data reports would be generated from these closely related data files. The functional managers relied on the users to clearly specify the type of information requested, and most users were unaware of the minute differences in data definitions. For example, the total number of graduates in a given period would be different from the total number of degrees awarded for the same period when some students completed two or more degree programs simultaneously. Another common problem was that the "head count" number of students was different from the "full-time-equivalent" number of students. The casual data user would not be able to distinguish the two different reported numbers of students; even some functional managers had difficulty understanding the later definition! The individual interpretation of data definitions and the subsequent requests for customize data reports, without clear guidelines for the applications of various data reports, created great confusion among the users. Users lacking training in Western practices would refuse to accept certain data definitions as appropriate outcome measurements. Many users eventually attributed the unfortunate chaos to the inferior design of the Data Management System. In the reality, management had never taken the time to develop a consistent and timely approach to report data in a format that was comprehensible to the users.

Challenge Four: Management must take leadership in establishing precise, formal data definitions, and communicate them to all potential data users, and those assigned roles in data distribution. This is especially important in a cross-cultural environment where mastery of languages, cultural predisposition, level of information literacy, and social attitude could strongly influence the group dynamic of data usage.

WHEN DATA IS FREE

As the custodian of the Management Database, the Computer Center confronted a major challenge in supporting the organization's need for data. While the Computer Center aggressively kept pace with the trend of electronic data and paperless operation, most workers in the organization still heavily relied on printed data reports. The Computer Center soon realized that its existing budget for data preparation could not support the expensive staff time and supply costs for producing printed data reports. The functional units faced the same dilemma of attempting to support the management mandate to distribute data without additional funding. However, the users have expected the availability of data reports as a free service. In a furious race for data reports, users freely requested printed reports, not giving thought to the costs of data report preparation. Delays in receiving data reports triggered the users to repeat multiple requests for reports to all available sources. The uncoordinated efforts to hunt down data reports often resulted in multiple requests for the same data report from different members of the same department. This resulted in the duplicated production of data reports for a single usage. Many data reports were never used. Some users relied on personal connections and arbitrary mandates to obtain reports for personal projects. The uncontrolled data requests eventually convinced the functional units more than ever to avoid data distribution activities that could be a bottomless drain on the limited functional resources.

Challenge Five: The increased complexity and frequency of usage of information reports is in reality, a severe drain in budgetary resources, and management needs to develop a mechanism to track data usage and adjust resources appropriately. This could be more challenging under cultural environments that lack sophistication in information processing.

CALL THEM OFFICIAL DATA

On-demand creation of data reports triggered data integrity issues. Some were time sensitive when the database was continuously updated. As a result, data reports differ depending on when the database was queried. There were times when impulsive senior officials publicized enrollment figures before the closing of registration activities. Other times a snapshot of the data set was hastily included in reports to funding agencies. The very nature of the public announcement of the data sealed them as official data. This undermined the integrity of the Management Database, which was used to generate reports for auditing activities. Discrepancies between information in the audit report and the "official" data were frequent sources of embarrassment. In the more serious cases, disagreement between the initial best available data set, and the final data set reported in subsequent years jeopardized funding. Users who were unaware of the time sensitivity of certain types of data questioned the integrity of the information system, while the data discrepancy problem could be the combined results of data query method, data analysis method, and data report generation timing. The result was a widespread distrust on the overall data quality of the institution.

Eventually, the Computer Center adopted the practice of data certification at predefined point in time. For example, a sample of all enrollment data two weeks after the end of registration period was set aside as the certified data. The certified data was recommended for all official data reports regardless of subsequent updates to the database. The certified data set protected the Computer Center from accusation of mismanagement of the database, and provided a consistent reference for generating external data reports. Unfortunately, the Institutional Research Office was designated to announce the official data. A vacant position of the Institutional Researcher left the university without official data for over two years! However, many users were unaware of the existence and the role of the certified data, and circulation of multiple versions of data reports continued.

Challenge Six: Management must take an active role in controlling the flow of organizational data, both within the organization and to the external environment. Management should consider endorsement of an official organizational data to ensure consistency rather than leaving official data report to random actions. This is especially important in cultural setting where it is impractical to correct public statements of social leaders regardless of facts.

DATA RELEVANCY PROBLEM:
DATA RICH BUT INFORMATION POOR

The Management Database was designed for operational support, and data elements were kept current to reflect the latest changes. However, the design of the database and the use of standard management reports created shortcoming in the capturing of planning data. The following example illustrated these shortcomings.

For a period, many senior level students were unable to graduate because they could not enroll in a freshman level course. An analysis of student enrollment data indicated that there was a decrease in the number of students in the program while the total number of seats for the freshman course has been kept at the same level. In fact, many sessions of the course were not at capacity according to enrollment data. The analysis did not support the opening of new sessions for the course. Furthermore, the course schedules from the previous year were reused because it was a "traditional practice" to do so to ensure "consistency."

Numerous requests from senior students for special permission to enroll in the course triggered a faculty member to investigate the enrollment situation. The research effort reviewed that mainly seniors were able to enroll in the freshman course in recent years. A greater surprise was that nearly half the recent enrollments were from students outside of the program! Further investigation showed that the course was always at full capacity by the end of the registration periods, explaining the number of students panicking to seek special permission. However, the traditional course schedule conflicted with other senior level courses explaining the great number of students withdrew from the course, leading to much lower enrollment figures at the end of the term.

The new information supported the offering of new sessions, and the design of new course schedules. Requests for special permission to enroll the course disappeared within the next 12 months. The average student enrolled in the course dropped to sophomore level within 24 months. Total enrollment for the course doubled in two years, outpacing the university enrollment growth. The irony was that the data was in the Management Database, some even reported to the academic units but ignored because there was no perceived information value for the data.

Challenge Seven: Management needs to play an active role in data planning, and closely align the information report designs for decision support. This is especially challenging in cultural environment that lacks appreciation for operational planning and control.

CHALLENGES IN INFORMATION
RESOURCES DEVELOPMENT

Visionary leaders at the University of Guam have realized the critical role of information technology in the continuous growth of the organization. Systematic acquisition of state of the art technology have allowed the university community to stay connected with the rest of the world in an otherwise isolated environment on a sparsely populated island. Despite the technical achievement in telecommunication, there is still limited understanding on the management of organizational information resources. There are a few lessons we could learn and a few challenges for organizations in cross-cultural environment. Firstly, management must develop understanding towards Information Resources Management. Secondly, management must recognize their critical role in Information Resources development. Lastly, the organization must develop appreciation for the value of Information Resources.

Information Resources as an Investment Issue

A common reaction to the deficient in organizational data is to seek capital investment for new technology, or to purchase an entire software system. The investment approach tends to neglect information resources development in areas such as system and facility maintenance, technical staff, user training and support, data architecture development, data quality assurance, and data distribution. The implementation of the information system is not matched with organizational readiness to use the system. Organizational issues become barriers in the deployment of the information system. Confusion arises as individual users are left to tackle the technology issues. Inflated expectation and unscrutinized usage of data services nullifies the value of the information system. Erratic funding pattern destroys development projects, making it extremely difficult to retain technical personnel. Poor maintenance damages equipment and threatens the integrity of the data system. Management eager to modernize without fully understanding the implications of information resources management would abandon their support for the information system under political pressure.

Information Resources Development by Delegation

Management desiring an easy fix to the organizational data problem mandated data compilation activities by the functional divisions. The practice of delegating the responsibility of data ownership to functional units has mixed results. While the capturing of data at the point of transaction is an efficient approach to acquire data, unmotivated functional managers present major obstacles to data quality assurance, and the timely distribution of data. The organizational database can never be completed without the fully cooperation of all functional managers. Turnover and retirement of administrators create further obstacles for the data development efforts. The decentralized approach to information resource management undermines the strategic role of information resources as a critical organizational asset. A huge gap remains in planning data and environmental sensing data.

Limited Appreciation for Information Resources

Information Resources can be compared to utility services, users begin to appreciate their value when there is a supply shortage. Individual managers instructed to practice data-driven decision making often underestimate the value of information. There is a need to development accountancy of the value contribution of information system, beyond periodic technical achievement. Benchmark studies should identify cost performance, as well as the proper usage of data and the strategic planning and accumulation of critical information resources within the organization.

FUTURE TRENDS

The historical development of information systems has followed the model of a rational manager, with emphasis on openness, clear structure, innovative practices and logical thinking. In regions where history and culture dominate the population, information system designer must consider the needs of emotional decision-makers, with heavy emphasis on tradition, relationship, and the maintenance of social and cultural harmony. Some culture demands tight control of information flow, while other culture is very casual about the absolute data quality. Some organizations integrate Information System as an organizational backbone, other preferred to separate information in isolated pockets. Some prefer a simple information system, while others invest in a sophisticated intelligence system. Information system for cross-cultural environment must deliver value to users with diversified backgrounds. Comparative study on information system features valued across cultural settings should improve the value delivery of the information system function.

CONCLUSION

After one decade of rapid technological development, information resource management is still a new concept to managers at the university. Data reports preparation is still a laborious activity, and accepted practices and administrative preferences still drive decision-making. Organizations that anticipate increasing exposure to multi-cultural environments should allow longer time for organizational adjustment to technical development. Information systems, originally developed as productivity tools for data processing and report generation, must undergo radical design evaluation to meet the diversified user expectations and information skills. Information resource manager must also carefully consider data ownership and data distribution issues. Cultural preferences and information values should be carefully considered in the justification of information services. Information system objective should be clearly distinguished from information system capabilities, especially with different cultural interpretation of information value. Management should play an active role in defining organizational data flow, with implementation of appropriate incentives. Special attention should be given to precise data definitions, especially with a workforce with different training backgrounds under different cultural and language settings. Lastly, it is critical to emphasize strict standards for data quality, due to difference in expectations for the information system performance.

REFERENCES

Applegate, L. (1995). *Designing and Managing the Information Age IT Architecture.* Harvard Business School Press, September 26.

Davenport, T. (1997). *Information Ecology: Mastering the Information and Knowledge Environment.* New York: Oxford University Press.

Duncan, G.T. (1999). Managing Information Privacy and Information Access in the Public Sector. In G.D. Garson (Ed.), *Information Technology and Computer Applications in Public Administration: Issues and Trends* (pp. 99-117), Hershey, PA: Idea Group Publishing.

Heeks, R. (1999). Management Information Systems in the Public Sector. In G.D. Garson (Ed.), *Information Technology and Computer Applications in Public Administration: Issues and Trends* (157-173). Hershey, PA: Idea Group Publishing.

Hofstede, G. (1980). *Culture's Consequences: International Differences in Work-Related Values.* Beverly Hills, CA: Sage.

Kepner, C.H. & Tregoe, B.B. (1965). *The Rational Manager.* New Jersey: Kepner-Tregoe.

McLeod, R.M., Jr. (1998). *Management Information Systems.* New Jersey: Prentice Hall.

O' Brien, J.A. (2002). *Management Information Systems: Managing Information Technology in the E-Business Enterprise.* New York: McGraw-Hill.

Osterman, P. (1991). Impact of IT on jobs and skills. In M.S. Scott Morton (Ed.), *The Corporation of the 1990s: Information Technology and Organizational Transformation,* New York: Oxford University Press.

Oz, E. (2002). *Management Information Systems.* Boston, MA: Course Technology.

Parker, M. (1996). *Strategic Transformation and Information Technology: Paradigms for Performing While Transforming.* New Jersey: Prentice Hall.

Raman, K.S. & Watson, R.T. (1997). R. T. National Culture, Information Systems, and Organizational Implications. In P.C. Deans & K.R. Karwan (Eds.), *Global Information Systems and Technology: Focus on the Organization and Its Functional Areas* (pp. 493-513). Hershey, PA: Idea Group Publishing.

Rocheleau, B. (1999). The political dimensions of Information Systems in Public Administration. In G.D. Garson (Ed.), *Information Technology and Computer Applications in Public Administration: Issues and Trends* (pp. 23-40), Hershey, PA: Idea Group Publishing.

Shea, T. & Lewis, D. (1996). The Influence of National Culture on Management Practices and Information Use in Developing Countries. In E. Szewczak & M. Khosrowpour (Eds.), *The Human Side of Information Technology Management* (pp. 254-273), Hershey, PA: Idea Group Publishing.

Schafer, S. (1995). How Information Technology is Leveling the Playing Field. *Inc. Technology, 4,* (92).

Chapter IV

Analysis of the Cross-Cultural Dimensions of National Web Portals

Sajjad Zahir
University of Lethbridge, Canada

Brian Dobing
University of Lethbridge, Canada

M. Gordon Hunter
University of Lethbridge, Canada

ABSTRACT

When new technologies become available and cultures adopt them, the result can be convergence or divergence when cultures adopt technology in different ways that maintain or even further accentuate their differences. An analysis of full-service national web portals from different countries, typically offering a search engine, directories of links on a set of selected topics, news items (including weather, sports, entertainment, and stock market results), advertisements and shopping, and free e-mail, shows evidence of both trends. While most national portals closely resemble the basic structure of Yahoo!, the original free full-service portal, there are also differences in appearance and features offered that can be attributed to cultural variations based on Hofstede's framework.

INTRODUCTION

Culture can be defined as the manifestation of "learned behavior consisting of thoughts, feelings and actions" (Hoft, 1996) formed under the influences of social, biological, psychological, economic and ecological environments over an extended period of time. But, as Hoft notes, culture is a complex subject encompassing many diverse concepts. By 1952,

Kroeber and Kluckhohn (1963) had already identified 164 definitions of culture, ranging from "learned behavior" to "ideas in the mind," "a logical construct," "a statistical fiction," and "a psychic defense mechanism" and claimed that over 300 existed (p. 291). Culture is a product of learning (Hoebel, 1971; Murdock, 1965), varying from place to place and changing over time. Such changes are accelerated by various social exchanges, direct and indirect, among peoples. Creative processes or innovations diffuse through cultures, so times of rapid technological innovation are likely to see accelerated cultural change.

When new technologies become available and cultures adopt them, there is a wide range of possible outcomes that can be described along a dimension of convergence to divergence. Sometimes, cultures become more similar as they adopt technology, leading to convergence. Alternatively, cultures may adopt technology in different ways that maintain or even further accentuate their differences. This creates divergence. Convergence theory, well summarized by Coughlin (2000), can be traced back to the 18th century. By the 1960s, convergence theorists suggested that economic development would mean that cultures should begin to become more similar in social organization, class structure, or family characteristics. While research shows that convergence is by no means inevitable, particularly in a simple linear fashion, the concept remains a useful way to view the impact of change on cultures.

Recently, the Internet has brought about a revolution in information and communication technology, affecting many aspects of the personal, professional and social lives of those connected through it. From its roots in the United States, the Internet has spread rapidly in the past decade and is now accessible in most parts of the world (although not to most people in the world). The Internet is changing the way we do business, obtain an education and learn other skills, gather information, bank and invest, pay bills, listen to music, see movies, buy and sell things, exchange greetings and communicate with others, express views, participate in debates and are entertained. These changes are likely to affect cultures. But are all cultures being affected in similar ways, leading to greater cultural homogeneity (i.e., convergence)? Is the Internet a "virtual cultural region," as Johnston and Johal (1999) suggest? Or are different cultural groups adopting this particular information technology in different ways consistent with their culture (i.e., divergence)?

To address these questions, this study examines national web portals in countries around the world. Portals are "gateways" to the Internet, web sites that provide some basic information and services themselves and, more importantly, provide access to selected sites in the Internet through links and to many other sites through search engines. Initially, there were only a few such sites (notably Yahoo!) suggesting a convergence view. But Yahoo! was quickly followed not only by American competitors, but national portals in many countries. This study was designed to identify both the similarities and/or variations among national portals and attempt to explain these findings. More importantly, the results will establish a foundation for further research of this type. The results at this relatively early stage of Internet usage are mixed. While national portals show considerable similarity, a closer examination reveals some important differences that do reflect local cultures.

BACKGROUND AND LITERATURE REVIEW

As the world becomes more connected through technology, two competing hypotheses have emerged regarding the effect of globalization on culture. These hypotheses are discussed in more detail by Webber (1969), Yang (1986), and Ronen (1986). One hypothesis, convergence, suggests that cultures will become more similar as they modernize because they must pass through a "relatively fixed pattern of development" (Coughlin, 2000, p. 422). In addition, "the rapid growth of telecommunications and computing technology … holds profound implications for possible societal convergence" (Coughlin, 2000, p. 428). The Internet could play a key role in this process.

The opposite hypothesis, divergence, suggests that cultures tend to resist assimilation and adapt technologies in culturally distinct ways. Furthermore, the cost of technological assimilation can be considerable, leaving "have not" cultures unable to participate to the same extent even if the population might wish to do so. In some cases, the same technology can result in both convergent and divergent outcomes.

One of the difficulties in researching convergence theory is determining where to look for it. For example, Coughlin (2000) identifies industrialization (including means of production, occupational mobility and differentiation, increased emphasis on formal education, and growth of cities), stratification of class structures and occupational prestige, demographic patterns, family life, education, and the welfare state as areas of interest. Most quantitative research has been cross-sectional, although longitudinal studies seem more appropriate (Williamson and Fleming, 1977).

Most research on global or international information systems takes a divergence perspective, pointing out the problems that can occur when cultural differences are ignored. For example, Fernandes (1995) and Del Galdo and Nielsen (1996) provide guidance on user interface design. Both books point out problems that have occurred when user interfaces designed for one culture have been applied to another. More recently, researchers have been interested in cultural implications of global e-commerce issues (e.g., Davis, 1999) from a similar perspective. Simon (2001) provides empirical evidence that differences in the perception of web sites and satisfaction with them do exist among different cultures (and between men and women).

However, when Ein-Dor, Segev and Orgad (1993) investigated the effect of culture on international information system construction, they found considerable consistency and thus support for the convergence view. Ito and Nakakoji (1996) provide an interesting example of convergence, showing how Japanese word processors follow a Western typewriter model. They also note that Japanese programmers began with English languages (e.g., Fortran) and were reluctant to switch later to Japanese programming languages. Thus, information technology can also be a force for cultural homogeneity.

Web pages are much less expensive to build than programming language compilers and corporate information systems and so provide a much better opportunity for cultural customization. Johnston and Johal (1999) suggest that the Internet is a virtual culture and, using Hofstede's (1980) dimensions, conclude that this culture is both evolving and converging. Marcus and Gould (2000) reviewed selected web pages from various cultures, basing their analysis on updated work by Hofstede (1991). They conclude that culture, as expressed by Hofstede's dimensions, does affect the design of web pages. Thus, we can also see examples of divergence as cultures adapt new technology in different ways to suit their own needs. Simon (2001) also uses Hofstede's dimensions to analyze how students from different cultures react to select web sites.

Hofstede (1980, 1991), based on extensive research, suggests that culture may be differentiated via five major dimensions. These dimensions are described in Table 1 (adapted from Hunter and Beck, 1997).

Table 1. Hofstede's cultural dimensions

Dimension	Description
Individualism Collectivism	Individualistic cultures expect their members to be independent and look after themselves. Collectivist cultures have a tightly knit framework of mutual dependencies and obligations.
Power Distance	High Power Distance cultures accept unequal distribution of power within its society. Low Power Distance cultures strive for equalization and participation.
Uncertainty Avoidance	Strong Uncertainty Avoidance cultures attempt to control uncertainty by strict rules and codes of behavior. Weak Uncertainty Avoidance cultures are not as strictly controlled and deviation is more acceptable.
Masculinity Femininity	Masculine cultures emphasize achievement, success, and assertiveness. Feminine cultures emphasize caring, close relationships, and harmony.
Long-Term Orientation Short-Term	Long-term oriented cultures promote the family, respect for older people, and virtuous behavior such as hard work and frugality. Short-term oriented cultures develop equal relationships, emphasize the individual, and promote creativity and self-actualization.

This research builds on the work of both Hofstede (1980, 1991) and Marcus and Gould (2000) by focusing specifically on national portals. Web portals are Internet sites intended to be the starting point (i.e., a virtual launch-pad) to locate information and services on the Web.

Yahoo!, which began as a search engine in 1994, is perhaps the best known example. Full-service national portals are designed to appeal to a more focused audience within a country or culture, typically offering a search engine, directories of links on a set of selected topics, news items (including weather, sports, entertainment, and stock market results), advertisements and shopping, and other services such as free e-mail services and web pages. Thus, a full-service national portal is a platform for a collection of activities that are enabled by Web technology and that serve its intended audience (or culture). National portals are well suited for this research because they are quite common (many countries have multiple national portals), are intended for a particular culture or nation (rather than the worldwide Internet community), and are likely to endure and evolve over time. National portals will reflect the culture and values of developers, but they are also commercial ventures that must be responsive to the culture of their intended audiences to be successful. Just as a magazine's content says something about both those who produce it and those who read it, so does that of a national portal.

Paralleling the tremendous growth of e-commerce and other Internet services, the role of portals will continue to evolve rapidly. Portals may become the major link to entertainment and informational video (as the Internet and television converge), telecommunications (offering video phone calls), financial transactions, and other key services. Therefore, portals have the potential to become a major public policy issue. For example, Canada has tried to protect its magazine industry against split-run American magazines (Magder, 1998). Other countries have had similar concerns and will want to take steps to protect their interests. Yet, major portal providers often provide "split-run portals" for major countries and groups. For example, as of July 2002, Yahoo! offers links to 22 national or regional portals from its main page plus sites for American Chinese and Spanish speaking people. Some offer considerable local content, but there are currently few regulations or monitoring agencies to control this. Who determines the content is unclear. Nevertheless, split-run portals provide at least some local content. A recent survey by MMXI Europe found that about a third of the most popular sites in Germany, France and Britain were American portals (NUA, 1999).

Indigenous national portals catering to the needs of distinct national and cultural groups should reflect the socio-cultural, technological and economic characteristics of their cultures and countries both in their appearance and the list of services they provide. Of particular interest are national portals in Europe and Asia that are not in English. About half of Web content is expected to be non-English by 2003, up from about 20% in 1999 (Burke, 1999). Different countries and cultural groups have their own buying habits, social pastimes, ways of reporting and accessing news, values about public media, modes of business transactions, and ethics and taboos that restrict social practices. Not all countries are at the same level of technological adoption, either. As the world adopts Internet technology, portal developers must balance pressures towards convergence (i.e., providing a site much like Yahoo! which its intended customers may already be using) and divergence (i.e., to reflect cultural variations in their indigenous portals).

Some limitations of using portals to reflect culture should also be noted. In some countries, only a small percentage of the population has Internet access. Internet users are likely to be younger, wealthier and better educated than the average citizen (Johnston and Johal, 1999). Some will have gone outside their countries, often to Europe or the United States, for their education and are thus more familiar with these cultures. Some national portals may even target expatriates. Thus, until access to the Internet greatly increases, an argument can be made that national portals are directed at a small (and not necessarily representative) segment of some cultures.

RESEARCH METHODOLOGY

To include as many national portals as possible, we started with search engines, posted a request to the IS World list requesting help and added suitable entries from Microwho (an existing directory of portals and related sites). We first narrowed the list down by focusing on 26 countries, including those analyzed by Marcus and Gould (2000). Then, using WebZip

Table 2. Common portal features

Directories	Display Items/Links	Other Features

Arts
Community
Education
Health
Media and
Newspaper
Music and
  Entertainment
Personals
Politics
Religion
Science and
  Technology
Tourism and travel
Women Issues
	Advertising
	Auction
	Games
	Horoscope
	Job listings
	News stories
	Shopping
	Sports News
	Stock quotes
	TV Listing
	Weather
		Customizable
		  interface
		Chat
		Discussion Groups
		Download options
		Free e-mail
		Free Home Page
		Arts
		Community
		Education
		Health

(available at www.spidersoft.com), a complete copy of the initial page of each national portal belonging to those 26 countries was archived. Next, a program was written in Visual Basic to count the number of links from the HTML code for each national portal. For countries with more than one national portal, the one with the most links was selected. This provided the final set of 26 national portals that were studied in depth. While somewhat arbitrary, the national portal with the most links is arguably the most "full-service" and thus the best fit for the criterion used in this study.

Table 2 lists the common features present in most national portals, including Yahoo!, which is taken as the standard in our research. Almost all of the national portals have layouts similar to Yahoo! (i.e., Multicolumn Directory/Subdirectory with links, occasional frames and animated objects) except in few cases where the layout is unique (e.g., go-jamaica which appears to be aimed partly at tourists). When using Yahoo! as a standard, extra features are those that a national portal includes but Yahoo! does not, while missing features are those found in Yahoo! but not the national portal (see Table 3).

Since national portals tend to be designed by and targeted towards individuals belonging to the same cultural group, we may reasonably believe intrinsic cultural traits have been incorporated in the visual design of the interface. Among the various visual effects offered by national portals, we focused on color and layout. Colors reflect strong cultural values, much deeper than mere appearance. For example, green is generally considered an Islamic color, saffron yellow as Hindu/Buddhist, and red-blue-white-gold are colors of the Judeo-Christian West (Marcus and Gould, 2000). They identify color as an important new issue for global web user interface design, and suggest that the use of color could be related to Hofstede's Uncertainty Avoidance Dimension. Color could provide redundant cues (to reduce ambiguity for high uncertainty avoidance cultures) or maximize information without redundancy (for low uncertainty avoidance cultures). Colors were visually inspected to determine which was dominant by counting patches of color and the number of distinct color blocks. This provides some indication of the colorfulness of the portals.

Table 3. Content diversity and variations in visual effects among national portals

Portal Name URL No. of Links	Country/ Language	Missing Items	Extra Interesting Features	Dominant Color/No. of colors
Ahijuna www.ahijuna.com.ar 171	Argentina Spanish	Women's issues, religion, TV, Auction, Free Home Page, Stock Quotes, Discussion	Economy, humor, erotic (Diosas)	Gold 9
Matilda matilda.aaa.com.au 250	Australia English	Email, free home page, women's issues, religion, personals, auction, stock quotes, horoscope	Economy, humor	Light yellow 4
Web Watch www.webwatch.be 90	Belgium French	Health, women's issues, religion, politics, free email, free home page, TV, auction, games, sports, stock quotes	Personal pages – sex sites	Gold 4
Terra www.terra.com.br 179	Brazil Portuguese	Arts, science, personals, music, religion, politics, free email, free home page, weather	Personal finance	Orange 6
Sympatico www1.sympatico.ca 197	Canada English	Arts, science, education, media, religion	Kids & teens, business, personal finance	White 5
Sina www.sina.com.cn 293	China. Chinese-Simplified	Media, religion, auction, free home page, horoscope	Business, military	Gold 4
Costa Rica www.info.co.cr 108	Costa Rica Spanish	Community, women's issues, personals, religion, free email, free home page, TV, weather, auction, shopping, jobs, stock quotes, discussion, downloads, horoscope, news, games, chart	Business, culture, history	Light blue 5
Egypt Search www.egyptsearch.com 96	Egypt English	Women's issues, personals, free email, TV, weather, auction, stock quotes, horoscope, downloads, games, chart	Egyptian culture	White 3
Canoe www.canoe.fr 173	France French	Education, health, community, personals, religion, free e-mail, free home page, auction, jobs, discussion, chat downloads	Pull down menus	Very dark blue 9
Ins-Netz www.ins-netz.de 195	Germany German	Arts, education, media, community, women's issues, personals, religion, politics, free email, free homepage, TV, auction, jobs, horoscope	Erotica, business, hobbies, real estate	Dark blue 6
Ghana Forum www.ghanaforum.com 34	Ghana English	Science, media, community, women's issues, music, religion, free e-mail, free home page, TV, weather, auction, shopping, job, stock quotes, discussion groups, horoscope, news, games	Business Main page has very little – need to use subsidiary pages	Light brown 5
123India www.123india.com 219	India English	TV, free home page, jobs, discussion groups, downloads	Emigration, dating, matrimonial, Bollywood	Light yellow 5
Catcha www.catcha.co.id 156	Indonesia English	Community, free home page, TV, auction, shopping, stock quotes, sports	Children's stories, business	White 5
Kataweb www.kataweb.it 279	Italy Italian	Science, women's issues, personals, religion, politics, auction, free home page, stock quotes	Business	White 5
Isize www.isize.com 239	Japan Japanese	Arts, science, media, health, women's issues, personals, music, religion, politics, free email, free home page, TV, auction, discussion, games, chat	Personal finance, real estate, marriage planning	White 12

Table 3.   Content diversity and variations in visual effects among national portals (continued)

Portal Name URL No. of Links	Country/ Language	Missing Items	Extra Interesting Features	Dominant Color/No. of colors
Malaysia Directory www.malaysia directory.com.my 184	Malaysia English	Customizability, Horoscope Download options, Top news stories, Women issues, religion,	Martial arts as sport, Koi Fish forum as hobby	Yellow 9
El Sitio www.elsitio.com/ elsitio/mexico 100	Mexico Spanish	Science, Politics	Entertainment including erotic entertainment is explicitly profiled	Blue Yellow 14
Menara www.casanet.net.ma 134	Morocco French	Religion, Games, Health in general, Politics, Education, Stock quotes are absent but financial news are covered, Auction	Soccer as sport is highly profiled, although an Islamic country, Islamic reference is non-existent implying a more secular trend in Moroccan society, woman's issues are well presented	Grey 7
Zoek www.zoek.nl 191	Netherlands Dutch	Auction, Free Web page,	Sex related matters and links are prominently profiled. Soccer as sport is noted.	Deep blue 11
Pinoy Central www.pinoycentral .com 121	Philippines English	Horoscope	Extensive links for immigration, Shopping site for remittance by the Philippinos working abroad	Blue 13
Onet www.onet.pl 210	Poland Polish		Indirect links to erotic sites and adult contents. Polish beauty pageants related displays are prominently displayed	Yellow 11
Aport www.aport.ru 291	Russia Russian	Stock quotes, Free Web page, Auction	Science coverage is substantial, erotic entertainments are explicitly linked, family is focused widely, Soccer and ice-hockey as sports are profiled	Blue 10
Genie www.arrakis.com 209	Spain Spanish	Politics, Jobs	Spanish cooking is well profiled, Soccer-mania is mentioned	Green 9
Spray www.spray.se 162	Sweden Swedish	Auction, Science,		Green 9
Mirago www.mirago.co.uk 113	UK English	Stock Quotes, Chat, Customizability, Free Web page, E-mail, Religion, Science, Auction		Yellow 10

The layouts of all the national portals are found to be very similar to that of Yahoo! (multiple columns in rectangular arrangements), with only the layout of Go-Jamaica being different (semicircular arrangement of items each being a circular object). Thus, no further analysis of layout was performed.

DISCUSSION

The Internet has emerged as a great equalizer in respect of global information access, access to global markets and gender equality (Hoffman, 1998). However, as shown in Table

3, not all national portals are the same. Color combinations, contents and level of details vary. Religion and politics are not profiled in all of the national portals. Women's issues do not receive much attention, either. However, in many countries, immigration to the West is a very significant process of social mobility and this is reflected in their national portals. Such countries have large expatriate communities. For example, Indian communities abroad can keep in touch with the latest gossip from the movie industry in Bombay (Bollywood) and about other celebrities. Arranged marriage is common in India and thus, as expected, matrimonial advertisements are prominent in their national portals. (In other cultures, the focus may be on dating rather than marriage.) Obtaining stock quotes is a common feature in many countries, while others do not have this option. The reason may be partially technical; obtaining real-time quotes may be difficult in less developed countries. Levels of stock ownership will also vary. Many countries have key national sports (e.g., cricket in India, soccer in Europe and Latin America, etc.) highlighted. Access to erotica and sex-related entertainment varies greatly from country to country. Central and Eastern Europe are more open, while even Yahoo! has avoided this area.

The color of hyperlinks is set to blue as the default in many software packages (e.g., FrontPage). Since this software package (a product of the USA) is perhaps the backbone of the Web technology commonly adopted by other countries, text links are overwhelmingly blue. In Table 3, we list any dominant color other than the hyperlink's blue. However, there are instances when color of the portal truly reflects a national color. For example, purple orchid is the national color of Thailand (e.g., Thai Airways), and this color dominates the Thailand.com portal. Similarly, green dominates the Pakistani portal and 123India has shades of saffron.

Yahoo!, which is a leading free American full-size portal, has apparently been followed en masse both in design and diversity of contents. AOL is also another comprehensive full-service portal, but available only to those who have a paid subscription to access it. AOL's design is different and technically more complex. We have not found any free national portal that uses a design similar to AOL.

Hofstede's Dimensions

Hofstede's (1980) initial research resulted in the identification of four cultural dimensions:
- Power Distance
- Individualism—Collectivism
- Masculine—Feminine
- Uncertainty Avoidance

A fifth dimension was subsequently added (Hofstede, 1991) relating to Long-term versus Short-term orientation. Hofstede's (1991) tables on Power-Distance (p. 26), Individualism (p. 53), Masculinity (p. 84), Uncertainty Avoidance (p. 113) and Long-Term Orientation (p. 166) were combined to create Table 4. The Rank shown in Table 4 is based on the original tables, which contain many more entries than the summary table provided here. When scores are tied (e.g., Argentina and Japan are both 26 on the Individualism-Collectivism measure), this is shown as a shared ranking (e.g., 22/23). The Long-Term Orientation dimension has not been included in our analysis because of the lack of available data from Hofstede's research related to the cultures reviewed in our research project.

Power Distance

The first of Hofstede's dimensions to be employed to analyze our data is Power Distance. This dimension relates to a culture's willingness to accept a difference in power over other members of the culture. Thus, high Power Distance cultures tend to be willing to accept differences in the distribution of power across cultural members. However, low Power Distance cultures will strive for an equal distribution of power. Examples from our data include the Philippines and Costa Rica, as shown in Table 5.

Thus, according to Hofstede, The Philippines is considered a high Power Distance culture, and members are willing to accept a difference in power distribution. Evidence of this is found on The Philippines' portal relating to the Extra Features noted in our data. This national portal provides the unique service of shopping for Filipinos working abroad. It should be noted that a vast number of Filipinos work outside of The Philippines and gain economic power through salaries that are significantly higher than those that are paid in The Philippines. Indeed, it is common for university-trained Filipinos to work as domestic helpers throughout Asia.

Costa Rica, however, is a low Power Distance culture on Hofstede's dimension, and members will strive for an equal distribution of power within the culture. Once again,

Table 4. Hofstede's indices of cultural dimensions (a selected sample)

PORTALS	PDI		IDV		MAS		UAI		LTO	
	Rank	Score	Rank	Score	Rank	Score	Rank	Score	Rank	Score
Argentina	35/36	49	22/23	46	20/21	56	10/15	86		
Australia	41	36	2	90	16	61	37	51	15	31
Belgium	20	65	8	75	22	54	5/6	94		
Brazil	14	69	26/27	38	27	49	21/22	76	6	65
Canada	39	39	4/5	80	24	52	41/42	48	20	23
China	-	-	-	-	-	-	-	-	1	118
Costa Rica	42/44	35	46	15	48/49	21	10/15	86		
Egypt										
France	15/16	68	10/11	71	35/36	43	10/15	86		
Germany	42/44	35	15	67	9/10	66	29	65		
Ghana										
India	10/11	77	21	48	20/21	56	45	40	7	61
Indonesia	8/9	78	47/48	14	30/31	46	41/42	48		
Israel	52	13	19	54	29	47	19	81	-	-
Italy	34	50	7	76	4/5	70	23	75		
Japan	33	54	22/23	46	1	95	7	92	4	80
Malaysia	1	104	36	26	25/26	50	46	36		
Mexico	5/6	81	32	30	6	69	18	82		
Morocco										
Netherlands	40	38	4/5	80	51	14	35	53	10	44
Philippines	4	94	31	32	11/12	64	44	44	21	19
Poland									13	32
Russia										
Spain	31	57	20	51	37/38	42	10/15	86		
Sweden	47/48	31	10/11	71	53	5	49/50	29	12	33
United Kingdom	42/44	35	3	89	9/10	66	47/48	35	18	25

Table 5. Power difference examples

	Rank	Score
Philippines	4	94
Costa Rica	42/44	35

evidence of this is found in the Extra Features section of the Costa Rica portal. Links are provided to information about Costa Rican culture and history. These links represent evidence of the country's willingness to equally share the information about itself.

Individualism—Collectivism

Within this dimension, Hofstede suggests that members of Individualistic cultures will tend to be independent and will feel responsible for looking after themselves. Collectivist cultures, however, will include members who maintain a series of close interpersonal relations and who feel a social obligation to do so. These relationships and obligations are most often manifest in extended families.

Australia and Indonesia represent interesting examples from our data, as shown in Table 6.

As an Individualistic culture, Australians would tend to act more independently. Evidence of this action is found in our data, which lists those items not included on their portal. That is, items such as Women's Issues, Religion, and Personals are noted as absent on the Australian portal. These items, in general, represent ways of bringing people together. Thus, Australians, according to this Hofstede dimension, do not feel the necessity to provide these group oriented services on their national portal.

Indonesia is considered a Collectivist culture from the perspective of Hofstede's dimension and members will attempt to maintain strong family ties. Evidence of this is found in the Extra Features section of our data. Here a link is provided for Children's Stories. This represents evidence of an attempt to provide, via their national portal, a family-oriented activity.

Masculine—Feminine

This dimension, Hofstede suggests, relates to the quality, rather than quantity, of life. Thus, Masculine cultures emphasize assertiveness and achievement, while Feminine cultures emphasize harmony and caring. Contrasting cultures are Japan and Sweden, as shown in Table 7.

An example from our data is on the following page.

Table 6. Individualism-collectivism examples

	Rank	Score
Australia	2	90
Indonesia	47/48	14

Table 7. Masculine-feminine examples

	Rank	**Score**
Japan	1	95
Sweden	53	5

Uncertainty Avoidance

Hofstede suggests that cultures will vary according to the members' willingness to deal with uncertainty. Thus, strong Uncertainty Avoidance cultures will adopt strict rules and codes of behavior in order to reduce the uncertainty encountered in daily activities. However, weak Uncertainty Avoidance cultures will adopt a less controlled approach. The example from our data, as above, includes both Japan and Sweden as shown in Table 8.

In both the dimensions of Masculine – Feminine and Uncertainty Avoidance, Japan has been rated as Masculine and strong Uncertainty Avoidance. Thus, according to Hofstede, the Japanese culture would include members who would tend to emphasize achievement within relatively strict codes of behavior. Evidence of this is found in the Extra Features section of our data. Here, specifically, the Japanese portal lists such links as Personal Finance, Real Estate, and Marriage Planning. These links represent the presentation of a common approach to what could be considered the most important activities an individual will engage in throughout the lives. The portal is suggesting a common approach to these important activities.

Another perspective that can be employed to analyze the data is by topic. This results in the emergence of two topic themes relating to Sports and Erotica. National portals with Sports links include Malaysia, The Netherlands, and Spain. These cultures when viewed using Hofstede's dimensions all score quite highly masculine on the Masculine – Feminine dimension. In general, sports are associated with activities that are more masculine.

National portals containing Erotica links include Argentina, Belgium, Germany, and The Netherlands. In this case, these cultures are ranked relatively high (in comparison to the other dimensions) on Hofstede's Power – Distance dimension.

CONCLUSIONS

This review of the content of national portals is an attempt to better understand the cultural variations of these portals and to comment on their design. We analyzed the contents of 26 national portals and mapped our findings unto the dimensions of cultural variability as presented by Hofstede. The detailed results have been discussed above. Both convergence and divergence forces were clearly apparent. The national portals all look very much like

Table 8. Uncertainty avoidance examples

	Rank	**Score**
Japan	7	92
Sweden	49/50	29

Yahoo! and often offer remarkably similar directory headings and other links. Now that these formats have been established, it may be difficult for newer forms to emerge even if they are more culturally appropriate. Nevertheless, we find evidence of divergence, where national portals are customized to fit at least some cultural characteristics.

National portals, and indeed the Internet itself, are relatively recent phenomena. By collecting data at this point and building an archive of portals, we can continually monitor developments within both cultures as well as the convergence and divergence that work across cultures.

REFERENCES

Burke, B. (1999). Whither To Portals? *NUA Analysis*, March/April. Retrieved on [Insert Date] from the World Wide Web: http://www.nua.ie/surveys/analysis/bimonthly/archives/1999/mar_april.html)

Coughlin, R.M. (2000). Convergence Theories. In E.F. Borgatta & R.J.V. Montgomery, (Eds), *Encyclopedia of Sociology*, (2nd ed.)(pp. 422-431) New York: Macmillan.

Davis, C.H. (1999). The Rapid Emergence of Electronic Commerce in a Developing Region: The Case of Spanish-Speaking Latin America. *Journal of Global Information Technology Management, 2*(3), 25-40.

Del Galdo, E.M. and Nielsen, J. (1996). *International User Interfaces*. New York: John Wiley and Sons.

Ein-Dor, P., Segev, E., and Orgad, M. (1993). The effect of national culture on IS: Implications for international information systems. *Journal of Global Information Management, 1*(1), 33-44.

Fernandes, T. (1995). *Global Interface Design*. Boston, MA: Academic Press.

Hoebel, E.A. (1971). The Nature of Culture. In H.L. Shapiro, (Ed.), *Man, Culture and Society,* (pp. 208-222) London: Oxford University Press.

Hoffman, K.E. (1998). Internet as Gender-Equalizer? *Internet World*, November 9, 32.

Hofstede, G. (1980). *Culture's Consequences: International Differences in Work-Related Values*, Beverly Hills, CA: Sage Publications.

Hofstede, G. (1991). *Cultures and Organizations: Software of the Mind: Intercultural Cooperation and its Importance for Survival*. New York: McGraw-Hill.

Hoft, H. (1996). Culture and Design. In E.M. Del Galdo & J. Nielsen, (Eds.), *International User Interfaces*, (pp. 41-73) New York: John Wiley and Sons.

Hunter, M.G. and Beck, J. (1997). A Cross-Cultural Comparison of "Excellent" Systems Analysts. *Information Systems Journal, 6*(4), 261-281.

Ito, M. and Nakakoji, K. (1996). Impact of Culture on User Interface Design. In E.M. Del Galdo & J. Nielsen, (Eds.), *International User Interfaces,* (pp. 105-126) New York: John Wiley and Sons.

Johnston, K. and Johal, P. (1999) The Internet as a 'virtual cultural region': Are extant cultural classification schemes appropriate? *Internet Research, 9*(3), 178-186.

Kroeber, A.L. and Kluckhohn, C. (1963). *Culture: A Critical Review of Concepts and Definitions*. New York: Vintage Books. (Originally published in 1952 as Vol. 47 No. 1 of the Papers of the Peabody Museum of American Archaeology and Ethnology.)

Magder, T. (1998). Franchising the candy store: split-run magazines and a new international regime for trade in culture. *Canadian American Public Policy 34*, 1-66.

Marcus, A. and Gould, E.W. (2000) Crosscurrents - Cultural Dimensions and Global User-Interface Design. *Interactions, 7*(4), 32-46.

Murdock, G.P. (1965). *Culture and Society.* Pittsburgh, PA: University of Pittsburgh Press.

NUA (1999). *U.S. Brands Dominate the European Net.* Retrieved on October 22, 1999 from the WWW: http://www.nua.ie/surveys/?f=VSandart_id=905355360andrel=tru

Ronen, S. (1986). *Comparative and Multinational Management.* New York: John Wiley and Sons.

Simon, S.J. (2001). The Impact of Culture and Gender on Web Sites: An Empirical Study. *Database for Advances in Information Systems, 32*(1), 18-37.

Webber, R.H. (1969). Convergence and Divergence. *Columbia Journal of World Business, 4*(3), 75-83.

Williamson, J.B. and Fleming, J.J. (1977). Convergence Theory and the Social Welfare Sector. *International Journal of Comparative Sociology, 18*(3-4), 242-253.

Yang, K.S. (1986). Will Societal Modernization Eventually Eliminate Cross-Cultural Psychological Differences. In M.H. Bond, (Ed.), *The Cross-Cultural Challenges to Social Psychology,* Newbury Park: Sage Publications.

Chapter V

The Retention of Women in Information Technology—A South African Perspective

Nata van der Merwe
University of Cape Town, South Africa

Adrie Stander
University of Cape Town, South Africa

ABSTRACT

The retention of women in Information Technology (IT) is a global problem. This chapter reflects on the results of a comprehensive study of women in the South African IT Industry. Areas covered are demographics, experience and qualifications, the work environment, discrimination, gender issues, technical abilities, mentors and other issues related to women in the IT industry. Factors affecting the retention of women in the South African IT Industry are identified, and popular beliefs with regard to the preferences of female IT employees are examined. The authors believe that the findings reported on in this chapter can provide valuable insights that can be used by companies world-wide to enhance employment policies as well as recruitment and retention strategies aimed at women in IT.

INTRODUCTION

This chapter reflects on the findings of a study that investigates women in the South African Information Technology (IT) Industry. In line with the rest of the world, women represent only 19 percent of IT employees in South Africa (Jovanovic, 2001). The objectives of the study were to find out how they, as a minority group in the IT-workforce, experience the industry and to establish the factors influencing the retention of women in the industry.

BACKGROUND

Worldwide, there has been a strong drive to promote IT as a career for women and to attract them to IT-related courses. As De Palma (2001) points out, a wealth of available literature speculates about the reasons that so few young women enroll in IT-related courses. Many studies (Myers and Beise, 2001; Cuny and Aspray, 2000) focus on attracting and retaining female students and suggest ways to increase the number of young women preparing for and entering the IT Industry. This groundwork would be futile when these women enter the IT industry and an effort is not made to retain them as part of the workforce.

Carver (2000) hypothesizes that in order to attract more women to IT, the workplace must have flexible hours, part-time career options, the possibility of reduced work-hours, work-from-home possibilities and childcare facilities. These and other issues related to women in IT are investigated in this study.

Data for the study was gathered from women currently in the IT industry. The study aims to separate myth from reality in terms of what women want, their perceptions of the industry and what keeps them there, and to recommend employment strategies and management policies.

METHOD

A Web-based questionnaire was used to collect data. To reach as many women in IT as possible, the questionnaire was presented to the IT industry through an article in ITWeb, an important IT news site for Southern Africa. Women completing the questionnaire were also requested to forward the URL to female colleagues. To encourage participation, anonymity was guaranteed. After submission, respondents had the option to provide an e-mail address for further contact, which was stored independently of the questionnaire details. Although the questionnaire was comprehensive in its coverage, questions were designed to be quick and easy to complete. It took on average 10 minutes to complete and was available for a three-week period from late November until mid-December 2001.

DEMOGRAPHICS

A total of 299 women, representing nine major industry sectors and eight of the nine provincial regions in South Africa responded, with 32 percent of the respondents from the Western Cape and 61 percent from Gauteng. These two regions are the economical strongholds of South Africa. Respondents are from across the racial spectrum, with 6 percent Asian, 6 percent Black, 5 percent Coloured and 82 percent White, while 1 percent elected the Other-category. The 17 percent non-white vs. 82 percent White respondents is a fair reflection of the racial imbalance existing in skilled jobs in SA.

Woman of all ages took part in the study, with 1 percent being under 20 years of age and 1 percent being older than 45 years. 42 percent of the respondents are between 20 and 30 years of age and 45 percent between 30 and 45 years. Of concern is the sharp drop in numbers in the over-45 category.

Forty-one percent of the respondents are single, 44 percent married, 12 percent divorced and 3 percent elected the Other-category. Of the respondents, 37 percent are taking care of children, while 10 percent care for disabled or elderly relatives.

EXPERIENCE AND QUALIFICATIONS

The average work experience in IT is nine years, while non-IT experience averages at five years. Sixty-one percent of the respondents have a formal IT qualification, which can be broken down as follows:
- Commercial course 41 percent
- Technical College 12 percent
- Technikon (Technical University) 18 percent
- University 38 percent
- Postgraduate 24 percent

Of the respondents, 27 percent hold a recognised industry certification (e.g., MCSE). 31 percent also have non-IT qualifications.

The fact that the respondents have a number of years experience in IT and are well qualified, contributes to the validity of the survey results.

TYPE AND CONDITIONS OF EMPLOYMENT

Most women (85 percent) are in permanent positions while 12 percent work on a contract basis, 2 percent are self-employed and 1 percent work part-time or on a freelance basis.

The woman overwhelmingly indicate that flexi-time, work-from-home and equal pay for equal work are very important, while reduced hours is not seen as important. Alarmingly, many women (72 percent) indicate that salaries of women are not on par with male colleagues.

Part-time positions are not attractive, with the respondents agreeing that women in part-time positions are exploited in terms of:
- Less pay for harder work (78 percent)
- Career advancement and/or promotion (85 percent)
- Self-development and/or training (79 percent)

Fifty-five percent of the respondents indicated that they are willing to accept the above to have a more balanced life.

ROLE MODELS AND MENTORS

Although most women (68 percent) do not have a mentor, more than half of them (53 percent) act as a mentor. The majority are motivated by women in IT success stories and they strongly agree that women role models are important. Unfortunately, as shown in the next paragraph, management positions are still dominated by men, which makes women's role models a scarcity.

ORGANIZATION AND INDUSTRY RELATED ISSUES

The results show that the average number of male team members is six and the average number of female team members is three. Management positions are however, more male-dominated with 78 percent of respondents indicating a male immediate superior, and only 22 percent a female.

Although they are mostly satisfied with the management style of their superiors, they are undecided about the general management style in the organization.

The majority of respondents (86 percent) feel there is still gender bias in the IT Industry and 71 percent agree that employers still have the attitude that women employees will at some stage leave and have a family, with 73 percent indicating that the fact that a woman could have a family affects her career path.

An alarming 73 percent indicate that they have experienced discrimination. An industry breakdown indicated that IT-companies (as opposed to Banking or Insurance) are the worst offenders.

Eighty-six percent of the respondents agree that women are under-represented in the IT field, and an overwhelming 94 percent agree that women are under-represented in the IT executive and management teams. Most organizations (83 percent) do not have equal representation of male and female managers. An explanation for the sharp decline of respondents in the over-45 age category may be the fact that 70 percent of respondents report a perceived glass ceiling for women in the industry.

Stress is a factor for women in IT, with 76 percent indicating that it is stressful to balance work and personal life. However, 63 percent of the respondents believe that the stress of the IT environment is worth the rewards, with 49 percent indicating that stress is a factor that will influence them to leave the IT-Industry.

Nearly all respondents (97 percent) believe that women have special skills that they can contribute to the work environment, but that these skills are not valued by employers (66 percent).

Most respondents (64 percent) agree that gender stereotypes influence women's decisions to enter the IT-Industry. While respondents are undecided about being treated differently when getting married (49 percent/51 percent), 79 percent agree that women are treated differently once they start a family or have other family commitments. These perceptions are confirmed by the agreement of the respondents with regard to the status of women in the IT industry being influenced by:
- Being a single woman (67 percent)
- Being a working mother (78 percent)
- Being an older woman (72 percent)

Many of the respondents (58 percent) feel issues faced by women in South African IT are the same worldwide.

PROBLEM AREAS

A number of areas that are often referred to as problem areas were rated by the respondents, in order to establish to what extend these problems are perceived or real. Areas of concern are:

- Time (70 percent).
- The management style of superiors (61 percent)
- Sexism (60 percent)
- The different roles women have (59 percent)
- Personal and professional trade-offs (58 percent)
- Training and re-skilling opportunities (54 percent)
- Higher administrative workloads than male counterparts (53 percent)
- Lack of childcare facilities at work (53 percent)
- Family commitments (52 percent)

Of less concern are:

- Having young children (47 percent)
- Higher (general) workloads than males (46 percent)
- Workplace flexibility (40 percent)
- Academic commitments (34 percent)
- Community commitments (24 percent)

SUPPORT

Family

The respondents rated family support as extremely important, and indicated that they receive a high level of support from their families in areas such as housework, childcare, and on an emotional level. While they are willing to make family sacrifices for career advancement, the respondents are in strong agreement (88 percent) that male colleagues do not make the same sacrifices for career advancement.

Organizations and Networking

The majority of the respondents (89 percent) agree that the existence of an "old-boys" network gives men an advantage and that women do not network enough (76 percent). Respondents prefer to network at functions (57 percent) and conferences (49 percent), while launches (33 percent) and the Internet (34 percent) are less popular.

The role of support organizations is rated highly, with 77 percent indicating that it is important to very important. They overwhelmingly (89 percent) indicated that they will support female network organizations, with preferences being electronic forums (51 percent), monthly meetings (51 percent), and mailing lists (49 percent), while chat rooms (13 percent) are clearly unpopular.

TECHNICAL EVALUATION

Contrary to popular belief, women indicated that they do not find the technical environment intimidating. Seventy-one percent of respondents also do not think that women are less knowledgeable in technical environments and the majority (84 percent) do not think that women are less qualified to enter technical fields. They overwhelmingly agree (97 percent) that women need technical skills other than programming, but more than half (59 percent) feel that their organizations do not do enough to improve the technical skills of women.

CONCERNS

Although most companies in South Africa have affirmative action policies, the low number of non-white respondents (17 percent) is a matter of concern. Another area of concern is the low number of respondents (1 percent) in the over-45 age category. This is the age-group where many employees (men) are in senior management and decision making positions and it would be very unfortunate if the IT-Industry is losing women when they have a wealth of experience. The low percentage of women in this category could explain the low number of women in senior management positions in the industry. This is consistent with global trends. In Ahuja, (2002) it is reported that both trade journals and academic research indicate that women in the IT industry fields are concentrated at the lower and middle levels in corporations and are under-represented at the higher levels. Insufficient networking and the lack of female role models are two further areas of concern, as both are important tools for obtaining information, sharing experiences and building camaraderie, which are essential for climbing the corporate ladder.

CONCLUSION

Researchers initially believed that since IT is a relatively young field, traditional barriers for the advancement of women existing in the more established or older professional fields, e.g., old boys' networks, the lack of female role models and mentors, and other established perceptions and biases leading to discriminatory practices, would not affect the IT Industry (Ahuja, 2002). However, the results of our study indicate that this is not the case.

The results of the study give a clearer picture of what women in the IT Industry really wants. It was found that contrary to popular belief; women do not want to work fewer hours or part-time and are not overly concerned about child-care facilities at work. Women, however, do want the following:
- Flexi-time
- Equal pay for equal work
- To work from home
- Respect for their technical abilities
- To be valued for the special skills that they can contribute to the work environment

Follow-up research is already underway to investigate the areas of concern and to gather more input to establish what would make the industry more attractive for women. Two of the most prominent related current research areas are: a study to get the male viewpoint, as well as an exploratory investigation into ethnic imbalances within the South African IT Industry.

REFERENCES

Ahuja, M.K. (2002). Women in the information technology profession: a literature review, synthesis and research agenda. *European Journal of Information Systems, 11*(1), 20-34.

Carver, C.L. (2000). Research Foundations for Improving the Representation of Women in the Information Technology Workforce. Virtual Workshop Report, Department of Computer Science, Louisiana State University, Baton Rouge.

Cuny, J. and Asprey, W. (2000). Recruitment and Retention of Women Graduate Students in Computer Science and Engineering. Computing Research association, San Francisco, CA, June 21-22.

De Palma, P. (2001). Why Women Avoid Computer Science. *Communications of the ACM, 44*(6), 27-29.

Jovanovic, R. (2001). *It still pays to be in IT.* Retrieved March 9, 2001 from the World Wide Web: http://www.itweb.co.za

Myers, M.E. and Beise, C.M. (2001). Nerd Work: Attractors and Barriers Perceived by Students Entering the IT Field. ACM SIGPR 2001, San Diego, CA.

Chapter VI

Software Confederations—An Architecture for Global Systems and Global Management

Jaroslav Král
Charles University, Prague

Michal Žemlička
Charles University, Prague

ABSTRACT

Many (especially the large) software systems tend to be virtual peer-to-peer (P2P) networks of permanent autonomous services (e.g., e-government should be supported by the network of information systems of individual offices). The services are loosely coupled, a service can join/leave the system quite easily. We call such networks software confederation (SWC). The paradigm of the SWC is orthogonal to the paradigm of the object-oriented methodology. The architecture of SWC is an engineering necessity in the case of global or very large information systems (IS) and provides many software engineering advantages like incremental development, openness, modifiability, maintainability, etc. SWC is a necessity in many other cases. SWC supports the trend of large enterprises or modern states to be decentralized, dynamic, and able to work in the time of globalization. Software confederations are the result of the tendency to globalization, and at the same time, the tool allowing of implementation of IS for a globalized society. SWC changes basic features of a CEO's work as well as a CIO's. In both cases, it supports the decentralization. This paper discusses the motivation of software confederations, the techniques of their design and implementation, including the use of XML (inclusive SOAP-UDDI), their software engineering advantages, relation to object-oriented technology and methodological consequences of their use. The main conclusion is that the concept of SWC is the crucial for the future software and information technologies and substantially changes the management tasks of the CIO and CEO.

INTRODUCTION

The last 15 years were impressive for the success of object-oriented (OO) software and OO methodology. The OO paradigm was so successful and has become a respected standard. A unified OO methodology known as UML (unified modeling language) was developed by OMG and included into successful CASE tools. The success of OO was so great that it has overshadowed cases when object-orientation is not the best technique to use. Examples are the integration of legacy systems as well as of third-party products providing permanent services. Such systems are used as black boxes. Such architecture becomes crucial for information systems in global world and for global management. The architecture is not properly supported by the standard OO paradigm formalized in UML.

It appears, but is not generally accepted, that OO is good for systems that are mainly sequential. These systems have been developed mainly from scratch (with the exception of the use of OO libraries) and as one logical unit for example, the developers have good knowledge about all the parts of the developed system or they can easily gain it; no large constituent parts of the system must be used as black boxes). The result is that the reusability of the object-oriented code is rather low (Finch, 1998). The number of cases when people must use a paradigm other than an object-oriented one is surprisingly large. This scenario occurs when information technology should support global activities or the cooperation between competing companies.

It is usually required and expected that company information systems should support all company activities. The company cooperates with many external subjects; the set of these subjects and the level of the cooperation with particular partners changes quickly. It is therefore not possible to have an inflexible company IS.

It seems reasonable to enable temporal groups of companies to build information systems supporting their cooperation needs and common activities. On the other hand, it is reasonable that information systems of the members of such groups (coalitions) should be insensitive to the environment changes and protected against the attacks of outsiders (e.g., hackers) on their systems and data.

The easiest way to complete this task is to implement interconnections of existing information systems of the cooperating companies. Access gates of the companies' information systems than can serve both as watchdogs against hacks and espionage and as data transformers (they e.g., can convert the communication protocols from the proprietary one to the public one—and vice versa).

The common feature of such systems is that they have the structure of a peer-to-peer (P2P) network of permanent services. We call such systems *software confederations* (SWC). We will show in what respect the SWC paradigm differs from the OO model and what challenges and promises for the management it offers.

Let us illustrate the essence of the problem on the typical phenomenon of the global economy, on the example of the purchasing coalition of leading car vendors. The coalition wants to optimize the supply chain of car parts for all the members of the coalition. The information system that supports such a coalition must be implemented as a P2P network with peers being information systems of member car vendors (ISV)(see Figure 1).

The level of collaboration of the members of the coalition can vary.

Some car large vendors (they are in fact competitors) formed lately an alliance to optimize purchasing of car parts (and supply chain management in general). The coalition should behave as a new large subject. The subject needs a support of some new information system (IS). This IS must communicate with the information systems of the members.

It is advantageous to construct the system of the alliance so that the information systems of the members communicate in a peer-to peer manner.

The information systems of individual members should have a unified interface for the communication with information system (IS) of the coalition. The formats of the messages taking part in the communication must be designed, agreed, and implemented.

The implementation of the IS of the coalition is then independent of the implementation details and/or the implementation philosophy of the IS of the coalition members (member IS in the sequel). The number of attached member ISs can vary. The condition is that member IS provides gates able to implement the communication rules and procedures.

ISVs (in Figure 1) generate purchase requirements and other information to newly implemented services optimizing the parts purchasing. It is clear, that ISV (*information system of car vendor*) must work as an autonomous unit providing some data and services to the information system supporting purchasing activities. If we need to do it automatically, any ISV must be equipped by an appropriate gate and should be permanently active. Due to reasons explained below, it is advantageous to concentrate the functionality of purchasing module into a new permanent service component ISC (*information system of the confederation*) implementing the functions of the purchasing systems and the user interface into a peer UC. The *purchasing information system* (PIS) is then formed by a P2P network consisting of the following peers:

- The information systems of the car vendors (ISV). Every ISV is equipped by a gate G performing the communication of the peer with other peers.
- A newly developed peer (ISC) collecting and optimizing car parts orders.
- A peer (UC) implementing the interface of the operator of the purchasing system. It can be again equipped by a gate.

It is not difficult to connect the system with the information systems (ISP) of parts suppliers.

ISP should be again a peer of the P2P network. This feature can be used to support activities known as *supply chain management* (SCM).

The interconnection of the peers must be supported by a proper middleware, e.g., by Internet.

Figure 1. An implementation of the IS of the purchasing coalition

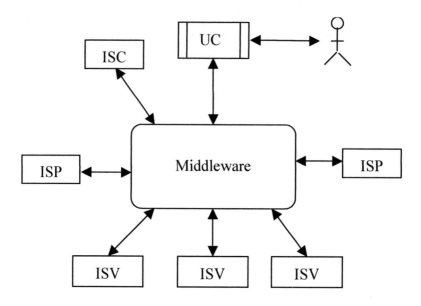

The structure of the system is shown in Figure 1.

Note that the integration or joining of a new peer is a quite simple task and can be performed via the programming of gates.

There are more cases when one must build a system similar to the just described one. For example, the system of flight tickets reservation has very similar properties - but it is simpler (ISC component is almost missing).

The software confederations like the one from Figure 1 have the following properties:

1. The system is a (virtual) P2P network of permanent autonomous services (called in the sequel *autonomous components*, AC) communicating via gates and a middleware. In our example ISV, ISP, and UC (user interface component) are autonomous components.

2. AC is ultimately integrated as a black box. It is the condition for the seamless integration of legacy systems and/or third-party products as well as for the modifiability, openness and other important software engineering properties.

3. New AC's can be easily added or excluded. This advantage can be used fully only in the case, that the interface provided by an AC *A* is very stable as the change of it influences all the components (partners) communicating with *A*. The problem is that sometimes it can be quite difficult to know all the partners (some can join the system later).

4. The communication between autonomous components is asynchronous. The messages between AC's have usually a quite complex meaning. The autonomous components can accept complex commands and/or provide a complex data queries.

5. The AC's provide often only a part of their functionalities or data; they can have its own users. They must be autonomous and should be developed/maintained independently.

6. The properties of the system can be adapted via changes of gates and via message routing.

7. Newly developed AC's can be developed autonomously and the whole system can be developed in an incremental way. If the structure of messages is agreed, e.g., via a specification of an XML dialect, the components can be tested using appropriate message generators. It simplifies development as well as management of the development.

8. The autonomy of components can be of different level from almost independent (as in above example or the system of flight tickets reservation) to highly dependent (examples are discussed below).

The number of cases, when the use of the architecture is the only feasible way leading to success is quite high. We will discuss some of them.

IS OF A STATE ADMINISTRATION

Any *e*-government must be based on a state information system (SIS). The SIS must satisfy many obvious requirements being unfortunately often (even worse - as a rule) not considered. The information system of any state administration is one of the largest software systems to be built in any country. The most important properties of the SIS are:

a) SIS should service all the citizens, enterprises, and/or state and municipal offices. It should provide data to anyone excluding the data excluded by law. The laws can specify different access rights for different users. The system must therefore be open and able to communicate with an unpredictable collection of collaborating systems outside SIS (banks, municipal systems, etc.). Any citizen should be able to communicate with all offices from one place. He should not bother with what offices should collaborate during the response to his request.

b) Secrecy and privacy rights must be supported.

c) SIS should support the collaboration of all state offices and majorities. Examples are the collaboration during the investigation of car robberies and/or document verifications.

d) The availability of many local functions of any (sub-) system need not depend on the global system and on the activities and services of the middleware.

e) SIS should be able to communicate with information systems of private companies at least at the territory of the state.

f) SIS should reflect almost in "real time" the changes in laws. Steady and seamless modification of the system is crucial. The modification process should not be too centralized, as then it would cause unacceptable delays. The central authority would then be a bottleneck.

g) The system should provide tools for the data filtering, mining, and analyzing. Various tools are necessary. It is very likely that many new tools will have to be added in the future.

h) As there are many systems used by particular offices, it is very difficult to rewrite them in time. The existing systems must be easily integrated into SIS without rewriting their application and data tier. The system cannot be developed from scratch, as it is too large. Such a system is difficult to develop and maintain in a centralized way as a monolith. If it is built as a monolith, then according to the known empirical laws, the development time must be long (it is proportional to the third root of the number of lines of the programs implementing the system (Boehm, 1981). The maintenance of such systems is very difficult and expensive, sometimes not feasibly implemented by any means.

i)   There are, however, more substantial reasons not to design the system as a monolith. No office will take responsibility for "its" (sub-) system if there is any doubt the subsystem supports its activities correctly. Any office can feel responsible for the data it produces and for the services it provides, only if it can trust the information system it uses. The office will therefore be required to influence or take part in the development and/or maintenance of its information subsystem. The office will oppose any changes of the kernel of the existing local (sub-) system if it works correctly. The office therefore tends to defend its subsystem. It usually implies that the office should take part in the (possibly autonomous) development and the modifications of "its" information system. Any actions and measures weakening the feeling of the responsibility of the office members for "their" (i.e., local) operations and data lead often to unpleasant consequences. We must also take into account such problems as prestige, lobbying, changes in political positions, corruption, etc. It is optimal under these conditions to prefer the integration of the existing (sub-) systems into the built confederation "as such," i.e., as black boxes.

It follows that any state information system should satisfy the following requirements:

i.   As the end user should not bother about the internal structure of the confederation, the user interface should be transparent; the users should need no knowledge about the internal structure and the implementation details and even implementation philosophy of the confederation and its components. The interface of the confederation should be easy to modify. Solution: Internet browsers and XSLT utility.

ii.   Security services (access rights, cryptographic services, rules of data replications, etc.) are provided.

iii. As the structure of confederations changes, the collaboration between autonomous subsystems should facilitate a quite easy modification and integration of components. So there must be a middleware supporting changeable complex message formats and standards for (meta-) data communicated between information subsystems.

iv.   As there are many different groups of users with different and changing needs, the regulations and methods how to implement communication and/or collaboration between components must be very flexible. The management of the SIS therefore need not and often should not take part in all the negotiations. Nevertheless, the management must develop the standards for the development of agreements and for the evidence of them as well as for the collecting the experience and development of generally acceptable standards.

It is not difficult to see that the communication subsystem (middleware) must offer further facilities like the data replication, general firewall tools, data warehouse facilities etc. Some services could be provided by components, some by the middleware. It is often not easy for the project management to decide what solution is better under given circumstances.

IS of a Global Company

Globalization enforces the international companies to be a worldwide network of relatively independent autonomous divisions (or autonomous enterprises). We shall call such enterprises *global enterprises* (GEN). The following features are typical for global enterprises:

i.   Dynamic changes of size. Quick changes of activity types. Heterogeneous activities.

ii.   Acquisition of previously independent companies (Hewlett-Packard bought Compaq).

iii.   A GEN often sells or outsources some its parts or it divides itself into several pieces (example: separation of health technologies from Hewlett-Packard).

iv.   The divisions of GEN's are usually active in countries with different legislatives and local cultures. Individual divisions can differ both by the kind of their activities and by their business culture.

v.   A seamless coordination with varying collection of business partners and state administration offices including the support of SCM (supply chain management), CRM (customer relationships management), purchase coalitions mentioned above, collaboration with existing and new business partners and/or customers.

vi.   The management of any global enterprise needs a wide support of analytical tools that should be obtained from specialized manufacturers (OLAP, workflow systems, statistical packages).

vii.   The partners should not need any knowledge o the structure of GEN. Points 1 and 2 imply the need of an easy integration of existing applications and IS (legacy systems) into the information system of the GEN. System changes, modification, and scaling should be easy.

Information systems of the divisions therefore ought to be autonomous and integration able. Heterogeneity and autonomy of constituent units of the GEN needs a rather big autonomy of the functions and an autonomous development of individual information subsystems (units). The reason is that some specific solutions are needed for the given unit only due to the diversity of the activities. The corresponding software entity must therefore be also autonomous, used as a black box, able to be integrated easily and eventually developed almost independently. In other words: any technical feasible structure of the information system of the GEN should have the mean features of software confederations.

There are many software engineering reasons for the use the architecture of software confederation in the discussed case. The development of a huge IS of a GEN as a monolith (one whole, no large parts are used as black boxes) is expensive, time consuming, and inflexible. If the subsystems are autonomous and loosely related (i.e., the system is a confederation), any possible failure of one of the subsystems need not necessary cause important consequences for other subsystems and for information system (IS) as a whole (compare the situation on WWW).

Splitting a company or selling out of some of its sub-units is substantially easier and economically more advantageous if it is possible to sell the sub-unit together with its IS. The possibility of the easy separation of such an IS and the possibility to sell it with as little knowledge about the IS of the whole GEN as possible is critical.

The connection between software components needs a powerful middleware. It can be used also for the communication with business partners and state authorities. The middleware should also allow end users (employees and business partners' agents) easy access to the information systems (e.g., to support *e*-commerce). An acceptable solution in the case of confederations discussed up to now is the Internet.

Activities in the countries with different legislative systems and culture have consequences also for the message formats. Heterogeneity of rules (e.g., shape and sometimes also the contents of invoices) forces the use of the data formats allowing the transformation of the document data into different forms.

We shall consider the IS like the IS of a GEN and/or of a state administration global information systems.

Shown facts imply following requirements on global information systems:

- Global information systems should be designed as a network of loosely coupled subsystems — it is as a confederation of subsystems.
- The subsystems offer permanent services.
- The subsystems should be autonomous — a failure of a subsystem should not spoil the run of the system as a whole.
- A parallel running of the subsystems is necessary; this is why asynchronous communication and the peer-to-peer philosophy should be used.
- There must be a powerful supporting middleware.
- The communication should allow exchange of data together with metadata to ensure flexibility needed for cooperation of the components in heterogeneous environments (countries). Some messages can be commands rather than data queries.
- The enterprise management often requires analytical tools. The easiest solution is integration of third-party products (e.g., OLAP or workflow systems) into the system.

There are many other cases when the use of confederated architecture is necessary or at least optimal. Give some of them:

- The information system of municipal offices
- Units of heath care systems
- Any enterprise having a decentralized architecture
- Information systems of large universities
- Education networks

Common Features of Global Information Systems

It follows from the above discussion that the following requirements are typical for global information systems. These requirements can be fulfilled by software confederations:

1. Incomplete, contradictory, often obscure, continuously growing and changing requirements due to changing business conditions or changing legislation.
2. The necessity to integrate third-party products as well as existing (legacy) systems.
3. The necessity to communicate with the software system of partners on different levels of interoperability varying from the communication between software entities of the organizational sub-units (e.g., divisions) to the communication with the software of a occasional customer.
4. The software supporting the activities of sub-units should provide local services also in the case when the whole system is down (e.g., the middleware does not work).
5. A changing, complex, and always growing set of users and user roles and the changing internal structure and the size of the software confederation.
6. The necessity to keep the autonomy of certain subsystems, e.g., a police information system inside the information system of state administration or an information system of a newly purchased company in the case of GEN. Besides it, there are many software engineering reasons for the autonomy of components.

7.   The necessity to collaborate with information systems of changing and unpredictable set of partner organizations (business partners in the case of a worldwide company, information systems of the companies residing on the state territory should communicate with IS of the state authorities).

8.   The distributed changeable user access rules and standards. The user interface should be easily modifiable and it should hide the system internal structure.

9.   As the number of components can be very large and some IS members need not be known at development time, it is not feasible to coordinate and/or to confirm the communication agreements between the components in a strictly centralized way.

10.   The continuous and seamless modification of the system is crucial. The modification process should not be too centralized, as it would cause unacceptable delays, as the bottleneck would be the central authority. It implies that the message formats (the syntax of messages) must be usually agreed in a decentralized way by the designers of the components. A feasible solution is a metatool able to define all the possible variants of the message syntax. A promising solution is XML. The problem is the optimal balance between the freedom in the choice of formats and the rules of standardization.

Note that Points 2, 4, 5 and 6 imply that the system must have the structure a network of large loosely coupled autonomous software units (autonomous components) providing permanent services interconnected by a powerful middleware.

All the components work like many services in human society or like www servers — i.e., they form a peer-to-peer network. The practice indicates that the network should be based on a middleware able to transport complex text messages. The messages are then words in a complex language having a quite rich structure and/or contents.

Autonomous component (AC) is usually a quite complex software entity, often provided by a third-party or it is a legacy system. AC is usually a complete application (often an IS) providing appropriate gates for the communication with other autonomous components of the network.

In business systems, a component can be OLAP or a complete warehouse control system. The inner structure of autonomous components is as a rule hidden. Autonomous components are therefore used as (total) black boxes. The only external knowledge on the AC is its interface defined via a complex language understood by their gates. The messages used in the communication should be rather declarative — they should specify what to do rather than how to do it. It facilitates the modifiability of the confederation. This feature can be strengthened if we use XSLT-based autonomous components as general message formats transducers. The architecture of the resulting systems can follow the principles shown in Figure 2.

Let us specify some details of the implementation of the communication between the components. A feasible solution is implemented via construction of gates opening the data and/or commands paths to and from the components. If a component is a three-tier (user interface tier, application tier, data tier, see Figure 2). The gate can be connected either to the application tier or to the data tier. In the former case, the messages addressed to the component will be rather command-oriented and can be sometimes specified by SOAP (Simple Object Access Protocol). In the second case, the messages will be data-oriented (their format will be based on some metadata based structure, e.g., UDDI or RDF). Both cases have their pros and cons. The command interface enables the access to all the functions of the

Figure 2. The gates of a three-tier information system

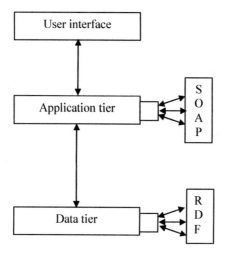

component but need not provide all the component data. It can be quite secure. Data gate provides in principle all the data, but not all functions.

Software Confederations in the Small

There is yet another variant of software confederations having origin in the design and development real-time (process control) systems like atom plant control systems, flexible manufacturing systems or simply the systems controlling a collection of automated house-hold devices in an automated family house. Such systems can work on one computer and can be quite small. Their middleware services are provided by the underlying operating system able to support symmetrical multiprocessing. We call these systems confederations in the small. The confederations discussed above will be called confederations in the large. The testing of real-time systems consists of:

a)   Software testing of the data correctness of the responses on the simulated signals of the controlled processes (i.e., the testing off line). Simulation uses software simulators. If the user interface is sophisticated enough, it can be used as a simulator.

b)   Off line testing of the timeliness of the responses with software simulators.

c)   Off line testing with hardware simulators. Some catastrophic cases are simulated as well.

d)   Testing the whole system, controlled process inclusive.

e)   During the system run, all the commands and reactions of the system operators must be logged.

The solution of the problem can be following one (see Figure 3). The system is designed as a confederation consisting of at least the following permanently active services (autonomous components, i.e., processes in the sense of a multiprogramming operating system allowing symmetrical multiprocessing):

1.   A component L containing the process control logic.

2.   A user (operator) interface component UC.

Figure 3. Structure of a real-time control system

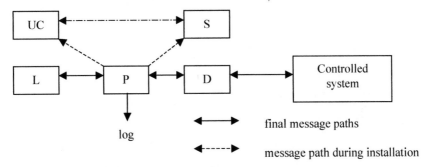

3. A component *D* containing all the I/O drivers. This is the only component communicating with the controlled system (process).
4. A communication component *P* called Post. All important messages in the system must be sent via the Post *P*. *P* sends the messages to the addressees and it can optionally log the messages. The messages can be redirected to other destinations (e.g., to a simulator or to UC) by a system administrator command.
5. Optionally, a simulator *S* containing some parts of the run time support of discrete event simulation languages like Simula 67 or at least the calendar of events. The task of *S* is to simulate the dynamics of the controlled system.

The point (a) can be implemented via redirecting messages to UC being able to accept and present them and being able to generate the messages for the logic *L*. UC is under these conditions used as a prototyping tool. The conditions are fulfilled if UC contains a browser. The point (b) can be implemented via redirecting messages to the simulation component *S*. The messages are logged together with the values TY-TS, where TY is the system time and TS is the cumulative time (duration) when the simulator *S* was active (running). It is not difficult to implement such a system.

Note that it is not necessary that *L* is one component only. If UC is sophisticated enough and *L* is formed by more than one component, then one can implement prototypes of the components not implemented yet via UC and via redirecting messages to UC. This is a feature very usable in the confederations in the large as well, but its implementation should be based on new tools allowing implement the concept of the Post as a modification of user interface components (see below).

The just described paradigm can and should be used in the case of quite small systems if the message administration is not too slow (ineffective). Such effectiveness problems appear, however, quite rare.

The implementation of real-time system described above is a very old application of the SWC paradigm.

COBOL SYSTEMS

In IT history, there is at least one parallel with SWC in the large. Surprisingly, it is the concept of systems written in COBOL developed according to the methodology of structured

Figure 4. DFD for a salary computation

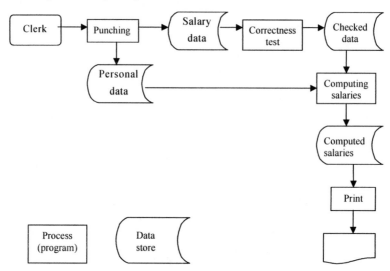

specifications. A key part of the structured specification and design are *dataflow diagrams* (DFD)(see Figure 4). DFD is a network of autonomous processes communicating via data stores (or files). Such COBOL systems can be characterized as a batch version of software confederations in the large.

COBOL-based systems have the structure of a network of autonomous programs implementing the processes (peer applications). Every autonomous program has as its input an *n*-tuple of files (datastores) and as an output another *m*-tuple of files/datastores.

What are common features of the software systems written in COBOL with SWC in the large? If the input data stores (files) are available, the output data stores (files) can be generated or modified autonomously — independently on other processes. Processes in COBOL programs are conceptually close to autonomous components in SWC, especially in this key feature.

Some further similarities between COBOL systems (we can call them *batch confederations*) and software confederations can be found also in the way the batch confederations are developed (i.e., in the corresponding software processes). The COBOL-masters created parametrizable processes as e.g., universal input reading and checking programs, report generating programs, various data transformers, etc. That was the main reason for COBOL's enormous success in programming history. The paradigm of batch confederation was the basic of the wonderful stability of the systems written in COBOL.

The most convincing proof of the stability of systems written in COBOL is the Y2K problem. It has appeared during the solution of Y2K problem that systems written in COBOL were used in the enterprises for many years without any maintenance. We cannot otherwise explain that there was an enormous need for COBOL programmers for the adaptation of COBOL programs to the new century (to be able to work with the year 2000 and more). Such an enormous lack can hardly be due to the peak of maintenance effort connected with the Y2K problem. In other words: the systems have been working without any problems for a very long time. Such a stability is often a dream only for present software systems. Let us note that reusability of COBOL programs was also (by some researches) better than reusability of object-oriented programs (Finch, 1998).

It is surprising how little have been this feature of COBOL appreciated by the software development theoreticians. They express themselves contemptuously about COBOL at all and especially about dataflow diagrams. Note that some constructs such as dataflow diagrams are planned for a new version of UML.

The above discussion indicates that many software theoreticians did not recognized the COBOL's main advantages. The theoreticians have enforced e.g., the use of object-orientation in situations when it disabled the application of the bath confederations. It has important consequences: Ideologized object-oriented view trying to expel from OO methodics dataflow diagrams spoils the knowledge needed for the development of large systems. The trend towards software confederations goes outside the research oriented to object-orientation (components based object-orientation inclusive).

It can lead to some improper managerial measures. Harry Sneed e.g., described during a discussion at Software Maintenance and Reengineering 2002 Conference (Budapest, April 2002) a case, when the CIO as well as the CEO of a large company insisted on the application of "modern" object-oriented paradigms during the development and maintenance of COBOL programs. They were surprised that even young new programmers were unable (did not will) to do it. Fortunately for the company, the programmers were wiser than the managers were.

ADVANTAGES OF SOFTWARE CONFEDERATIONS: CONSEQUENCES FOR THE CEO

Let us give the list of advantages of software confederations following from the above discussed facts.

1. Software confederation can be developed incrementally via adding new autonomous components.
2. Some components can be outsourced. The outsourcing can be easily revoked.
3. The confederation can be easily adapted to the current organizational structure of the enterprise using it. The confederation supports changes to modern organization structures. It should be the aim of CEO to promote such positive changes.
4. Software confederation is the only feasible solution of the support of many managerial problems and/or activities like company splitting, forming coalitions of vendors, selling of organizational sub-units, acquisition of firms, the use of analytical tools of third parties, etc. The software confederations are able to support modern decentralized organizational structures and support vertical as well as horizontal links and collaborations. The resulting structure is not merely the flattened original one neither it is reduced in another way (see Figure 5).
5. SWC can well support modern management practices and activities like CRM, SCM, etc.

The CEO, therefore, should require software systems to be confederated as a crucial precondition of modern management practices and techniques. The influence of the technology on the properties of the software systems is critical. Note that systems provided by many

Figure 5.   Changes of organizational structures

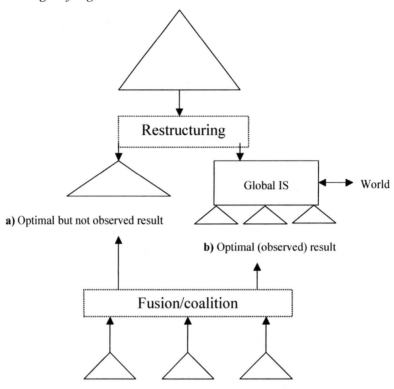

a) Optimal but not observed result

b) Optimal (observed) result

software vendors are invisibly confederated.

On the other hand, the advantages of the software confederations can be fully used up only in the case when the structure of the enterprise is decentralized and flexible and allows the autonomy of organizational sub-units and the vertical as well as horizontal variants of cooperation.

The use of software confederations changes substantially the tasks of CIO as well. In order to explain it, we must discuss some further technical details.

USER INTERFACE IN CONFEDERATIONS IN THE LARGE

Any dynamically changeable network of autonomous components can be used efficiently only when it contains a programmable, easily modifiable user interface supporting system (UC). It should support integrated interface to all components communicating with any user. WWW browsers have many good properties for such a purpose.

New utilities based on XML, especially the XSLT, allow to transform message formats, to integrate messages from various autonomous components into one message for screen, and vice versa to decompose the messages from the screen into several messages to be sent to several autonomous components. It allows designing a transparent user interface hiding the internal structure of the confederation if we use the attitude shown in Figure 6.

The user interface is to be implemented as a permanent service (i.e., autonomous component) transforming HTML messages from presentation software (browser) into *n*-tuples of messages in XML dialects (see Figure 4). The XML messages are sent to the gates of destination components and vice versa. HTML messages for the browser are composed from answers from several components. XSLT is a powerful tool working on syntactic trees specified by XML. We do not sufficiently understand its power yet. The knowledge of formal language theory is advantageous, but not yet widely used.

The XSLT based components can be used to enhance the modifiability and reusability of components. Let us discuss the problem:

The gates G1, G2, and G3 in Figure 6 should provide the full functionality provided by the corresponding components. If a component C is designed in the object-oriented way, its gate G tends to provide an object-oriented interface — i.e., (remote) method invocations. If C is a database system, the language of G will be probably a modification of a 4GL language. In other words, the communication partner must know a lot of information on the structure of the component to obtain the required service. Such a requirement is unrealistic since the set of collaborating partners of any component can vary and is unknown prior to development of the component. We say that gates providing full public functionality are basic ports (or basic gates). Any basic port provides all the services that the component may offer. The direct use of the basic ports has some drawbacks:

- The use of basic ports is too complex for many users due to the too fine granularity of their commands. Specific groups of users need a specific (often small) set of services

Figure 6. Parallel user access to multiple components

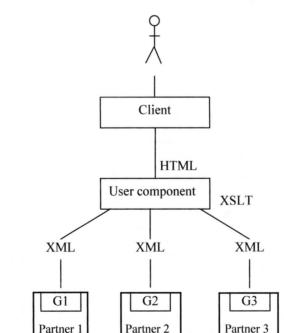

expressed in the terms of user problem domain. The users therefore need a specific problem-oriented messages formulated in a language in which the user is familiar.

- The basic port discloses too much information about the architecture of the component. For example, it is usually necessary to know that such a component is a relational database or an object-oriented application. It limits the possibility to replace the component by another one having different implementation. The main problem is that the change of the implementation philosophy can imply changes in all the components (partners) possibly communicating with the given one. As noted above, it is a quite difficult task, as the partners need not be known during the system development phase.

- The basic ports tend to use fine grain commands. If they are directly used, it increases the effort needed to design a dialog with the component. It also often increases the load of the communication infrastructure.

We must cope with the dilemma that we must somehow use the basic port, but we are not happy with it. The way out can be based on the following observation. The commands for the basic port of a component C can be viewed as elements of a "quite simple" implicit language L_C (a high level analogy of assembly languages).

As pointed out above it is required that the messages from a sender can be in a sender specific language L. L should be able to formulate the commands or queries in a form specifying 'what' to do rather than 'how' to do it (L is problem domain oriented). The syntax and semantics of L should fit the needs, knowledge, and habits of senders. The way to implement the requirement is to direct the messages from sender to a new autonomous component transforming the messages in L into (sequences of) messages in L_C and sending the messages in L_C to the basic port of C. We can view any message M in L as a command or a query for the component C generated by M. The message in L must be translated into "program" in L_C or interpreted via sequences of commands in L_C. The front-end gate can be a new component (Figure 7) used as a front-end processor of C. It is not difficult to see that *front-end gate components* (FEC) have functions quite similar to the functions of the user component in Figure 6.

Any component can have more than one FEC. The development of FEC's should be as easy as possible as there can be many FEC's and they should be easily modifiable.

Now we can use the results of the theory of syntax directed translation and compilation and syntax directed interpretation (Aho and Ullman 1972, 1973, Bison system). The FEC can have the following structure (see Figure 7):

1. The data specifying the syntax directed transformation — i.e., syntax and associated semantic symbols. We can use some compiler writing system. It requires, however, a specific knowledge. It is open whether we should use a dialect of XML, something like XSLT, for this purpose. Simple transformations can be obviously defined via XSLT. The use of XML and XML-based tools could broaden the number of people able to design new FEC's.

2. Outputs of the FEC are external messages in some problem-oriented language L (e.g., in a dialect of L). The sequences of commands in L_C can be viewed as the interpretation of the external messages in L.

The FEC can translate sequences of messages in L_C into messages in L. The techniques known from front-ends of syntax directed compilers could be used.

Figure 7. The extended component scheme

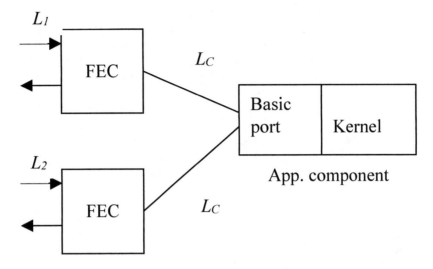

The open question is whether the XSLT systems are powerful enough to fully cope with such problems.

Our discussion indicates it is meaningful to distinguish three types of autonomous components:

1.   Application autonomous components (AAC) providing the main functionality of the system.
2.   Front-end gate components (FEC) enhancing the middleware services.
3.   User interface components (UC).

All the components are standard peers of the network forming a software confederation. They differ only in the functions they provide.

The use of syntax-directed FEC could substantially simplify the design and the modifications of the confederated systems. It supports the generation of multiple interfaces of a component. The interfaces can be quite declarative (i.e., problem oriented). The use of FEC implies a greater freedom in modifications of components (there is a greater chance that a modification of a component does not influence "declarative" front-end interface) and simplifies the design of the communication. The use of the syntax directed (compiler writing) techniques substantially simplifies the development of the FEC's. It is believed that the implementation of syntax-directed FEC in the YACC/Bison style could be specified via a new XML dialect (i.e., in XML). A good candidate can be a system combining the philosophy of XSLT and compiler writing systems. The advantages and/or limits of such a solution are the topics of future research.

It is quite easy to add log facilities mentioned above to the functions of FEC; it provides one the main functions of the Post discussed in the section *Software Confederations in the Small*. This is a very useful tool for system maintenance. Any problems analysis starts from the analysis of log files. Properly used statistics can indicate whether some component is in the "worn out" stage, i.e., if it should be rewritten.

CIO ISSUES

The CIO should use the software confederation principle not only as the tool enhancing the user oriented properties of the confederation, but also as a paradigm enhancing the quality of software processes and offering new software engineering tools.

1.   The central task is to accept the paradigm of software confederations and to find an optimal balance between the design in the large (as confederations) and in the small (e.g., using object-oriented attitude) and an optimal balance between developing and purchasing the components of the system. The confederate attitude substantially changes engineering and business properties of the resulting system as well as the processes of its development. The most important is the possibility to develop the system incrementally and to use legacy systems and third-party products. The CIO should decide what components will be developed and what purchased or outsourced. The outsourcing can be component-vise and therefore easily changeable.

2.   Another task is to decide the optimal size of components that should not be further decomposed into a federation and should be developed using standard development methods like OO analysis and programming. The effectiveness issues can influence the decision.

3.   The main emphasis is on the activities that can be characterized as the enhancing of existing middleware services. It requires new skills of programmers. The main problem is that software developers should be able to understand the knowledge domains being background of the functions of the components. It is important for the decision what components to integrate as well as what message formats to use in front-end components (when to use command-oriented interface, e.g., SOAP, and when data-oriented, e.g., RDF or UDDI; it is open whether SOAP is always the best solution for command oriented interface). It implies the abilities of software developers to have some interdisciplinary knowledge as well as to be able to use mathematical statistics in data mining and software processes (compare CMM methodology). For many programming-oriented persons, the ability to use statistics is a very difficult and unpleasant task. It is the task of CIO to cope with this problem. A sound knowledge of mathematics and mastering of natural (mother) language is often needed during the requirements specification, but often missing.

4.   The CIO must find an optimal balance between centralized and decentralized activities. It is especially important for the policy of the standardization of message formats. The decentralized decisions are more flexible and often more optimal, but it can result into a Babel of formats. A similar situation is in the case of data. Data should be in the responsibility and localized near to they producers or main users. CIO should support the decentralized solution and decide the strategies of data replication.

5.   *Ad hoc* modeling diagrams for software confederations must be used, as there are no satisfactory CASE tools for software confederations. Usable are Use Case diagrams, diagrams modeling the behavior of system users. Diagrams able to visualize the internal dynamics of software confederations are not available yet. Some variants of Petri net diagrams and/or a modification of data flow diagrams can be used. The use of UML is limited.

6.   The decision what security transaction and authorization services where to implement/ use (standard middleware, front-end components, components providing main appli-

cation functions). In Rowe (2002), for example, the transactions (rollback inclusive) are controlled by a generalized user interface components (user gates).

OPEN ISSUES

The CIO must take into account that in the case of confederations, there are few well established practices and generally accepted solutions. It is mainly due to the fact, that the concept of software confederation is so powerful that it does not require sophisticated methods beyond its basic principles. Nevertheless, the developers should be aware of the open issues. Let us give a short overview of them.

Configuration Management for Confederation

SWC is open and very dynamic. If it is formed by a large number of components, (it is now fortunately a rare case) something like configuration control must be implemented and used. However, until now, only ad hoc solutions have been found. Again, an optimal balance between flexibility and security must be found.

Transactions

This is a quite difficult problem. As the components can accept commands influencing real world some commands cannot be revoked (rolled back). The dynamic structure of the confederation implies that even in the case, that all the actions of a transaction can be rolled back, the control of the rolling back should be performed by no central authority but rather by the component initiating the transaction. Often it will be a user component (compare Rowe, 2002).

Moving and Cloning the Components

It is not difficult to move the components around the underlying computer network to work on different hosts to achieve a better performance of the system (response times or costs). It is even possible to clone components (i.e., to make copies of them) and to move the copies around to optimize the system behavior.

Similar tasks are solved in distributed database system when the system administrator must decide where the data and/or their replications should reside.

We did not find any theory and any satisfactory implementation of such an idea, allowing performing the optimization in a semi-automated way. We have no current satisfactory criteria function (Fisher et al., 2000).

Languages of Messages — XML

There can be tens and even hundreds of components in a large confederation. Many components can have a very complex interface. New components can be added quite easily. The functions of particular components can vary. It is therefore impractical to standardize all the message formats and to successfully use such standards. Message formats must be very flexible and specified by the parties involved in particular collaboration modes. The format agreements must be realized in a rather decentralized way. The idea is not to standardize formats, but to standardize a "metatool" for the format definition seems to be a very good idea, as well as its implementation in the Extensible Markup Language, XML. It is not clear, however, how to use the tool properly (for example, whose XML dialects are necessary).

A confederation providing the services of an information system should have the classical three-tier architecture: user interface, application logics provided by a network of components, and a data tier. We need different XML dialects for all three tiers:

1. The dialects for user interface (XSL and XSLT).
2. The application specific dialects for specific groups of activities (see e.g., ebXML, RIXML, GML) or the object-oriented command interface (SOAP, Simple Object-oriented Access Protocol, 2001). These dialects are used in the definition and construction of gates to application tiers. It is not clear what format is optimal. SOAP supports object-oriented attitude, but it is not clear whether it is too programming-oriented (and not enough application-oriented) and as such, not optimal for the partners of the given component. The use of SOAP can limit the modifiability and openness of the confederation, as it implies object-oriented architecture of the application tier, and it need not be true.
3. The data-oriented dialects like RDF (1999) for metadata definition; various query formats (XQL) see e.g., Pokorný (2000) and especially metadata-oriented formats like UDDI (Universal Description, Discovery, and Integration, 2001).

The present number of XML dialects induces the hesitation whether a new Babel will not appear (compare the problems of TeX). Should the definition of dialects be more centralized or at least coordinated? The messages in XML dialects can be interpreted as declarations/data definitions and/or programs. It is not clear when and why it is better to treat a message as a command and when as a meta-data. We believe that the XML dialects will be often used as programming languages (languages of commands) — especially in the case of the design of component gates allowing using component functions.

The communication between components is based on the exchange of texts in an appropriate language L that can evolve. Therefore, the components communicate like people in a human group. This is the situation forecast by Winograd and Flores (1986).

The collaboration of components is more complex than the merely simple exchange of messages. A multiparty discussion and/or complex coordination (workflow) process is often necessary. Like in the human society, the process can be implicit, i.e., based on the implicit knowledge of individual components how to react on particular input messages (stimuli), or explicit — controlled in an explicit way by a specific data structure (workflow specification) interpreted by a middleware service. It is open what attitude is more feasible.

Addressing Strategies and Dynamic Configuration Control

As mentioned above the communication of components should be in the language of a very complex syntax. The syntax of the messages can be used to identify the correct addressees. The proposal WSDL (Web Service Definition Language) can be used. The addressee can be any component able to understand the message, i.e., able to parse the syntax of the message to process it. This schema can be used to find the components all over the WWW. The chosen components form the system, which in turn exists only virtually. These issues must be solved:

- Can be such a schema implemented effectively enough?
- Can be the identification of the components robust enough (i.e., can be the identification of components in the sense of configuration control reliable enough)?
- Can the process of acceptance of new components be secure and to what degree it can be automated?
- Is SOAP a good solution for complex commands? Note that in databases, we use SQL or UDDI instead. It indicates that the question is relevant.

Components as Software Agents

The majority of tasks performed by a confederation must be implemented/supported by a 'team' (group) of components. It must be supported by appropriate tool allowing starting the cooperation of the components from the group. There are several possibilities:

1. The collaboration is implicit, i.e., organized because of the activities of the components without any explicit support of the middleware. Any component knows to what components send messages as a response to some particular message and the given history.
2. The identification of the components involved in the group are somewhat coded into the messages implicitly like in collaboration diagrams in UML (1999).
3. A negotiation strategy similar to the strategy of negotiation between software agents known from multi-agent theories (Weiss, 1999; Fisher et al., 2000) is used. Unfortunately, no effective implementation of the theories applicable in a confederation is known at present. It is unclear, whether the results valid for a multi-agent system can ever be used in a confederation, as the components differ from SW agents in the usual sense.
4. It is open how to control that a task was successfully finished and how to implement transactions for software agents. We can use results for distributed databases. However, it is unclear, whether known algorithms work successfully for components with complex activities.

INTERCONNECTIONS BETWEEN THE PARADIGM OF SWC AND OBJECT ORIENTATION

It is often argued why to introduce or invent a new paradigm — e.g., a software confederation paradigm — when object-oriented paradigm works fine. We must point out that the SWC paradigm was invented long time ago and have been used in practice with very good results. It is an optimal tool for large and/or real-time software systems. The SWC paradigm is applicable in the domain where object-oriented paradigm is not optimal and vice versa.

It follows from the above discussion that object orientation and confederation orientation are substantially different paradigms. Let us repeat the main differences (compare Table 1):

1. Object orientation is not based on the concept of massively parallel systems implemented as an open P2P network of permanent services and utilities. Object-orientation

started from sequential programs; object-oriented programs are not massively parallel. They have a controlled level of parallelism (compare the activity diagrams in UML).

2.   Basic building units in OO are methods encapsulated into classes. The practice indicates that in well-written OO programs, the methods tend to be rather (very) simple. Therefore, the complexity of class methods is also very low. It implies that the developers must remember a very large number of interfaces and methods. The OO programs must be therefore understood and visible in quite small details. The concept of UML components is trying to change it, but the success is still not too convicting. The most important consequence is that under these circumstances, the system must usually be designed as one logical entity without black boxes inside. It does not exclude the possibility that it is distributed. It increases development effort, limits the modifiability and openness of the developed system.

On the other hand, the confederative orientation need not be an optimal attitude for the development of very small systems. It is usually optimal to apply object orientation during the development of the small systems for which it is not effective to use confederative architecture (we call such systems atomic ones).

UML is not as an object-oriented tool not fully applicable in the case of SWC. Applied cannot, it seems, be the diagrams describing the implementation details like class diagrams an sometimes the state transitions diagrams.

Useful are the diagrams describing the interaction of the system with the environment, especially:

•   Use Case Diagrams.
•   Diagrams able to describe scenarios like sequential diagrams, activity diagrams and collaboration diagrams.
•   A modification of data-flow diagrams intended to be included into new UML standard.

It follows that there are no available diagrams describing the internal dynamics of software confederations. Due to the properties of a SWC-like message routing, the diagrams should describe only some chosen activities of the confederation.

Table 1. The comparison of autonomous components an object-oriented components

	Middleware orientation-autonomous components	Object orientation-object-oriented components
concurrency	Inherently parallel	Tend to be sequential, parallel rather an added feature
interface	Interface asynchronous, message oriented, messages have complex syntactic structure	Primarily synchronous, procedure call oriented, syntax - procedure calls only
building units	Components rather large, autonomous, components used as black boxes	Building units (objects, components) tend to be small; system usually designed as a whole and then decomposed by grouping building units
middleware	Middleware properties and/or services should be explicitly specified	Middleware properties used mainly implicitly

CONCLUSIONS

The architecture of software confederations should be applied in the following cases:
- Cooperation of independent economic entities (also competing ones - see Ex. 1).
- State/municipal administration network
- Health care
- Information systems of large enterprises
- Information and control systems containing real world process control like systems of automated (family) houses

In addition to the above described systems, software confederations should be used also when the SW system:
- Requires usage of third-party subsystems or legacy systems,
- Is too large to be developed and maintained as a monolith,
- Some software confederations' development techniques are needed, or
- Purchased information systems need to be extended by new (for given application specific) functions.

The SWC paradigm is becoming quite common in practice. It is due to the current situation in software that can be characterized by the following key facts:
1. SW systems become global and support activity of organizations composed by/from distributed organizational units with different level of autonomy (like state administration offices, health care institutions, international enterprises, and coalitions of independent and often competing subjects). The organizational units and/or independent subjects can (and often must) have their autonomous information systems. The collection of the units or alliance members can be very large and can vary.
2. There is a growing need to integrate third-party products like statistical packages, legacy systems, workflow systems, etc., into the system.
3. The structure of such systems changes dynamically. The systems are open — they have a changing number of users. It (along with many more reasons) means that it is necessary to build the systems as SWC's.
4. There are very powerful communication networks and middleware software allowing a high capacity data transfer all around the world and offering a broad collection of services (message formats transducers like XSLT, flexible message formats specification tools like XML, security and routing services, etc.).
5. Powerful user interface tools (Internet browsers) are available.

The first, second, and third points imply that it is desirable to build the system as a network consisting of almost independent information systems (IS) of individual organizational (sub-) units and of almost independent applications. Due to many reasons, the constituent software subsystems must be integrated into a confederation such that it should support many local activities as if there were no SWC (e.g., all local functions should be available for local use — see Figure 1). The constituent information systems can be (at least for some time, often forever) also used in the way they had been used before they were integrated into the confederation. It can be easily achieved if the network is a P2P one with nodes being permanently available services (compare Internet, see e.g., Král and Žemlička (1999).

The fourth point indicates that such a solution is technically feasible. The fifth point is important for the construction of the integrated transparent interface of the whole confederation.

The dynamic character of the confederation (Král and Žemlička, 2000, 2001a) enforces a flexible format of messages. This problem is solved by XML and its dialects (compare Král and Žemlička, 2000).

The paradigm of SWC changes substantially managerial problems connected with the use as well as with the development and maintenance of software systems, especially of information systems. We have now a methodology enabling the construction of systems of the complexity comparable with the size and complexity of such technical products like power plants. SWC is the way for software to be a high-tech product of the quality and stability comparable with other high-tech products like planes, cars, and boats.

The use of the SWC paradigm is not too difficult, but it requires changes in habits, skills, and knowledge of software designers. Some prejudices should be overcome.

There is some hidden opposition from software vendors as SWC can imply less dependence of software users on software producers.

It is the time for software researchers and CASE system designers to develop tools applicable during the development of software confederations.

REFERENCES

Aho, A.V., and Ullman, J.D. (1972). *The Theory of Parsing, Translation, and Compiling, Vol. I:* Parsing. Englewood Cliffs, NJ: Prentice Hall.

Aho, A.V., and Ullman, J.D. (1973). *The Theory of Parsing, Translation, and Compiling, Vol. II*: Compiling. Englewood Cliffs, NJ: Prentice Hall. ISBN 0-13-914564-8.

Aho, A.V., Sethi, R., and Ullmann, J.D. (1986). *Compilers, Principles, Techniques, and Tools*. Reading, MA: Addison Wesley.

Bednárek, D. (1999). Using Petri nets in processor modelling. Technical report No. 99/9 of the Department of Software Engineering, Prague: Faculty of Mathematics and Physics, Charles University.

Boehm, B.W. (1981). *Software Engineering Economics*. Englewood Cliffs, NJ: Prentice Hall.

Booch, G., Rumbaugh, J., and Jacobson, I. (1995). *The Unified Method for Object-Oriented Development, Version 0.8. Metamodel and Notation.* Santa Clara, CA: Relational Software Corporation.

Finch, L. (1998). So Much OO, So Little Reuse. Dr. Dobb's Journal, also at Dr. Dobb's Web site. Retrieved from the World Wide Web in May 1998: http://www.ddj.com/oped/1998/finc.htm.

Fisher, K., Oliveria, E., and Stěpánková, O. (1999). Multiagent systems: Which research for which applications. Private communication.

Král, J., and Žemlička, M. (1999). Middleware orientation - Inverse software development strategy. Presented at the ISD99 Conference, Boise, August 1999, also in Wojtkovski, W. et al. (Eds.), Systems Development Methods for Databases, Enterprise Modeling, and Workflow Management, NY: Kluwer Academic, (385-396).

Král, J., and Žemlička, M. (2000). Autonomous components. In: Hlaváé, V., Jeffery, K.G., and Wiedermann, J. (Eds.), SOFSEM 2000: Theory and Practice of Informatics. (pp. 375-383) Milovy, Berlin: Springer Verlag.

Král, J., and Žemlička, M. (2001a). Necessity, challenges, and promises of peer-to-peer architecture of information systems. Presented at the ISD 2001 Conference, Royal Holloway U. London, Egham, September 5-7, 2001. Published in G. Harandranath, W. G. Wojtkowski, J.

Král, J., and Žemlička, M. (2001b). Electronic government and software confederations. In: A M. Tjoa and R. R. Wagner (Eds.), Twelfth International Workshop on Database and Experts System Application (pp. 383-387) Los Alamitos, CA, USA: IEEE Computer Society.

Král, J., and Žemlička, M. (2002a). Component types in software confederations. In: M. H. Hamza (Ed.), Applied Informatics (pp. 125-130) Anaheim: ACTA Press.

Král, J., and Žemlička, M. (2002b). Software confederations and the maintenance of global software systems. In the proceeding of the conference: Software Maintenance and Reengineering, Budapest, (March 2002, pp. 61-66).

Löwe, W., and Noga, M.L. (2002). A lightweight XML-based middleware architecture. In: M. H. Hamza (Ed.), Applied Informatics (pp. 131-136) Anaheim: ACTA Press.

Parsons, J., and Wand, Y. (2000, June). Emancipating instances from the tyranny of classes in information modelling. ACM Trans. on Database Systems, 25(2), 228-268.

Pokorný, J. (2000). XML functionally. In B. C. Desai, Y. Kioki, and M. Toyama (Eds.), Proceedings of IDEAS2000, IEEE Comp. Society, pp. 266-274.

Rowe, D. (2002). e-Government Motives and Organisational Framework. In: J. Pour and J. Vorísek (Eds.), Systems Integration 2002, Conference Presentations. Prague: Prague University of Economics.

Sneed, H. (2002). A contribution in the discussion at CSMR 2002 conference (case studies). Budapest, Hungary.

Tai, S., and Rouvellou, I. (2000). Strategies for Integrating Messaging and Distributed Object Transactions. In Sventek, J., Cuolson, G. (Eds.), Middleware 2000, (pp. 308-330) New York: Springer Verlag.

UDDI (2002). Retrieved from the World Wide Web: http://www.uddi.org/ Home page of UDDI project.

W3C (1999). Retrieved from the World Wide Web: http://www.xml.com/xml/pub/ Extensible Markup Language. A proposal of W3C consortium.

W3C (2000). Retrieved from the World Wide Web: http://www.rdf.com/, Resource Description Framework. A Proposal of the W3C consorcium.

Weiss, G. (1999). Multiagent systems. A modern Approach to Distributed Artificial Intelligence, Cambridge, MA: The MIT Press.

Winograd, T., and Flores, F.C. (1986). *Understanding Computers and Cognition - A New Foundation for Design. Norwood*, NY: Ablex Publishing Corporation.

Chapter VII

An Investigation of GISM Issues for Successful Management of the Globalization Process

Yi-chen Lan
University of Western Sydney, Australia

ABSTRACT

This chapter investigates issues related to the global transition of an enterprise through the application of information technology and information systems. It starts with the discussion of the issues that are critical to the successful transition of an enterprise to transborder business operations using information systems. The expected outcome of such transition would be a globalized organization that would not be limited by geographical and time zone barriers, nor restricted by cultural differences. The global transition issues are further classified into five categories embracing business information systems management, information technology management, people management, end user management, and culture. It is then followed by a comprehensive examination of individual issues that is vital in understanding their impact on the transition and how to alleviate that impact. The chapter concludes by indicating a future research direction that might augment the development of this emerging field.

INTRODUCTION

The rapid growth of information technology (IT) is one of the key drivers forcing organizations toward globalization. The meaning of "globalization" to an organization seems no longer to be a business vision but a crucial strategy as the global market becomes a single

Figure 1. Research framework

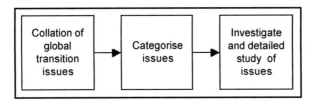

entity. Nevertheless, to be capable of successful in the global transition process and sustain in the global competitive environment, the organizations require more than just applying information technology. Without a clear understanding of the issues in relation to the management of global information systems, organizations are most likely to fail in this transition.

The key objective of this chapter is to investigate the global transition issues through the collation and categorization of global IT management literature from the past decade. It intends to provide readers a comprehensive view of the problems faced in the organization's IT globalization process. The research framework used is illustrated in Figure 1.

BACKGROUND

During the global transition, organizations often face many tacit as well as explicit factors that could delay or, in worst cases, even destroy the globalization process. In order to eliminate these unnecessary incidents, enterprises need to identify the possible issues that will impede the process of globalization before it takes place.

In the past decade, researchers have put in significant efforts in identifying the global information systems management (GISM) issues. Most notable are Senn's six key information technology issues (Senn, 1992), and the eight multinational categories of global information technology issues by Palvia and Saraswat (1992). In addition, a number of issues have been identified in various areas, including culture (Burn et al., 1993; Ein-Dor et al., 1993; Sauter, 1992; Yellen, 1997), human resource management (Agocs and Suttie, 1994; Boudreau et al., 1994; Harrison and Deans, 1994; Niederman, 1994; O'Connell, 1997; Pucik and Katz, 1986), individual country and region (Palvia et al., 1992; Watson et al., 1997), business strategic planning (Cheung and Burn, 1994; Ives et al., 1993; Gibson and McGuire, 1997; Kesner and Palmisano, 1996; Minor and Larkin, 1994; Neo, 1991; Sethi and Olson, 1992; Unhelkar, 1999), practical issues (Edberg et al., 2001), and technology (Klein, 1999; Passino and Severance, 1990; Sankar and Prabhakar, 1992; Waples and Norris, 1992).

Based on the implication of issues on the process of globalization, five categories are identified to facilitate classification and collation of the GISM issues. The core concept of categorization intends to provide the organizations an abstract overview of concerns in relation to the transition to globalization. These categories are labeled as:

1. Information technology management
2. Business information systems management
3. People management
4. End user management
5. Culture

Figure 2. Global information systems and transition issue categories

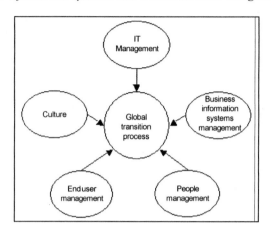

The criteria of grouping and forming GISM categories are based on the intention and affiliated field of individual issue. Coincidentally, the first four categories match the emphasis of management IT issue categories developed by Khandelwal and Warrington (1999). Culture, the fifth category, is identified to ensure the completeness focus of cross-border and global information systems distribution and management. Figure 2 shows the overall schematic of transition issue categories and the global transition process. The following sections provide detailed study and explanation of each GISM issue category and the underlying issues in relation to global transition process.

INFORMATION TECHNOLOGY MANAGEMENT ISSUES

The implementation of global information systems is based on the coordination and inter-communication of software applications, hardware components, telecommunications, networks infrastructure, and network management in a cross-border business environment (Sankar and Prabhakar, 1992). Rapid evolution of technologies causes efficient and effective performance of global information systems as a result of real-time and accurate transborder data flows. Organizations need to realize and understand the technological issues involved in order to adopt the most suitable technologies for global information systems. The essential technological issues and implication of global transition that need to be considered are telecommunication availability, network infrastructure, security, systems equipment, data resources utilization, systems standards, software applications availability, systems integration, and systems recovery.

Furthermore, the review of the global IT literature and issues suggests that an organization's IT architecture is generally divided into four classes. This is based on the fundamental properties of an organization's IT environment, and they are global IT infrastructure (refers to hardware and operation systems), global business applications (refers to software), global telecommunication network (refers to communication), and data/information systems improvement (refers to data and applications). Knowles (1996) and Passmore

Figure 3. IT management classes

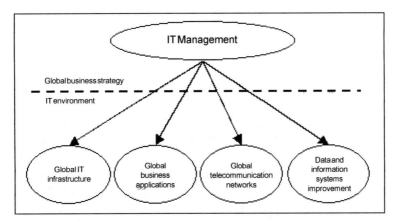

(1997) have described the IT architecture as the underlying technology platform that supports all data and applications, including hardware, systems software and communication. Accordingly, the fundamental properties of an organization's IT architecture are essentially related to hardware, software, network, and data/information. Figure 3 illustrates these four classes.

The criteria of correlated issues of each class are outlined as follows.

Global IT infrastructure – this class covers the development, implementation and maintenance of global information architecture components such as hardware, equipment, technology platform, and supports.

Global business applications – this refers to all the development, management, implementation, maintenance, integration, and improvement of global business application softwares.

Global telecommunication network – this class includes all the network communication structures, facilities, supports, and management to provide the business data flowing within and between organizations.

Data and information systems improvement – this applies to the enhancement of data or information in terms of quality assurance, integration, security, contingency plan, and effective utilization.

BUSINESS INFORMATION SYSTEMS MANAGEMENT ISSUES

In the process of globalization, business and information system strategies are often senior executives' major concern. The alignments of global information strategy and the new business visions are crucial to the success of global business operations. Areas in this category and the transition implication contain information systems planning, information systems organization alignment, information systems effectiveness, productivity measurement, business reengineering, competitive advantage, information quality, office automation, identification of global business opportunities, systems reliability, availability, and transferability (Lan, 2002). The following sub-sections investigate and explore these issues in details.

Information Systems Planning

A global information system is a piece of art that facilitates cross-border business operations by integrating both social and technical elements. Introducing a new global information system involves not only the hardware and software, but also the changes in job specifications, skills requirements, management, and organization structure. All these changes should not be any surprise to all parties involved in the development and implementation of the new systems. In fact, the anticipated changes related to the new systems should be documented and the business plan drawn to reflect all stages. Before the global transition process, the organization needs to develop an information systems plan to precisely state the specifications and requirements of each phase and ensure the plan matches the organization's strategic vision. As per Laudon and Laudon (2002), the information systems plan refers to: "A roadmap indicating the direction of systems development: the rationale, the current situation, the management strategy, the implementation plan, and the budget."

To develop an effective global information systems plan, the organization should first, understand the current business status in terms of the strengths and weaknesses, recognize all issues faced in the global transition process, and clearly outline short-term and long-term business strategies.

Information Systems Organization Alignment

As mentioned earlier, it is imperative for the information system function to align itself with the business processes, strategies and goals of the organization. Information systems are developed based on the requirement, behaviors and activities of all business parties who have intercommunicated with the organization's core business functions and objectives. These parties include suppliers, customers, government agencies, and even competitors. The goals and strategic visions of these business entities must be incorporated in the development of information systems. In addition, the alignment of information systems with business functions in a global organization must also take into account the organizational type or structure. Information systems organization alignment in the global organization is not just following business processes and conducting analysis and design, but it also requires understanding of abstract level of business strategic vision and cooperation with all business entities.

Information Systems Effectiveness

Developing effective global information systems requires more than an understanding of business processes and applying the latest information technology. It needs the participation of people who will be using the information systems from all areas through the entire development life cycle. These users include senior managers, operational staff, salespeople, customers, suppliers, and many other general employees. All these users should be invited to participate in different development phases in accordance with the job related processes or tasks. Thus, ascertaining the user involvement through the development phases is crucial for an effective global information system.

Productivity Measurement

An efficient and productive enterprise is built upon matured business processes. Accordingly, the measurement of productivity in the global organization should focus on benchmarking of business processes and information systems that facilitate these processes. The measurement of process maturity as set by ISO (International Organization for Standardization), and the CMM (Capability Maturity Model) can be used as software quality measurement. ISO 9000:2000 standard is the latest version of quality assurance system. It concerns quality systems that are assessed by outside auditors, and it applies to many kinds of production and manufacturing organizations. It covers documentation, design, development, production, testing, installation, servicing, and many other general business processes.

The Capability Maturity Model is developed by the SEI (Software Engineering Institute of Carnegie Mellon University). It is a model of five levels of organizational maturity that determine effectiveness in delivering quality information system software.

Business Reengineering

As organizations pursue globalization, changes are foreseeable in four areas:
1.   Fundamental organization structure
2.   Business processes
3.   Management concepts
4.   People and skills

Of the previous four, changes in business processes are tightly coupled with the design of global information systems. Organizations must understand and recognize that business processes in global context are significantly different from the traditional or existing ones. In order to design the appropriate information systems to facilitate business operations in global environment, organizations should rethink and redesign the business processes to align with the global business strategic vision, in accordance with Hammer and Stanton's (1995) "official definition" of reengineering which is "the fundamental rethinking and radical redesign of business processes to achieve dramatic improvements in performance."

Four key words (fundamental, radical, dramatic, and processes) contained in the definition are identified to further explore its significance in globalization perspective.
1.   Fundamental – in preparing for business process reengineering, organizations must ask themselves questions in relation to the current and future business operations and strategic vision. These questions can be as simple as "What are the current business processes?" "What are the new business processes that would emerge after the global transition?" and "What are the activities involved in the processes (both current and future)?" and so forth. By asking these questions, organizations are forced to map an overall picture of ways they are expecting to conduct their global businesses.
2.   Radical – refers to the design of business process from its roots. Which means not redesigning the business processes by just making modifications or improvements to the existing ones. Instead, the key concept of reengineering is to remove the old ones and rebuild the new processes to cope with the global operations.
3.   Dramatic – refers to the deepness of changes to the existing business processes. Dramatic improvement differs from the marginal improvement as the former requires giving up the old ones and replacing with something totally new, while the later requires only fine-tuning of the existing processes.

4.   Processes – are the objects of the reengineering concept. A business process refers to a collection of activities that carry out operations to achieve business routines and satisfy customer requirements. In a global business environment, many business processes are accomplished through collaborative teams across borders. Hence, the view of transborder business processes is crucial to successful in the business reengineering process for global organizations.

In addition to Hammer and Champy's reengineering, Bill Gates (1999) has introduced the concept of a digital nervous system as the basis of business communication network to facilitate the transformation or reengineering of business processes into new digital business processes.

Most of the business enterprises focus on a few essential elements such as customer, supplier, product and services, costs, employees, and skills. Each of these areas contains a collection of business data. Through human intelligence, the data is interpreted and transformed into meaningful information to assist people in all levels for making decisions. However, if the interpretation and transformation are performed significantly by the use of information technology, then the organization has a digital nervous system. Gates describes *digital nervous system* as, " the digital processes that closely link every aspect of a company's thoughts and actions.... The immediate availability of accurate information changes strategic thinking from a separate, stand-alone activity to an ongoing process integrated with regular business activities."

In thinking of business reengineering, Gates suggests organizations to consider three imperative concepts. At first, organizations should review their current business processes periodically; secondly, they should try to have the least number of people involved in the decision making of each business process; and thirdly, they should consolidate procedures and activities to decrease the failure rates.

Multinational corporations often find that some similar or even identical processes are implemented in various transborder business units. This would result in the duplication of jobs, inappropriate allocation of human resources, and the ambiguous global management responsibilities. Although creating a new business process or reengineering an existing one is a complex and sophisticate project in a global business organization, the process owners in all transborder business units should define a unique global process that would be adopted throughout the organization. Furthermore, the globalized business processes streamline the transition in outsourcing situation.

Competitive Advantage

Attaining global competitive advantage, organizations require competence in changes in areas such as organizational structure, skills, and resources. These competences are crucial to attaining competitive advantage, but perhaps even more importantly, making sure the competitive advantage is always through a value-added product or service to the customer. Ford Motor Company is a good example to illustrate how the changes have taken place (Leontiades, 2001). In order to reach the global competitive advantage, Ford transformed its organizational structure through five stages of changes in its competence.

In the first stage, competence of overseas business unit was based on products, designs and methods provided by home country (the headquarters). In Stage 2, competence of the overseas business unit was based on its own production with the designs and methods provided by the home country. When the overseas business unit had the capability of production and designing products locally, then it had reached the third stage. In the fourth and fifth stages, the capability of production and designing were based in regional and global respectively. In accordance with the above stages, the competence of changes became the key driver for the organization towards globalization, while customer requirement became the trigger of transformation from stage to stage. Furthermore, to maintain the global competitive edge, the organization needs to ensure the reorganization of the organizational structure and its business strategy have met the customer satisfaction in the global transformation process.

Besides the changes in competence, Porter (1998) also introduced the diamond theory of competitive advantage. The diamond constitutes four attributes that determine the environment, the inputs of production, the availability of resources, the requirement of necessary skills, the business strategy, and structure of the organization. These attributes are labeled as factor conditions, demand conditions, related and supporting industries, and firm strategy, structure and rivalry. Using the diamond of competitive advantage concept in the globalization context (see Figure 4), the determinants of four aspects of the competitive advantage can be defined as follows.

1. Factor conditions – factors of production are the fundamental input to competition. The advantage arises from the high quality inputs such as global market and products knowledge, diverse acquisition of technology and infrastructure and variety of human and capital resources.

2. Demand conditions – advantages arises from the characteristic of global market and products. In a global market, customers demand products from anywhere in the world. Redesigning of products or services is essential to fulfill the global conditions and satisfy the global customer requirement. Thus, the global products can be manufactured anywhere and distributed to the nearest market.

3. Related and supporting industries – advantages in increasing productivity arises from the availability of global resources (specialized suppliers and related industry). Through the global supplier channel, organizations are able to find required supporting materials and services with at reduced costs. The presence of global resources even works better with the global production strategy. That is, the selected global suppliers provide the required materials or services directly to the closest global production sites.

Figure 4. Diamond of competitive advantage in the global organization

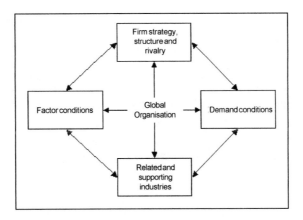

It results in the reduction of time required for transportation and thus shortens the production cycle.

4. Firm strategy, structure, and rivalry – the diverse and multicultural conditions in the global business environment present advantages to enterprises in organizing, structuring, and managing the business strategy and structures to survive in the global rivalry.

Information Quality

Information is a direct product of processes that capture knowledge about the persons, places, things and events discovered while conducting business transactions (English, 2001). In a global organization, the sources of information are enormous. Information is virtually produced by everyone from any level in the organization. As a result enterprises are often facing the situation such as missing or inaccurate information. These would cause business processes to fail and increase costs in reproducing of information. Hence, organizations must apply quality principles to effectively manage information. However, managing and controlling information and its quality seem to be a complex and challenging task. Clikeman (1999) defines a number of dimensions that are critical to maintaining the information quality in the global organization; they are relevance, accuracy, timeliness, completeness, coherence, format, accessibility, compatibility, security, and validity.

Office Automation

Office automation involves the planned application of integrated information handling tools and methods to improve the productivity of people in office operations. Although managing information by office people is the focus of office automation, other aspects of the office are also affected. These include factors such as the structure of business functions and lines of reporting, training for new methods, work space design, locations of subsidiaries or business units, home versus office work, hours of work, employee morale, and job classifications. Organizations that harness office automation products will need to deal with many more than just technological issues.

Three major roles of an office identified by Laudon and Laudon (2002) are:

1. Coordinate and manage the work of local professional and information workers within the organization.
2. Link the work being performed across all levels and functions throughout the organization.
3. Couple the organization with the external environment.

Generally, there are five major office activities can be identified including managing documents, scheduling individuals and groups, communicating with individuals and groups, managing data on individuals and groups, and managing projects. The computing and information technologies that support each activity should be identified and made available for all business units in planning for globalization.

1. Managing documents – it involves tasks such as creation, storage, retrieval, and dissemination. The technologies supporting these tasks include word processing, desktop publishing, document imaging, Web publishing, and work flow managers applications.

2. Scheduling individuals and groups – the technologies facilitate this activity include electronic calendars, groupware, and intranet.
3. Communicating with individuals and groups – the tasks include initiating, receiving, and managing data in the format of voice, image, digital, and text. The supporting technologies may consist of e-mail, voice mail, digital answering systems, groupware, and intranets.
4. Managing data on individuals and groups – this activity mainly focuses on the management of data and information of employees, customers, vendors, suppliers, or even competitors. The enabling technologies include database systems and spread-sheet applications.
5. Managing projects – it refers to the management of collaborative work and projects in both local and global environments. The technologies that can be applied to this activity may include groupware, teamware, and project management applications.

Identification of Global Business Opportunities

With rapidly advancing technology, the business and information technology community are encouraged to consider many more innovative business models. These emerging innovative business models can be defined in a number forms such as mergers and alliances, differentiation of products and services, e-business (electronic business), economic value added focus, productivity process, order fulfillment and customer demand management, and globalization of markets.

1. Mergers and alliances – these refer to the need for individual organizations to increase in size either by internal growth or by alliances with external parties (other organizations).
2. Differentiation of products and services – refer to the need to provide products and services to customers that are, at the same time, unique, value efficient, and reasonably priced.
3. E-business – refers to development, acceptance, and usage of the Internet business tools in overall or partial company operations (such as virtual organization), sourcing and supply strategies.
4. Economic value-added focus– refers to the increasing financial pressure on organizations to achieve high process performance as they affect or are affected by sourcing and supply, and increasing focus on economic value-added.
5. Productivity process – refers to the growing emphasis by top management on cost control, reduced cycle time, increasing flexibility, and the profit picture and process economics.
6. Order fulfillment and customer demand management – refers to the fundamental changes in distribution, and the need to change the methods used in customer order fulfillment and customer demand management.
7. Globalization of markets – refers to the need to adopt standard processes for producing, selling and distributing products and services.

Systems Reliability, Availability, and Transferability

Information systems should be reliable in terms of withstanding the use by various types of users through a variety of platforms or environments. This refers to the capability of incorporating diverse error handling strategy to react any possible and unforeseeable situations in information systems. Moreover, the availability and transferability of information systems are considered as important as the systems reliability in the global organization. Due to the multinational business units in the global organization, each business unit may need to access the information in different periods. The maintenance strategy needs to cope with this multinational characteristic to eliminate the consequences of the systems downtime. If the implementation of global information systems is through the Internet, users expect the systems to operate in a 24/7 manner. The components and modules of global information systems should also be designed flexible enough to transfer and adapt from one business unit to another without further technical modifications. This portable and transferable concept should be built into the development architecture to enhance the reusability and to reduce the development and maintenance costs.

PEOPLE MANAGEMENT ISSUES

People are major players in designing, implementing and utilizing information systems. When investigating the human resources management in the global business environment, a number of areas need to be considered as crucial to the success of globalization. These areas are recruiting, training, organizational learning, cross-cultural skills development, and global team development (Lan, 2002).

Recruiting

Hiring employees for a global organization is not as easy as for domestic companies. The recruitment process requires careful planning to provide the best strategy for the global organization in obtaining suitable employees for appropriate positions and locations. For example, Unhelkar (2002) has suggested the importance of "best fit" approach to recruitment. In preparation of the global recruitment plan, the organization's human resources department needs to firstly transform itself into the global operation. Traditionally, human resources is quite independent and unique system for each subsidiary in multinational corporations (MNCs). For example, the human resources department in the Sydney subsidiary may have no relationships or connections with the human resources department in Tokyo of the same MNC. In addition, each subsidiary's human resources department may maintain its own operations that may be enough to fulfill the local requirements, but certainly would not have the flexibility to facilitate the management of employees in the global scale. This uniqueness of human resources function in the traditional organization leaves the organization with no centralized control and standardized operations in regard to people management. By implementing a global human resources system, MNCs would benefit in efficiently managing geographical by dispersed employees as well as standardizing the organizations' employment policies.

In the global recruitment aspect, the Internet seems to be the appropriate operating platform. The implementation of corporation's careers Website is considered the key success factor in improving the speed, efficiency and effectiveness of the overall recruiting process. Further, the careers Website has a profound impact on the organization's global recruitment strategy in the following areas (Jones, 2001):

1.   Branding and sourcing – it provides the potential candidates a comprehensive and concentrated source of information and branding experience on the organization as an employer.

2.   Response management – it provides a standardized application for candidates from various sources and maintains a centralized database for the ongoing relationships.
3.   Assessment – to reduce the organization's costs and time, extra features can be incorporated into the careers Website for pre-screening and filtering the candidates.
4.   Processing – it streamlines the processes of people/employee management by connecting the careers Web site to the organization's back-end systems.

Training

Training is a critical agenda for organizations to continuously improve the quality perspective in products, services and management aspects, and strengthens organizations in the global competitive edge. In designing and developing the training programs, a number of factors are identified to ensure the appropriateness and effectiveness. These factors include:

1.   Stage in the global transition process – as there are various stages in the global transition process, the training development needs to reflect to the various skills required by employees carrying out tasks in different stages.
2.   Target employee domains – different levels and types of employees would play different roles in the organization's global transition process. Considering the types of employees and their respective situations, the suitable training programs could be developed to enhance the employee skills and serve the requirements of globalization.
3.   Methods of training – implementing training programs across national borders have significant level of complexity and budget requirements. By applying technology (such as computer based training programs, or online training) to develop and deliver the training programs would allow the employees to participate in learning anywhere and anytime. However, the standardized training programs may require some variations, for example in languages and cultural aspects to fit in the foreign subsidiary contexts.

Organizational Learning

In today's challenging business marketplace, organizational learning seems to become one of the prominent aspects that enterprises would like to focus on and incorporate in their business strategies. As the enterprise evolves, many changes have transpired and demanded for resolutions. These changes are often associated with leadership and management styles, implication of technology, and the business environment. Because of swift technological development, enterprises are capable of applying knowledge management, and through the online learning environment to promote organizational learning. Laudon and Laudon (2002) define knowledge management as "the process of systematically and actively managing and leveraging the stores of knowledge in the organization." The key information systems that support knowledge management include office automation systems (OAS), knowledge work systems (KWS), group collaboration systems, and artificial intelligence systems (AI).

Cross-Cultural Skills Development

In multinational corporations, business units and subsidiaries are often spread across nations and have quite distinct cultural attitudes and characteristic. Hence, employees in global companies are more likely to have greater chances of dealing with foreign colleagues than non-multinational companies. In order to smoothen the communications and information flows between employees from different cultural backgrounds, global corporations should consider the introduction of multi-cultural skills development programs. These programs may consist of language and communication learning, and recognizing and understanding of culture differences.

Global Team Development and Leadership Styles

Collaboration and coordination are the two imperative ingredients of successfully conducting teamwork in the global organization. Coordination refers to the extra tasks required for amalgamating tasks performed to accomplish the final goal, while collaboration deals with multiple teams working jointly toward the same objective. In global projects, teams or even members of the team mainly come from different countries or regions. In order to succeed in global coordination and collaboration, there is a need to establish the common standards in terms of communication method, language, management rules, and information technologies (hardware platforms and software applications).

Four possible team organizational models (see Figure 5) can be applied in the global projects namely pyramid, breakthrough, open architects, and synchronous paradigms (Thomsett, 1994).

1. Pyramid – has its roots in the industrial age. Projects are decomposed into functions, similar to how a business is decomposed into business functions, such as R&D, engineering, manufacturing, marketing, sales, distribution, accounting, and finance, with all the functions reporting to the same executive. A single person, the project manager, is responsible for the project and has the authority to make decisions. All team members are directly accountable to the project manager.

2. Breakthrough – involves teams of random creative independents. Team members do not wait for guidelines or directions, and have clear objectives in mind. For better performance, the breakthrough model requires freedom from interference, and freedom to investigate problems. This model is suggested for small-sized, short-term, and simple projects that do not require intensive coordination of interdependent units.

3. Open architects – Members of this team model work collaboratively toward the project objectives. Functional roles are well defined in the team and rotated among team members. Software development teams are suggested to adopt the open architects model for making collaboration and consensus engineering more efficient and controllable (Constantine, 1995).

4. Synchronous paradigm – Team members share the common vision with the leader. The level of alignment with the common value and vision is the key to eliminate the tight control of any kind and increase the efforts made by each individual. Hence, the leader of this team model has less workload in supervising and guiding the team members to carry out their responsibilities.

Figure 5. Four global team organizational models

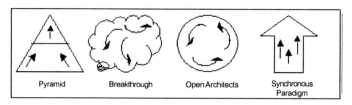

END USER MANAGEMENT ISSUES

The end users are the ultimate group of people using the global information systems on a regular basis. The task of managing and supporting end user groups is not only in maintaining business information operations but is the key to evaluating and improving the global information systems. The fundamental concerns of the end user management category in globalization context (Lan, 2002) include managing end user computing facilities, end user computing education, introducing and learning new global information systems, help desk support, and end user involvement in global information systems development as mentioned in the "Information Systems Effectiveness" section.

Managing End User Computing Facilities

Controlling the end user computing equipments and facilities is a complex assignment especially in the global organization where business units are dispersed across nations. Managing end user computing facilities should be taken into account when planning and designing the global information systems. Tasks involved in the end user facilities management may include the identification of facilities in each business units and subsidiaries, verification of facilities availability, development of standard maintenance procedures, and the development of standard facility purchasing, logistic and distribution procedures.

End User Computing Education

In the modern business environment, employees' capability of using computers to perform business tasks seems to be part of the job requirements. The basic computing skills such as producing documents, sending e-mails, and browsing the Internet are required in most office environments. However, the level of employees' computing education in the global organization varies from subsidiary to subsidiary. Thus, there is a need to incorporate end user computing education plan in the global transition process. The main objective of the plan is to ensure that the employees' have obtained required computing skills in all business units. It may consist of the identification of the employees' current computing skills and levels, identification of essential computing skills development of training programs, and implementation of training programs.

Introducing and Learning New Global Information Systems

When the development of global information systems reaches a certain level (such as the testing and deploying stages), the training programs should be introduced. The training programs should be developed through the systems development teams and the human resources department collaboratively. In order to develop the appropriate training programs for the respectable end users, the initial stage is the mapping of the organizational hierarchy in terms of the end user types and responsibilities to the systems functionality.

Help Desk Support

As per many other business information systems, help desk plays a key role in keeping the users satisfied of performing business tasks through the global information systems. To provide an effective help desk service, two fundamental concepts may be incorporated in the

Figure 6. Global help desk structure

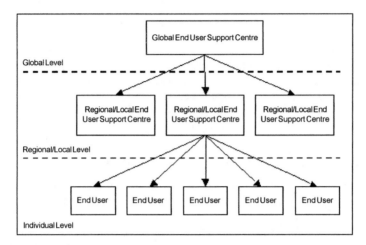

help desk function – a clear understanding of what are the services the users anticipate, and accurately and timelessly responding of problems reported by users. Figure 6 illustrates a proposed a help desk structure to accommodate the global information systems help services. It includes a centralized global end user support center and various regional or local end user support centers. The global end user support center takes care of problems and requests dealing with transborder activities in global context and manages the regional/local end user support centers. In the regional/local centers, the main services are to firstly define the scope of request (global or regional/local) and secondly provide help on issues relating to local or regional activities. If the problem relates to the transborder activities, the regional/local center will divert the request to the global end user support center for resolution.

End User Involvement in Global Information Systems Development

Users' perception and information requirements drive the entire development of global information systems effort (Laudon and Laudon, 2002). Users must have sufficient control over the design and development of global information systems to ensure that business functions and operations are accurately incorporated. Moreover, the design of global information systems should be based on all stakeholders. In other words, lack of users involvement in the design of global information systems is the major cause of systems failure.

There are always benefits by involving users on information systems development teams. However, it is even more important to engage users in global information systems development. As mentioned above, users are people who understand the business functions and operations. Involving various type of users through the entire global information system analysis and design phases is crucial as it helps in making sure the global information system would appropriately implement business processes and bring extra value to the business. It is also believed that users who have been involved in the design and development phases would become change agents for the introduction of new systems. The change agents play the role of disseminating the concept of new systems to members in their local business unit and who may be involved in developing training programs.

CULTURE ISSUES

When addressing information systems and technology globally, culture is an important aspect to be considered as it influences the success or failure of global transformation. In the new challenge of globalization the reality of cultural diversity is not avoidable. Instead, organizations should be encouraged to embrace diversity and turn the multicultural characteristics into strategic advantages. Understanding this diversity is crucial to conducting any global business. As Kincaid correctly points out (Kincaide, 1999) doing business "requires a deep respect of the country's culture, religions and institutions." Furthermore, understanding the cultural issues and variables will provide organizations a certain level of competitive edge in the global business environment. O'Hara-Devereaux and Johansen (1994) introduced a multifaceted lens concept – a way of peering through the fog of cultural diversity. The multifaceted lens concept is based on the identification and understanding of various cultural dimensions including:

Language – refers to the vocabulary, structure, and meanings of oral and written communication. For example, a standardized global customer relationship management (CRM) application may require multiple interfaces designed in different language characters (such as English, Chinese, or Japanese) for subsidiaries in different countries. However, in a global organization it is very difficult for the internal communications to take place without an agreed common language.

Context – refers to the entire array of incentives surrounding every communication event. The measurement of context can be assigned either high or low. High-context cultures assign meaning to many of the incentive surrounding and unambiguous message. On the other hand, low-context cultures leave out many of those incentive and focus on the objective communication event (O'Hara-Devereaux and Johansen, 1994). For example, high-context culture refers to an individuals *context* or their relationship with other people (e.g., families and friends) as more important (that is the context in which the individual relates to people/ families) than the individuals themselves do. Low-context culture means it is less important whom an individual is related to (i.e., the context in which the person operates), but more importantly, what the individual does.

Time – the concept of time and time management differ widely from culture to culture. As per Edward and Mildred Hall (1990) described, cultural time differences can be thought of either *monochronic* or *polychronic* categories. In monochronic time category, people tend to do one single thing at a time, however, in polychronic time category, people can perform multiple tasks at once. Another aspect in relation to the time is the orientation. The time orientations are generally partitioned as past, present and future. According to O'Hara-Devereaux and Johansen (1994), cultures are either future-oriented or past-oriented. This means the current operations of business activities are designed to influence the future events or to be influenced by past events. Different cultures would have different emphases on time orientation. For instance, Asian cultures are inclined to be oriented toward a more distant future. On the other hand, many Latin cultures are heavily influenced by the past. When planning for cross-culture collaborative works, for example the global information systems development teams with members across nations and culture backgrounds, organizations need to consider the employees' attitudes toward time categories and orientations and derive a balanced "Time" solution for maximizing the performance in the global collaborative situation.

Power equality – refers to the degree of power and authority distribution and understanding of equality in different cultural perspective. Organizational units in various cultures may have diverse perception of power, authority, and equality to employees. For example, some cultures might demonstrate higher respect to professional, skilled employees than to general unskilled workers. Thus, skilled professionals would derive more power than unskilled workers would. In this dimension, organizations ought to carefully adjust the power, authority, and equality given to employees in diverse cultural backgrounds while maintaining equivalent level of distribution (power, authority, and equality) among business units.

Information flow – refers to the methods and paths of transferring information and data between people across levels and regions within the organization. Information flow is critical in productively carrying out business operations and achieving business objectives in a cross-cultural business environment. Global organizations need to realize the cultural impact on the information flow and ensure that information travels from one part of the organization to another within expected time, sequence, and format.

Additionally, many recent research publications have reported that the knowledge of culture and cultural environments is crucial for the success of the globalization process. In addition, a number of global information systems management issues related to culture and culture differences have been outlined by researchers (Burn J. et al., 1993; Ein-Dor, Segev and Orgad, 1993; Sauter, 1992; Yellen, 1997). These issues aim to draw organizations' attention intending to pursue globalization. There are several aspects pertaining to culture that need to be heeded by an organization planning to globalize its information systems management. These include education levels, geographical and time zones, religion aspect, demographic perspective, individual significance and objectives, communication, and leadership style. To recognize the importance of these, each aspect is further explored and discussed in the following sections.

Education Levels

The education level in relation to the information technology and globalization depends upon various aspects of a country's vision. In some developing countries such as China and India, information technology seems to be the main agenda in the national education strategy as the rationale of competing with developed countries. However, some other countries have much less emphasis on information technology education. A company's transition to globalization can be impacted significantly based on the level of education in the regions it operates.

Geographical and Time Zones

Geographical by dispersion of business units with respective time zone ranges are natural characteristics of organizations that operate their business globally. These can be both helpful and detrimental. These can be helpful because of round-the-clock information systems development scenario. On the other hand, the geographical and time zone differences could be detrimental. In videoconference and telephone conference situations, for instance, an inter-organizational meeting scheduled at two o'clock in the afternoon in Sydney would cause difficulty for people to participate in New York (as it would be the middle of the night there).

Religion

Sometimes religion has major influence on the daily schedule of business operations. For example, in the Islamic world, Friday is considered the holy day and is part of the weekend instead of Sunday. Business units or subsidiaries in Islamic areas must align their business hours to the religious activities. Religious events also affect organizations' non-working (holiday) periods. For instance, most of the Western world would have a one-week Christmas holiday; India will be in holiday season during Diwali, somewhere in between the end October and early November; Arab countries and China also have different holiday periods. Organizations with business units or subsidiaries operating in different countries need to ensure that there are no scheduled business activities during the times and days for religious activities and festivals.

Demographic Perspective

The focus of demographic aspect in global culture category is specifically associated with age and gender perspective. Age distribution can be quite different in every social culture. The general perceptions and values of age groups are also different from culture to culture. For example, many Western cultures value young people over the elders, whereas elders are revered in most Asian cultures. In the gender perspective, masculinity and femininity are the two key categories to be considered. In masculine cultures, gender roles are strictly distinguished; therefore, competitiveness and strength tend to be appreciated in organizations. In feminine cultures, values such as cooperation, caring and nurturing are valued and there is less demarcation between gender roles.

Although there is no perfect and standard solution to overcome the various cultural differences in age and gender aspects, organizations are strongly recommended to comprehend the meaning of these aspects in each culture and fine-tune the appropriateness to their working environment.

Significance and Objectives of the Individual

No matter where the employee is located or the position of the employee as a human being, an individual has its own objectives and meaning of the life. These objectives can be identified in three aspects: personal, social, and professional. From time to time, the emphasis of these aspects is changing, or conflicting with each other. For instance, an individual's personal objective is to spend more time with the family, but a promotion opportunity is given to the individual with the condition of working several months overseas. Hence, the individual has to decide whether to take the promotion opportunity and sacrifice the family commitment. Similarly, each organization has it own objectives and these objectives may conflict with employees' personal objectives. To overcome this conflict, the organizations must realize their employees' objectives, and negotiate with a realignment strategy to achieve a win-win situation.

Communication

As in the earlier discussion of O'Hara-Devereaux and Johansen's cultural lenses, communication primarily refers to languages in either verbal or written forms. Although English is the common language for business communication around the world in both written and verbal formats, there are other languages prominent in specific regions. For example, Chinese is the widespread language in greater China region (includes mainland China, Taiwan, Hong Kong, and Singapore); Spanish is the common language used in most Latin American countries. Adopting a language to be used across a multinational organization is a challenge task in the global transition process. In addition to language itself, methods used to flowing messages also play an import role in global business communication. The traditional ways of transferring messages amongst organizations are telephone conversation, fax and telex. On the other hand, e-mails, Web cam, and mobile SMS (Short Message Service) are the technological ways of transferring messages between companies.

Communication is always a major concern in most global organizations. Enterprises should ensure a standard communication topology is embedded in the policy and implemented in daily operations.

CONCLUSION

Globalization has become an essential business strategy for many enterprises in the current environment. It requires detailed planning, preparation, and investigation of issues before the implementation of global transition process can take place. In order to move the enterprise towards globalization, senior executives need to realize the impact of GISM issues on the globalization process. To provide a comprehensive view of the global transition issues, this chapter presents a number of factors identified by other researchers as cultural, human resource management, business strategic planning, quality assurance, systems development, and technological issues. These issues are classified into five categories: information technology management, business information systems management, people management, end user management, and culture. Each of these categories is explored and discussed in a number of associated factors. Further, suggestions and recommendations have been made to address these factors.

REFERENCES

Agocs, C. and Suttie, P. (1994). Just doing business: Managing human resource information in the learning organization: Strategic responses to the global environment. In C.P. Deans and K.R. Karwan (Eds.), *Global information systems and technology: Focus on the organization and its functional areas*. Hershey, PA: Idea Group Publishing.

Boudreau, J. W., Broderick, R. and Pucik, V. (1994). Just doing business: Human resource information systems in the global organization. In C.P. Deans and K.R. Karwan (Eds.), *Global information systems and technology: Focus on the organization and its functional areas*. Hershey, PA: Idea Group Publishing.

Burn, J. et al. (1993). Critical issues of IS management in Hong Kong: A cultural comparison. *Journal of Global Information Management, 1*(4), 28-37.

Cheung, H. K. and Burn, J.M. (1994). Distributing global information systems resources in multinational companies – A contingency model. *Journal of Global Information Management, 2*(3), 14-27.

Clikeman, P. (1999, June). Improving information quality. *Internal Auditor*, 32-33.

Constantine, L. L. (1995). *Constantine on peopleware*. NJ: Prentice Hall PTR, 84.

Edberg, D., Grupe, F. H. and Kuechler, W. (2001). Practical issues in global IT management. *Information Systems Management, 18*(1), 34-46.

Ein-Dor, P., Segev, E. and Orgad, M. (1993). The effect of national culture on IS: Implications for international information systems. *Journal of Global Information Management, 1*(1), 33-44.

English, L. P. (2001). Information quality management: The next frontier. Milwaukee, WI: Annual Quality Congress Proceedings, 529-533.

Gates, B. (1999). *Business @ the speed of thought: Using a digital nervous system.* England: Penguin Books Ltd, 15.

Gibson, R. and McGuire, E. G. (1996). Quality control for global software development. *Journal of Global Information Management, 4*(4), 16-22.

Hall, E. T. and Hall, M. R. (1990). Understanding cultural differences: Germans, French, and Americans. Yarmouth, ME: International Cultural Press, 16.

Hammer, M. and Stanton, S. A. (1995). The reengineering revolution. MA: Harvard Business School Publishing, 3.

Harrison, J. K. and Deans, P. C. (1994). The design and development of modules for an international human resource information system (HRIS). In C.P. Deans and K.R. Karwan (Eds.), *Global information systems and technology: Focus on the organization and its functional areas.* Hershey, PA: Idea Group Publishing.

Ives, B., Jarvenppa, S.L. and Mason, R.O. (1993). Global business drivers: Aligning information technology to global business strategy. *IBM Journal, 32*(1), 143-161.

Jones, S. (2001). Going global: How international firms are using the Internet to recruit. *Canadian HR Reporter, 14*(21), 21.

Kesner, R.M. and Palmisano, P.F. (1996). Transforming the global organization: Integrating the business, people, and information technology at Camp Dresser & McKee, Inc. *Information Strategy, 12*(2), 6-15.

Khandelwal, V. and Warrington, J. (1999). *Management of information technology in Australian enterprises: Critical success factors of CEOs.* University of Western Sydney, Nepean, Australia.

Kincaide, J. (1999, February). A CT passage to India. *Computer Telephony*, 100-114.

Klein, B.D. (1999). A spreadsheet project for integrating global issues in the software tool kit course. *Journal of Computer Information Systems, 40*(1), 64-68.

Knowles, J.H. (1996, July). Build an IT architecture on a business foundation. *Datamation*, 25.

Lan, Y. (2002, June). GISM issues for successful management of the globalization process. *Proceedings of the Third Annual Global Information Technology Management World Conference*, 224-227.

Laudon, K.C. and Laudon, J.P. (2002). *Management information systems: Managing the digital firm.* (7th ed.), NJ: Prentice-Hall, Inc.

Leontiades, J.C. (2001). *Managing the global enterprise.* London: Pearson Education Limited, 58-65.

Minor III, E.D. and Larkin, M. (1994). Information technology and global operations integration, planning, and control. In C.P. Deans and K.R. Karwan (Eds.), *Global information systems and technology: Focus on the organization and its functional areas.* Hershey, PA: Idea Group Publishing.

Neo, B.S. (1991). Information technology and global competition: A framework for analysis. *Information and Management, 20*(3), 151-160.

Niederman, F. (1994). Information systems personnel, human resource management and the global organization. In C.P. Deans and K.R. Karwan (Eds.), *Global information systems and technology: Focus on the organization and its functional areas*. Hershey, PA: Idea Group Publishing.

O'Connell, S. (1997). Systems issues for international business. *HR Magazine*, March, 36-41.

O'Hara-Devereaux, M. and Johansen, R. (1994). Globalwork: Bridging distance, culture, and time. CA: Jossey-Bass Inc., 61.

Palvia, S. and Saraswat, S.P. (1992). Information technology and the transnational corporation: The emerging multinational issues. In S. Palvia, P. Palvia and R. Zigli (Eds.), *The Global Issues of Information Technology Management*. Hershey, PA: Idea Group Publishing.

Palvia, S., Palvia, P.C. and Zigli, R.M. (1992). Global information technology environment: Key MIS issues in advanced and less-developed nations. In S. Palvia, P. Palvia and R. Zigli (Eds.), *The Global Issues of Information Technology Management*. Hershey, PA: Idea Group Publishing.

Passino Jr., J.H. and Severance, D.G. (1990). Harnessing the potential of information technology for support of the new global organization. *Human Resource Management, 29*, 69-76.

Passmore, D. (1997, February. The need for architecture. *Business Communications Review*, 18-19.

Porter, M.E. (1998). *On competition*. MA: Harvard Business School Publishing, 166-167.

Pucik, V. and Katz, J.H. (1986). Information, control, and human resource management in multinational firms. *Human Resource Management, 25*(1), 121-132.

Sankar, C.S. and Prabhakar, P. K. (1992). Key technological components and issues of global information systems. In S. Palvia, P. Palvia and R. Zigli (Eds.), *The Global Issues of Information Technology Management*. Hershey, PA: Idea Group Publishing.

Sauter, V.L. (1992). Cross-cultural aspects of model management needs in a transnational decision support system. In S. Palvia, P. Palvia and R. Zigli (Eds.), *The Global Issues of Information Technology Management*. Hershey, PA: Idea Group Publishing.

Senn, J. (1992). Assessing the impact of Western Europe Unification in 1992: Implications for corporate IT strategies. In S. Palvia, P. Palvia and R. Zigli (Eds.), The Global Issues of Information Technology Management. PA: Idea Group Publishing.

Sethi, V. and Olson, J.E. (1992). An integrating framework for information technology issues in a transnational environment. In S. Palvia, P. Palvia and R. Zigli (Eds.), *The Global Issues of Information Technology Management*. Hershey, PA: Idea Group Publishing.

Thomsett, R. (1994, December). When the rubber hits the road: a guide to implementing self-managing teams. *American Programmer, 37*-45.

Unhelkar, B. (1998). Transactional analysis (TA) as applied to human factors in object-oriented projects. In Saba Zamir (Ed.), *Handbook of Object Technology*. FL: CRC Press.

Unhelkar, B. (2002). *Process Quality Assurance for UML-based Projects*. MA: Addison-Wesley.

Waples, E. and Norris, D.M. (1992). Information systems and transborder data flow. *Journal of Systems Management, 43*(1), 28-30.

Watson, R. T. et al. (1997). Key issues in information systems management: An international perspective. *Journal of Management Information Systems, 13*(4), 91-115.

Yellen, R.E. (1997). End user computing in a global environment. *Journal of End User Computing, 9*(2), 33-34.

Chapter VIII

A Framework for Narrowing the Digital Divide

Alexander Osterwalder
Université de Lausanne, Switzerland

Mathias Rossi
Université de Lausanne, Switzerland

Minyue Dong
Université de Lausanne, Switzerland

ABSTRACT

The bridging of the so-called digital divide is an important issue in today's development efforts of international and non-governmental organizations and developing countries. This does not only concern access to new information and communication technology (ICT) such as the Internet, but also access to the knowledge how to use these technologies for economic development. This chapter outlines the business model framework and the business model handbook that shall help to develop a knowledgeable class of e-entrepreneurs that are able to use ICT and to detect the opportunities of the Internet era.

INTRODUCTION

The use of Information and Communication Technology (ICT) is not a panacea for all development problems. Several obstacles that make it difficult for Small- and Medium-Sized Enterprises (SMEs) in developing countries to adopt ICT and particularly, Internet business tools. However, detailed analysis of experience around the world reveals ample evidence that, used in the right way and for the right purposes, ICT can have a dramatic impact on achieving specific social and economic development goals as well as play a key role in broader national development strategies (DOI, 2001). One of the greatest impacts of ICT is the mobilization of worldwide knowledge and expertise and their knowledge transfer to the actors of developing economies (World Bank, 1996).

The goal of this chapter is to focus on the development of human capacity in ICT and Internet use for businesses in developing countries. Building a critical mass of knowledge workers, increasing technical skills among users and strengthening local entrepreneurial and managerial capabilities are essential for countries to participate in the information economy. The Business Model Handbook for Developing Countries, which we propose and explain in the following pages, relies on extensive research on e-business models (Osterwalder et al., 2001). This Web-based knowledge transfer tool should show SMEs and local entrepreneurs the relevant business issues in the information society and help them find new business opportunities. With this tool they could, for example, learn about new value propositions, how to streamline business and improve productivity or understand how to reduce operational costs by decreasing material, procurement and transaction costs, resulting in lower prices for intermediate and finished goods. Finally, they should also understand how to use more and better information to improve the value of their output.

In short, the Business Model Handbook for Developing Countries should be an openly accessible resource on the Web addressing the following three points:
- Understanding business issues of the Information Economy.
- Understanding the relationship between business logic and structure, ICT and particularly, the Internet in developing countries.
- Storage of case studies of SMEs in developing countries that illustrate the business issues and the use and adoption of ICT.

Following this introduction, the next section explains the problem of the so-called digital divide. Then we insist on the importance of knowledge transfer and the development of entrepreneurial capacities. To achieve these goals, we outline the Business Model Framework (BMF) for Developing Countries. On top of this framework, we propose the Business Model Handbook (BMH), a tool that allows a better understanding of the firm in the Internet era.

DIGITAL DIVIDE

Simply put, the term *digital divide* means that between countries and different groups of people within countries, there is a wide division between those who have real access to ICT and are using it effectively, and those who do not[1]. Since ICT is increasingly becoming a foundation of our societies and economies, the digital divide means that the "information have-nots" are denied the option to participate in new ICT jobs, in e-government, in ICT improved healthcare, and in ICT enhanced education. More often than not, the "information have-nots" are in developing countries, and in disadvantaged groups within countries. In this chapter, we particularly focus on bridging the digital divide for companies of developing countries. We try to provide a tool that helps these firms understand how ICT influences company structure and how it opens up new business opportunities.

ENTREPRENEURSHIP

Human capacity development and entrepreneurship promotion are central issues in bridging the digital divide. Besides, the majority of recent publications of International Organizations stress the fact that the encouragement and support of e-entrepreneurship is indispensable if developing countries do not want to miss out on the possibilities of ICT (DOI, 2001; Dot Force, 2001; UNCTAD, 2001; World Bank, 2001; UNDP, 2001). Local businesses need to acquire a strong awareness and understanding of the business opportunities these technologies make available. Entrepreneurship plays a particularly critical role during periods of rapid economic change, as small, agile firms increase the ability of an economy to quickly respond to new challenges. Unfortunately, most developing countries have a poor environment for entrepreneurship. In general, there is a lack of knowledge with respect to the new business models that characterize Internet-centered businesses. And people that combine skills and creativity in Internet site creation, business know-how, access to finance and knowledge of local community needs are still relatively rare worldwide, but particularly in developing countries (infoDev, 2000). Nevertheless, as stated in the final report of the Digital Opportunity Initiative it is far from inevitable that ICT will have a negative impact on developing economies; in fact, with the right policies and practical actions, ICT can be a powerful enabler of development (DOI, 2001). Creativity and entrepreneurship in Brazil, India, Thailand, Niger and elsewhere have made the development of software for illiterate users and low-cost, solar-powered wireless devices possible (UNDP, 2001). But two essential conditions for entrepreneurship development are access to knowledge tools for business architects and a better understanding of the existing opportunities arising out of new ICT. In the following two sections we try to outline a framework and some tools that address these issues.

BUSINESS MODEL FRAMEWORK

The Business Model Framework is a rigorous building-block-like methodology that defines the essential concepts in e-business models and shows the relationships between them. Our framework has been inspired in some ways by the different enterprise ontology projects described in academic literature (Toronto Virtual Enterprise, Enterprise Ontology, Core Enterprise Ontology) (Bertolazzi et al., 2001). These ontologies mainly concentrate on processes and organizational representation. The work of the Edinburgh Group (Ushold, 1995), for example, is aimed at proposing enterprise ontology, i.e., a set of carefully defined concepts that are widely used for describing enterprises in general and that can serve as a stable basis for specifying software requirements. The group has developed tools for modeling, communicating and representing enterprises and processes in a unique way. The focus of this work is on the logic and concepts of value creation, at a higher level of abstraction, which is the business model. This allows a much better and more structured transfer of business knowledge to entrepreneurs in developing countries.

Our Business Model Framework is the conceptualization and formalization into elements, relationships, vocabulary and semantics of the essential issues in the business model domain. The framework contains several levels of decomposition with increasing depth and complexity. On the following page, we describe the first and second level of decomposition.

The Business Model Framework is founded on four main pillars:

* The *products and services* a firm offers, representing a substantial value to the customer, and for which he is willing to pay.

Name of BM-Element	e-BUSINESS MODEL FRAMEWORK (root element)
Consists of	• PRODCUT INNOVATION • CUSTOMER RELATIONSHIP • INFRASTRUCTURE MANAGEMENT • FINANCIALS
Level of decomposition	0 (root element)

- The **infrastructure and the network of partners** that is necessary in order to create value and to maintain a good customer relationship.
- The **relationship capital** the firm creates and maintains with the customer, in order to satisfy him and to generate sustainable revenues.
- The **financials**, which are transversal and can be found throughout the three former components, such as cost and revenue structures. The four main elements are then further decomposed (see Figure 1).

Product Innovation

The *Product Innovation* pillar of the framework covers all product-related aspects. The main elements are the **value proposition** a firm wants to offer to specific **target customer segments** and the **capabilities** a firm has to be able to assure in order to deliver this value. This is described on the following page.

Target customer segment. The value proposition a firm offers on the market should target a specific customer segment. The arise of new affordable communication technologies such as the Internet, have given firms in developing countries access to completely new markets. If companies had to pass by several intermediaries to access the final clients for their products and services in the past, they can now often address them more directly. For example, Chincheros, a small village in Peru, increased its income five-fold to US$1,500 per month when the village leaders formed an Internet-enabled partnership with an export company in 1996. The village vegetables are now sold daily in New York (DOI, 2001). Through PEOPLink's global artisans trading exchange[2] local craftspeople in developing countries are increasing their incomes particularly because the wholesaling intermediaries for their produce have effectively been removed. They now receive up to 95 percent of the selling price for their produce, when previously they received only 10 percent (DOI, 2001). Several similar initiatives, offering indigenous peoples opportunities to globally market their traditional crafts and farm products exist on the Web (World Bank, 2002). In general, the Internet could erode an important advantage now enjoyed by firms in industrial countries: proximity to wealthy customers (World Bank, 2001).

Figure 1. Business Model Framework

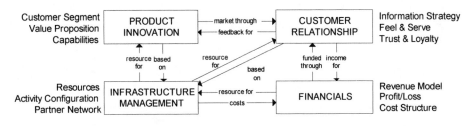

Name of BM-Element	PRODUCT INNOVATION
Child of	Root Element: Business Model
Consists of	• TARGET CUSTOMER SEGMENT • VALUE PROPOSITION • CAPABILITIES
Level of decomposition	1
Related to	• *Marketed through* CUSTOMER RELATIONSHIP • *Based on* INFRASTRUCTURE MANAGEMENT

Value proposition. This refers to what business the company is in and what bundle of products and services it offers on the market. It is important for firms and entrepreneurs in developing countries to understand that ICT opens them up a whole new world of opportunities. For example, rather than exporting products over the Internet, which demands an efficient and functioning logistical infrastructure, they could export digitally deliverable services. In e-transcription or e-editing, firms would receive audio files over the Web, split them into sections and format them by several employees in a parallel working mode. The electronic document could be returned in 24 hours. A one-hour tape, which equals about five to six typed pages, goes at US$60 to 100 per hour in North America (Rostenne, 1999). Another often-cited example is the case of Indian firms that rely on cheap software developers or accountants to provide outsourcing services to Western firms, particularly to multinationals. Further, through customization (Piller, 2000) firms could propose value tailored to the demand of a single customer. Small firms in developing countries have a substantial competitive advantage if they provide customized handmade products or customer-tailored services at low prices. The Internet makes it possible for a tailor in Shanghai to hand-make a suit for a lawyer in Boston and then FedEx it to him (The Economist, 2000).

Capabilities. To deliver a value proposition, firms must be conscious that they have to possess the range of capabilities that underpin the proposed value. This is particularly important for firms in developing countries, where ICT infrastructure and general infrastructure are not always satisfying and still often very expensive.

Infrastructure Management

The *Infrastructure Management* element, describes the value system configuration (Gordijn et al., 2001) that is necessary to deliver the value proposition. This comprises the *value configuration* of the firm, in other words the activities to create and deliver value, and, the relationship between them, the in-house *resources and assets* and the firm's *partner network*.

Value configuration. The main purpose of a company is for the creation of value for which customers are willing to pay. This value is the outcome of a configuration of inside and outside activities and processes. To define the value creation configuration in a business model, there are three basic trajectories. The first is the *value chain framework* by Porter et al. (1985) and its extension, as defined by Stabell et al. (1998), who add the concept of the value shop and the value network. Understanding the value creation process is indispensable for streamlining business and for identifying the right software and Internet tools. Firms in developing countries can also benefit from the Open Source software movement that delivers powerful, cheap ICT tools.

Resources and assets. In order to create value, a firm needs resources (Wernefelt, 1984). Grant (1995) distinguishes tangible, intangible, and human assets. Companies in developing

Name of BM-Element	INFRASTRUCTURE MANAGEMENT
Child of	Root Element: Business Model
Consists of	• RESOURCES • ACTIVITY CONFIGURATION (or VALUE CONFIGURATION) • PARTNER NETWORK
Level of decomposition	1
Related to	• *Resource for* PRODUCT INNOVATION • *Resource for* CUSTOMER RELATIONSHIP • *Cost for* FINANCIALS

countries have to analyze where they have competitive advantages, in order to focus on a precise and limited range of resources and assets. For everything else, ICT opens up new ways of partnering and outsourcing.

Partner network. The partner network outlines which elements of the activity configuration are distributed among the partners of the firm. Shrinking transaction costs make it easier for firms to vertically disintegrate and to reorganize in partner networks. CatGen, for example, provides software that enables local artisans to easily capture and transmit digital images of products over the Internet with minimal training and in conditions of poor connectivity. The solution is feasible due to the existence of public access points such as cyber cafes and telecenters (infoDev, 1998).

Customer Relationship

Through the use of ICT firms can redefine the notion of *Customer Relationship*. First, they can get a feel for and understand the customer by outlining an ***information strategy***. Second, firms can exploit new ways to deliver value and expand reach by covering new and multiple ***channels***. Third, companies must understand that ***trust and loyalty*** has become one of the most important elements in a business world that is increasingly a virtual one and has less face-to-face contact. This is described at the bottom of the page.

Information strategy. Collecting information on customers and their behavior has become essential for understanding the market and offering adequate products and services. Better knowledge of its customers allows a firm to establish a personalized relationship tailored to the needs of every single customer. However, companies in emerging markets are often wary of introducing continuous-relationship marketing because of the sophisticated IT systems, customer records, and marketing expertise it is said to require. In reality, things are not as complicated, as shown by Chung et al. (Chung et al., 2002). One mobile-phone operator in Asia, for example, cut customer churn by more than 40 percent by offering a special discount to just the customers identified as the most likely to cancel. An East Asian retail bank increased its credit card profits by targeting a direct-marketing campaign at high-income

Name of BM-Element	CUSTOMER RELATIONSHIP
Child of	Root Element: Business Model
Consists of	• INFORMATION STRATEGY • FEEL & SERVE • TRUST & LOYALTY
Level of decomposition	1
Related to	• *Feedback for* PRODUCT INNOVATION • *Based on* INFRASTRUCTURE MANAGEMENT • *Income for* FINANCIALS

customers who were heavy ATM users, having discovered through the use of CRM that they were four times as likely to take up a credit card offer as the people in a control group.

Feel & Serve (channels). This element refers to the way a firm "goes to market" and how it actually "reaches" its customers (Hamel, 2000). As shown above, direct selling over the Web can improve margins and selling through new Internet mediation services, so-called cybermediaries (Sarker et al., 1995) can mean new market opportunities. AfricanCraft.com[3] is a Web site dedicated to bringing the arts and the artisans of Africa online. By supplying information on online shops, craftspeople, artists and designers in Africa, and by setting up on-line classrooms on subjects such as Kente paper weaving or loom construction, this Web site positions itself as a portal for African craftsmanship. This illustrates one of the best known and mostly applied aspects of e-business: providing information on products and value-added services over a Web site. A firm can easily supply its customer with a wide range of basic information on products, prices and availability, or even offer him customized real-time information (i.e., delivery status, product lifecycle management). African countries for example, could have stopped their diminishing export performances, which were largely attributed to non-prices factors on the demand side (Oshikoya et al., 1999), if they had used the Internet for marketing information on prices and used the Web for after sales services and quality amelioration. A successful example of a new cybermediary is the Chinese Web site, alibaba.com, which matches international customers with Chinese suppliers. This is very helpful for Chinese manufacturers that often have little knowledge of how to address international export markets.

Trust & Loyalty. For businesses in developing countries it is indispensable to find ways to establish trust between business partners if they want to survive in the virtual market space, particularly if they are in the export business. In online auctions, more often than not a lack of credibility makes it difficult for firms in developing countries to access customers. Purchasers need to have confidence that suppliers will provide input on time and in conformance with specifications, and product quality may not be known ex ante. More than half of 35 large firms using online auction or exchange sites said that they would not do business through online Web sites with firms they did not know (Forrester Research, 1999). Interview results indicate buyers—typically firms in industrial countries—see an especially high risk in purchasing from firms in developing countries (World Bank, 2001). Therefore it is important to use the existing mechanisms to build trust in e-business environments, such as virtual communities (Hagel et al., 1997), performance history, mediation services or insurance, third party verification and authorization, and, clear privacy policies (Friedman et al., 2000). Finally, customer loyalty emerges out of the customer's trust and satisfaction.

Financials

The *Financials*, the last pillar of our framework is transversal because it is influenced by all other pillars. This element is composed of the *revenue model* of the firm and its *cost structure*. The formerly mentioned determine the firm's *profit or loss* and therefore its ability to survive in competition.

Revenue Model. This element measures the ability of a firm to translate the value it offers its customers into money and therefore generate incoming revenue streams. Firms can compose their revenue model of different revenue streams that can all have different pricing models. Companies in developing countries must understand that the Internet has had an

Name of BM-Element	FINANCIALS
Child of	Root Element: Business Model
Consists of	• REVENUE MODEL • COST STRUCTURE • PROFIT/LOSS
Level of decomposition	1
Related to	• *Resource for* INFRASTRUCTURE MANAGEMENT • *Funded through* CUSTOMER RELATIONSHIP

important impact on pricing and has created a whole new range of pricing mechanisms (Klein et al., 2000).

Cost structure. This element measures all the costs the firm incurs in order to create, market and deliver value to its customers. It sets a price tag on all the resources, assets, activities and partner network relationships and exchanges that cost the company money.

Profit/Loss. This element is simply the outcome of the difference between the revenue model and the cost structure. It can be seen as the culminating point and as an expression of the entire business model. Whereas product innovation and customer relationship shall maximize revenue, an effective infrastructure management shall minimize costs and therefore, optimize the profit model.

THE BUSINESS MODEL HANDBOOK FOR DEVELOPING COUNTRIES

The Business Model Handbook (BMH) for developing countries is a proposition for a tool that has the goal to help Small and Medium Sized Enterprises (SME) and local entrepreneurs to design business models in the context of developing economies that use ICT and particularly the Internet. The BMH should be a Web-based tool that relies on the Business Model Framework (BMF) outlined above. It is essential that this tool is driven by user demand and realized through direct participation of targeted end users. It should not be perceived as a kind of Trojan horse (Afemann, 2000) to impose business and ICT concepts of rich countries. ICT use should be proportional to the capacities of its adopters. In other words, firms should only use technologies if they effectively bring advantages. The relationship between costs and opportunities should remain realistic.

The goal of the BMH for Developing Countries is threefold. The first goal consists in the transfer of business knowledge for better understanding the information society. ICT has had an important impact on business and enterprise structure and therefore make it necessary to rethink the way a firm builds it business. Business model design relying on the BMF detailed above shall allow local SMEs and entrepreneurs to be competitive in a increasingly global economy (see Figure 2).

The second goal of the BMH is to help SMEs and local entrepreneurs identify new opportunities arising through ICT deployment in developing countries. Firms in emerging economies have several competitive advantages, such as low wages, that they could not exploit without profiting of the recent ICT evolution. Government agencies and Non Governmental Organizations (NGOs) should be involved in the supplying of local/regional information and should be consulted in the construction of a BMH for a specific country or

Figure 2. Business Model Handbook

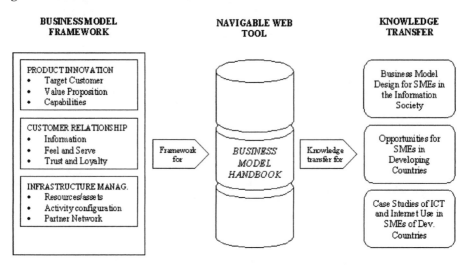

region. Typically, this concerns information on local taxes, specific trade regulations and other legal frameworks.

The last goal and probably the most important aspect of the BMH is the collection of successful case studies of firms in developing countries that have adopted ICT in their businesses. The goal of this repository is to make replicable, transportable and scalable cases of ICT adoption in developing countries easily available. These cases would be different from similar existing Web-repositories of international organizations and NGOs. The cases would be decomposed and formally described by using our framework, based on a building block-like approach. This scenario has the advantage because cases can be searched and analyzed according to their different business model "blocks." One entrepreneur might want to know what kind of value proposition has been adopted by other firms in developing countries, whereas a manager might want to learn more about digital distribution channel strategies and a third one might want to understand more about the opportunities in infrastructure management or partner networks. This project shares with the *Process Handbook* project of the MIT (Malone et al., 1999) the key idea that a repository and the associated computerized tool can significantly enhance the creativity and the efficiency of business model designers (process model designers in the case of the MIT).

CONCLUSION

We agree with Emmanuel Castells, who said, "technology per se does not solve social problems" (Castells, 1998). We also agree "the availability and use of information and communication technologies are a pre-requisite for economic and social development in our world. They are the functional equivalent of electricity in the industrial era." Therefore, the goal of this project is to use ICT for knowledge sharing and transfer. The main contribution of the BMH is to make a comprehensive business model framework available that allows transferring knowledge in the domain of ICT use in developing countries. This could be achieved through a Web-based business tool we call the Business Model Handbook (BMH) for Developing Countries. The implementation of such a tool would be an attempt to create a development dynamic to accelerate the creation of a critical mass of motivated entrepreneurs and people with business expertise that can leverage new opportunities (Digital Opportunity Initiative, 2001).

ENDNOTES

[1]   This definition of the digital divide and a pool of related information can be found on the Bridges.org Website at http://www.bridges.org. Retrieved on August 7, 2002.

[2]   http://www.peoplink.org/EN/0.html. Retrieved on August 7, 2002.

[3]   http://www.arficancrafts.com. Retrievd on August 7, 2002.

REFERENCES

Afemann, U. (2000). Internet and Developing Countries – Pros and Cons. International Workshop Social Usage of Internet in Malaysia. Retrieved August 7, 2002, from the World Wide Web: http://www.interasia.org/malaysia/workshop_afemann.html

Afuah, A. & Tucci, C. (2001). *Internet Business Models and Strategies.* McGraw Hill.

Benjamin, R.I. & Wigand, R.T. (1995). Electronic commerce: Effects on electronic markets. *JCMC 1*(3).

Bertolazzi, P., Krusich, C. & Missikoff, M. (2001). An approach to the definition of a core enterprise ontology: CEO. *OES-SEO 2001, International Workshop on Open Enterprise Solutions: Systems, Experiences, and Organizations.* Rome, September 14-15.

Brandenburger, A. & Nalebuff, B. (1996). *Co-opetition.* Doubleday.

Castells, M. (1998). Information Technology, Globalization and Social Development. UNRISD Conference on Information Technologies and Social Development. Retrieved August 7, 2002, from the World Wide Web: http://www.unrisd.org/unrisd/website/events.nsf/(httpEvents)/373F79257FE8665880256B810060276B?OpenDocument

Chung, S. & Sherman, M. (2002). Emerging marketing [Electronic version]. *The McKinsey Quarterly, 2.*

Daly, J. & Miller, R.R. (1998). Corporations' Use of the Internet in Developing Countries. IFC Discussion Paper Nr.35, The World Bank.

Dhawan, R., Dorian, C., Gupta, R. & Sunkara, S.K. (2001). Connecting the unconnected [Electronic version]. *The McKinsey Quarterly*, Nr.4 Emerging Markets, Retrieved from the WWW: http://www.mckinseyquarterly.com/ article_abstract.asp?tk=351136:1110:22&ar=1110&L2=22&L3=77

DOI: Digital Opportunity Initiative. (2001). *Creating a Development Dynamic: Final Report of the Digital Opportunity Initiative.* Accenture, Markle Foundation, UNDP.

DOT Force. (2001). Digital Opportunities for All: Meeting the Challenge. *Report of the Digital Opportunity Task Force.*

The Economist (2000). Falling through the net? September 21.

Elotu, J. (2000). ITU Brings Telemedicine to Uganda [Electronic Version], Retrieved from the World Wide Web in December/November 2000: http://www.isoc.org/oti/articles/1100/uganda.html

Forrester Research. (1999). *Managing e-Marketplace Risk.*

Friedman, B., Kahn, P. & Howe, D. (2000). Trust online. Comm. *ACM, 43*(12), 34-40.

Goodman, S. & Kelly, T. (2001). Electronic commerce in Nepal [Electronic version]. Retrieved from the World Wide Web in March/April 2001: http://www.isoc.org/oti/articles/0401/press.html

Gordijn, J., Akkermans, J. & van Vliet, J. (2000). What's in an electronic business model? *Knowledge Engineering and Knowledge Management - Methods, Models, and Tools, LNAI 1937*: 257-273.

Gordijn, J., Akkermans, J. & van Vliet, J. (2001, July/August). Designing and evaluating e-business models. *IEEE Intelligent Systems, 16* (4), 11-17.

Grant, R.M. (1995). *Contemporary Strategy Analysis.* Malden, MA: Blackwell.

Hagel, J. & Armstrong, A. (1997). *Net Gain - Expanding Markets through Virtual Communities.* Harvard Business School Press.

Hamel, G. (2000). *Leading the Revolution.* Harvard Business School Press.

InfoDev. (1998). Implementing a global e-commerce network for artisan groups [Electronic version]. infoDev Project Proposal, Project Number 289-980521.

InfoDev. (2000). The networking revolution – Opportunities and challenges for developing countries. Infodev working paper. Global Information and Communication Technologies Department of the World Bank Group.

Klein, S. & Loebbecke, C. (2000). The transformation of pricing models on the web: examples from the airline industry. *13th International Bled Electronic Commerce Conference,* Bled, (June 19-21).

Malone, T.W., Crowston, K., Lee, J., Pentland, B., Dellarocas, C., Wyner, G., Quimby, J., Osborn, C.S., Bernstein, A., Herman, G., Klein, M. & O'Donnel, E. (1999). Tools for inventing organizations: Toward a handbook of organizational processes. *Management Science, 45*(3), 425-443.

Oshikoya, T.W. & Hussain, M.N. (1999). Information technology and the challenge of economic development in Africa. African Development Bank Group Economic Research. Paper No.36.

Osterwalder, A. & Pigneur, Y. (2002, June). *An e-business model ontology for modeling e-business.* 15th Bled Electronic Commerce Conference.

Panos (1998). *The Internet and Poverty: Real Help or Real Hype?* Panos, London.

Piller, F.T, Reichwald, R. & Möslein, K. (2000). Information as a critical success factor for mass customization or: why even a customized shoe not always fits. *ASAC-IFSAM 2000 Conference*, Montreal, Canada.

Porter, M. (2001). Strategy and the Internet. *Harvard Business Review, 79*(3), 62-78.

Porter, M. & Millar, V. (1985) How information gives you competitive advantage. *Harvard Business Review 63*(4), 149-160.

Rappa, M. (2001). *Managing the digital enterprise - Business models on the Web. Retrieved* from the World Wide Web on August 7, 2002: http://ecommerce.ncsu.edu/business_models.html

Rostenne, J. (1999). Internet for Business – Making Money on the Web, a Specialized Workshop for Executives and Entrepreneurs. African Development Forum.

Sarkar, M., Butler, B. & Steinfield, C. (1995). Intermediaries and cybermediaries: A continuing role for mediating players in the electronic marketplace. *Journal of Computer-Mediated Communication 1*(3).

Stabell, C.B. & Fjeldstad, O.D. (1998). Configuring value for competitive advantage: On chains, shops, and networks. *Strategic Management Journal, 19,* 413-437.

Tapscott, D., Lowi, A. & Ticoll, D. (2000). *Digital Capital Harnessing the Power of Business Webs.* Harvard Business School Press.

UNCTAD. (2001). E-Commerce and Development Report.

UNDP. (2001). Human Development Report.

Ushold, M. & King, M. (1995). Towards a methodology for building ontologies. *Workshop on Basic Ontological Issues in Knowledge Sharing*, held in conjunction with IJCAI-95, Montreal, August 20-25.

Wernefelt. (1984) A resource-based view of the firm. *Strategic Management Journal, 5,* 171-181.

World Bank (2001). *Global Economic Prospects and the Developing Countries 2001.*

World Bank (2001). Harnessing information for development: a proposal for a World Bank Group vision and strategy, Information Technology for Development, 6(3/4), 145-188.

World Bank (2002). *Global Coalitions for Voices of the Poor Web Guide: E-Commerce to Support Grassroots Entrepreneurs.*

Chapter IX

Managing Information Technology Component of Knowledge Management: Outsourcing as a Strategic Option in Developing Countries

Adekunle Okunoye
University of Turku and TUCS, Finland

ABSTRACT

Information technology and social-cultural, organizational variables are considered major components to support knowledge processes in knowledge management. These components have to be carefully managed and be supported in balanced proportion for organization to create and retain greater value from their core competencies. The peculiar situation of developing countries, where there is lack of adequate information technology infrastructure, emphasizes the importance of strategic management of organizational information technology. Using a case study, we discuss the possibility of outsourcing the management of the information technology in order to have more focus on the other components in knowledge management.

INTRODUCTION

Knowledge management (KM) could be defined as the ability to create and retain greater value from core business competencies (Duffy, 2000; Bhatt, 2001; CIO, 2000). IT is one of the enablers of knowledge management. Its availability, management, and right application could increase the success rate of knowledge management efforts of organizations. Due to lack of human resources with required skills and lack of adequate IT infrastructure (ITI) in sub-Saharan Africa, IT outsourcing could be a better approach to IT management for an organization considering KM. In this chapter, we present part of the outcome of an empirical research and an in-depth analysis of a case organization where IT outsourcing seems to contribute to a high performance in knowledge management efforts. We suggest that organizations in sub-Saharan Africa that are considering knowledge management could look at the possibility of outsourcing the management of the information technology component in order to have more focus on the other enablers of KM

Information technology is one of the enablers of knowledge management and its management could have a great effect on the knowledge management efforts of organizations. IT management in sub-Saharan Africa is posing problems to some organizational activities in the face of low resources and expertise (Odedra et al. 1993; Moyo, 1996). Outsourcing IT has attracted a lot of attention in IT literature (e.g., Lacity and Hirschheim 1993; McFarlan and Nolan, 1995; Hirschheim and Lacity 2000). It could allow organization to focus more on development efforts such as reengineering process, just-in-time, total quality management, benchmarking, etc. For these reasons, IT outsourcing has become very popular. There is much evidence of its success after the understanding of the problems associated with earlier agreements (Shepherd, 1999). Firms focus on their core capabilities to have competitive advantage especially in today's dynamic, volatile business environment. When a firm focuses on core businesses that add unique value to its customers, it may outsource activities for which it lacks core capabilities (Quinn and Hilmer, 1994).

In our empirical study of six research organizations on ITI and KM in sub-Saharan Africa, two organizations presented exceptions to our assumption that organizations with high ITI capability are also likely to have effective knowledge management. In one organization, high level of IT infrastructure capability was not accompanied by high KM efforts while in another research institute, there were high KM efforts at instance of low IT infrastructure capability. Upon closer inspection of the later, the IT outsourcing strategy of the organizations with low ITI seems to be responsible for the high performance in knowledge management activities. Could the IT outsourcing strategy directly relate to the performance in KM efforts? We examine KM from core competence perspective and argue about the difference between the strategic and operational view of organizational IT. We illustrated this with a case organization upon which we will draw our conclusions and suggestions for further studies.

IT OUTSOURCING

Outsourcing is the transfer or delegation of the operation and day-to-day management of a business process to an external service provider. IT outsourcing can be regarded as the practice of transferring IT assets, leases, staff, and management responsibility for delivery of services from internal IT functions to third-party (Hirschheim and Lacity, 2000). According to Hitt et al. (1999), outsourcing is a strategic concept, a way to add value to the business that converts an in-house cost center into a result oriented service operation. The motivation for IT outsourcing is widely discussed in the literature. Shepherd (1999) provides a summary where he included financial restructuring, reduction or stabilization of costs, overcoming cultural and organizational problems, concentrating on core competencies, access to world class expertise, concern with economies of scale and scope, and possibly growth expectation. Generally, virtually all organizations are seeking the strategic value that can be captured through effective outsourcing.

IT outsourcing evolved from the early 1960s data processing service bureau to the contract programming approach of 1970s. The 1980s witnessed more focused efforts on vertical integration and internal control and a slowdown in outsourcing (Ketler and Willems, 1999). The 1990s are characterized by a renewed interest in outsourcing, following Eastman Kodak's much written-about outsourcing deal of 1989. At turn of the century, with various IT related problems (e.g., Y2K, skill demands, etc.) and developments (e.g., e-commerce) and the need for organizations to be more competitive and responsive, IT outsourcing has become a generally acceptable practice in various forms and scopes. Both small and large-sized organizations are taking advantage of outsourcing opportunities.

Since only few organizations if any, possess the resources and capabilities required to achieve competitive superiority in all primary and support activities, more especially with respect to information technology which required keeping with the dynamism of the industry and changing expertise (Hitt et al., 1999). IT outsourcing enables an organization to focus on their core competence and it provides possibility to make a right strategic decision that directly affects the work. It enables access to new technology and keeping up with the trends in the ever-changing world of IT (Ketler and Willems, 1999; Goo et al., 2000). In a situation where there is low availability of human resources, it relieves the organization of the burden of continuous recruiting due to the high turnover rate in the sector (Slaughter and Ang, 1996). Thus, we also agree that IT outsourcing could be a good decision for an organization that does not use IT for strategic purposes, but mostly for operational functions (Currie and Pouloudi, 2000), especially in a region where there is lack of adequate expertise to support in-house IT management.

According to Ang and Straub (1998), organizations apply selective outsourcing analysis in which outsourcing relationships are focused on specific IT activities where external providers supply expertise that is currently lacking. Also, organizations apply selective outsourcing analysis is applied where outsourcing relationships are focused on external providers that furnish assets or competencies for which they have a comparative advantage in terms of economies of scale. Analysis is also applied to external providers that take on responsibilities for IT activities not considered mission critical so that the organization can deploy released resources into strategic activities. Using the last option could enable an organization to nurture few core competencies and thus, increase the organizations probability of developing a competitive advantage or a tremendous improvement in a particular process (Chesebrough and Teece, 1996).

Although outsourcing IT to India and other developing countries has attracted attention, the outsourcing arrangements within developing countries are less written about. In the case of non-profit research organizations, IT could be viewed as a set of operational tools. The scientists are mainly interested in getting their work done and they may have little interest in state-of-the-art-IT. Their core competence is far from IT, though in the modern world where they operate, IT use appears essential. In as much as they are able to carry out their primary duties with IT, the kind of IT installed or the style of its management might not in any direct way provide competitive advantages to them. In fact, these non-profit organizations do not consider other organizations as competitors, but rather collaborators. They need IT to support the process of their work, communication, collaboration and coordination. For these reasons, it could be convenient for the research organizations to outsource their entire IT management functions.

INFORMATION TECHNOLOGY INFRASTRUCTURE (ITI)

IT infrastructure is a major business resource and a source for attaining sustainable competitive advantage (Broadbent et al., 1999; Keen, 1991; McKenney, 1995). It is increasingly seen as a fundamental differentiator in the competitive performance of the organizations, its investment leads to new competitive strategies and progression through higher levels of organizational transformation. IT infrastructure capabilities enable the emergence of new organization forms, facilitate electronic commerce and knowledge management; it is critical to globally competing firms (Broadbent et al., 1999). Strategically, the importance of an organization's information technology infrastructure capability is increasingly recognized as critical to an organization's competitiveness. These infrastructures are important for organizations going through dynamic change, for organizations reengineering their business processes, managing individual and organizational knowledge and for those with multiple business units or extensive international or geographically dispersed operations (Broadbent et al. 1999). IT infrastructure, according to Broadbent and Weill (1997) is the base foundation of information technology capability, delivered as reliable services shared throughout the firm. ITI is coordinated centrally, usually by the information systems group or external people when outsourced. They use a pyramid to illustrate the different components of information technology infrastructure (see Figure 1).

At the base of the pyramid there are components such as computer and communications technologies (hardware and software), that are largely commodities and readily available for

Figure 1. Elements of IT infrastructure (Broadbent and Weill, 1997)

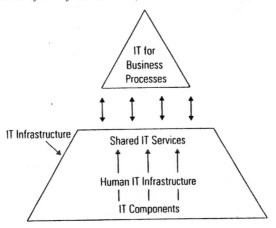

purchase and hire. The second layer comprises of a set of shared services such as management of large-scale data processing, provision of electronic data interchange (EDI) capability, groupware, Internet or management of firm-wide databases. The human resources turn the components into reliable, shared information technology infrastructure services. Each of these components could be outsourced completely or in part, the decision depends on the factors already described above.

They also identified four views of IT infrastructure with different benefits and investments: none, utility, dependent, and enabling. None view implies that an organization does not invest in IT infrastructure at a firmwide level. The utility view primarily considers investment in IT infrastructure as a way to reduce costs through economies of scale. The dependent view ties the investment in IT infrastructure to the current organizational strategies and the enabling view is a dependent view with extra investment to cater for long-term goals and developments (Broadbent and Weill, 1997). It has earlier been recognized that ITI can be a significant barrier or enabler in the practical options available to planning and changing organization processes like KM (Broadbent et al., 1999), thus adequate support of enabling technologies and platforms is an important factors in the success of organizational changes. Therefore, organizations that consider IT as part of their core strategies are likely to take the dependent and/or enabling views. On the other hand, while organizations that consider IT as operational tools are likely to take the none and /or utility view, thus, they are likely to outsource their IT without fear of losing knowledge and have more time to concentrate on core capabilities.

KNOWLEDGE MANAGEMENT (KM)

Several authors acknowledge that the ultimate goal of KM is to improve organizations efficiency and productivity, hence profitability (APQC, 1996; Davenport and Prusak, 1998). For the purpose of this chapter, we lean towards the definition that KM is the ability to create and retain greater value from core business competencies (CIO, 2000) and a practice that finds valuable information and transforms it into necessary knowledge critical to decision making and action (Beveren, 2002). This could be achieved by various strategies to provide the right knowledge for the right people at the right time (APQC, 1996). Organizations are using various approaches to achieve these goals. Some are focusing on management of people and others on the management of information (Sveiby, 1996).

Tyndale (2000) further explained Sveiby's view, using the terms codification and personalization. He used codification to explain KM that is IT focused. This strategy includes attempts to codify knowledge and carefully store it in a database where it can be accessed and used easily by anyone in the company. This approach considers knowledge as objects that can be identified and handled in information systems. Personalization was used to explain KM that is people-focused. This approach regards knowledge as a process that is closely tied to the person who developed it. This kind of knowledge is shared mainly through direct person-to-person contacts. In this approach, technology is only used as the infrastructure that enables the capture, storage, and delivery of contents to those who need it when they need it. Bhatt (2001) also suggested that exclusive focus on codification or personalization does not enable the firm to sustain its competitive advantages but rather it is the interaction between technology, techniques and people that allow an organization to manage its knowledge effectively.

KM AND IT OUTSOURCING

The focus of previous studies on the relationship between IT outsourcing and KM has been on the knowledge issues between the contracting parties. For example Currie and Pouloudi (2000) relate the outsourcing decision to the value the organization attaches to their knowledge-based assets, they conclude that consideration of the value of knowledge-based assets, knowledge creation, growth, and retentions could affect the outsourcing decision. Their conclusion also supports the view that organizations that considered IT as core competence are likely to insource while organization that think otherwise may likely outsource. However, they did not elaborate further on whether the outsourcing decision allows the organizations to focus more on their core competency. Although it is the core competencies that really distinguish a company competitively and reflect its personality. According to Hitt et al. (1999), core competencies emerge over time through an organizational process of accumulating and learning how to deploy different resources and capabilities. Like in product development where organization can focus on their core competency, organization could also focus on the issues that they understand better in a dynamic organization change like knowledge management.

Although KM is currently being viewed as a combination of the technological component and the social-cultural, organizational component, relatively little attention has been paid to the issue of outsourcing the IT component. Balancing these components could yield effective KM and improve productivity, efficiency, innovation and competence of an organization. In the knowledge management components described by Alavi (1997), effective KM occurs at the intersection of the technological component and social-cultural and organization component (Figure 2).

Therefore, for an organization to have an effective KM practice, there should be a balance between the technological component and the social-cultural, and organizational component. Technology is often considered to be the easier component. Dan Holthouse in his foreword to Information technology for Knowledge management (Borghoff and Pareschi, 1998) remarked on this: "Technology is the easier piece of the problem to solve, it's far more challenging to change people's behavior and to create a learning environment that fosters the expansion of individual's personal knowledge. Therefore, organization could do better if the internal resources [were] focused on the people aspect and allow an external organization that has the adequate [expertise], to handle the (easier piece of) technology."

Figure 2. Knowledge management components (Alavi, 1997)

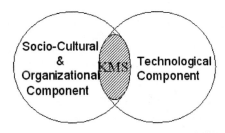

THE EMPIRICAL STUDY

As part of a study to investigate how information technology infrastructure generally affects knowledge management efforts of research organizations in sub-Saharan Africa, we conducted a multiple case study (Yin, 1994) using six different organizations in two countries in sub-Saharan Africa (Okunoye and Karsten, 2001). Three of the organizations are international: International Institute of Tropical Agriculture (IITA), Nigeria, Medical Research Council (MRC) Laboratories, and International Trypanotolerance Center in The Gambia. Three are national: National Agricultural Research Institute (NARI) in The Gambia, Nigeria Institute of Social Economic Research (NISER) and Nigerian Institute of Medical Research (NIMR) in Nigeria.

The national organizations are primarily dependent on the national government for their basic funding. Usually the international organizations enjoy supports from various sources around the world. They have a substantial number of expatriates working in them and have better support for the IT. The multiple-case study was conducted between January and March 2001. We interviewed, observed and presented questionnaires to research scientists, management staff, librarian, and IT staffs on knowledge management and use of ICTs. We interviewed the head of IT where applicable and the people responsible for IT department. KM was evaluated using the knowledge management diagnostic (KMD) created by Bukowitz and Williams (1999) and ITI was assessed using the approach developed by Broadbent and Weill (1997) where IT infrastructure is linked to the business by maxims, which reflect the company's strategic context. The KM assessment and ITI capability has been fully described in Okunoye and Karsten (2002).

INFLUENCE OF IT ON KNOWLEDGE MANAGEMENT

Four of the organizations appear to correspond to our expectations on the influence of IT on KM: In NARI in the Gambia and in all Nigerian organizations, the ranking in IT is similar to ranking in KM. Two exceptions to this consistency were found. In MRC, a high level of ITI existed with low level of KM. In ITC, a high level of KM existed despite low level of ITI capability.

The ranking of IITA and NISER in both KM process assessment and their IT infrastructure capability tallied and reflects the way they have been able to apply the available IT infrastructure in supporting their knowledge management efforts. IITA had a well-developed IT infrastructure. NISER had a reasonable level of infrastructure, which is put into proper usage. In these two organizations, people have been able to put the IT infrastructure into proper use for the purpose of their work. NIMR and NARI had low IT infrastructure rank and they were also low in their KM assessment, thus showing the relationship between IT infrastructure and KM processes similar to IITA and NISER. MRC needs to be studied further to find out their specific deterrents to efficient KM despite high ITI capability. The performance of ITC in KM efforts could be explained by their strong focus on organizational efficiency and on research, leaving all the IT management of the small organization to be taken care of by an outside vendor (see Table 1).

ITC is the smallest among the case organizations, with about 122 staff members and attracts visitors and researchers from major agricultural research laboratories with interest

Table 1. Nature of IT management, IT infrastructure capability and KM rankings

Name	IT Unit	Status of the Head	Outsourced services	IT Staff No.	Est. expenditure on IT per year (in US dollars)	Total Staff Strength	ITI capabilities ranking	KM efforts ranking
MRC	Yes	Expatriate	Some	7	$ 142 243	600	2	5
NARI	Yes	Local	Some	2	Not known	211	5	4
ITC	No	N/A	All	N/A	Not known	122	4	2
IITA	Yes	Expatriate	Some	10	$ 200 000	1400	1	1
NISER	Yes	Local	Some	8	$ 8 900	500	3	3
NIMR	Yes	Local	Some	4	Not known	130	5	6

in tropical agriculture. Due to their small size and their view towards IT, they do not see the need for running in-house IT department, as remarked by one interviewee. Hence they outsource the management of the IT unit to local companies.

> *"If your staff strength is not high, the cost benefit is not there... We have IT support from ITS and other ISP, that is better for us, because again of critical mass, there is no point hiring a permanent staff, if no computer breaks down in a month then he sits down idle. If there is a problem, then we call our engineers."*

The Gambia is one of the smallest countries in the sub-region. There is a shortage of IT personnel. It also shares other difficulties facing the countries in the sub-region in the areas of training and low expertise. Nevertheless, there are a few IT companies serving the needs of local businesses. We do not go into detail of the kind of agreements ITC have with the outsourcing partners. However, they tried to avoid opportunism and monopolistic bargaining by using multiple competing vendors strategy (Ngwenyama and Bryson, 1999). From our interview, we are aware that they use at least two different outsourcing partners, the Internet service provision is from one company while the regular IT management services are from another.

> *"Now it is difficult and we have asked for a network and we are hoping, a man was just here from QuantumNet or ITS to make a budget for Network."*

IT OUTSOURCING –
A STRATEGIC CHOICE FOR KM

Even though ITC had a low infrastructure services, they performed well in their knowledge management efforts. Their outsourcing decision is likely to be responsible for it. They were able to concentrate on the particular infrastructure required for their work. In ITC, the Internet is enabling collaboration among the staff and connecting them to external sources of knowledge that used to require travelling abroad in the past.

> *"That used to be quite a difficult thing, it was a problem, the only way you could get access to journals would be either to go to Europe in person and then do a literature search. I normally go to Wageningen every year, that's my almamater, but now I can liase with the Royal Tropical Institute in Amsterdam. I only send keywords of research topic and they will do the relevant search and send back to me abstracts. I will request the document I am interested in and they will send it to me... I get table of contents of recent journals and if something is of interest to me, I send to them by email and they send it back to me."*

ITC have extended their computing infrastructure by using the Internet to exchange files even to next door.

> "...we don't want to go into the cost of having a LAN, so even for me to send things next door, I go through the Internet."

Technology is seen to a vital role in knowledge management, but that technology on its own cannot make knowledge management happen (Hibbard, 1997). This was evident with ITC: their low ranking in IT infrastructure capability did not affect their KM efforts, because knowledge actually resides in people, technology can only assist in making things work more efficiently. Moreover, there was a presence of a minimum IT infrastructure supported by their outsourcing partner, which they were able to balance with other variables as suggested by Leavitt (1965). While the availability of IT infrastructure is important, support for its applications, usage, and technical components can significantly lower its usefulness.

CONCLUSION

We have discussed how IT outsourcing appeared to be having a positive effects on KM efforts of a research organization in sub-Saharan Africa. As an exception to a consistency that the availability of IT infrastructure has a direct relationship with KM efforts, we examined the concerned organization further. The outsourcing of the IT management seems to enable them to put the available IT infrastructure into proper usage and the main success factor in their KM efforts. It would be appropriate to study several organizations that have a similar arrangement to see if a similar pattern could be found before we could make any generalization. Nevertheless, there is an implication of this finding for the organizations in sub-Saharan Africa considering knowledge management as part of their strategy. This chapter implies that they might fare well by focusing on the social, cultural and organizational issues while outsource the technological component. For the researchers with interest in IT outsourcing and knowledge management, this chapter raises additional issues to be considered in the IT outsourcing and knowledge management relationship.

REFERENCES

Alavi, M. (1997). Knowledge Management and Knowledge Management System. In *Proceedings of 18th International Conference on Information Systems*, (December 14-17) Atlanta, GA.

American Productivity and Quality Center (APQC). (2000). Knowledge Management: Consortium Benchmarking Study Final Report 1996. Retrieved from the World Wide Web on April 3rd, 2000: http://www.store.apqc.org/reports/Summary/know-mng.pdf

Ang, S. and Straub, D. (1998). Production and Transaction Economies and IS Outsourcing: A Study of the U.S. Banking Industry. *MIS Quarterly, 22*(4), 535-552.

Beveren, J. (2002). A Model of Knowledge Acquisition that Refocuses Knowledge Management. *Journal of Knowledge Management, 6*(1), 18-22.

Bhatt G. (2001). Knowledge Management in Organizations: Examining the Interaction Between Technologies, Techniques, and People. *Journal of Knowledge Management, 5*(1), 68-77.

Borghoff, U. and Pareschi, R. (eds). (1998). *Information Technology for Knowledge Management.* Berlin: Springer- Verlag.

Broadbent, M. and Weill, P. (1997). Management by Maxim: How Business and IT Managers can Create IT Infrastructures. *Sloan Management Review*, Spring, *38*(3), 77-92.

Broadbent, M., Weill, P. and Neo, B. (1999). Strategic Context and Patterns of IT Infrastructure Capability. *Strategic Information Systems*, 8, 157-187.

Bukowitz, W.R. and Williams, R.L. (1999). *The Knowledge Management Fieldbook.* London: Pearson Education Limited.

Chesbrough, H. and Teece, D. (1996). When is Virtual Virtuous? Organising for Innovation. *Harvard Business Review*, *74*(1), 70.

CIO (2000). Knowledge Management: Collaborating for a Competitive Edge. CIO White Paper Library 2000. Retrieved July 26, 2001 from the World Wide Web: http://www.cio.com/sponsors/0600_km/index.html

Currie, W. and Pouloudi, A. (2000). IT Outsourcing: A Challenge for the Management of Knowledge as a Resource. In J. Edwards and J. Kidd (Eds.), *The Proceedings of The Knowledge Management Conference*, (pp. 364-375) The Operation Research Society, Birmingham, UK.

Duffy, J. (2000). The KM Technology Infrastructure. *Information Management Journal*, *34*(2), 62.

Goo, J., Kishore R. and Rao, H. (2000). A Content-Analytic Longitudinal Study of the Drivers for Information Technology and Systems Outsourcing. *Proceedings of 21st International Conference on Information Systems* (ICIS) 2000, (pp. 601-611) Brisbane Australia.

Hibbard, J. (1997). Knowing What We Know. *InformationWeek*. October 20, 46-64.

Hirschheim, R. and Lacity, M. (2000). The Myths and Realities of Information Technology Insourcing. *Communications of the ACM*, *43*(2), 99-107 .

Hitt, M., Ireland, R. and Hoskisson, R. (1999). *Strategic Management: Competitiveness and Globalisation.* Ohio: South Western College Publishing.

Keen, P. (1991). *Shaping the Future: Business Design through Information Technology.* Massachusetts: Harvard Business School Press.

Ketler, K. and Willems, J. (1999). A Study of the Outsourcing Decision: Preliminary Results. In *Proceeding of ACM SIGCPR 99*, (pp. 182-189) New Orleans, LA.

Lacity, M. and Hirschheim, R. (1993). *Information Systems Outsourcing Myths, Metaphors and Realities.* Chichester, UK: John Wiley & Sons.

Leavitt, H.J. (1965). Applied organisational change in industry: structural, technological, and humanistic approaches. In J. March (Ed.), *Handbook of Organisations*, Rand McNally & Co., Chicago, 1144-1170.

McFarlan, E. and Nolan, R. (1995, Winter). How to manage an IT outsourcing alliance. *Sloan Management Review, 36*(2), 9-26.

McKenney, J. (1995). *Waves of Change: Business Evolution through Information Technology.* Massachusetts: Harvard Business School Press.

Moyo, L. M. (1996). Information technology strategies for Africa's survival in the twenty-first century: IT all pervasive. *Information Technology for Development*, 7, 17.

Ngwenyama, O. and Bryson, N. (1999). Making the information systems outsourcing decision: a transaction cost approach to analyzing decision problems. *European Journal of Operational Research, 115(2)*, 351-367.

Odedra, M., Lawrie, M., Bennett, M. and Goodman, S. (1993). International perspectives: Sub-Saharan Africa: A technological desert. *Communications of the ACM, 36*(2), 25-29.

Okunoye, A. and Karsten, H. (2001). Information technology infrastructure and knowledge management in sub-Saharan Africa: Research in progress. *Second Annual Global Information Technology Management (GITM) World Conference*, June 10-12, 2001, Dallas, TX.

Okunoye, A. and Karsten, H. (2002). ITI as enabler of knowledge management: empirical perspective from research organizations in sub-Saharan Africa. In *Proceedings of the 35th Hawaii International Conference on System Sciences HICSS*, January 2002, Hawaii.

Quinn, J. and Hilmer, F. (1994, Summer). Strategic Outsourcing. *Sloan Management Review, 35*(4), 43-55.

Shepherd, A. (1999), Outsourcing IT in a changing world. *European Management Journal, 17*(1), 64-84.

Slaughter, S. and Ang, S. (1996). Employment Outsourcing in Information Systems. *Communications of The ACM, 39*(7) 47-54.

Sveiby K. (1996). What is Knowledge Management? Retrieved from the World Wide Web on March 4, 1996: http://www.sveiby.com.au/KnowledgeManagement.html

Tyndale, P. (1997). The knowledge development cycle: from knowledge creation to knowledge distribution. In *Proceedings of the 1st European Conference On Knowledge Management*, Bled, Slovenia, 2000. Retrieved from the World Wide Web on July 31, 2001: http://www.mcil.co.uk/2a-eckm-papers2000.htm

Yin, R. K. (1994). *Case Study Research: Design and Methods,* (2nd ed.) Newbury Park, CA: Sage Publications.

Chapter X

The Leapfrog Effect: Information Needs for Developing Nations

Stewart T. Fleming
University of Otago, New Zealand

ABSTRACT

Developing countries have special needs for information and communication. In the rush towards globalization of economies and communications, there is a danger that developing nations will get left behind. If we are to close the gap between the "information rich" and "information poor," then we must take these specific needs into account. This chapter gives an account of some development problems and current initiatives and describes ways in which advancing technology can be manipulated by the developing world to gain social advantage. The term "leapfrog effect" is introduced to explain how advancement can be made in a revolutionary fashion, not incrementally. The chapter draws on the author's direct experiences in Papua New Guinea, but many of the examples given and lessons learnt are applicable to many other developing nations.

INTRODUCTION

"What do I think of Western Civilization? I think it would be a very good idea."
–Mohandas K. Ghandi

A developing country is one that has the potential for economic strength, but lacks skills, capital or technical equipment to immediately exploit its own resources. People of these nations may have poor healthcare, limited education and inadequate nutrition. The developing nations are those at the low- and low-to-medium end of the United Nations Development Index (UNDP, 2002).

Some developing countries are in a post-colonial state of development, or dependencies that are gradually distancing themselves from governing nation-states. The poorest nations are the ones that did not benefit from 19th century globalization (colonization) because they had no resources to be exploited.

The most important aspect of globalization for a developing country is the sustainable management of its own socio-cultural and natural resources. The growth of the Internet as an influence in globalization runs the risk of replacing the diverse cultural resources of individual countries with a few dominating languages and cultures.

Developing countries frequently encounter three different barriers to development: political, technological and social. Development aid requires political will to go ahead and to actually be delivered as intended. However, the spread of technologies such as the Internet and the World Wide Web make information easier to obtain and can span national boundaries. The general populace can be empowered and to an extent, many political problems sidestepped. The deployment of technology can be for monetary gain, or more importantly as highlighted at the recent IT 2002 Summit in Kathmandu (Rao, 2002), can be deployed to solve social problems.

The emphasis on growing social capital rather than monetary-oriented capitalism raises further problems. Investors may be more reluctant to provide funding for projects where they see no direct financial return. Although the developing world represents a large proportion of the world's population, it is not economically strong enough to provide a lucrative market to be exploited.

In the developed world, we have perhaps become used to the constant, rapid change in technology, particularly Information Technology (IT). If the developing world were starting behind the developed nations, how would it ever catch up? The answer lies in the ability to bypass incremental steps on the technology curve – what has been termed here the leapfrog effect. Developing nations can use this effect to their advantage to keep pace with advancements in technology without necessarily incurring the economic impact of incremental change.

SOCIETY AND TECHNOLOGY: ISSUES AND TRENDS

Globalization

Current economic trends are towards globalization of markets, convergence of currencies and consequent alignment in social policies (Zarsky, 1997). For developed nations, international economic union is one way to grow their markets.

However, economic union creates greater interdependence and homogeneity while the global economy is still fragile. Temporary problems, often due to natural causes, which affect key economic indicators such as interest rates, can lead to massive outflows of capital. Developing countries are particularly vulnerable to such effects.

In particular, strategies based on economic, not geographic, principles do not tend to empower local populations. Rather, they can lead to a sense of helplessness that the local voice cannot be heard or does not influence events.

The Internet and (separately) the World Wide Web (WWW) are powerful forces in the growth of globalization. A consideration of the economic forces behind globalization indicates that the result is homogeneity of geography and of cultures. Market forces act to eliminate the differences between peoples and societies, not to enhance diversity. How can the Internet and access to information in general act as a force for change, particularly in developing nations, to enhance diversity?

At worst, the Internet has no government, no legal system, economic policy or elected representation. At best, it is controlled by voluntary organizations such as the Internet Engineering Task Force (IETF), the World Wide Web Consortium (W3C) and a mix of private enterprise and public service to implement address and domain name allocation.

Capitalist market forces are driving the rush towards globalization (Greider, 1997, p. 11) As a force for economic change and development; the Internet has many of the characteristics of these market forces. There is little government of the Internet and it does advance under its own momentum.

In order to establish a true global market, legal and regulatory frameworks are needed. However, at present, there is little or no government on the Internet and the Web is held together by a loose consortium of corporations held together by techno-centric 'geek' factors. I believe that if the Internet is to become established as a real force in the global economy, it will have to adopt some form of governance over all or part of its domain.

Bandwidth is becoming thought of as a commodity, to be bought and sold, aggregated and the costs involved to be offset against the potential benefits of information (Cavanaugh, 1998).

Bandwidth is generally more limited in developing countries than in developed nations. Many developing countries have less bandwidth for the entire nation than commercial Internet providers do. In PNG, the bandwidth for the commercial service introduced in 1996 was only 256Kbps. Between 1996 and 1998, the University of Technology in PNG operated its entire Internet and email service over a 9.6Kbps analogue leased line.

Low bandwidth connections may preclude access to some services, limiting the access to potentially valuable information. How can you build a so-called "knowledge economy" when your infrastructure lacks the capacity to communicate effectively with all your people?

Literacy and Computer Literacy

Adult literacy is a major barrier to the uptake of Information Technology in the developing world. There is a significant challenge here for Human-Computer Interaction (HCI): to be able to design and create interfaces to complex systems for use by illiterate or low-literate peoples.

The Cybertracker project (www.cybertracker.co.za) involves the use of mobile computers for use by bush trackers to record the movements of wild animals. One of the designers of this system spent time in the bush with native trackers, learning some of their craft and sharing their experiences. The development of this system demonstrates truly participatory design.

Intuitive iconic interfaces have great application here. Reading skills and comprehension of pictures are separate (Fordham, 1995). Simple icons and pictures can convey information of direct relevance to users. Complex information can be communicated by referring to ideas already introduced. The approach of eliciting requirements described by Pimenta and Faust (Pimenta, 1997) has a lot to offer in this regard since it emphasizes both *mutual learning* and a *language-centred* style.

In Papua New Guinea, spoken or written English may be a second or even third language. Rural schools often use local languages first, and then introduce English at provincial or national high school levels. The COMNET project is working to introduce communication and translation of simple texts at an early stage in education. The system uses simple pictures accompanied first by text in the child's own language and then by text in other languages.

Primitive peoples can also be educated. Negroponte cites Sheik Yamani's observations on the differences between primitive and uneducated peoples:

> *"The answer was simply that primitive people were not uneducated at all, they simply used different means to convey their knowledge from generation to generation, within a supportive and tightly knit social fabric. By contrast, he explained, an uneducated person is the product of a modern society whose fabric has unraveled and whose system is not supportive."*
>
> *–Sheik Yamani, cited in Negroponte (1995)*

Primitive peoples do have their own cultures, societies and abstract thoughts. To support people and empower them with technology, we simply cannot eliminate our differences. We must understand their minds through observation of the customs, traditions and methods that have been handed down, often over centuries.

Literacy is a major problem in trying to establish a technological foundation in developing nations. How can you use a computer if you cannot read? The answer appears to be to provide entertaining and useful content and to rely on incidental learning by children to acquire basic computing skills (Mitra, 2000).

Sugata Mitra conducted two experiments in incidental learning of computer skills amongst subjects with only rudimentary education and limited knowledge of English. In one, a computer with a touch-screen was installed in a hole in the wall in a New Delhi slum to allow access by street children. In another, a computer system was introduced at the roadside in rural India, without announcement or instruction. Mitra discovered that learning of computer skills occurred in an incidental fashion and suggests that the natural curiosity of children is an important motivator for acquiring such skills.

Many researchers have used a "Wizard of Oz" technique in experimental design to allow highly sophisticated activities to be performed by a less-skilled user e.g., Good (1984). Such a technique is finding practical use in villages in India where villagers pass requests for information to a mobile technician. Some time later, the technician returns with answers to the queries culled from browsing of the Internet. In this scenario, the skilled individual acts as a filter of information to engage with the higher technology and must provide and explain the information to the clients in a form that they can understand.

The Simputer initiative (PicoPeta, 2001) aims to bridge the digital divide by providing a simple user interface based on sight, touch and sound. Resembling a PDA, the powerful hand-held computer provides users with low education a way to engage with the digital world.

Such a resource is intended to be shared among a number of owners. The stumbling block to the widespread introduction of such a device appears to be the lack of investor support for the target markets – the rural poor of India (Srinivasan, 2002).

Donor Issues

The players in the business of foreign aid are those such as national governments. Some of those players are: the World Bank, International Monetary Fund (IMF), World Trade Organization (WTO), Organization for Economic Cooperation and Development (OECD), global extra-national government organizations under the auspices of the United Nations and regional forums such as the Commonwealth, Asia-Pacific Economic Consortium (APEC) and Association of South-East Asian nations (ASEAN). There is no shortage of power brokers in the economic world.

Donor agencies offer overseas aid to tackle global poverty and promote sustainable development. Large-scale funding initiated by governments appears to be out of fashion. Government-sponsored donations are falling amongst OECD nations. Non-government organizations and private sources account for increasing amounts of funding. In Papua New Guinea, the Australian Agency for International Development (AusAID) is increasing the amount of "tied aid" – funding committed to specific projects that must be matched by national government funds. All donor organizations are becoming more concerned about the need for positive evaluation of sponsored projects.

Donor funding can be a boon and a curse to a developing nation. Aid given in the form of loans will incur the burden of debt servicing. Unless real benefits are achieved using the funding, this will lead to a negative flow of funds. However, aid tied to specific projects must be done in a way to make those projects sustainable.

For example, donor funding to acquire computers for education may provide the initial capital, but no recurrent funding for training or maintenance. Such a project may fail when the full burden of support falls on the recipient.

Developmental aid given to develop a nation should benefit that nation more than it does the donor. It is common to hear tales of "boomerang" aid where money given to one country is used to purchase goods and services from the donor nation.

Donor aid can only provide for the first generation. Technical aid should be devoted towards training the next generation of planners and staff. The goal of any expatriates contracted to a developing nation should be to train their own replacements.

Technological Issues

The devices that we take for granted when interacting with personal computers – system units, storage devices, mouse, screen and keyboard – are actually fragile and prone to failure in an adverse environment. The breakdown of equipment causes intense frustration, particularly amongst those learning computer skills for the first time.

Difficult environmental conditions put up barriers to high-capacity, low-cost, reliable telecommunications. Sabotage of telecommunications or power equipment can occur during disputes over land ownership and royalty payments from public utilities to landowners. The infrastructure of a developing country may not have extra capacity or backup systems to take account of network failures. The uptake of technology will be limited unless personal computer manufacturers achieve significantly higher reliability in an uncontrolled environment.

Supply of electrical power is a problem, particularly to rural areas. In PNG, the domestic supply voltage is 240V AC on *average*, not nominal. Over-voltages, brownouts and blackouts are common. The infrastructure does not extend to rural areas, forcing them to fall back on generators, solar power or batteries. Much of the rural population is without any source of electrical power. The inadequate power infrastructure is a major barrier to foreign investment in many nations.

Even a technology as simple as reliable electric lighting can be a major advance. In many societies based on intensive agriculture, daylight hours are spent laboring. Solid-state lighting projects have been proposed and initial field-trials conducted to demonstrate how low-power lighting can be achieved without conventional electricity supply (Halliday, 2001). Clockwork radios and even laptops have been developed to provide advanced technology based on more primitive power sources.

It is clear from the environmental situation that information technology deployed in harsh environments cannot be of the same form as that installed in clean, air-conditioned, westernized offices. Hardware manufacturers should work to improve robustness and reliability of equipment, and to reduce power requirements or make the use of renewable or alternative sources a viable alternative to mains power.

THE LEAPFROG EFFECT

"We follow the industrialized countries, especially USA, so we can choose the winners and avoid the expensive market experiments ... There is a leapfrog effect, given that a lot of companies are just beginning to manage their workflow through Intranets, or even their connections with providers and/or distribution channels with extranets, and they don't have legacy systems that slows introduction of new technology."

–Anthony Rodriguez Chapa (Chapa, 1998)

In the developed world, we are inured to rapid change in IT. Advances tend to be made in an incremental fashion, with one small refinement made on a chain of backwards-compatible products. The cost of following this path, in terms of change management, administration and training, is significant.

Developing countries simply cannot sustain progress along this incremental path. However, due to the lack of investment in legacy systems, hardware and software, they can be in a good position to "leapfrog" over some of the incremental steps and to select a new position on the technology curve, as noted above.

The precise nature of this "leapfrog effect," particularly in relation to sustainable development, is worthy of further study. In this regard, it is worth noting that donations of outdated or discarded equipment from developed nations are often unsuccessful as they limit or prevent the occurrence of this effect.

Leapfrogging Moore's Law

In 1965, then-Chairman of Intel, Gordon Moore, made the prediction that the number of components on a microprocessor integrated circuit roughly doubled every year. In 1975, he revised this prediction to the number of transistors doubling roughly every two years. This

Figure 1. Actual and projected trends of computing power from Moore's Law[1]

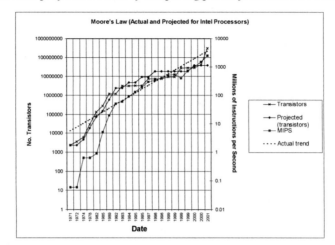

prediction has held true against the empirical evidence from 1971, right through to the current generation of Pentium processors offered by Intel.

Figure 1 shows the increase in the number of components in microprocessor integrated circuits for a period of some 30 years. The actual trend is very close to that what was predicted, with the number of transistors on microprocessor devices doubling roughly every two years. However, there are some aspects of this graph that deserve comment.

If we focus on the period between the introduction of the original 60-MHz Pentium processor in 1993 and the introduction of the 1.5GHz Pentium 4 in 2000, we can observe that:
a)   The actual increase in numbers of transistors fell below the projected trend.
b)   The number of different microprocessors introduced over this seven -year period (13) was greater than the number of processors introduced in the previous 11 years (8).

If we pick the points on the curve in this period where the projected trend was closely approached or exceeded, we can identify "leapfrog points". These are points at which there is a suitable technology whose capabilities are not significantly exceeded by the next incremental offering.
1.   The original 60-MHz Pentium introduced in 1993 (60 MIPS).
2.   The 300-MHz Pentium II introduced in 1997 (300 MIPS).
3.   The 1.5GHz Pentium 4 introduced in 2000 (1500 MIPS).

These leapfrog points represent a five-fold increase in computing power over a four - year cycle. For an organization depreciating capital expenditure on Information Technology over the same period, making purchasing decisions at these points would be appropriate.

This period where the trend drops below that predicted corresponds to the widespread uptake of personal computers, especially those adopting Microsoft Windows as the operating system. The larger variety of processors introduced during this period corre- sponds to the demand from different markets (e.g., servers, desktops, laptops, embedded computing) that exploded at this time.

Some of the processors offered were clearly, what might be termed "market experiments" and some failed. In particular, the Pentium III was consistently underpowered in all varieties and provided no real incentive for an end-user to upgrade hardware.

For developing countries, not only is there no incentive to upgrade, there is no capital available with which to do so. A common scenario is for an organization – commercial or educational – to struggle along with whatever equipment they have until it fails totally and then to install the current best hardware. This corresponds to leapfrog along the technology curve and the effects can be quite dramatic[2].

Moore's Law is of interest because it is almost unique in industry. No other technology save telecommunications exhibits such a dramatic increase in capability over a short period. The consistency of Moore's Law is due to a number of factors:

- Technological control of a physical process (etching of semiconductor substrates by various photo-lithographic processes).
- Incremental refinement of the manufacturing process through experience.
- Improvement on a single aspect of the manufacturing process yielding improved performance (e.g., by decreasing the feature size, more transistors can be packed on the same area, providing a more complex processor).

In fact, experience gained through the manufacturing process and the volume of manufacture lead to cost reductions over time. As the power of processors has increased dramatically, the average cost of a personal computer has reduced over the same period. As personal computers crossed the threshold of affordability in the developed world, demand increased further, permitting greater volume of manufacture. In fact, a positive feedback loop drives Moore's Law. The feedback forces the semiconductor industry to keep pace by introducing new fabrication techniques and continually reducing costs. At least until the physical limits are reached, the consistency of the law for the foreseeable future is assured.

Since an organization can rely on the consistency of the law (projected out until 2007, it still holds), they can make decisions about depreciation, purchasing and/or proposals for technological aid. They are able to hold position on the technology curve without fear of being left dramatically behind; knowing that a suitable landing spot for the leapfrog jump will appear in due course.

The implication of Moore's Law is useful for technology development projects that may be spread over several years. It makes sense to specify allocations of funds for computer hardware, rather than specifying particular technologies at the proposal stage. Purchasing decisions should be delayed as long as possible, leaving only sufficient time for procurement, delivery and installation. Clear policy decisions should be set out in funding proposals for replacement of hardware after specific periods of time.

Microprocessor development over the past 30 years has striven to maintain backward compatibility. Indeed, only the 2001 release of Intel's Itanium processor breaks the link of compatibility that extends from the Pentium back to the 4004. In part, this is due to the incremental nature of semiconductor manufacture – using past experience to drive cost-reductions and new technologies. In part it is due to the need to protect the investment that consumers have made in the technology. This is in sharp contrast to many of the software applications that have been developed throughout the personal computer revolution.

Leapfrogging Software – The Arms Race

The advantage that hardware has over software (at least for the manufacturer) is that it wears out, develops faults and eventually becomes obsolete. No matter how reliable we think our computing equipment might be, it is still prone to catastrophic failure, loss or physical damage. Software has no such characteristic – if software is functioning at a particular time, performing some function, it will continue to perform that function at some other time. The set of instructions that software follows can be regenerated by compilation, or copied perfectly as a collection of bits. Software manufacturers therefore have a problem – if they release a single version of a software product, then the market will eventually reach saturation. After an initial peak, sales will gradually drop as new computer users adopt the product. There is limited potential for cash-flow. Software manufacturers therefore must continually provide new releases or new versions of their software in order to protect their source of income.

In a very real sense, there is an "arms race" (Thimbleby, 2001) between users and software vendors. The vendor has limited interest in providing backward-compatibility between software versions since they wish to drive demand for the latest version. As users adopt the later versions, they find it more and more difficult to exchange information with those who still maintain the earlier versions.

This kind of software incompatibility is a major barrier, especially for developing nations who are more likely to lag behind on the technology curve. They are forced to upgrade software in order to communicate with others, thus they are forced onto the incremental path. Worse still, if a software upgrade requires a hardware upgrade for which there is no budget, an organization can find itself left further and further behind.

This software barrier to the leapfrog effect goes some way to explaining why donations of older computing equipment from developed to developing nations are often unsuccessful. The older hardware immediately sets the recipient years backwards on the technology curve and since it is unlikely to support the newer software, cuts them off even from the incremental upgrade path.

SATISFYING REAL INFORMATION NEEDS

The deployment of technology in the developing world finds greatest utility where it is applied to solve social problems. The real information needs of those populations are in widespread education, greater empowerment and independence and hence the growth of social capital. However, the deployment of such technologies may meet resistance from traditional societies and raise some tensions.

Communication for Development

Valuable information must be made available to those who need it in order to solve their own problems. There are particular groups who can benefit from wider access to information. Young people and women who may be left out of the traditional decision-making processes of their societies may find a voice in the "information society."

Developing countries often have a great reliance on agriculture. The same problems, solutions and resources can often be found in geographically disparate regions. National

Agriculture Research Centres can act as agents to support local access by farmers to participate, gain access to resources and tools that they need to solve their own problems, set their own agendas and empower themselves through knowledge.

The barriers here are language and other cross-cultural factors. In Papua New Guinea, there are over 800 separate languages. Communication between people from different regions, indeed even adjacent villages may be possible only through recourse to common tongues of English, Melanesian Pidgin or Motu. Children growing up in villages learn their own village or local language (*tok ples*) first, then Pidgin and English if they are lucky enough to attend high school. Literacy among the older generations is low. For effective communication amongst peoples, if the solution is to adopt a common tongue, then diversity will be lost.

Local and regional content is important in a developing country. That is, content that is provided by nationals of those countries intended primarily for their peers or for others in the region. Publication of this information for the external world is secondary when the information is of greatest importance to those in similar situations.

Some aspects of foreign cultures may be completely unacceptable. The separate cultures in PNG have their own taboos and their own ways of making decisions. Pornographic material is illegal in PNG, but is widely available on the Internet. Clearly, there must be some control, but how is that to be achieved? Government control over Internet content as seen in China and Singapore is one approach that can control access to some material. But how will a cooperative society cope with technology that empowers individuals, or empowers women?

Sustainable Development

Land is an important resource for developing nations. A good understanding of land ownership issues is essential for the responsible exploitation of natural resources, however traditional landowner rights often conflict with macro-economic development. Cadastral systems link land titles to accurate surveys of the terrain to formally establish ownership. A cadastral system is essential for the transition of a developing country to "developed" status (Williamson, 1997). Work is ongoing in PNG to establish a digital cadastre (Burrage, 1997).

The work of the MASP project to document Agriculture Systems in PNG provided valuable information to assist with relief aid during the recent frosts and droughts in PNG (Bourke et al., 1997). The work of researchers on the social and economic impact of the Lihir gold mine in New Ireland highlight the importance of wealth distribution. Payment of royalties and issues relating to land rights were major factors in the Bougainville conflict over the Panguna mine.

Rural Telecommunications

Telecommunication is an important link in the development process (Hudson, 1995). Electronic commerce and the Internet assume the widespread availability of low-cost global telecommunications. In developing countries, a regulated telecommunication industry acts as a barrier to competition whilst providing ready profits for governments (often valuable foreign currency). The market forces of the Internet demand competition amongst telecommunications providers and ready access at the point of need.

Rural telecommunications can be hard to guarantee effectively in rural areas. The cost of hard-wiring telecommunications services to remote locations has led many organizations to explore digital wireless telephony as a more effective solution.

Wireless local loop (WLL) developed by the Indian Institute of Technology demonstrates an effective solution for low-cost access in rural areas (Jhunjhunwala, 1998). The Bushnet project (www.bushnet.net) in Africa uses HF radio to distribute Internet and email services to remote subscribers. NGOnet (www.ngonet.org) is an initiative to create Internet access for NGOs in Africa to enhance communication and provide access to information.

Rural telecommunications do not necessarily have to support high-rate communication. Email is still the most valuable form of communication for many individuals. Even though they have access to the Web, the complex graphics and heavy content of many pages act as a significant barrier to information access.

The obvious beneficiaries of widely available telecommunications are rural commercial enterprises and educational institutions. Healthcare can benefit from a reliable communication infrastructure for tele-medicine and to improve access to medical records (Fleming, 1998).

Local providers will spring up to meet the demand, once there is deregulation. In Papua New Guinea, the initial round of five licensed Internet Service companies in 1996 was augmented a year later by a second round to allow any private enterprise to distribute Internet access. In Egypt, 11 Internet companies immediately began providing access when commercial licensing began in 1996. Across Africa, private companies and individuals are exploiting technologies as systems become deregulated.

People will use the Internet if it provides them with answers to their questions, or practical solutions to their problems. They will not use it if it presents them with social, cultural or intellectual barriers that they cannot or will not cross.

CONCLUSIONS

The overall picture of the informational needs for a developing country is quite different from one in the developed world. Access to relevant information at the point of need is critical for the empowerment and development of rural people. Robust computer systems and low-cost rural telecommunications are required to establish points of presence in remote areas.

HCI practitioners must work to consider the needs of low-literate or illiterate peoples and find ways to deal with multi-lingual cultures. Approaches to eliciting requirements must involve a dialogue between end-user and designer. It is difficult to establish common ground between disparate cultures, but we must try.

Developing nations must adopt the Internet, but not at the expense of their own culture. The entire information society must value diversity and not seek to eliminate differences by imposing a monoculture. Emphasizing the social benefits of technology is important, because it encourages individuals to be producers *and* consumers of information. A technology that values the culture of its users will be more widely accepted than one that merely acts as a conduit to a foreign culture.

Globalization proceeds to reduce the differences between peoples and between nations. The net effect is to make nation-states interdependent and more homogenous. While the East-West divide may have lessened in recent years, the economic gap between "North and South," "developed versus undeveloped" will cause friction in the process of globalization.

In economic terms, there is a gap between rich and poor. In technology, there is a gap between "information rich" —those with ready access to relevant information—and "information poor," for whom accessing information and communicating is a real struggle. We have not even begun to address these gaps in the design of information systems. There is a danger that the globalization accelerated by the Internet and the Web will end with the homogenization of socio-cultural resources.

On the positive side, while a developing country may be lacking in modern infrastructure, technological developments have the potential to progress in leaps and bounds, rather than incremental steps. Indeed, in order to keep up with the current trend towards globalization, the developing nations will need to "leapfrog" in order to close both the economic and information gaps.

ENDNOTES

[1]   Source: Intel Inc.
[2]   This author has observed a leapfrog of 13 years (upgrade from 80386 to Pentium II hardware) in an educational establishment in Papua New Guinea. The author is currently using hardware and software that is five years and three processor generations behind the cutting-edge.

REFERENCES

Allen, B.J. & Bourke, R.M. (1997). *Report of an assessment of the impacts of frost and drought in Papua New Guinea.* Port Moresby: Australian Agency for International Development.

Burrage, K. (1997). The digital cadastre database for PNG: designing a sustainable DCDB in a developing country. *Cartography, 26*(2).

Cavanaugh, K. (1998). Bandwidth's new bargainers. *Technology Review, Nov-Dec*, 62-65.

Chapa, A.R. (1998). Paper presented at the Nikkei Global Information Online Summit.

Fleming, S.T. & Vorst, D. (1998). *Putting your finger on it - patient identification in a multi-name society.* Paper presented at the IRMA International Conference, Hershey, PA.

Fordham, P., Holland, D. & Millican, J. (1995). *Adult Literacy: A Handbook for Development Workers*: Oxfam, UK.

Good, M.D. (1984). Building a user-derived interface. *Communications of the ACM, 27*(10).

Greider, W. (1997). *One World, Ready or Not: The Manic Logic of Global Capitalism.* New York: Simon and Schuster.

Hudson, H. (1995). *World Bank Report on Economic and Social Benefits of Rural Telecommunication* .

Irvine-Halliday, D. & Craine, S. (2001). *Does the overdeveloped world appreciate the win-win-win opportunities for HBLEDs in the developing world?* Paper presented at the LEDs 2001 - The Strategic Summit for LEDs in Illumination, San Diego, CA.

Jhunjhunwala, A. (2002). Making the telecom and IT revolution work for us. *Science and Technology in India* (July 2002).

Mitra, S. (2000). *Minimally Invasive Education for mass computer literacy.* Paper presented at the CRIDALA 2000, Hong Kong.

Negroponte, N. (1996). *Being Digital*: Knopf.

PicoPeta Simputers Pvt. Ltd. (2001). *PicoPeta Press Release.*

Pimenta, M.S. & Faust, R. (1997). HCI and requirements engineering - eliciting interactive systems requirements in a language-centered user-designer collaboration: a semiotic approach. *SIGCHI Bulletin, 21*(1).

Rao, M. (2002). *Rural Community Networks - Growing Social Capital Via Interactive Technologies*: University of St.Gallen.

Srinivasan, S. (2002). Computer for the poor struggles. *MSNBC*.

Thimbleby, H. (2001). *The Computer Science of Everyday Things.* Paper presented at the Proceedings of the 2nd IEEE Australasian User Interface Conference.

United Nations Development Programme. (2002). *United Nations Development Index.* New York: United Nations.

Williamson, I. (1997). The justification of cadastral systems in developing countries. *Geomatica, 51*(1), 21-36.

World Bank. (1991). *World Development Report: The Challenge of Development.*

Zarsky, L. (1997). Stuck in the Mud? Nation-States, Globalization and the Environment, *Globalization and Environment Study*: OECD Economics Division.

Chapter XI

Harmonizing IT and Business Strategies

Kevin Johnston
University of Cape Town, South Africa

ABSTRACT

This chapter proposes that all business strategies should be harmonized into a single strategy, rather than attempt to align IT strategy with business strategy. It focuses on two hypotheses: firstly, that IT strategy is not widely aligned with business strategy; and secondly, that IT is still thought of as "something different" in businesses. The chapter proposes that rather than attempt to align IT strategy with business strategy, the strategies should be harmonized into a single strategy. The chapter attempts to use lessons from geese to outline the process of strategic development.

INTRODUCTION

The alignment of business strategy with IT strategy has been a concern of CIOs (Berkman, 2000; Conarty, 1998; Croteau & Bergeron, 2001; Crowley, 2001) CEOs (Mesoy, 1999), academic researchers (Henderson & Venkatraman, 1999; Reich & Benbasat, 2000; Tallon & Kraemer, 2000) and research companies (Broadbent, 2000; Croteau & Bergeron, 2001; Meta Group, 2001) since the age of vacuum tubes. In surveys (Mesoy, 1999) of IT management (CIO) concerns, alignment has consistently been rated as a major issue of concern. A Cutter study in 2000 (Crowley), reported that business-IT alignment was "the number one problem facing IT."

Many authors (Burgleman et al., 2001; Croteau & Bergeron, 2001; Hartman et al., 2000; Reich & Benbasat, 2000) agree that it is important to align IT strategy with the organization's business strategy. Although the importance of strategic alignment of IT is acknowledged and widely accepted, it remains an issue within many organizations.

In a recent study by Crowley (2001) of 253 large IT organizations, 52 percent of organizations claimed to have a 'good to excellent alignment between e-business and IT strategies.' Crowley (2001) admits the results are contrary to how business-IT alignment is usually rated, and speculates that the reason may be that non-IT departments sponsored 76 percent of e-projects.

Burgleman et al. (2001) state, "Technological issues only occasionally are included explicitly in typical corporate strategy reviews, and only rarely are they among the regular inputs to corporate planning and development." Gates (1999) wrote, "It is impossible to align IT strategy with business strategy if the CIO is out of the business loop."

Many managers have poor knowledge and poor attitudes towards IT, they assume the IT staff have the knowledge, and allow the IT staff to decide on the organizations needs. Management's attitude towards IT and IT strategy need to be changed (Cosgrove Ware, 2001). A 'model of attitude change' described by Nash et al. (2001) lists five steps to effect an attitude change.

- Attention and awareness. Managers are subjected to advertising, publications and word of mouth about IT.
- Comprehension and Knowledge. Managers are taught about IT and its uses.
- Yielding, managers actually try out the IT.
- Use of IT, management actually uses the IT.
- Reinvention, where IT is improved or its use is varied for maximum benefit.

The lack of IT alignment with business can result in late market entry, lost market opportunities or an unsustainable market advantage (Conarty, 1998).

Some (Bocij et al., 1999), view IT strategy and business strategy as two distinct strategies, with IT strategy either supporting or influencing business strategy. Other authors such as (Pukszta, 1999), stress that IT strategy must be completely and seamlessly integrated with business strategy at all organizational levels.

IT and Business strategies should not be aligned, but should in fact be one harmonious strategy. Alignment is defined by Dictionary.com as an "Arrangement or position in a straight line or in parallel lines." Harmonizing is defined by Dictionary.com as "A pleasing combination of elements in a whole or being as one." IT and business strategies have to be as one. IT strategy has to lose its distinctness; in this way it will gain prominence and exert greater influence (Pukszta, 1999) within organizations. Each organization should have a single harmonized strategy.

This chapter examines why IT planning should be in harmony, not merely aligned with business strategy. The analogy of flying, and lessons from geese is used to enhance the ideas presented.

"As each goose flaps its wings, it creates an 'uplift' for the birds that follow. By flying in a 'V' formation, the whole flock adds a 71 percent greater flying range than if each bird flew alone" (Clark, 2000). The lesson we can learn from this is that "People who share a common direction and sense of community can get where they are going quicker and easier because they are traveling on the thrust of each other" (Clark, 2000).

IT and business have to share a common direction, and should therefore plan to fly in harmony, not in parallel.

WHY FLY? (WHY DEVELOP STRATEGIES?)

Geese migrate for several reasons (Why Files, 1996), changing climatic conditions, seasonally fluctuating food resources and to create more geese. The geese that prepare for migration, and then move in the right direction at the right time, survive.

Similarly, organizations need to recognize changing business climates, fluctuating resources, and the need to expand or grow (Heske, 2001). Organizations have to plan where they want to take the business and to prepare accordingly. All factors including IT have to be considered and taken into account holistically.

There is no balance in nature; there is perpetual disruption, as organisms and environments transform each other. Organizations, structures, careers, products, markets, and suppliers are all subject to continual change (Kelly, 1998). Change is a natural and creative force that both destroys and creates. Organizations need to develop strategies to cope with and survive change.

Key tasks of managers within an organization are to acquire, develop and allocate organizations resources, and to develop and exploit the organizations capacity for innovation (Burgleman et al., 2001). The acquisition, development, allocation and exploitation of IT should be part of any business strategy. Many new products and services such as on-line banking, airline reservation systems, and voice mail have been based on IT (Laudon & Laudon, 2002). IT can contribute to the overall performance of the organization by synergistically tying operations of various business units together so the organization can act as whole (Laudon & Laudon, 2002). This could lower costs, increase customer access; speed up the marketing process of new products and services. IT can assist an organization develop a central core of competencies by allowing knowledge to be shared across the organization (Laudon & Laudon, 2002). It is unlikely that these contributions and possible innovations will occur by chance; they need to be planned.

Hammer and Champy (2001) presented a way of improving organizational, team, and individual performance by first getting a birds-eye view of how work gets done. They advocated rethinking and redesigning business processes to improve an organizations performance.

Tallon and Kraemer (2000) found that organizations with focused IT goals achieved higher payoffs from IT. Their results indicate that unfocused organizations achieve consistently lower payoffs at each point along the value chain than focused organizations. Organizations must formulate and implement an Internet Strategy (Afuah & Tucci, 2001) as part of their overall strategies.

Linear planning is useless; organizations must plan holistically (Hartman et al., 2000) or harmoniously in order to survive.

WHERE TO FLY?

Where should an organization do business, locally, nationally or internationally? Organizations should rather be thinking in terms of where it makes good business sense, where the organization will survive. A vision of where the organization is going to needs to be developed and communicated, and everyone in the organization needs to understand the vision, as they have to implement it (Rollins et al., 2002).

An important goal of strategic planning is to anticipate change beyond the control of the organization, so change within the organization can be initiated and controlled (Ivancevich & Matteson, 1999).

A strategy needs to be defined that includes all the capabilities (forces/tools/resources) of an organization, so that approved plans may be executed as effectively as possible (Henderson & Venkatraman, 1999). Strategy articulates ways in which opportunities can be exploited using the organizations capabilities (Burgleman et al., 2001). Strategy without capabilities is meaningless (Burgleman et al., 2001), and excluding the IT capability from the organizations strategy renders the strategy less effective at best. Similarly having capabilities without strategy makes them aimless (Burgleman et al., 2001). The IT capability must therefore be part of the overall strategy or IT will become an aimless capability of the organization, or at best, will be run according to the IT manager's aims. Managing the IT resource is a basic business function (Burgleman et al., 2001), which should be the responsibility of all managers within an organization.

A number of elements must fit together in a balanced way in order for an organization to function effectively. Sawy (2001) uses the Leavitt Diamond framework to illustrate the balance. The framework has four sets of organizational variables: IT use, organizational form, people skills, and business processes. When any one of these is changed, the other three need to be adjusted to maintain 'functional harmony' (Sawy, 2001).

Organizations need to define exactly where they are going, and ensure that all stakeholders know why, and where the destination is.

HOW TO FLY? (FORMATION)

A requirement for successful migration is for the geese to successfully navigate and reach their destination. Geese have been recorded flying as high as 29,000 feet. Geese change altitudes to find the best wind conditions (Why Files, 1996). Geese use several formations when flying, V-formation, column or cluster. Researchers (Rible, 2000) suggest that it is a mixture of aerodynamic benefits and the ability for the flock to communicate and see one another.

"When a goose falls out of formation, it suddenly feels the drag and resistance of flying alone. It quickly moves back into formation to take advantage of the lifting power of the bird immediately in front of it." The lesson according to Clark (2000) is "if we have as much sense as a goose, we stay in formation with those headed where we want to go. We are willing to accept their help and give our help to others."

"When the lead bird tires, it rotates back into the formation to take advantage of the lifting power of the bird immediately in front of it." The lesson is that, "It pays to take turns doing the hard tasks and sharing leadership. As with geese, people are interdependent on each others' skills, capabilities, and unique arrangements of gifts, talents, or resources" (Clark, 2000).

Like geese, organizations need to decide on formations or structures in which to fly. Geese fly faster and further in formation. Formation, structure, and order are necessary for the survival of the geese and the organization (Schwein, 2000).

"A gap has developed between the power and choice enjoyed by individuals as consumers and citizens on the one hand, and that available to them in the workspace on the other" (Chowdhury, 2000). This gap will have to be reduced. Consumers are allowed to design/personalize products/services within a range of options; this is the age of the individual. However, employees are seldom given any choices in the workplace, other than compliance or exit. Organizations will have to include employees in decisions regarding the formation and structure of the organizations. Free enterprise needs to accommodate the free person.

Organizational design and structure have always been important factors that influence the behavior of groups and individuals. It is through structure that management establishes expectations of achievements for individual employees and departments, and decides how the organizations strategy is to be accomplished. The purpose of structure is to regulate, or reduce, uncertainty in the behavior of employees (Ivancevich & Matteson, 1999). Where and how IT is placed in the organizational structure determines the role and influence of IT.

Each organization is a formation, and when that is ignored, the organization will not be able to crawl, much less fly! No organization will last if everyone acts independently; a structure needs to be developed preferably with the employees, which will support the strategy and vision of the organization.

WHO TO FLY WITH?

A goose cannot fly in formation alone. Similarly, employees cannot survive alone within an organization; they need to be in some sort of "flock." Often the collection of employees is more a group than an organization. Geese in groups are called a "gaggle" when not in flight. Geese only become a flock when they are flying in formation. Similarly, organizations only 'fly' when all the employees are in formation.

Organizations need tradition, ritual, and structure to retain their identity. Before geese take off, they have a pre-flight takeoff ceremony in which they encourage one another (Schwein, 2000). An organization in which the author worked had a daily meeting in which employees met each other and offered encouragement, support, guidance and feedback. The meetings were stand-up affairs that lasted 15 to 30 minutes, with a fixed regular program. On Mondays, projects and work for the week ahead was discussed; Tuesdays were Thinking days on which employees had to solve puzzles in groups; Wednesdays were Learning days where one employee had to teach the others something; Thursdays were set aside to announce and discuss change; and Fridays were for external focus or external speakers. Although the author coordinated and organized the meetings, every employee had an opportunity to lead a Tuesday and Wednesday meeting. Rollins et al. claim that 50 percent of all employees receive no formal feedback on their performance, and of the 50 percent who do receive feedback; only 20 percent believe that it is effective.

"Geese flying in formation honk to encourage those up front to keep up their speed."

Lesson – "We need to make sure our honking is encouraging. In groups where there is encouragement, the production is much greater. The power of encouragement (to stand by one's heart or core values and to encourage the heart and core values of others) is the quality of honking we seek" (Clark, 2000).

Organizations need to fly with employees who want to be in the organization, who know where the organization is headed, and who want to fly in formation.

DO WE LET OTHERS FLY FOR US?

Would a flock of geese let a turkey or an eagle fly for them? Organizations outsource IT (or parts thereof) for various reasons. Bocij et al. (1999) list the main reasons as to achieve cost reduction, improve quality, and enable organization to focus on core business, to reduce risks of project failure and to implement a strategic objective. Outsourcing IT can create problems for an organization such as loss of control, cost increases (Laudon & Laudon, 2002), security issues, and employee morale (Bocij et al., 1999). Dell (1999) states "our partners are treated as if they're inside our company" and "bringing our supplier-partners into our business virtually has become a key component of our success."

The debate about outsourcing (and in-sourcing) will no doubt continue with pros and cons for both sides. Each organization must carefully consider their strategy and make a call. If IT is strategic to the organization (Croteau & Bergeron, 2001) can it be outsourced?

WHEN TO FLY?

Geese fly before winter sets in, when the seasons tell them its time to move on. Geese understand that they cannot change or fight the seasons. Similarly, organizations need to develop strategies anticipating 'winter', and start flying before winter sets in. Organizations must respond to external demands quickly, adapt their organizations and redirect their employees and IT to achieve competitive advantage (Rollins et al.).

Organizations need to understand that IT change is one external factor, which affects competitive position. In order to survive, organizations need to adapt timeously to change. Therefore, strategic planning must be a dynamic process, and IT and IT change must form part of the process. Successful organizations balance a well-defined business focus with the willingness, and the will, to undertake major and rapid change. Immobility is the most dangerous behavioral pattern (Burgleman et al., 2001).

Organizations need to be ready to fly. Four prerequisites for organizations wishing to embark on e-business are leadership, governance, competencies and technology (Hartman et al., 2000). The first prerequisite is leadership; outstanding companies are associated with their leaders (Welch, Gates, Bezos). Leaders create a vision that is shared and accepted within the organization. Governance is the operating model that defines the organization. The formation or structure of the organization must be clear. People roles, responsibilities, and authority levels must be defined. Organizations need to have methods for assessing, selecting, allocating and monitoring resources. Competencies are the ways in which the organization responds to change, exploits available resources and opportunities, and accommodates reality. Technology needs to be robust and comprehensive.

"The reality of a strategy lies in its enactment, not in those pronouncements that appear to assert it" (Burgleman et al., 2001). Strategic intent needs to be converted into strategic action to be meaningful.

HOW TO HANDLE OBSTACLES EN-ROUTE?

During migration, geese encounter and overcome many natural obstacles such as predators and weather disturbances, as well as many man-made obstacles.

"When a goose gets sick, wounded, or shot down, two geese drop out of formation and follow it down to help and protect it. They stay with it until it dies or is able to fly again. Then, they launch out with another formation or catch up with the flock." The lesson we can learn is to stand by and help each other in good and in bad times (Clark, 2000).

Organizations need strategies to deal with obstacles and may, in some cases, need to revise their strategies in order to be successful.

HOW TO DECIDE IF THE FLIGHT WAS SUCCESSFUL

If a large percentage of the flock reaches the destination in a condition to continue, the flight has been a success. The organization like the geese has to expect some casualties. To succeed, the energy, creativity and resources of the organization must have been used. If there are parts of the organization that have not being used, the question must arise, *why are they in the organization*?

Burgelman et al. (2001) ask and answer the question "what strategies, policies, practices, and decisions result in successful management of high-technology enterprises?" Six themes of success are listed: (1) business focus, (2) adaptability, (3) organizational cohesion, (4) entrepreneurial culture, (5) sense of integrity, and (6) hands-on top management. All are controlled or influenced by the organizational strategy. Unless each and every one of the organizations resources is in harmony, an organization cannot have succeeded. If IT strategy (and all other strategies) are harmonized into a single business strategy, then the organization can claim to have a holistic business focus, to have organizational cohesion, and to have a sense of integrity. Integrity can be defined as "the state or quality of being entire or complete; wholeness; entireness; unbroken state; as, the integrity of an empire." A disharmonized strategy certainly cannot be regarded as being honest, fair or open, other attributes of integrity.

CONCLUSION

Organizational success must include the ability to align the organization and mobilize the work force (Reich & Benbasat, 2000). Organizations and individuals can only realize their potential for greatness and goodness when they join the flock, fly in formation, and contribute something for the common good (Nash et al., 2001; Sawy, 2001). IT strategy must be one of the components of the organizations overall strategy.

REFERENCES

Afuah, A. & Tucci, C.L. (2001). Internet Business Models and Strategies. McGraw-Hill, Singapore.

Berkman, E. (2000). Why we're still talking about alignment. Retrieved from the World Wide Web in March 2002: http://www.cio.com/archive/010101_talking.html

Bocij, P., Chaffey, D., Greasley, A. & Hickie, S. (1999). *Business Information Systems, Technology, Development and Management.* Pearson Education, Harlow.

Broadbent, M. (2000). Today's CIO energizes, enables, executes and exploits. Retrieved from the World Wide Web in March 2002: http://www4.gartner.com/ UnrecognizedUserHomePage.jsp

Burgleman, R.A., Maidique, M.A. & Wheelwright, S.C. (2001). *Strategic Management of Technology and Innovation*. Singapore: McGraw-Hill.

Chowdhury, S. (ed.). (2000). *Management 21C*. London: Prentice-Hall.

Clark, D. (2000). Leadership – *Lessons from geese*. Retrieved from the World Wide Web in March 2002: http://www.nwlink.com/~donclark/leader/geese.html

Conarty, T.J. (1998). *Alignment for success: Information technology and business strategy*. Presentation at IISI-32. Retrieved from the World Wide Web in March 2002: http://www.worldsteel.org/events/proceed/IISI-32_1998/PR_conarty1.html

Cosgrove, W. L. (2001). *Measuring IT Alignment*. Retrieved from the World Wide Web in March 2002: http://www.cio.com/archive/040101/tl_numbers.html

Croteau, A.& Bergeron, F. (2001, June). An information technology trilogy: Business strategy, technological deployment and organisational performance. *Journal of Strategic Information Systems*, *10*(2), 77-99.

Crowley, D. (2001). Business-IT alignment – A turn for the better. September 18, 2001, The Cutter Edge, Cutter Information Corp.

Dell, M. (1999). *Direct from Dell. Strategies that revolutionized an industry*. New York: Harper Business.

Dictionary.com. Retrieved from the World Wide Web in March 2002: http://www.dictionary.com

Gates, B. (1999). *Business @ the speed of thought*. London: Penguin.

Hammer, M. & Champy, J. (2001). *Reengineering the Corporation: A Manifesto for Business Revolution*. New York: Harper Business.

Hartman, A., Sifonis, J. & Kador, J. (2000). *Net Ready*. New York: McGraw-Hill.

Henderson, J.C. & Venkatraman, N. (1999). Strategic alignment: Leveraging information technology for transforming organizations. *IBM Systems Journal*, *38*(2-3), 472-484.

Heske, P. (2001). Leaders, lemmings or laggards. *Computing SA*, September 17, 10.

Ivancevich, J.M. & Matteson, M.T. (1999). *Organisational Behaviour and Management*. Singapore: McGraw-Hill.

Kelly, K. (1998). *New rules for the new economy*. London: Fourth Estate.

Laudon, K.C. & Laudon, J.P. (2002). *Management information systems*. Upper Saddle River, NJ: Prentice Hall.

Mesoy, T. (1999). Transforming IT to position the IT function as a valued and respected business partner. Presentation at 21st Century IT Alliance Forum. Sun City, South Africa.

Meta Group. (2001). *Top CIO issues for 2001*. Retrieved from the World Wide Web in March 2002: http://www.metagroup.com/cgi-bin/inetcgi/search/displayArticle.jsp?oid=23211

Nash, J., Gwilt, D., Ludwig, A. & Shaw, K. (2001). *The use of technology to support decision-making in South Africa*. University of Cape Town Paper.

Pukszta, H. (1999). Don't split IT strategy from business strategy. *Computerworld*, January 11, 1999, *33*(2), 35.

Reich, B. & Benbasat, I. (2000, March). Factors that influence the social dimension of alignment between business and information technology objectives. *MIS Quarterly, 24*(1), 81-113.

Rible, J. (2000). Canada Goose. Retrieved in March 2000 from the World Wide Web: http://www.sou.edu/library/jim/wildlife/cangoose.htm

Rollins, T., Bognanno, M.A. & Lockwood, M. (2002). The strategy-focused workforce: Using the Balanced Scorecard to align people with strategy. Retrieved from the World Wide Web in March 2002: http://rm.haygroup.com/balanced.htm

Sawy, O. (2001). *Redesigning Enterprise Processes for e-Business.* Singapore: McGraw-Hill.

Schwein, W.M. (2000). *Looking at the birds of the air.* Retrieved from the World WideWeb in March 2002: http://www.carmelumc.org/sermons/Serm_000806.htm

Tallon, P.P. & Kraemer, K.L. (2000). *Executives' Perspectives on IT: Unravelling the Link between Business Strategy, Management Practices and IT Business Value.* Center for Research on Information Technology and Organizations, University of California.

Why Files. (1996). Retrieved from the World WideWeb in March 2002: http://whyfiles.org/006migration/fact_sheet.html

Chapter XII

Software Outsourcing Prospects for Small Developing Countries

Stewart Bishop
University of the West Indies, Barbados

ABSTRACT

Developing countries have been utilizing information and communication technologies in the management of their business and administrative affairs to improve efficiency and effectiveness; at the national level also, they have been innovative with the establishment of information services sectors. From the initial provision of data entry services some developing countries, as participants in the global software outsourcing movement, have embarked on the development of software for export. Many challenges ranging from insufficient skilled personnel to becoming competitive in a fierce marketplace will be faced. This chapter examines the participation of two small Caribbean countries and describes education and training initiatives and other policy approaches taken by them. The consensus is that, while they will hardly ever make a significant impact on global outsourcing, such small developing countries can achieve substantial economic benefits, stimulate their domestic Information Technology environment and attain an enhanced technological capability.

INTRODUCTION

Since the early seventies, developing countries have sought to harness information technology to attain social and economic development. Benefits have been realized in
- efficiency through the automation of administrative functions and
- effectiveness through the provision of improved information for decision-making purposes.

Some countries in the Caribbean have additionally attempted innovation in IT utilization through the creation of new products and services and the establishment of new relationships with corporations in the developed world. In their creation of an Information Services Sector three decades ago, these countries initially were content to start at the lowest rung of the ladder with data entry. The intention was to progress toward software development and other professional services at the upper end, through a gradual upgrading of skills and technical capability. According to the Development Plan 1983-1987 of the Barbados government's investment agency, these upper end services would expand the sector's contribution to the economy and provide better employment opportunities (Nurse, 1996).

The provision of the lower end offshore services was targeted at North American markets and Caribbean countries possessed several advantages:
- Affordable labor cost
- Reasonably high quality, if not competitive, telecommunications services
- Linguistic and cultural affinities
- Time-zone affinities
- Transport convenience
- Open environment for investment

Over a decade ago, Barbados and Jamaica, satisfied with their progress in the provision of lower end services and in the diffusion of IT in their respective public and private sectors, decided to become involved in software development for export. In both countries, much of the utilized software was developed in-house. This was a reflection both of the types of applications implemented and of a desire to develop the programming competence and confidence of their programmers.

The success of India, Ireland and a few other developing countries in software development for export also served to motivate these Caribbean countries to stake their claim for a piece of the pie. This would call for adherence to standards and deadlines such as had seldom been required with software development for domestic entities. In their attempt to tackle software development for global markets they were apparently convinced of their ability to leverage their initial success in the Information Services sector. Meanwhile in the private sector, accounting and billing applications were now commonplace and some software houses were engaged in the initial stages of software provision for the local and regional markets.

Planners in these countries were influenced by a number of factors:
- An eagerness to leverage their successes at creating locally a technological awareness and developing competence at the basic entry level of the software industry.
- Queries for software services that were made at their investment offices in North America.
- Their near-shore location that benefited investors who wished to be able to visit the home offices of their outsourcing partners.

However, it is doubtful whether at those early stages policymakers appreciated the difference between involvement in data entry operations and participation in global software outsourcing movement. There were a few local software companies which initially seemed to be creating a good impression with the quality of software provided, in some cases, for Fortune 500 corporations. These software companies, like many others globally, would experience hard times, forcing them to scale down operations or even relocate to other developing countries where operating costs are cheaper.

This chapter reviews how two small developing countries have attempted to exploit IT in the management of their public and private affairs. The emphasis is mainly on the efforts to participate in the software for export movement. The many challenges faced from breaking into the movement to human capital development are examined. Specific IT initiatives undertaken and incentives provided by government are discussed.

Governments for their part anticipate direct benefits through significant inflows of much needed foreign currency earnings. Among other lasting benefits for these Caribbean countries of Jamaica and Barbados would be the enhancement of their human capital development and the creation of the appropriate legal and regulatory environment to meet the higher standards required for success in a competitive global climate. In particular, there was a cadre of competent professionals who could serve on local software project teams and ultimately help to create a local technological capability. As electronic commerce and electronic government take a firm footing in the region, these trained professionals would be able to take leading roles in any software development needed.

BACKGROUND

Global Perspective

The availability of appropriate software has been a major factor in the diffusion of information technology into almost all aspects of the current environment. Cane (1992) classified software and its utilization as follows:

- Embedded software for the electronic products and telecommunications industry
- Customized software for commercial and financial sectors and for government services
- Packaged software, the driving force behind many personal computers employed in all areas of human endeavour in today's information age

The acquisition of computers for use in business was concentrated primarily in large corporations where centralized computing was successfully implemented. As technological improvements came in the form of mini computers and later PCs, small and medium sized businesses and eventually homes were able to afford to acquire computers. Three market segments for software development could be identified:

- Large corporations that favoured the building of proprietary systems from scratch using basic languages such as COBOL to provide systems for the management of their operations. Maintenance and upgrading of the legacy systems constituted an important activity.
- Small and medium sized businesses for which packaged software was ideally suited. Application software has included spreadsheets, accounting and other management packages, which were bought and then adapted to the special needs of the business.

- The personal computer market for which off-the-shelf products and user-friendly programs mainly on CD-ROMs were mandatory.

This assessment of the market for software globally reflects the overall situation that prevailed up until the start of the Internet era. Web-based business opportunities have for the past five years been sought by corporations and small businesses alike. In this radically new environment, software applications and services utilize easy to use graphical web browsers with new companies constantly seeking to network their businesses.

For those which seek a mere presence on the web all that is required after the page has been designed, possibly by the client, is the integration of the graphics and sound. To achieve greater benefit there will have to be the integration of the web page with the databases and the legacy systems. Successful entry into the electronic commerce environment necessitates a complex information technology environment. There is, according to Hoch et al., a coexistence challenge as one seeks greater advantages from the web technologies. Several platforms, programming languages and strong *de facto* standards coexist and often must be managed in parallel. The high level of complexity in the IT and communications architectures along with variable commitment to standards in software production have led to difficulties in the management of today's IT infrastructure (Hoch, 2000).

The industry has become quite fluid and unstable with the frequent entry and demise of companies and constant search for innovation among the leading players. The ever-present threat of viruses and worms and the persistence of hackers have not helped the management of current systems.

Another challenge relates to the business skills competence of current software developers in this networked environment. A decade ago software engineers would most likely have had experience in the development of information systems for businesses prior to their involvement in software for export. They would have been quite knowledgeable about business applications. Today's software developers brought up in this networked and object-oriented environment and fast-tracked into dealing with web-based applications are less likely to be familiar with basic business practices.

This trend poses difficulties when, in electronic commerce applications, web-based interfaces to legacy systems have to be developed and maintained. Such challenges must be addressed in the education and training of current software developers. In particular greater emphasis on business skills and project management should be reflected in the respective training programmes.

Domestic Market

In both Jamaica and Barbados, businesses entered the computer era using in-house software and with expertise and experiences gained moved on to the acquisition of packaged software that had to be customized. U.S. software corporations mainly supplied these packages, although companies throughout the Caribbean have acquired a few local packages. In a few cases major businesses, such as a utility company in Barbados, which have successfully implemented computer applications now feel ready to acquire best practice software globally and modify their procedures to fit the software.

The banking sector has been a major user of information technology with the internationally affiliated banks using the same systems as found in their respective head offices. The indigenous banks have attempted to innovate with their systems which are developed by local or international software producers.

In the public sector, which is a major user of information technology the specialized nature of their information systems has meant that, until recently, most systems had to be developed in-house. Local software developers and others from North America have also been contracted to develop application packages, mainly payroll and national insurance systems, for government departments. With growing demand for better information provision expected in an electronic government environment much interest is being shown in Intranets and Internets.

One particular area where a local demand for software is expected in the near future in both countries is in the education sector as both have committed themselves to greater implementation of educational technology. Over a decade ago, a few companies were developing courseware for the North American education system but they have all ceased operations, mainly due to the high cost of production. It is uncertain how much of the available software can be described as being culturally relevant or desirable or whether domestic production of courseware will be required. Any production of courseware for the local environment would have to be preceded by substantial training in an area where there is already much concern about current quality. Unfortunately, the focus has been on the purchase of hardware with considerably more complex questions of software evaluation and acquisition being given minimum attention.

Software Engineering Process

The software engineering process consists of various phases and has, over the past decades, been modified in a continuing effort to arrive at a more efficient model. However there is commonality among the various approaches as described in the following five phases by Reichgelt (2000):

- Problem definition where the problem to be solved is formulated as accurately as possible and in terms relevant to organizational needs.
- Requirements analysis where the requirements of the software are described.
- Specifications phase where the detailed specifications of what the software will look like and how it will meet the requirements are outlined.
- Programming phase where those specifications are converted into program code.
- Maintenance phase where bugs detected during operational use of software are fixed and modifications are introduced to improve and optimise the software's functionality.

The first three phases, representing analysis and design, are deemed to require higher skills and often reflect subjectivity including cultural values of the organization and its environment. The other two phases, representing programming, are seen as requiring relatively lower skills in that a prescribed algorithmic outline has to be coded in the language of choice.

The maintenance phase, in spite of the continuing enhancement efforts including automation of the software process, remains a very labor intensive one. As applications have moved from the earlier accounting ones with specific and static processes to modern online ones incorporating complex decision making aspects, it has proven very difficult to cater for these multiple and dynamic requirements. As a result software maintenance accounts for over 50 percent of the programming effort for most software projects and developing countries have benefited from the outsourcing of this maintenance work.

The pattern has therefore been that the analysis and design for software projects have tended to be confined to the developed countries. Reasons for this pattern include:

- A desire to incorporate cultural affinity and values that can best be ensured by utilizing IT professionals from the same developed countries.
- A lack of trust in unknown and inexperienced IT professionals from developing countries whose work ethic has unfortunately been seen as not being up to the same standard of professionals in developed countries. There is, however, ample evidence from companies in the Information Services Sector to negate this suggestion.

In the competitive global software environment, critical project management skills are needed to complete projects on time, within budget and to the required quality assurance level. Programming, on the other hand, is a relatively more prescribed and objective activity where competence in the particular hardware and software environments are mandatory. This competence can more readily be acquired from education and training in academic and professional institutions. Universities in developing countries after years of insistence on traditional Computer Science programs have modified their offerings and are now able to provide basic and even advanced programming instruction suited for the professional software development. In addition initiatives in the form of short, high-impact and focussed training have been undertaken recently by the governments of Jamaica and Barbados to enhance the professional programming competence in these countries (Bishop, 2001).

Off-Shore Development

Yourdon (1994) was one of the earliest to recognise the potential of developing countries for producing world-class software and possibly becoming a threat to the American programmer. He identified the following growth stages for foreign software industries:

- Body shopping with offshore programmers working on-site in U.S. corporations;
- On-site systems analysis and design done in the U.S. with programmers working offshore to develop that software;
- Offshore development of generic software products to be marketed in the U.S. and in other developed countries; and
- Global marketing of indigenous applications developed offshore. Egypt with its multimedia cataloguing of its historical and cultural artefacts and Singapore with its port management systems have been successful in this area.

India, with its large numbers of trained scientists and programmers, has been the only developing country capable of promoting body shopping as a development strategy. Most developing countries have had to be content with utilizing their relatively cheap labor resources to provide programming support in collaboration with partners in the developed countries.

Typically the applications which are outsourced have tended to be of a financial nature and are based on on-line, web-based and multimedia technologies. In many developing countries, only a few applications, for example in the banking sector, depend heavily on these technologies. Programming standards and practices vary greatly in the two markets with world-class expectations for the export market. Another key requirement would be the existence of an appropriate legal and regulatory environment to safeguard against piracy and copyright infringements.

Global Software Outsourcing

Global software outsourcing is the outsourcing of software development to subcontractors or developers who operate away from the client's home country. Clients tend to be mainly U.S. corporations but may originate from Europe or even Asia. India can claim to be the original developer and, with over 800 IT service firms, has dominated the market, its share being worth almost $4 billion (U.S.) in 1999/2000 (Heeks, 2001). However almost 50 countries now participate as developers with Ireland, Israel and Singapore being among the more successful ones. In the Caribbean Jamaica and Barbados have been the leaders in this pursuit.

Global software outsourcing has been undertaken by the clients for two main strategic reasons, namely cost considerations and access to a larger pool of competent professionals. This has meant that business relationships have had to be established and maintained between these clients in the developed countries and the developers who might be, physically and otherwise, poles apart. Various studies have been undertaken to evaluate the strategies for achieving the most satisfactory relationships.

Global software outsourcing has been fraught with difficulties, chief of which are communication between partners and coordination of the various tasks in the software development process. Distance between the partners can play a major role in exacerbating the problem. Modern communications technologies, it has been claimed, can remove physical or geographical distance as a constraining factor. However experience has shown that, with respect to communication between business partners, video-conferencing and other technologies cannot substitute for actual face-to-face contact. Carmel et al. have identified, in addition to physical and temporal distance, national, cultural and organizational differences as factors that reduce the effectiveness in coordinating the several tasks (Carmel, 2001).

Developers in the Caribbean clearly have great advantages with North American clients in having English as the spoken language and through close cultural and business ties. To capitalize on this Caribbean countries would be advised to market themselves as "near-shore" rather than offshore developers.

Strategies for Involvement

Schware's Strategy

Schware's "walking on two legs" proposition has been advocated as a development strategy for developing countries wishing to become involved. The production of software for domestic markets, he argues, provides opportunities for domestic companies to develop their skills, capabilities and possibly market niches. This could result in the establishment of successful consultancies. The transition to software for export can then be approached with greater confidence and expertise gained from the domestic production effort (Schware, 1992).

There is great variability between developing countries according to their size, stage of economic and technological development and such factors. Thus, the application of Schware's proposition to any particular developing country would depend on the similarity between its domestic applications and those being demanded by corporations in developed countries.

Indigenisation

Heeks (1992) posits that developing countries need to indigenise their software production efforts for the following reasons:

- To avoid reliance on the whims and fancies of foreign suppliers and operators through the creation of technological awareness.
- To allow adaptation of the technology for local conditions. Certain software could be adapted to local languages and scripts.
- To ensure the development of a local capability at both the low- and high-skilled aspects of software production.

Here Heeks is emphasizing hands-on experience for workers rather mere involvement in training sessions. A representative measure of a country's indigenous IT industry development is its technological capability, which he defines as the general ability to undertake a range of tasks that involve the consumption and production of any particular technology. These tasks are:

- Choice and use of a technology
- Adaptation without production, that is, product modification and minor product innovation for local needs
- Basic production, that is, copying and assembly using existing products and processes
- Inward-looking skilled production, that is, modification, redesign or innovation to meet local needs
- Outward-looking skilled production, that is, modification, redesign and innovation to meet global needs
- Global production to compete through innovation

Technological development in a country then is the growth in its technological capability as evidenced by movement up the various levels listed earlier. When applied to IT production or more specifically, to software production, this quantitative measurement of indigenous development is similar to the Software Engineering Index developed at Carnegie-Mellon University which is currently regarded as the industry's standard.

Small developing countries cannot attain the technological development of larger ones such as India and thus have to set for themselves more modest and realistic goals in their involvement in software for export. There has therefore been a reliance on multinationals or collaboration with foreign institutions and organizations to develop their local capability. Governments have offered incentives such as tax concessions and subsidized office space to foreign investors, sometimes in excess to those available to local IT companies. This reliance on multinationals and other foreign investors has proven to provide mixed results. Appropriate advice in this regard should be:

- Approach foreign investors with caution since they bring hidden costs as well as benefits.
- Monitor and evaluate the role of foreign investors.
- Assist local technological development through negotiation with these investors to provide transfer of technology or training as condition of their access to government incentives.

PARTICIPATION IN SOFTWARE FOR EXPORT

Unfortunately, the reality of participation in global software development brings these challenges and difficulties that have been often minimized or even ignored by many officials who promote software production in developing countries like Barbados or Jamaica. Their desire often is to have their country regarded as being a technological capable country that has been able to bridge the digital divide. The reality, however, is that such basic questions that have to be answered include:

- What software can or should be produced?
- Will the user-interface be acceptable?
- How and where will it be marketed?
- How will it be supported?
- Are relevant tools and people available?
- Is documentation adequate?

Software development also takes place in the Information Services Sector where companies at this higher value-added end of the sector undertake programming contracts with many North American corporations. These companies may be affiliates of U.S. corporations taking advantage of the generous investment concessions granted by government, local companies or joint venture companies formed between local and North American entities.

From the perspective of a small developing country such participation has become an attraction for two main reasons:

1. Successes gained from their initial involvement in the provision of lower end services have made them aware of the possibly greater gains to be made through advancement to higher-valued services such as software development. Jamaica's National Industrial Policy document suggests that successful performance in the provision of data entry services to U.S. clients and software services to the local private sector could be a basis for seeking to penetrate the international market.

2. Many computer science graduates from these developing countries, imbued with an entrepreneurial spirit, armed with PCs and with contacts in the U.S., now seek to become global 'infopreneurs' (Heeks, 1999). Involvement at this level provides an excellent opportunity for these graduates to experience the latest technologies. IT professionals in local companies eagerly expect to function with such novel technologies. Overall the presence of these high tech operations has a positive effect on the domestic IT environment.

For such countries, successful participation will be determined largely on the contribution of foreign currency earnings to the national economy. Concerns about securing employment opportunities for their citizens and the earning of foreign exchange still dominate the thinking of governments in developing countries. It follows that while a new software product at a major U.S. developer, according to Yourdon, only shows up as a 'blip' in their accounting system when it generates $50 million annually, a small developing country would readily grasp such an earning opportunity. The global software pie was estimated at US$400 billion in 1997. Any country that can provide reliable and efficient software services at competitive prices can expect to get at least a small contract for software production. Therefore, with the pie being worth so much, almost any slice would represent a success for any small country. In light of the many likely challenges, serious consideration of a strategy for involvement should be given.

Strategies

Schware's strategy and Heeks' indigenisation thrust have been suggested earlier as means of assessing a developing country's capability of becoming involved in the production of software for export. Both, however, seem to be less applicable in the current environment where virtual or global software teams are commonplace. Their proliferation is due mainly to more sophisticated and advanced technologies being less costly and so permitted collaboration between partners and individual team members from different cultural and geographical regions.

Heeks (2001) and Dafoulas (2001) have examined some of the issues such teams have to confront. Critical factors that affect and determine their success include:

- Cultural values between team members
- Frequency of communication
- Frequency of meetings
- Actual roles allocated to team members

This last factor was an important concern in the strategies outlined earlier. Without enhanced local technological advancement, team members from the developing countries could still be relegated to performing the lesser roles of programming with only minor involvement in analysis and design.

Various authors have outlined possible development strategies for involvement of developing countries in software for export (Heeks, 1999; Yourdon, 1994; Reichgelt, 2000). The following reflects a Caribbean perspective on the issue, but should provide useful insight for small developing countries elsewhere.

- Market existing locally developed software. This was usually custom-written for a single client and hence, tended to be unsuitable for mass packaging. At one time, some thought was given to marketing some public sector software in other developing countries in the Commonwealth that had adopted the British administrative systems for that sector. Fuller analysis led to the abandonment of this idea. The few software packages already written and implemented regionally would have had much difficulty competing against similar but globally written packages after considering continued maintenance, support and purchase costs. When a local software system was marketed throughout the region, it was found that a help desk had to be provided.
- Develop software locally, explicitly for an identified overseas market. Even if the technological capability and competence existed in a small developing country, major factors such as venture capital support, product identification and marketing would prove to be major hurdles. Opportunities had been identified in the past through the initiatives of government investment agencies stationed in developed countries. These agencies hired consultants in developed countries to seek out outsourcing contracts on their behalf. IT conferences were held with North American speakers invited, to which potential investors from developed countries were also specially invited with a view to making on-the-spot assessments and contacts with partners. With the possibility of the project exceeding the capability of a single developer in Barbados, it was necessary to satisfactorily address the formation of project teams from among individual software entities. The actual project management was a major concern. In Barbados, a project implementation unit, called Project INFOTECH, was contemplated as a means of assisting locals firms that sought to become involved in

software development for U.S. corporations. A team of IT professionals was nominated to serve as a liaison between the client and the developers and to provide any further professional assistance. This well-intentioned initiative was short-lived as difficulties arose with the establishment of consortium teams of small local software units to tender for software projects. While the engagement of a consultant could be seen as a positive step, the fear, uncertainty and doubt experienced by U.S. clients in doing business with developers in the developing countries would present a virtual roadblock. Participation in joint ventures with software developers from the developed countries may be the only logical course of action. The question of technology transfer remains a debated one.

- Develop software locally in collaboration with an overseas company as a sub-contractor, in a joint venture partnership or as a participant in a global software team. The major advantage with this arrangement is that the overseas company would handle the marketing function, secure contracts and provide specialist tools and training as required for each project. Contract work would generally originate in the U.S. and would feature the same level of technology found in U.S. corporations. A certain minimum technological competence would be expected from local counterparts in the global team. Training initiatives toward this goal are being implemented in both Jamaica and Barbados. Reichgelt (2000) suggests that the best way to approach participation in software for development is through the establishment of joint ventures with recognized international software vendors.

- Seek out market niches to take advantage of a country's unique expertise. Reichgelt (2000) has suggested that, in the case of Jamaica, the development and marketing of application software related to all-inclusive hotel operations in the tourism sector, an area where that country is a world leader, could be considered. A few years ago, the millennium bug provided developing countries with a good opportunity to earn valuable foreign currency. Their programmers seemed more *au fait* with the COBOL language, in which many legacy systems were written, than those from the developed countries. Provision of data conversion services remains an option, but recently, opportunities for web site development, hosting and maintenance became widely available.

Challenges and Solutions

As small developing countries contemplate greater involvement in software for export, it must be appreciated that the requirements will far exceed current practices and expectations for software for domestic use. Many challenges will have to be overcome if the expected benefits are to accrue from involvement in software for export.

Training

Bishop (2001) examined the human resource capability needed for successful involvement in the information services sector. He reported that, based on a recent survey in that sector, increased training should be provided in areas such as systems analysis and design methodologies, case tools, Java-based programming, project management and documentation. An initial improvement should be seen in the quality of the system development process with more formalized procedures being applied. Better management control of the development process will ensure the quality assurance so necessary in a competitive environment. Other improvements should also be evident in cost management and in the ability to measure specific processes.

In Jamaica and Barbados the respective governments have, in collaboration with universities in the U.S. and U.K. and with companies in their Information Services Sectors, established special training institutions to assist with human capital development. These feature short, high-impact and modular courses specially oriented toward the applications found in this sector in respect of the languages and methodologies studied.

The University of the West Indies at its campuses in these two countries has been modifying its Computer Science programmes to pay greater attention to areas such as information systems and software engineering. Management and Accounting Options and separate courses in these disciplines are now available to Computer Science majors.

In the event of an absence of software business incubators, the involvement of IT corporations in the design and even teaching of web-based courses and other programs should be encouraged. Job attachments for tertiary-level students with companies in the information services sector are now a regular feature in the training of IT personnel.

Availability of Programmers

The size of the pool of competent software developers has been seen by Reichgelt (2000) and others as a major challenge since it is known that there have been large software projects that have absorbed hundreds of software engineers. Indeed Reichgelt argues that a necessary condition for the establishment of vibrant software engineering project is the availability of a large pool of highly trained individuals. He however admits that small developing countries such as Singapore, Israel and Ireland have become important players in the global market.

For a better appreciation of the prospects of small developing countries, one should note that the actual size of typical software teams is quite small. For example, in India over 75 percent of companies have had fewer than 25 professionals and in Egypt company size has varied from being one to five persons up to a maximum size of 50 to 100 professionals. The existence of global software teams suggests that generally programming modules are being assigned to individual teams which can be quite small.

One common project in today's networked environment is the development and maintenance of a web site for a corporation. This can be undertaken in a small developing country by a company with only a few professionals. Technical competence, along with the requisite teamwork appears to have a greater impact on the eventual success of the project than the actual size of the team.

In both countries, there have been attempts to bring in IT professionals from other developing countries, mainly India, to boost the numbers of trained personnel. These have been unsuccessful because of the cultural differences between these and the local programmers and also due to the desire of these migrants to seek greener pastures in the U.S.

Regulatory Framework

A major difference for smaller developing countries between participating at the lower and upper ends of the Information Services Sectors is the mandatory existence, in the case of the latter, of the requisite legal environment. Intellectual Property and Anti-Piracy legislation and an up-to-date Computer Misuse Act are basic requirements if corporations in the developed countries are to be comfortable with having their software projects undertaken by companies in developing countries partners. Governments in the two Caribbean countries have taken this issue seriously and in addition to the introduction of actual legislation, have supported public discussion on such topics as intellectual property and the legal requirement for electronic trading.

Telecommunications

Monopoly companies have for a long time controlled the telecommunications services in most developing countries but strenuous attempts are being made to correct this practice. Jamaica has enacted legislation to fully liberalize those services there, while in Barbados consultations and deliberations are in the final stages before the enactment of such legislation. The problems with telecommunications would therefore appear to be about to be resolved. Unfortunately, companies in the Information Services Sector in Barbados still relate horror stories about the cost of such services, a charge vehemently denied by the monopoly service provider. Government's role then is a critical one. In a situation where there has been little experience with such technical matters, government officials are unable to properly confront the service provider. Friendly persuasion has been their preferred approach, but meanwhile, affected companies continue to complain that they are unable to maximize their contributions to the economic development of the country. At least one other Caribbean has taken a more radical approach in the attempt to liberalise its telecommunications sector. It is still too early to assess the consequences of that course of action.

Sustainability

The area of software production has come to be regarded as one where the continued existence of an entity is a problem. As indicated starting such an IT operation is easy and relatively inexpensive and appeals to those with an entrepreneurial flair. However, in this fast-paced, dynamic and very competitive environment business changes come too quickly even for large corporations and suppliers of well-known products. As an example WordPerfect's share of the word processing market decreased from 46 percent in 1990 to 17 percent in 1997 (Hoch, 2000).

The picture from the Caribbean tells a similar tale. The U.S. custom-software design company PRT set up operations in Barbados in 1996, staffed by some 300 programmers from India, but only a few Caribbean nationals who were recruited both from inside and outside of the region. It was suggested that regional IT personnel, though well educated, were not capable of software production to the desired level. It provided software for Fortune 500 corporations in the U.S. and had a Level 3 rating in its software development. Within just two years it was being hailed as the flagship for software in the Caribbean. However by the end of 2000 only a skeleton staff of less than 50 remained with the company. Another company, providing web-based business solutions, relied entirely on local personnel. After some initial success it too collapsed with managerial problems, according to anecdotal evidence, being cited as a major cause. There has been similar but less high profile failures recorded throughout the region in both domestic and export-oriented companies.

In any attempt to try to determine the causes of these failures, a key factor has been the quality of management of the company. The selection and retention of competent software professional continues to be a major problem as better jobs with higher salaries from North American companies are constantly being offered. The ability to retain secure financing is also a major problem. It has been suggested that while many entrepreneurs have good ideas for business start-ups and are able to create effective software products, few are able to complete the transition to become successful managers of those companies.

There however seems to be some hope for a small company which is able to enter the global market through the provision of products and services in a restricted area and to a few clients. Management of such companies is much less complicated, and profit margins can still be recorded. The practice of web page hosting and maintenance has been successfully undertaken in a small country like Bermuda.

Role of Foreign Investors

Multi national companies and foreign investors have been at the heart of any successes by developing countries in the export of software. They must also be at the core of the enhancement of local technological capability through their involvement in the design and implementation of programmes and courses offered by educational and training institutions. On-site training at offices in developed countries has proven to be very beneficial and this practice must be extended to include more companies in the Information Services Sector. Governments must insist that all foreign corporations, through conditions attached to their gaining access to training and other incentives, provide for the transfer of technology that would enhance local technological capability.

PROSPECTS

Software development represents the ultimate attainment for developing countries which for almost three decades have endeavoured to create Information Services Sectors to earn foreign exchange and provide employment for their citizens. Software for export presents several challenges for these countries yet about 50 of them have ventured into the arena.

These two Caribbean countries, Jamaica and Barbados, have as joint venture partners or in global software teams, contributed as developers to the global software outsourcing movement. In the process they have had to improve their educational and training programmes for IT personnel. Companies in the Information Services Sector have influenced curriculum changes at the various institutions for the development of software engineers. They have actually taught courses at these institutions and have afforded job attachments for students within their companies. Recent university graduates have also benefited from stints in the clients' North American software factories. The impact on human skills development for IT utilization has been considerable. One notes the adoption of system development tools and methodologies and the adherence to programming standards which have been evident in the production of domestic software. Some domestic companies now feel compelled to adopt best practices in their systems planning and have even opted to modify existing procedures so that best practices software can be acquired globally.

In the pursuit of the dream of software for export there has been a heightened interest in strategic national IT planning. Also closer public-private sector cooperation about IT utilization has ensued.

One unfortunate feature however has been the veil of secrecy that surrounds organization in the sector. This has not only affected the assessment of real financial contribution to the economy but has limited access to information on critical issues about the general operations of these companies. The true picture about the sustainability of individual companies and of the sector itself is difficult to determine. There still continues to be too heavy a reliance on anecdotal evidence as one seeks to evaluate the true contribution of IT companies to the local economy.

However government's investments agencies in both countries continue to market these as good locations for the establishment of near-shore operations. With the growth of electronic commerce and of networked organizations the prospects for these countries and similar small developing countries seem bright once the correct training, legal and telecommunications infrastructures are put in place.

REFERENCES

Bishop, S. (2001). Human Capital Development for an ISS. *Proceedings, IRMA 2001 Conference.* Toronto, Canada.

Cane, A. (1992). Information Technology and Competition Advantage: Lessons from the Developed Countries. *World Development,* 20(12), 1721-1736.

Carmel, E. & Argarwal, L. (2001, March/April). Tactical Approaches for Alleviating Distance in Global Software Development. *IEEE Software,* 22-29.

Dafoulas, G. & Macaulay, L. (2001). Investigating Cultural Differences in Virtual Software Teams. *Electronic Journal on Information Systems in developing Countries* 7(4), 1-14. Found at http://www.ejisdc.org (active on July 15, 2002).

Heeks, R. (1992). Strategies for Indigenizing IT Production in developing Countries. In S. Bhatnagar & M. Odedra (Ed.), *Social Implications of Computers in DCs.*

Heeks, R. (1999). Software Strategies in developing Countries. *Communications of the ACM,* 42(6), 15-20.

Heeks, R., Krishna, S., Nicholson, B. & Sahay, S. (2001, March/April). Synching or Sinking: Global Software Outsourcing Relationships. *IEEE Software,* 54-60.

Hoch, D., Roeding, C., Purkert, G. & Lindner, S. (2000). *Secrets of Software Success.* Harvard Business School Press.

Nurse, L. (1996). Information Services in National Development Strategy: The industry in Barbados. *Barbados Investment and Development Company Report.*

Reichgelt, H. (2000). Software Engineering Services for Export and Small developing Economics. *IT for Development,* 9(2), 77-90.

Reichgelt, H. & Girvan, N. (1998). Local Software Development - Current State and Future Possibilities. *Proceedings, Jamaica Computer Society Conference 1998,* Kingston.

Schware, R. (1992). Software Industry Entry Strategies for Developing Countries: A "Walking on Two Legs" Proposition. *World Development,* 20(2), 143-164.

Yourdon, E. (1994, June). Developing Software Overseas. *Byte,* 113-120.

Chapter XIII

The Ten Commandments for Global Electronic Commerce Success in Small Business

Nabeel A.Y. Al-Qirim
Auckland University of Technology, New Zealand and
Deakin University, Australia

ABSTRACT

Small to medium-sized enterprises (SMEs) contribute significantly to national economies and employment levels and represent a viable source for inventions and innovations. The emergence of electronic commerce in the early 90's could provide different opportunities to the small business sector to overcome its inadequacies. However, in view of the electronic commerce/business (EC) literature in organizations in general and in SMEs specifically, EC research is scarce. Available research portrays a gloomy picture about EC uptake and use by SMEs. Therefore, this chapter attempts, by reviewing recent EC research, to depict an agenda for EC success in SMEs made up of ten influencing factors. Thus, an attempt is made to develop deeper understanding about the factors influencing EC success in SMEs. By following the suggested guidelines in this chapter, SMEs would be in a better position to assess the viability of the new EC perspective to their organizations. The same factors are highly important to researchers, SMEs, professionals (including educational institutions) and policymakers in driving SMEs and EC forward.

INTRODUCTION

Small- to medium-sized enterprises (SMEs) constitute 95 percent of enterprises and 60 to 70 percent of employment within the countries of the Organisation for Economic Cooperation and Development (OECD, 1997) and other countries across the globe. Accordingly, SMEs contribute significantly to the economies of the different countries and to the employment level (Cameron & Massey, 1999). SMEs are usually the source for most of the profound inventions and innovations in these different countries (Iacovou, Benbasat & Dexter, 1995).

The recent emergence of the Internet in general and the World Wide Web in particular has revolutionized business activities (Abell & Lim, 1996). At the outset, despite the apparent media hype (Premkumar & Roberts, 1999), and enthusiasm among academicians (Adam & Deans, 2000; Abell & Lim, 1996; Infotech Weekly, 1997; Poon & Swatman, 1999a) and professionals (Deloitte, 2000; IDC, 1998; PWHC, 1999) about electronic commerce (EC), the published research about EC in general provided little insights about EC penetration and success in SMEs.

In a recent study, 73 percent of surveyed small businesses are connected to the Internet; however, the potential use of the Internet in business was rarely explored (Waikato, 1999). Findings from another survey study indicate a lack of knowledge among SMEs about EC and its applications (Deloitte, 2000; PWHC, 1999). Despite the high adoption rates of e-mail, domain names, and Web sites, SMEs are lagging other larger businesses in the use of EC in business and in the adoption of EC-technology in general (Deloitte, 2000) and the extent of such laggardness varies from one country to another. Overall, the above portray a gloomy picture about EC uptake and use by SMEs and hence, investigating the reasons behind such laggardness in adopting and in using EC effectively is very essential.

In line with the above discussion, this chapter attempts to unveil different factors influencing EC adoption and use in small business and hence, influence its success and penetration in SMEs. By reviewing relevant literature about EC, it is expected to develop factors that would assist SMEs in resolving many of the ambiguities surrounding the new EC field. Thus, an attempt is made to further bridge the existing gap between SMEs and EC.

A RECIPE FOR ELECTRONIC COMMERCE SUCCESS IN SMES

The Dilemma of Electronic Commerce Benefits

In the SMEs scenario, different research emphasized the different EC advantages to SMEs (Abell & Black, 1997; Abell & Lim, 1996; Adam & Deans, 2000; Deloitte, 2000; Poon & Swatman, 1997, 1998, 1999a, 1999b; PWHC, 1999):

- The Internet is an efficient communication medium and a vast resource for information. The SMEs could use the e-mail technology to communicate efficiently with their buyers and suppliers, reducing many of the communication cost including buying of expensive equipment (e.g., fax/telex).
- The Internet provides value-added services to customers/partners/suppliers by providing different primary/supplementary information about the organization's industry, products and services on their Web sites. This could result in increasing the

loyalty and the stickiness (CRM) of their customers. The preceding tangible/intangible tactics are of strategic importance to retain and/or increase their customer base by increasing the switching costs.

- The Internet would provide new opportunities to SMEs, otherwise not possible before the introduction of the Internet, such as the ability to reach global markets and the ability to mass customize products and services to appeal to the different tastes of global consumers.
- SMEs would adopt EC for image-enhancement purposes. Having an Internet account (URL, dot.com, Web page), e-mail address on business cards and letterheads was reported as a major driver as well. Whether the SMEs were able to elevate from such initial depiction to a more strategic posture in adopting more strategic EC initiatives such as selling and buying online is worth further investigation from the perspective of the different countries.

On the other hand, the main impediments are:
- Technological impediments, e.g., security (privacy concerns, viruses, ePayments), legalities (enforceability of contracts, confirmation of receipt, prosecutions), policy (lack of global or unified standards), telecommunication services (bandwidth, convergence, reliability and quality of services (QoS)).
- Organizational impediments: cost, busy nature, small size and limited resources, lack of knowledge/expertise about EC. All of the preceding hindrances may force the SMEs to cast away from EC and hence, view it as not critical to their businesses.
- Environmental impediments: relating to the lack of regulatory frameworks pertinent to the above technological impediments highlighted above, either at the one country level or even at the global level.

In the light of the above advantages and impediments, most of the existing EC research found most of the SMEs not witnessing real benefits (direct sales and tangible profits) in the short run due to difficulties in selling products over the Internet as yet (Adam & Deans, 2000; Poon & Swatman, 1998, 1999a). The face-to-face interactions with customers and buyers proved to be more dominating than electronic interfaces (Ba et al., 1999; Poon & Swatman, 1997). They found the key motives for SMEs to adopt EC are the long-term indirect benefits, e.g., ongoing business transformation and new business initiatives (new opportunities), which could resemble a preparatory stage (infrastructure) for the long run direct benefits stage (secure returning customers and long term business partnership) (Poon & Swatman, 1998, 1999a).

However, the biggest challenge for the SMEs here is to succeed in moving from such simple and preparatory EC initiatives (driven mostly by media and researchers hype) to the more sophisticated and strategic initiatives (e.g., efficiency → effectiveness → strategic advantage).

Can You Afford the Investment in Electronic Commerce?

Despite the advent of economical personal computers (Cragg & King, 1993; Poon, 1999; Naylor & Williams, 1994), most of the research which examines this feature pertaining to SMEs found that scarce financial resources are one of the main inhibitors to IS and EC adoption (Blili & Raymond, 1993; Behrendorff & Rahman, 1999; Burgess, 1998; MOED, 2000; Poon, 1999;

Poon & Swatman, 1995; Poon & Swatman, 1999a; Soh, Yap & Raman, 1992; Thong, 1999) including New Zealand SMEs (Cragg & King, 1992, 1993; Peters & Paynter, 1999).

On the one hand, having EC requires an apparent investment in different areas: technological infrastructure upgrades or replacement, EC integration with existing systems, EC consultants, investments in bandwidth and applications (Web site, intranet, extranet, etc.). However, this considerable investment in the EC infrastructure is necessary to make it possible to process information efficiently, handle heavy traffic, and deliver satisfactory performance. SMEs would perceive this to be an expensive endeavor and hence, represent a barrier to EC adoption (MOED, 2000; PWHC, 1999). It is worth mentioning here that unlike the investment on IS/IT, which requires high initial investment and smaller ongoing maintenance and support costs, EC would require considerable continued investments on upgrading, new, overhauling, and/or replacing the whole EC system with an innovation or new design.

On the other hand, most probably the investment in EC would materialise in the long term only as highlighted earlier (Poon & Swatman, 1998, 1999). However, this depends on different factors, among them the ability to develop economies of scale (Ba et al., 1999; Poon, 2000), e.g., having a well-established online customer base and ongoing business that enables the firm to sell massively and cheaply at the same time.

The EC field is very vast and mining its perspectives for different saving opportunities is possible and is therefore, highly recommended. Overall, a thorough cost-benefit analysis should provide many insights concerning the investment path on EC – where it should be highly stressed that tangible profits should not be necessarily the main driver for adopting EC. SMEs, for instance, could achieve cost savings in marketing their business over cyberspace as a cheaper means than the regular physical channels (Ba et al., 1999), which require a considerable regular investment (e.g., catalogues or TV ads).

Despite the lack of such tangible benefits, interestingly recent research found that most of the SMEs willing to continue adopting EC viewed the EC technology as a necessity for business like any other technologies existing in the office such as fax and telephone (Poon & Swatman, 1998). It is as if the earlier hype (mentioned above) about EC drove the SMEs to explore its perspectives and hence, believed in its importance as an efficient communication mean. However, other research found that most of the SMEs did not even experience any savings in communication costs by adopting the Internet and e-mail (e.g., ISP, hardware, software) (Poon & Swatman, 1999b).

However, how far the earlier assertion about IS/IT applies to a considerable investment in EC infrastructure and whether the business would be able to sustain that investment for a long time is highly questionable, unless it proves viable to the business. This represents the greatest challenge for SMEs in balancing their investments on EC in the light of the anticipated advantages or value sought. That is, if EC proved its absolute effectiveness to the business in the first place.

Change Your MindSet

Recent EC research found fear of technology and management resistance to change hindering EC adoption and use within SMEs. With the introduction of new EC technology like the Intranet, Internet-EDI, Extranet, Web site, etc., there would be some fundamental changes in work processes and current practices (Alexander, 1999; Behrendorff & Rahman, 1999).

EC is not only a new way of selling and marketing, but also a new way of thinking, which requires a change of mindset. Teo, Tan and Buk (1998) pointed to the fact that organizations attempting to adopt the Internet should expect a possible change in communication and culture patterns. The Internet provides rich and accessible information to organizations and this could result in removing the existing segmented walls of knowledge in organizations. The new pattern of communication may disturb the internal power structure (status quo) and culture of the existing firms.

On the other hand, other research found the compatibility factor (compatible with the internal value, beliefs, and system of the organizations) significant to Internet adoption and hence, SMEs adopting EC (e.g., Web site) perceived it compatible with their organizations. The result indicated the importance of the fit between the innovation and the organization in the EC adoption and use scenario.

Issues pertaining to the technology itself may lead to a loss of confidentiality and to the leakage of SMEs vital information to hackers or snoopers. In light of a non-existing regulatory framework, this will deter many SMEs from going to EC. If SMEs perceive that their employees will misuse the Internet, this may create many incompatibilities within SMEs and hence may raise barriers to EC adoption.

On the other hand, small business faces the two-sided problem of asymmetric information, where in the marketplace customers meet buyers and develop basic trust and rapport through eye contact, bargaining, shaking hands, etc., but this kind of interpersonal interaction does not exist on the Internet (Ba et al., 1999). Such loss of the interpersonal interactions on the Internet will deter SMEs and suppliers/buyers from transacting over the Internet.

The above challenges would represent major barriers for SMEs in moving from their initial EC initiatives, or even deter them completely from adopting EC in the first place.

Be Small but Think Big, Think Smart

SMEs will always have much simpler structure, resources and capabilities than larger firms (Poon, 1999; Thong, 1999). Therefore, it is expected that SMEs will always lag behind larger business in adopting EC (Premkumar & Roberts, 1999).

Interestingly, most of the earlier IS literature found that larger SMEs are more likely to adopt IS and IT than smaller ones. Recent EC research found the same (Adam & Deans, 2000; Al-Qirim & Corbitt, 2002; Deloitte, 2000; Premkumar & Roberts, 1999) but other research found that smaller SMEs are as capable as larger ones in adopting EC (Abell & Lim, 1996) and this could be attributed to their enthusiasm for the technology and to their agility and flexibility in making fast decisions. Remember that most of the start-ups on the Internet were SMEs.

The open standards of the Internet bring electronic commerce (EC) within the reach of the smallest of firms and help reduce the gap between large and small firms (Kalakota & Whinston, 1996; MOC, 1998). Traditionally, the availability of such EC infrastructure was within the reach of the large enterprises only. The availability of such economical infrastructure is becoming more of an essential tool for organizations in general, and for SMEs businesses in particular, in gaining competitive advantage and in accessing global markets (Poon & Swatman, 1995). It is expected that SMEs will not be able to develop EC capabilities alone and hence, outsourcing part or all of their EC stake to the outside to a trusted EC vendor/ consultant (discussed later) will assist the SMEs in developing their EC strategies and in reaching online markets quickly. The emergence of this new technological innovation is changing the way business is conducted - even it is expected to changing our lives and daily activities in the long run.

Look Internally

EC is changing the way business is conducted even with individual customers. Firms that are able to streamline their products or processes or delivery agent on the Internet will be able to shift entirely to the pure EC arena (Choi et al., 1997). The success stories of small business using the Internet are quite apparent and are publicized and reported by the media.

Most of the businesses existing on the Internet are not necessarily transacting information-based products only, but rather complementing the sale and/or the delivery of a physical product with such things as publishing information about the usability of a physical product (e.g., user manuals), tracking the shipment, etc. (Teo et al., 1998). Product characteristics appeared to have an effect on EC adoption being physical or digital (e.g., software download), where Poon and Swatman (1997) indicated that there are other activities, which could be implemented over the Internet to supplement the physical delivery of products. For instance, the Internet could be used to transact information pertaining to delivery or acquisition of physical products.

Thus, using the Internet to transact products is dependent on how efficient and effective the Internet is in coordinating transactions between senders and receivers of the product or the service (Poon & Swatman, 1998). Characteristics include:

- the physical or information component
- usability in electronic form (e.g., music, video)
- gain in effectiveness, and efficiency during the transaction process
- value added during the transaction process (e.g., freeware)
- customer preference between different forms of the same product and the related transaction process.

The Manager

Most of the IS literature in SMEs (Blili & Raymond, 1993; Cragg & King, 1992, 1993; Harrison et al., 1997; Jarvenpaa & Ives, 1991; Thong, 1999; Thong & Yap, 1995, 1996) and EC in SMEs (Poon & Swatman, 1997, 1998, 1999a, 1999b) emphasises the role and the characteristics of the manager (usually the owner) as a product champion. Poon and Swatman (1998) highlighted the importance of the following two main determinants on EC success in small business:

- Management involvement: most of their respondents were either owners or managers who have direct involvement in adopting the Internet and using it for business; and
- The entrepreneurial perspective: Poon and Swatman observed the entrepreneurship characteristics among their Internet-active users, are always searching for change, responding to it, and exploiting it as an opportunity, ability to create, innovate, bear risk, manage and achieve targets.

Be Involved in Electronic Commerce

Poon and Swatman (1998, 1999a) point to the manager's role in their EC study, where they found direct management involvement was the norm in the different cases. Although the managers of small business lacked formal IT qualifications and training, they were champions in adopting EC specifically in micro-businesses, where the sole decision-maker was the director of the business. Poon and Swatman emphasized the importance of the manager's involvement as being vital to EC success.

Peters and Paynter (1999), however, point to the lack of senior management involvement with computerization and to the low positioning of the IT function in the firm which further highlights the importance of the manager's involvement perspective on EC success.

Further, due to the multi-perspectives that characterise EC, which requires the collaboration of different departments within the organization (e.g., IT, marketing, management), top management involvement and ownership is essential to overcome any political frictions that may arise in the introduction of EC.

Be an Innovative Manager

In adopting a closer stance to the IS literature, Thong (1999) and Thong and Yap (1995, 1996) considered the following measures for the CEO's innovativeness (based on Kirton's (1976) theory of innovativeness): introducing new original ideas, always looking for something new rather than improving something existing, and risk taker. Such features are at the heart of the entrepreneurial literature, in emphasising features pertaining to entrepreneurship and to entrepreneurs.

Due to the recent nature of EC, it is expected that the adoption decision for EC would include some sorts of high-risk elements and hence, the adoption decision for EC would require a risk taking manager.

Poon and Swatman (1997, 1998, 1999a) found that the entrepreneurial perspective differed between the different firms in their study. Managers/owners embraced EC technology and attempted to exploit it to the maximum. The managers who championed Internet adoption in their organizations demonstrated an innovative and a risk-taking attitude towards EC despite lacking formal IT training.

Reassess the Competition and New Entrants

Two main issues are reported for the elements of competition in EC: firstly, Adam and Deans (2000) in their Australian/New Zealand study found that only the SMEs which operated with overseas businesses perceived the greatest benefits from adopting EC.

Poon and Swatman (1998) pointed to the market scope of small business, where SMEs transacting with international markets would perceive many advantages from the Internet, such as cost savings and market communication in comparison with other SMEs operating in local markets. Teo et al. (1998) showed that SMEs planning to expand their business globally would face high set-up costs and high levels of risk. The Internet, on the other hand, would provide a relatively low-cost alternative for SMEs for advertising and for finding new partners and suppliers around the world.

Poon and Swatman (1998, 1999b) report that some SMEs reported having a competitive advantage on the Internet. This was only a perception and the SMEs failed to produce financial evidence endorsing the competitive advantage assertion. The SMEs did not maintain customer counts and comparison sales figures to show they performed better than their competitors, but indicated that their competitors were either not connected to the Internet or their own Web site was reporting higher hit counts on search result lists.

The literature on small businesses suggested that the greater the perceived intensity of competition in the industry, the more likely EC would be adopted by SMEs (Poon, 2000; Poon & Swatman, 1999a; Teo et al., 1998), specifically if the innovation directly affects the competition (Premkumar & Roberts, 1999).

Get Closer to Your Buyers and Suppliers

Pressure from buyers/suppliers could be divided into pressure from consumers and pressure from other businesses. SMEs in the consumer business (SMEs-to-consumers (S2C)), e.g., retailers, would establish, e.g., Web sites to provide different products and services to their existing customers. At the same time, SMEs will anticipate reaching the masses existing on the Internet for the chance of increased sales and revenues.

SMEs in selling-to or buying-from other businesses [SMEs-to-business (S2B) or business-to- SMEs (B2S) respectively or S2S if both businesses are SMEs], e.g., wholesale trader, manufacturer, etc., are usually encouraged (sometimes forced by larger businesses) to adopt EC to enhance the collaboration with other businesses. Such collaboration could result in having different EC activities such as sending purchase-orders, monitoring delivery status, price and inventory enquiries, and stock monitoring (Poon, 2000).

The type of relationship between SMEs and other businesses could be established on a continuous basis, where SMEs leverage their inter-organizational systems (IOS) and extend them to link with their buyers and/or suppliers for automating large parts of the manual processes and transactions. Accordingly, the pressure from suppliers/buyers would influence the type of technology adopted as well. Poon and Swatman (1999a) asserted that if a small business retained a high percentage of customers and competitors online, this would increase the chances of adopting EC.

Select the Right Technology Vendor

External support refers to the availability of support for implementing and using the innovation (e.g., EC), where organizations are more willing to risk trying new technologies if they feel there is adequate vendor or third-party support for the technology (Premkumar & Roberts, 1999). SMEs will lack the availability of technical resources and IS expertise in-house.

Due to the expected growth in EC SMEs will be further encouraged to adopt EC (Mcdonagh & Prothero 2000). On the other hand, the field of EC is relatively new and the actual functioning and utilization of EC-technologies are still unknown to most organizations (Teo et al., 1998) including SMEs. Therefore, it is expected that SMEs planning to adopt EC would seek assistance from consultants/vendors in the industry in different areas such as planning and strategy, training, development, and implementation (Deloitte, 2000). Consultants and technology vendors can add significant value to business planning by SMEs (Mcdonagh & Prothero, 2000). Poon & Swatman (1995) found SMEs relied on external support for their EC initiatives. Thus, the availability of such external support is essential for SMEs and will further encourage them to adopt EC (Alexander, 1999). How far efficient technology vendors in providing feasible and well-integrated EC products and services to SMEs are worth further investigation. For instance, Fichman and Kemerer (1993) point to the lack of unbiased information sources about the different innovations as provided by the different technology vendors. Technology vendors tend to aggressively promote their own products, which are sometimes "masked in new vocabularies that are explainable only by a self-selected cadre of experts." Thus, selecting a suitable innovation and/or a technology vendor for the SMEs would be a very difficult task. Above all, how the SMEs viewed technology vendors in the first place is worth further investigation as well (Al-Qirim & Hanoku, 2002).

Figure 1.   The evolution of EC in SMEs

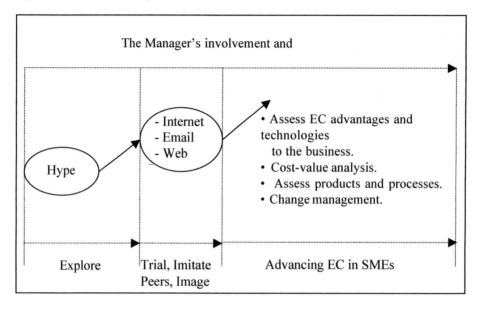

DISCUSSION

Being a new technological innovation, EC would provide diverse opportunities to SMEs to enlarge their scope and market share. However, these advantages will not accrue if SMEs do not know about these advantages (and disadvantages) in the first place, which emphasizes the importance of spreading the awareness of the technology and e-business models among the SME community

Most of the EC literature points to high adoption rates for the Internet, e-mail and Web pages among the SMEs. Whether this initial adoption is driven by media hype, pressure from peers, image enhancement, or by push from technology vendors or other concerned stakeholders is worthy of further investigation. It is worth noting that the adoption of the preceding EC technologies is not costly and does not require fundamental changes in work processes or practices (Figure 1).

On the other hand, due to the low anticipated benefits from EC among the SMEs' community, this would deter many of the SMEs from advancing to more sophisticated EC initiatives. Kalakota and Robinson (2001) indicate that the impact of EC is happening in phases. The first phase (1994-1997), the EC hype was about having Web presence regardless, whether large or small businesses were aware of what they were doing or not with EC. The second phase (1997-2000) of EC was about conducting transactions where businesses started to realise some benefits out of EC such as selling and buying goods online. The third phase (2000) focuses on increasing the profitability of the online business model and how the new technology could be used strategically to maximize customer value and profits. Looking at Figure 1 above, it could be argued that SMEs are still locked in the first phase of EC. Unless something is done about this concerning fact, the gap between SMEs and EC will keep increasing (Al-Qirim & Corbitt, 2002). This chapter proposes ten factors that would assist the SMEs in progressing with EC and hence, increase their success with EC.

Knowing the real benefits that would accrue from having EC in the present and/or in the future is of importance to SMEs in order to plan their EC acquisition plans properly and not to waste valuable resources. This should be achieved in parallel with the understanding of the real impact of EC on their organizations (products and processes) and on their business environment (competition and customers/suppliers).

Despite the existing optimism among the SMEs about EC, the lack of EC profitability in the short-term will further endanger many of the EC initiatives if they base their analysis on financial cost-benefit "return on investment" measures only. On the other hand, striking a balance between the investments made on EC and the value (either tangible or intangible) accruing from having EC will further judge the success or the failure of the different EC initiatives in SMEs. Thus, an initial investment in EC, e.g., a Web page, might be motivated by an image-enhancement criteria and might not develop any further to a strategic one.

It is observed thus far that SMEs are still experimenting with the technology (adopting Internet, e-mail accounts, and Web site presence only) and are still avoiding a considerable investment in the technology (Teo et al., 1998; Waikato, 1999) (Figure 1). One possible explanation, however, is that when greater convergence of technologies and critical mass and interdependence occur, then SMEs may use electronic commerce strategically (Peters & Paynter, 1999).

However, more evidence is needed to have better insights into EC from the SMEs' perspective. Despite these impediments, recent EC literature reported wide enthusiasm for the technology and in pursuing new opportunities, which highlights seriousness in exploring the potential benefits of EC to small business. The preceding hype and interest in EC would represent the foundation for the wide diffusion of EC in SMEs provided the SMEs take into consideration the different factors highlighted in this chapter.

EC seemed a logical extension to SMEs operating within international markets; having high information-content products; technology-based or Internet-related vendors (Poon & Swatman, 1997, 1999, 1998; Abell & Lim, 1996); driven to have EC by supplier/buyer/partner; and facing intense competition over the Internet. It is worth noting that the information-content of products has led to the emergence of new businesses (mostly SMEs) over the Internet. SMEs with excess resources (usually larger ones) are more able to experiment with the technology and to sustain it for a longer time.

Most of the literature in small business highlighted the importance of the manager's role (usually the owner) in IS/EC success being the single point of authority and decision-making. The field of EC is relatively new and the actual functioning and utilization of EC-technologies are still unknown to most organizations. Thus, highly emphasizing the importance of the manager-owner innovativeness and involvement on EC success. This is necessary to guarantee EC adoption and diffusion and in providing resources, motivation, and transformation-empowerment (Figure 1).

SUMMARY

This chapter attempted to highlight the main issues that would accelerate or hinder the wide adoption and diffusion of EC in SMEs. These factors would prove useful to SMEs in their potential uptake and use of EC. Specifically, these points are addressed to the manager-owner of the SMEs in identifying the different perspectives surrounding the new innovation. Therefore, it is left to the managers of the SMEs to consider the importance of the above factors on their current and future plans in adopting and/or using EC.

The issues raised by this chapter are of importance to researchers working in the same field, policymakers interested in devising means and measures to encourage the small sector in embracing EC, and to professionals including vendors, consultants and education institutions in targeting the small sector.

REFERENCES

Abell, W. & Black, S. (1997). Business use of the Internet in New Zealand: A follow-up study. Retrieved August 8, 2000 from the World Wide Web: http://www.scu.edu.au/ausweb96/business/abell/paper.htm

Abell, W. & Lim, L. (1996). Business use of the Internet in New Zealand: An exploratory study. Retrieved August 8, 2000 from the World Wide Web: http://www.scu.edu.au/ausweb96/business/abell/paper.htm

Adam, S. & Deans, K. (2000). Online business in Australia and New Zealand: Crossing a chasm. AusWeb2k-The Sixth Australian World Wide Web conference, Rihga Colonial Club Resort, Cairns, 12-17 June 2000. Retrieved August 8, 2000 from the World Wide Web: http://ausweb.scu.edu.au/aw2k/papers/adam/paper.html

Alexander, A. (1999). Tuning small business for e-commerce: Consultants say business consulting is essential, even in e-commerce. *Accounting Technology, 15*(11), 48-53.

Al-Qirim, N. & Corbitt, B. (2002). An empirical investigation of an e-commerce adoption model in small to medium-sized enterprises in New Zealand. *Forthcoming in the proceedings of the 6th Pacific Asia Conference on Information Systems (PACIS 2002): The next e-What? For business and communities.* Tokyo, Japan, September 2-4.

Al-Qirim, N. & Hanoku, B. (2002). IT and e-commerce outsourcing in small- to medium-sized enterprises in New Zealand: An exploratory research. *Proceedings of the fifteenth Bled electronic commerce conference (Reality: Constructing the economy)*, Bled, Slovenia, June 17-19, 537-551.

Ba, S., Whinston, A. & Zhang, H. (December, 1999). Small business in the electronic marketplace: A blue print for survival. *Texas Business Review.* University of Texas, Austin.

Blili, S. & Raymond, L. (1993). Information technology: Threats and opportunities for small and medium-sized enterprises. *International Journal of Information Management, 13,* 439-448.

Behrendorff, G. & Rahman, S. (1999). Adoption of electronic commerce by small to medium enterprises in Australia. In F. Tan, P. Corbett & Y. Wong (Eds.). *Information technology diffusion in the Asia Pacific: Perspective on policy, electronic commerce and education* (pp. 130-147). Hershey, London: Idea Group Publishing.

Burgess, S. (1998). Information technology in small businesses in Australia: A summary of recent studies. Retrieved June 27, 2000 from the World Wide Web: http://www.sbaer.uca.edu/websonar/WebSonar.acgi$SearchCommand

Cameron, A. & Massey, C. (1999). Small and medium sized enterprises: A New Zealand Perspective. Auckland: Addison Wesley Longman New Zealand, Ltd.

Choi, S., Stahl, D. & Whinston, A. (1997). *The economic of electronic commerce.* Indiana: Macmillan Technical Publishing.

Cragg, P. & King, M. (1992). Information systems sophistication and financial performance of small engineering firms. *European Journal of Information Systems, 1*(6), 417-426.

Cragg, P. & King, M. (1993, March). Small-Firm computing: Motivators and inhibitors. *MIS Quarterly*.

Deloitte Touche Tohmatsu. (2000). Deloitte e-Business survey: Insights and issues facing New Zealand business. Retrieved August 8, 2000 from the World Wide Web: http://www.deloitte.co.nz/images/acrobat/survey.pdf

Iacovou, C., Benbasat, I. & Dexter, A. (1995, December). Electronic data interchange and small organizations: Adoption and impact of Technology. *MIS Quarterly, 465-485.*

Infotech Weekly (1997, April). New Zealand Internet use. Retrieved May 15, 2000 from the WWW: http://www.nua.net/surveys/index.cgi?f=VS&art_id=863080905&rel=true

International Data Corporation (IDC) (1998). Ecommerce booming in New Zealand. Nua Internet Services: Retrieved April 30, 1998 from the World Wide Web: http://www.nua.ie/surveys/index.cgi?f=VS&art_id=905354498&rel=true. Retrieved May 15, 2000 from the WWW: http://www.nua.ie/surveys/index.cgi?f=VS&art_id=905354498&rel=true

Jarvenpaa, L. & Ives, B. (1991, June). Executive involvement and participation in the management of information technology. *MIS Quarterly, 15*(2), 205-227.

Kalakota, R. & Robinson, M. (2001). *eBusiness 2.0: Roadmap for success.* Boston, MA: Addison-Wiley Publishing Company, Inc.

Kalakota, R. & Whinston, A. (1996). *Frontiers of electronic commerce.* Reading, MA: Addison-Wiley Publishing Company, Inc.

Kirton, M. (1976). Adopters and innovators: A description and measure. *Journal of Applied Psychology, 61*(5), 622-629.

Mcdonagh, P. & Prothero, A. (2000). Euroclicking and the Irish SME: Prepared for e-commerce and the single currency. *Irish Marketing Review, 13*(1), 21-33.

Ministry of Economic Development (MOED) (October, 2000). Electronic commerce in New Zealand: A survey of business use of the Internet information technology. Policy Group Competition and Enterprise branch. Retrieved May 16, 2001 from the World Wide Web: http://www.ecommerce.govt.nz/ecat/resources/index.html

OECD (1997). Small business, job creation and growth: Facts, obstacles and best practices.

Peters, D. & Paynter, J. (1999). Application of electronic commerce in New Zealand. In F. Tan, P. Corbett & Y. Wong (Eds.), *Information technology diffusion in the Asia Pacific: Perspective on policy, electronic commerce and education* (pp. 148-162). Hershey, London: Idea Group Publishing.

Poon, S. (1999). Small business and Internet commerce: What are the lessons learned? In F. Sudweeks & C. Romm (Eds.), *Doing business on the Internet: Opportunities and pitfalls* (pp. 113-124). London: Springer-Verlag London Ltd.

Poon, S. (2000). Business environment and Internet commerce benefits –A small business perspective. *European Journal of Information Systems, 9*, 72-81.

Poon, S. & Swatman, P. (1995). The Internet for small businesses: an enabling infrastructure for competitiveness. Retrieved June 27, 2000 from the World Wide Web: http://inet.nttam.com

Poon, S. & Swatman, P. (1997) Internet-based small business communication. *International Journal of Electronic Commerce, 7*(2), 5-21.

Poon, S. & Swatman, P. (1998) A combined-method study of small business Internet commerce. *International Journal of Electronic Commerce, 2*(3), 31-46.

Poon, S. & Swatman, P. (1999a). An exploratory study of small business Internet commerce issues. *Information & Management, 35*, 9-18.

Poon, S. & Swatman, P. (1999b). A longitudinal study of expectations in small business Internet commerce. *International Journal of Electronic Commerce, 3*(3), 21-33.

Premkumar, G. & Roberts, M. (1999). Adoption of new information technologies in rural small businesses. *The International Journal of Management Science (OMEGA), 27*, 467-484.

PWHC (Pricewaterhousecoopers) (1999, September). SME electronic commerce study (TEL05/97T). Retrieved April 10, 2000 from the World Wide Web: http://apec.pwcglobal.com/sme.html

Soh, P., Yap, S. & Raman, S. (1992). Impact of consultants on computerisation success in small business. *Information & Management, 22,* 309-313.

Swanson, E.B. (1994). Information systems innovation among organisations. *Management Science, 40*(9), 1069-1092.

Teo, T., Tan, M., & Buk, W (1998). A contingency model of Internet adoption in Singapore. *International Journal of Electronic Commerce, 2* (2), 95-118.

Thong, J. (1999). An integrated model of information systems adoption in small business. *Journal of management information systems, 15*(4), 187-214.

Thong, J. & Yap, C. (1995). CEO characteristics, organisational, characteristics and information technology adoption in small business. *Omega, International Journal of Management Sciences, 23*(4), 429-442.

Thong, J., & Yap, C. (1996). Information technology adoption by small business: An empirical study. In K. Kautz & J. Pries-Heje (Eds.), *Diffusion and adoption of information technology* (pp. 160-175). London: Chapman & Hall.

Waikato (The University of Waikato Management School) (1999, September). SME benchmarking survey. Management Research Centre, 3rd quarter.

Chapter XIV

Culture and E-Business in Thailand

Suttisak Jantavongso
Monash University, Australia

Raymond Koon-Ying Li
Monash University, Australia

Benedict Tootell
Monash University, Australia

ABSTRACT

Surveys of Western literature identify law, infrastructure, tax, payment processes, consumers, suppliers, education and business culture, as the key factors in the successful adoption of e-business. A survey of Thai business executives confirmed that culture and society are additional factors. Twenty of these factors were identified and examined. Organizational infrastructure and English literacy were also found to be major internal and external barriers respectively. The research findings provide the foundation for future research aimed at developing a holistic framework to guide business in Thailand and other countries, to successfully implement the new generation of e-business activities. The new generation of e-business activities include operation-centric e-business, virtual business and Application Service Providers (ASPs).

INTRODUCTION

Over the past few years, the widespread use of the Internet has lead to tremendous expansion in electronic business (e-business) worldwide, especially in South-East Asian countries (Input, 1999). E-business over the Internet is a new and fast-growing way of conducting business and, although only a few years old, is rapidly developing into a major economic activity (Legard, 2000). The ability of e-business to link companies within the global market overcomes traditional barriers to business transactions caused by geography, location and distance.

Surveys of Western literature identify eight key factors that contribute to successful e-business: law, infrastructure, tax, payment processes, consumers, suppliers, education and business culture.∹ Countries and businesses that want to be successful in the new economy must undertake careful study in these areas before launching their e-business endeavors. The Singaporean government is an example of a body that has successfully achieved this goal.

Thailand, which has just begun the initial stages of its e-business development, was selected as the case study for this chapter (Business in Thailand online, 1999a, 1999b). Thailand has a good mixture of foreign and local investors, healthy import and export markets, and an existing strong business environment. Thai culture and society contain many unique characteristics. As in other countries in Asia, e-business activities in Thailand are rapidly growing.

A survey of Thai business executives was conducted during the course of this study. The survey findings confirmed that in addition to the eight key contributors to successful e-business identified in Western research, there are a number of cultural and social issues that are often ignored by current researchers. Twenty of these social and cultural issues· are identified and examined in this chapter. From the survey, organizational infrastructure and English literacy were found to be the major internal and external barriers respectively to the adoption of e-business in Thailand.

The findings contained in this study provide the foundation for future research and the development of a holistic framework to guide e-business development in Thailand. The findings can assist both Thailand and other countries in similar stages of e-business development to successfully implement e-business initiatives. Such initiatives encompass many of the new generation of e-business opportunities, including operation-centric e-business, virtual business and Application Service Providers (ASPs). The chapter concludes with a discussion covering the new generation of e-business and predicted future trends in e-business.

BACKGROUND

In this study, e-business is defined as any form of commercial transaction involving goods and services, conducted over a computer network (Evans, 2000). It covers the buying and selling of products and services over the Internet, including those that facilitate online transactions and those enabling the dissemination of information over the Internet. It includes all online interactions between buyers and sellers. A survey of Thai business executives was conducted. The objective of the survey was to identify issues considered by Thai business to be important to the adoption of e-business.

E-BUSINESS: A WESTERN VIEW

Surveys of Western literature identify eight key factors deemed essential to the successful adoption of e-business: law, infrastructure, tax, payment processes, consumers, suppliers, education and business culture.

Law Related to E-Business

A legal framework is required to support e-business. It can enhance or inhibit the development of electronic trading. Legal issues include: support for the use of digital signatures and digital certificates in virtual transactions; ease of licensing; and the degree of regulation governing conduct of online transactions. The legal and regulatory environments required to support growth in the digital economy are significantly different to those needed to support traditional enterprises (IDA Singapore, 1998). This presents specific challenges to the government, who must also adapt both national policy and international strategy to effectively deal with the new digital economy. The government must provide transparent, market-favorable regulation and legislation. Suitable environments must be set in place to support security, secrecy and non-repudiation of digital transactions. Existing regulations must not be allowed to interfere with the growth of new or existing markets over the Internet. New regulations should be flexible enough to cater for global policy shifts and further changes in technology.

E-Business Infrastructure Requirements

E-business infrastructure can be defined according to network connectivity, logistics, transportation, telecommunications structure, and the standards, guidelines, components and services required to support e-business activities. E-business cannot function without adequate telecommunications and Internet infrastructure (Sowinski, 2001). Global e-business requires a modern, seamless and reliable global telecommunications network. Research in this area reveals that in many countries, delays in the establishment of sound telecommunication policies has affected the development of advanced digital networks (IITF, 2000).

Tax Related to E-Business

Taxation of e-business is a difficult area to address. The global nature of electronic business raises issues of international tax legislation that should be examined by both national governments and international bodies. According to the National Computer Board (Mauritius, 2001) most international tax authorities believe that current tax systems and structures, founded on basic principles of neutrality, fairness, certainty and simplicity, will continue to be appropriate to cater for the changes brought about by electronic transactions. In May 1998, members of the World Trade Organization (WTO) agreed to refrain from applying customs duties on electronic products and services delivered electronically across national boundaries.

Payment Process of E-Business

Payment and logistics systems form the backbone of e-business transactions. E-business requires the support of secure, reliable and efficient electronic payment mechanisms including those for handling online credit card transactions (Sowinski, 2001). Security is the most discussed e-business issue and concerns the confidentiality and protection of sensitive information. Electronic payments represent a new form of payment and doubts have been raised regarding the potential risks and lack of security associated with such transactions. Credit cards are the most common form of payment on the World Wide Web (WWW). Securing e-business transactions, however, involves more than simply encrypting the transactions. Businesses must also ensure that sensitive consumer information, such as credit card numbers, cannot be abused by employees and that unencrypted credit card information is stored on a secure system (Hong Kong Productivity Council, 2001).

Consumer of E-Business

The Internet presents new challenges to business by providing new ways to find, develop and interact with customer bases. The Internet has enabled customers to access information on products and services from vendors around the world. Information from competitors is now readily available to customers to allow them to make more informed purchase decisions.

It is therefore important that organizations involved in e-business understand what the needs of their customers are and how to respond to these needs as they arise. To be successful in e-business, organizations must be able to clearly define who their e-customers are and be aware of the changes that the World Wide Web has brought to marketing. They must also be educated in successful on-line interaction methodologies and understand the best ways to market products and services to their e-consumer base (Agarwal, 2001).

Vendors of E-Business

Companies involved in conducting business internationally have to deal with clients from different cultures. Successful e-business providers rely on their ability to satisfy the requirements of their customers, provide secure transactions, and deliver goods in a timely and reliable manner. The usability and personalization of their web sites is also an important consideration.

Education

E-businesses require their customers to have the ability to navigate the WWW. It follows, therefore, that a country's level of education and literacy determines the number of people with the necessary skills to navigate the web and, consequently, utilize e-business. Education and literacy are a necessary pre-condition to e-business uptake. Education and training are also important factors in ensuring that entrepreneurs, managers and employees, both present and future, have the necessary skills to perform successfully in an electronic business environment (National Computer Board-Mauritius, 2001).

Business Cultural

Merrill Lynch & Co, Inc. (2001) stated that gaining a clear understanding of global business culture . was essential in operating a high quality e-business. Culture is defined as the sum of learned beliefs, values and customs that guide the behavior of members within a society. Business culture can exist at both a national level, as well as at various other levels within a country (Pornpitakpan, 2000). As e-business is global in nature, cross cultural business issues must be addressed. Ignoring alternate ways of thinking can seriously impede successful business negotiations. Kammeyer (2001) believes business cultural differences are significant and are often the most troublesome variables in business negotiations. Acquiring a good knowledge of intercultural/cross-cultural business issues and etiquette through training can mean the difference between business success and failure. Failure in e-business may not be due to technical or professional incompetence, but rather a lack of understanding of cross-cultural business issues and the inability to adjust accordingly.

Cultural fluency is the term most often used to describe a person's ability to understand the traditions, assumptions and values of other cultures. Failure to identify and account for the cultural issues associated with e-business can lead to the development of culture shock and the possible failure of the business enterprise. Understanding the importance of managing business cultural differences is therefore a key to building a successful global e-business.

E-BUSINESS IN SINGAPORE AND THE EIGHT KEY FACTORS

Singapore is a unique country. Whilst geographically situated in the East, much of its culture has been strongly influenced by the West. Yet as a very conservative society, preferring conformity and obedience to individuality, Singapore differs considerably from many Western democracies. Singaporeans have a general belief in working together for the good of the country, despite the clear division of the population into three major ethnic groups (Chinese, Malays and Indians/Pakistanis). Operating under a single system of government and sharing English as a common business language, each of the major ethnic groups has managed to retain distinct cultural traditions. National citizenship, however, always comes before ethnicity. The direct result of this approach is that it eliminates many of the cross-cultural business issues one might expect when undertaking business. Singapore also has the advantages of a well-educated and technologically literate workforce, essential for the wide-spread successful adoption of e-business.

Over the past decade, Singapore has strived to become an international electronic business center where Electronic Business transactions from the region and around the world are processed. It now controls the necessary infrastructure to support an international transactions hub and is well-connected to the rest of the world. The legal infrastructure for electronic commerce is also in place. The Singaporean Government has worked closely with business and industry to create a safe investment environment. Together they have built the necessary infrastructure required to become a digital economy, where buying and selling can be done completely electronically. The government is continuing to review policy and regulatory issues relating to such factors as electronic identification, payment, electronic business policies, and security. Some of the country's achievements are as follows:

Legal

The Singaporean government is committed to creating an environment of trust, predictability and certainty so that companies can feel safe and secure in conducting their business online. The Singapore Electronic Transactions Act (ETA), instituted on July 10, 1998, deals with the legal aspects of electronic contracts, the use of digital signatures, and concerns for authentication and non-repudiation. It covers the use of electronic applications, licenses for the public sector and the liabilities of service providers. The Evidence Act, amended in 1997, allows for the use of electronic records as evidence in the court. To protect knowledge and intellectual capital, the Copyright (Amendment) Bill was passed in 1999.

Network Infrastructure

The Singapore Telecom Internet eXchange (STIX) is an Asian Internet Hub connected to more than 15 countries in the Asia-Pacific Rim and the European Internet backbone.

Singapore also has a 45 Mbps direct Internet connection to the US Internet backbone. Internally, Singapore ONE provides an ATM backbone and broadband access to homes, libraries and kiosks. The Infocomm Development Authority of Singapore (IDA) Infrastructure for Electronic Identification (IEI) initiative provides required secure communication and identification using digital certificates and digital signatures.

Taxation

Singapore has a clear policy on Goods and Services Tax (GST) relating to online business. All physical goods supplied over the Internet and goods delivered locally attract the present rate of 3 percent GST. Exported goods are not charged GST. If the supplier is from overseas and the value of the goods exceeds $400 (Singapore), then the GST does apply.

Payment

The commercial deployment of SET (MasterCard and VISA) was initiated in March 1998. CashCard for Open Network E-Business (C-ONE) was launched in January 1998. This innovation by the Network for Electronic Transfers (NETS) makes Singapore among the first countries in the world to introduce a smart card-based payment system in cyberspace. According to Chua (2000), online payment in Singapore is secure. There are sufficient mechanisms in place to ensure that information transmissions are safe.

Customers

According to Tan (2000), the consumer can buy just about anything online from Singaporean retailers: from books to durians, alcohol to Nonya beaded slippers, and groceries to watches.

Vendors

While many Singaporeans are already surfing and buying from vendors abroad (for example, Amazon.com), demonstrating their acceptance of e-business, many local online vendors have not yet developed a web strategy and require help in this area.

Several e-business services now exist, including online payment, security and bureau services.

In summary, the Singaporean Government has played an active role and succeeded in providing the legal infrastructure, safe investment environment and excellent technological infrastructure required for e-business to flourish.

E-BUSINESS IN THAILAND

E-business is not new to Thai businesses. According to Koanantakool (2000), it has existed for much of the past decade. Earlier forms of e-business were conducted through closed networks, for example, internal networks (Intranet), mainly in the form of electronic data interchange (EDI) and electronic funds transfer (EFT).

With the rapid growth in the Internet and the WWW, recent attention has been focused on e-business conducted over the Internet. In response to this, many Thai companies have begun exploring various e-business methodologies and attempted to identify issues associated with the adoption of e-business. Institutions and private organizations are working collaboratively to develop a framework for e-business implementation (Koanantakool, 2000).

THE RESEARCH

Thailand has its own unique culture and religion, as well as a low level of English literacy. The authors believe that these factors are of equal importance to determining the successful adoption of e-business as are the eight key factors identified by Western researchers.

The Hypothesis

The eight key factors identified by Western researchers are based on findings relating to the Western model of business Western. Thailand, like other countries in Asia, has its own unique educational system, culture, religion and social framework. Education, society and culture (including business culture) may have therefore a strong influence on the adoption of e-business and e-business activities in Thailand.

The Objectives

The main objective of this research is to validate the above hypothesis. The other major objective of the research is to attempt to establish the following in relation to Thailand:
- The current status of e-business
- The reasons for businesses to start e-business initiatives
- Cultural factors and their relative importance
- The main difficulties in driving e-business initiatives

The findings from this research will lay the foundation for future research aimed at developing a holistic framework to guide e-business development in Thailand. The framework will assist countries in a similar developmental state to successfully implement new endeavors and support the next generation of e-business environments.

The Method

One hundred Thai businesses in the Bangkok region were randomly selected to participate in the study. Forty companies finally agreed to participate. An executive was selected from each company and interviewed either face-to-face, over the phone, or through the mail.

The Survey Population

Of the 40 companies who agreed to participate, more than half were small- and medium-sized enterprises (SMEs). SME are defined as companies with less than 50 employees. Around 20 percent can be considered to be large firms (with more than 500 employees (see Figure 1). Around 50 percent of the companies had less than 10 IT staff (see Figure 2).

The majority (60 percent) of the companies surveyed were traditional companies involved in manufacturing, retail, wholesale, financial services, travel, communication/information and government service. The remaining 40 percent were in the Information Technology (IT) sector (see Figure 3).

184   Jantavongso, Li & Tootell

Figure 1. Number of employees

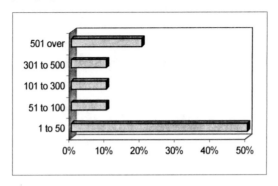

Figure 2. Number of IT

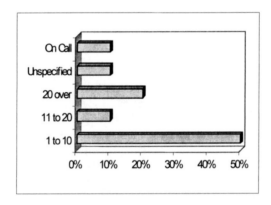

Figure 3. Industry sectors of the surveyed company

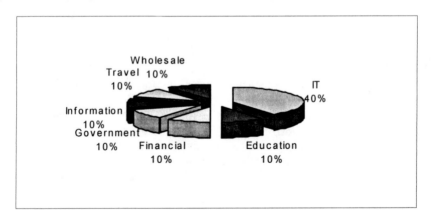

Table 1. E-business initiatives reasons

Market expansion - Advertisement	33.3%
Competition	16.7%
Real-time response to meet the customer demand	11.1%
Company's image	5.6%
Cost efficiency	5.6%
Increased profitability	5.6%
Information fulfillment	5.6%
Internet requirement from end users	5.6%
Catching up with technology	5.6%
Common Practice	5.6%

General Findings

All the senior executives agreed with the definition of e-business (as defined earlier in this chapter). All the executives interviewed agreed that e-business in Thailand was still in its early stages; though most believed that e-business was here to stay. They agreed that e-business would increase competition.

The survey showed that approximately 56 percent of the organizations had short and long-term plans for e-business. The remainder had no immediate plans to introduce e-business activities. The executives felt that there was little encouragement from the Thai Government in the form of support for private sector e-business activities.

Table 1 shows the survey results relating to the reasons for adopting e-business. The top three reasons for Thai organizations to introduce e-business initiatives were market expansion (33.3 percent); gaining advantage over competitors (16.7 percent); and real-time response to meet customer demand (11.1 percent).

Specific Findings

Issues Associated with E-Business in Thailand

Table 2 displays those e-business issues identified by the executives of the surveyed companies as being of most importance. The survey revealed that education and culture were the main issues for e-business activities in Thailand. This finding agrees with the hypothesis stated earlier.

Table 2. E-business issues

Education & Culture	28.57%
Payment Processes (Banking Practice including secure transaction)	23.81%
Law (Legal and regulations)	19.05%
Infrastructure (Accessibility to Computer & regional differences)	9.52%
Infrastructure (Telecommunication & Technology)	9.52%
Infrastructure (Delivery Systems)	4.76%
Government Support	4.76%

The survey also indicates that Thai executives believed e-business technology in Thailand would eventually catch up with the rest of the world. They expressed a strong desire for further research in education and culture in relation to e-business activities.

Cultural Factors that Effect E-Business Activities in Thailand

During the survey, all executives were asked to list the social and cultural factors that they believed related to e-business activities in Thailand. Twenty factors were identified. Table 3 shows the survey findings which revealed that business culture and Web page presentation were considered by the Thai executives to be the main factors determining the success of Thai e-business initiatives. They agreed that developers of e-business applications had to respect cultural factors.

Comments on the Identified Culture Factors

As expected, business culture heads the list of cultural influences. Thai businesses often do not have refund policies; have unique warranty and information secrecy policies;

Table 3. Culture factors

Business Culture (After Sale Services, Warranty, Refund Policy, Information Secrecy)	12.37%
Web page Presentation (Color, Format, Layout, Font)	10.31%
Price (Including Credit Card & Delivery Charge)	9.28%
Payment (Including Credit Card, Banking systems)	6.19%
Response Time	6.19%
Trust & Sincerity	6.19%
Web pages Contents	6.19%
Government Support	5.15%
Security	5.15%
Company's Image (Including Creditability, Location, Product Brand)	4.12%
Convenience	4.12%
Education	4.12%
Product Category (Variety)	4.12%
Cross Culture	3.09%
Delivery	3.09%
Languages	3.09%
Laws (Including Copyright)	3.09%
Technological Apprehension	2.06%
Fashion	1.03%
Web pages Address (Easy to remember)	1.03%

and often have poor after-sale service in comparison to Western companies. Factors relating to credit cards and banking systems appear high on the list (third and fourth positions) and the authors believe that this is directly related to the issue of trust (the sixth position on the list).

Impact of Cultural Factors – Fonts, Color and Diagrams

Web page presentation occupies a high position on the list of cultural influences.

Graphical components on a web page are there to support users' understanding of the product and thereby encourage them to purchase from the company. Graphics, such as charts, diagrams and illustrations, need the support of text and color. The letters of the alphabet and numbers can be presented using various typeface styles. Each typeface style is designed to cater for different requirements. Some are created for legibility and to be easy on the eyes. Some styles are created to make use of space efficiently. Colors have the power and ability to influence emotions, perceptions and moods. They can alter behavior and trigger different emotional responses. Kang and Corbitt (2001) suggested that web page designers maximize the benefit of using colors, symbols and graphics on the web page.

Kang and Corbitt (2001) also stated that color and screen design directions have dissimilar psychological and social associations in different cultures. Users with different cultural backgrounds have different concepts of screen usage. E-business is a global business and therefore, users can be from a wide variety of different cultural backgrounds. The use of particular fonts, colors and diagrams in web page presentation can express the national identity and business culture of an organization.

Below are examples of how fonts, colors and diagrams were used to illustrate national and business culture in a web-based e-business application. Various web page presentations from the Makro Asia company chain, which operates in various different countries, were used. Makro Asia is a distributor for food and non-food products in the Asian region.

Figure 4 is a screen capture of the "Siam makro" retailer Web page application. It was designed for local Thai consumers using Thai cultural and social contexts. The lady performs the traditional Thai greeting *Wai*. *Wai* is a way of saying hello and of showing thanks or respect for people. In this case, it means, "Welcome." The smile is used to express friendliness.

Figure 4. Thai local firms – makro

Source: http://www.siammakro.co.th/

Figure 5. Mackro in Taiwan

Source: http://www.makrotw.com.tw/

The background color is used to create an atmosphere of warmth. Text fonts used are in the Thai language.

In contrast, the Web pages designed by the same company for Taiwan, the Philippines and Indonesia are different to those of Thailand. As shown in the diagram below, there are clearly cultural issues involved. Although different fonts, color and diagrams are used, these Web pages still identify the "makro" company chain.

E-Business Language Support

Language as a factor was rated surprisingly low. This may be because English remains the main language of e-business Web pages in Thailand (Table 4). The authors believe that this ranking was influenced by the survey being conducted from the executive view-point. As most of the Thai population has a poor command of the English language, it is believed that interviewing a broader cross-section of the Thai populace would have resulted in a higher ranking for this cultural factor.

Badre (2000) identified 168 native-languages used to build web pages around the world. According to Global Internet Statistics (by Language), as of March 2002, there were

Figure 6. Makro in Philippine

Source: http://www.makro.com.ph/

Figure 7.   Makro in Indonesia

Source: http://www.makro.co.id/

approximately 561 million people online. Of this number, 40.2 percent spoke English, while 26.1 percent of non-English speakers spoke Asian languages (Global Reach, 2002). For any business to extend beyond its national boundaries, language is an essential and often difficult obstacle to overcome.

E-Business Security

Security is always a big concern with Internet technologies (Biscontri, 2001). The survey revealed that security was ranked reasonably high on the list. Surprisingly, most Thai executives surveyed claimed that their current e-business activities were secure, even though 37 percent of those being asked the question were not clear how the security of their Web sites was being achieved.

Cross Culture

The survey revealed that the majority (67 percent) of Thai executives agreed that cultural issues had a strong impact on running e-business activities. This finding supports the findings by Fleenor and Raven (2002), which stated that culture and sensitivity to cultural differences plays a critical role in successful international business and international e-business. Understanding how the Web page fits into a country's culture is necessary to forming successful customer relations.

The survey also revealed that Thai executives believe as businesses go online, cross-cultural issues become more important. The position of Thailand in the early adoption stages of e-business explains the current position of cross-cultural issues towards the bottom of the list.

Table 4.   Language used in Thai web pages

English	47.06%
Thai	29.41%
Others: Malaysian, Chinese, Swedish, Norwegian, Danish	29.41%

Table 5. E-business initiatives barriers

Internal Factors	45%
Organization infrastructure	20%
Employees	10%
Web pages development	10%
Capital Investment	5%
External Factors	35%
Education - including English literacy	15%
Communication Infrastructure - including online payment	10%
Customer	10%
No difficulties	20%

The Main Difficulties Encountered in Driving E-Business Initiatives

The survey indicates that the main barrier to driving e-business initiatives in Thailand came from internal constraints (45 percent) of which 20 percent is accounted for by organizational infrastructure (see Table 5). This finding comes as no surprise, as most of the companies surveyed operate as family-run entities in which the owner is the sole decision-maker for the organization. A common cultural feature shared by many Thai business executives is that if something is operating, regardless of its level of efficiency, it should not be tampered with.

Table 5 indicates that of the external influences on Thai e-business, education and English literacy also play an important role (15 percent of total). English and education, especially computer literacy, were the main concerns shared by Thai executives.

FUTURE TRENDS IN E-BUSINESS

As mentioned earlier, the findings of the Thai business survey will be used to support future research and to develop a holistic framework to guide e-business developments. The aim is to assist Thailand and other countries in a similar stage of the their e-business development cycle, to implement more effective e-business strategies. In this section, a new direction for e-business is explored.

Figure 8 provides an overview of present e-business. This study focused on only the e-commerce section of e-business. Figure 9 presents a possible future trend in e-business activity. As shown in Figure 9, virtual business (v-business), Application Service Providers (ASPs) and operational centric e-business (e-business of business) will be the main driving forces of future e-business.

In recent years, the concept of virtual business has gained much popularity (Introna, 2001). V-business is defined as a business conducted over the Internet that has no physical office location. A v-business can be supported by one or more Application Service Providers (ASPs). At this stage, a virtual business is yet to become a reality. Yet the authors believe that a future trend of e-business activity in Thailand and other developing countries will be

Figure 8. Overview of electronic business

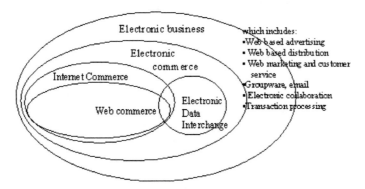

Source: http://www.dfat.gov.au/apec/ecom/CIRCIT1.html

Figure 9. A possible direction of e-business

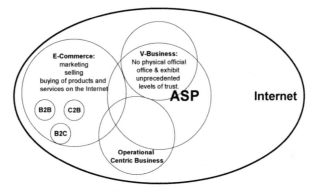

the increased adoption of the virtual business, as there are low set-up costs involved and such models are ideal for small company operations.

An ASP is a company that offers individuals or enterprises access over the Internet to applications and related services that would otherwise have to be located in their own personal or enterprise computers. ASP services are expected to become an important alternative to traditional methods of e-business and will be an important element in supporting v-business activity in Thailand. The use of ASPs will prove attractive because of minimal set-up costs and comparatively low running costs. It also enables resources and expertise to be shared among companies using the same ASP. It releases company IT resources and allows the company to concentrate on its main focus, that is, the running of the business.

Figure 10 illustrates the interrelationships between v-businesses and ASPs.

The current study has highlighted that cultural and social factors are important issues that needed to be taken into consideration when handling the adoption of e-business. These issues will be more profound when v-business and ASPs are included in the e-business model. Figure 10 shows the inter-relationships between the e-customer, ASPs, v-Businesses and vendors. The simple relationship between the company and its customers, or company and its vendor, now becomes much more complicated. A v-business is a virtual business

Figure 10. Relationships between v-business and ASPs

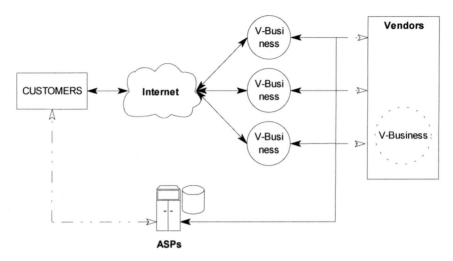

supported by an ASP, of which the customer has no knowledge of the ASP's identity. The issue of trust among the three players as shown in Figure 11 should become a very important issue.

Without trust, there will be no business. Trust is always a fundamental enabler of successful e-business.. To survive, virtual companies must demonstrate and sustain trust. Trust will continue to be important and for this reason must be embraced by the entire organization (Figure 12).

If a virtual organization is to be adopted as a viable business model, it is important to have suitable frameworks to support this new organizational form.

The issue of trust is an important cultural and social factor. If virtual business is to be adopted in Thailand, it is important that the holistic framework support this new form of organization. There is a need for further research to further understand social and cultural factors and their impacts on the new generation of e-business activities.

Conclusion

Surveys of Western literature revealed eight key factors that contribute to a successful e-business. They are: law, infrastructure, tax, payment processes, consumers, suppliers, education and business culture. Countries and businesses that want to be successful in the new economy must study these areas carefully before launching their e-business endeavors.

Figure 11. Trust relationship in v-business

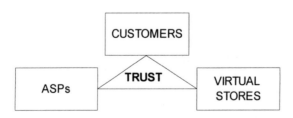

Figure 12. Critical success factors for virtual business

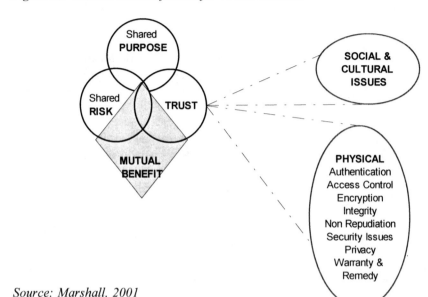

Source: Marshall, 2001

A survey of Thai business executives was conducted during the study. Twenty social and cultural factors were identified and examined. The survey findings confirm that in addition to the eight key factors identified by Western commentators, culture and social issues Western have had a significant impact on the adoption and the success of e-business in Thailand. Organizational infrastructure and English literacy were found to be the major internal and external barriers respectively to the adoption of e-business in Thailand.

Most e-business concerns currently relate to economic, technological, legal and regulatory issues. There should be more research into the social and cultural issues associated with electronic business. The business and technology focus needs to be complemented by greater attention to social and cultural considerations. V-business and ASPs are the latest additions to the e-business economy. Cultural and social issues, and in particular, *trust* will become more profound under the new generation of e-business activities. It is therefore recommended that more research be aimed in this direction.

REFERENCE

Agarwal, B. (2001). Defining the e-business model. Retrieved on October 16, 2001 from the World Wide Web: http://www.tanning.com/pressroom/publications/EBM_Final.pdf

Badre, A. B. (2000). The effects of cross cultural interface design orientation on World wide web user performance. *GVU Technical Report*, GIT-GVU-01.03.

Biscontri, R. (2001). Cutting through the business of culture. *Australian CPA, 71*(3),54-56.

Business in Thailand Online (1999a). On a slow boat to e-business (*Welcome to Business in Thailand Magazine*). Retrieved on August 21, 2000 from the World Wide Web: http://www.businessinthailandmag.com/archive/july99/4_editor.html

Business in Thailand Online (1999b). Thailand's journey to e-commerce (*Welcome to Business in Thailand Magazine*). Retrieved on August 21, 2000 from the World Wide Web: http://www.businessinthailandmag.com/archive/july99/34_infor.html

Chua, H. (2000). Don't be afraid to buy online (IT AsiaOne). Retrieved on September 4, 2000 from the World Wide Web: http://it.asia1.com.sg/specialsWire/shop002.html

Evans, C. (2000). E-strategy: A framework for e-business (World Capital Forum) Retrieved on January 21, 2001 from the World Wide Web: http://www.worldcapitalforum.com/esframforeb.html

Fleenor, C. P. & Raven, P. (2002). Barriers to effective e-business in developing countries. *The International Business & Economics Research Journal*, *1*(4), 39-47.

Global Reach (2002). Global Internet Statistics (by Language) Retrieved on July 15, 2002 from the World Wide Web: http://global-reach.biz/globstats/index.php3

Hong Kong Productivity Council (2001). A guide to personal data privacy and consumer protection on the internet. Retrieved on October 16, 2001, from the World Wide Web: http://www.hkispa.org.hk/pdf/guide-e.pdf

IDA Singapore (1998). Controller of certification authorities (untitled document). Retrieved on September 5, 2000 from the World Wide Web: http://www.cca.gov.sg/aboutus/bot_aboutus.html

Information Infrastructure Task Force IITF (2000). A framework of global electronic commerce. Retrieved on October 16, 2001 from the World Wide Web: http://iitf.doc.gov/eleccomm/execsu.htm

Input (1999). Buyers' guide to electronic commerce in south Asia (input). August. Retrieved on October 10, 2001 from the World Wide Web: http://www.input.com/buyers_guide/pc19s/pc19s_main.cfm

Introna, L. (2001). Recognizing the limitations of virtual organization. In S. Barn and B. Hunt, *E-Commerce & V-Business.* Oxford: Butterworth-Heinemann (pp. 268-277).

Kammeyer, M. (2001). The Other Customs Barrier: Cultural Research Avoids Business Blunder. Retrieved on February 13, 2002 from the World Wide Web: http://www.ita.doc.gov/exportamerica/Volumepercent202/Aprilpercent202001/im_customs.html

Kang, K.S. & Corbitt., B. (2001). Effectiveness of graphical components in web site e-commerce application - a cultural perspective, *EJISDC*, *7*(2), 1-6.

Koanantakool, T. (2000). Electronic commerce development in Thailand. Retrieved on December 17, 2001 from the World Wide Web: http://www.nectec.or.th/users/htk/e-commerce/intro.html

Legard, D. (2000, February). Outlook strong for Asia-Pacific e-commerce (IDG News Service). Retrieved on September 17, 2001 from the World Wide Web: http://www.security-informer.com/english/crd_data_439563.html

Marshall, P., Burn, J. & McKay, J. (2001). Structure, strategy and success factors for the virtual organization. In S. Barn and B., *Hunt E-Commerce & V-Business* (pp. 171–129). Oxford: Butterworth-Heinemann.

Merrill Lynch & Co., Inc. (2001). *Economic globalization and culture, a discussion with Dr. Francis Fukuyama.* Retrieved on February 13, 2002 from the World Wide Web: http://www.ml.com/woml/forum/global.htm

National Computer Board (Mauritius) (2001). Electronic commerce (Mauritius e-commerce hub). Retrieved on June 22, 2001 from the World Wide Web: http://ncb.intnet.mu/ncb/ecom/lmbarriers.htm (Last Updated January 17).

Pornpitakpan, C. (2000). Trade in Thailand: A three-way cultural comparison. *Business Horizons*. Retrieved on July 15, 2002 from the World Wide Web: http://www.findarticles.com/cf_0/m1038/2_43/61891232/p1/article.jhtml?term=trade+in+thailandpercent3A+A+three-way+culture+comparison

Sowinski, L. (2001). Global online supplement - Which countries are best positioned in the e-business race? Retrieved on October 16, 2001 from the World Wide Web: http://www.worldtrademag.com/CDA/ArticleInformation/features/BNP Features Item/0,3483,63039,00.html

Tan, K. (2000). E-commerce in Singapore (CNET Singapore). Retrieved on September 4, 2000 from the World Wide Web: http://singapore.cnet.com/Briefs/Guidebook/Ecommerce/

Chapter XV

The Impact of E-Business on the Competitive Landscape– Case of Automotive Industry in Asia

Amir Albadvi
Tarbiat Modarres University, Iran

ABSTRACT

This chapter focuses on the power and challenges of e-business in enhancing the competitive advantage in developing countries' industries and reports of some survey results in the Asian auto-industry. The study confirms that as many web-based businesses are learning that the real value of e-business comes not in the form of sales, but in removing inefficiencies in traditional business models. The study shows that currently, most auto manufacturers in Asia use e-business only for internal administration; despite all the talk of e-business, the development in Asia is slow. The current infrastructure in the industry is largely internally focused, incongruent with the customer-orientation of e-business. Furthermore, the author concluded that due to the uncertain nature of e-business, few companies understand how to integrate e-business into their corporate strategy in Asian developing countries. Companies need a clearly planned vision, starting with basic solutions. From there, the strategy will evolve to solutions in wider marketplaces.

INTRODUCTION

E-business is defined as a variety of market transactions that are enabled by information technology and represents the entire collection of actions that support commercial activities on a network (Zwass, 1999; Applegate et al., 1996). E-business is taking root in the competitive landscape. It is changing the shape of competition, the speed of action and the nature of leadership. It has already revolutionized the traditional way of doing business and has implied the redesign of core processes, e.g., in purchasing and marketing. It also introduced the important transformation and reaction of external relationships with partners and customers. Based on the new information and communication technologies, e-business can successfully be used to redefine a company's competitive position and to take advantages of new opportunities. Thus, the issue of whether and how to participate is high on the corporate agenda.

E-businesses are already allowing companies to dramatically cut their procurement costs. E-business enables seamless communication and collaboration between constitutions across vast distances. Along with horizontal integration, e-business facilitates vertical integration along the supply chain. Costs are lowered and market response time is reduced. Companies are able to find customers outside of a company's regular footprint. Forecasting the demand specifications are enhanced and industry standards are lifted and disparate channels and markets are integrated. Despite the plunge in business-to-business Internet stocks, many corporate leaders cling to the hope that their stakes in big e-marketplaces will give a boost to their companies' market capitalization. E-marketplaces will create value, but participants - not the e-marketplaces themselves - will capture the lion's share of that value. This economic reality will affect how e-marketplaces evolve and which ones will survive. The surviving e-marketplaces will be either major, broad-based players or niche competitors that provide specific products or functions (Lowy, Ticoll & Tapscott, 1998). The most cited reason why one might expect electronic markets to be more efficient than conventional markets is a reduction in information asymmetrics that arise from lower search costs. Economic theory predicts that high consumer search costs will lead to prices above marginal cost in equilibrium (Hotelling, 1929; Salop, 1979 for example). If electronic markets allow consumers to more easily determine retailers' prices and product offerings, these lower search costs will lead to lower prices for both homogeneous and differentiated goods (Bakos, 1997; Bakos & Brynjolfsson, 1999).

Low procurement costs and potential windfalls are not the reason why the emergence of business-to-business e-marketplaces matters. Procurement savings are important, but a large proportion of them will ultimately be passed on to the end customer. What does matter, is competitive advantages. E-business will have a tremendous impact on the competitive landscape. Online business-to-business marketplaces are growing very quickly, but realizing benefits will take more work and time than what many companies may recognize. Online collaboration services, the most promising area for e-businesses, are only beginning to come to the surface and just the most basic services are being offered today. Realizing the promised benefits of more sophisticated collaboration services will require companies to implement changes in systems, processes, culture, and behavior - a formidable task.

Naturally, the automotive industry has eyed these developments with great interest. The automotive industry today ranks among the most established and mature industries of the world. Recent consolidations will only further the well-established dominance of the big corporations. It is a global industry. Parts production, system and module composition, and car assembly take place virtually all over the world before a car is sold off the dealer's lot. Although car makers may not be the champions of fast change, the promise of e-business – and the companies that have recognized and exploited it – has set even the biggest car makers in motion. When all these changes take hold, it will alter irrevocably relationships throughout the automotive value chain. E-business in the Asian automotive industry is also emerging in many places, but on a smaller scale.

This chapter helps to explore the changes the e-business brings about and outlines the consequences for the corporations in Asian auto-industry. First, it underpins some challenges in this trend. It focuses on the power and challenges of e-business in auto industry and subsequently reports some results of a survey from Asian developing countries (including Japan) in this area. The main objective of this chapter is to gain insights from the survey on how car manufacturers in Asia are organizing and deriving benefit from e-business. The real value of e-business in Asian auto industry comes not in the form of sales but in removing inefficiencies in traditional business models.

THE RISE OF E-BUSINESS IN GLOBAL AUTO-INDUSTRY

Electronic linkages to support in global chains are typically implemented in auto-industry using Electronic Data Interchange (EDI), which provides a standardized format and structure for business documents in electronic form. While this standardization of the electronic documents provides some independence and generality among the auto-industry trading partners, the actual implementations, nonetheless, tend to involve a high amount of relationship specific investment (Lee, 2000). For the auto-industry where change is more dynamic, such relationship specific investments can become a hindrance to change. One of the most complex challenges for global auto-industry is in the area of global supply chains. In these cases, trading relationships are not only with other companies, who have similar competitive pressures, but also with a variety of governmental agencies involved in the regulation of import and export. The other challenges in this industry are customer-centric interactions. The Web offers unparalleled opportunities for customer-centric interaction in auto-industry, from data-mining behavioral information to using 'infomediaries,' incentives, and loyalty programs to provide and support mass customization (Raisinghani, 2000). According to a study of 250 Fortune 500 web sites by Palmer and Griffith (1998), marketing activities and strategies of corporations have been greatly affected by the internet. The internet has created a new marketing environment and a new distribution channel that enable organizations to establish a closer relationship with their customers. Global auto-industry is no exception.

Many authors (Cunningham and Tynan, 1993; Dearing, 1990; Johnston, 1998; Rochester, 1989) recognize that the significance of business-to-business electronic commerce in the supply chain is not just its ability to reduce direct operational costs (Colberg, 1990; Dearing, 1990), but also as an enabling technology for business process simplification (Johnston, 2000). At present, the main value of e-business in global auto industry comes from removing inefficiencies along the entire value chain and increasing direct customer communication. It facilitates:

- Improved forecasting of demand and market trends
- Fully integrated enterprise resource planning
- Possibility to integrate downstream industries
- Reduced inventory, cost and time
- Integrated customer relationship management

Many business analysts estimate substantial savings through e-business application in automotive industry. Savings per car derived from e-business applications in the US can add up to more than 10 percent of an average vehicle retail price. The savings mainly come from back end supply chain and direct online sales. Another five percent lies ahead in the built-to-order production which through flexible production planning offers a compromise between the differing needs of the sales and production functions. Built-to-order production is expected to cut excess production costs as well as lionizing customer demand by delivering timely, cost-effective products.

Funk (2001) provides an overview of the innovations the auto-industry has implemented thus far and will need to implement in response to the rise of e-business. He illustrates how these innovations change the automotive value chain in four different levels. At the first level, for car manufacturers to reach online customers, they must innovate in marketing. Manufacturers and independent parties initially created Web pages using multiple-choice options and 3-D virtual showroom technologies that enabled potential car buyers to configure their cars before entering the physical showroom. At the same time, manufacturers used advanced data mining techniques to identify which customer type is interested in which equipment features of the car. The second step in innovation is provided by the aforementioned online referral services for dealers. These innovative e-business models threaten to relegate traditional dealerships to mere pickup points for car buyers. In the third step of the innovation process, manufacturers have set up their own online services, planning and production can be optimized so that a new product can evolve. This development could conceivably branch off in a totally new direction, such as an Internet-equipped and information technology-stuffed vehicle – the PC on wheels. Finally, the sector arrives at the fourth level of innovation, where the entire business model can shift. Car manufacturers transform from product manufacturers to integrated service providers. The vehicle remains at the core of the offering, but it is surrounded by additional services such as mobility concepts and wireless internet access.

The above trend will also have tremendous impact on the value chain. E-business provides the efficient and timesaving tools to speed information from consumers to manufacturers and suppliers. The business-to-consumer interface is improved through the marketing innovations of car configurators or one-stop shopping opportunities that include financing, insurance, and extended warranty. The business-to-business interfaces between the manufacturer and first-tier suppliers of modules or systems, as well as suppliers on the following tiers, are organized through electronic marketplaces. Two mutually connected extranets will reduce coordination and modification costs and realize the targeted order-to-delivery time span (Funk, 2001).

In North America and Europe, there are already many examples of e-activities in key business areas of automotive industry; e.g., collaborative engineering, electronic marketplaces, improved supply chain and distribution. In this regard, e-business is going to reshape the competitive landscape of auto industry in these areas, the companies that transform their businesses most aggressively to use e-business and influence their evolution, stand to gain the most. Sellers can use the new markets to change competitive dynamics more than they realize. And as buyers are beginning to recognize, e-marketplaces represent more than a means of exacting lower prices from suppliers. Over time, many of the benefits gathered by e-business will flow to the end customer. This means that early movers that can overcome the implementation challenges will have the greatest opportunity to capture and retain most of the benefits.

TRENDS FOR THE FUTURE

Berger and Gattorna (2001) considered the future trends in automotive industry while envisioning the future of supply chains, and identified different key trends that they believe will continue to transform automotive industry. They stated that the traditional bricks-and-mortar car and component manufacturers need to reinvent themselves to embrace the age of the Internet. Change in these companies will be driven by the growing visibility of the best getting better and the rest getting worse. As traditional companies realize the implications of the changes required to remain competitive, there will be a new wave of outsourcing and alliances that will fundamentally change the nature and composition of auto-industry.

The trend toward new types of supply chain service providers is likely to accelerate and be dominated by two types of companies: those that specialize in owning and operating core assets and those that specialize in supply chain optimization services in auto-industry. The supply chain asset companies will focus on consolidating assets that serve multiple companies across the industry. Their competence will be rationalizing assets and providing low-cost service operations. Asset operations will become more global once the earlier stages of regional rationalization are achieved. Supply chain companies that specialize in supply chain optimization are still in early stages of development. They have their roots in clicks-and-mortar concept and develop their expertise by applying advanced information technology to optimization problems such as effective 24-hour delivery of slow-moving parts on a global basis. A new type of smarter supply chain operator will be driving these companies. The supply chain optimization specialists will take responsibility for managing complex cross-company optimization services, collecting data from multiple organizations in auto-industry, and analysing and optimizing operations on a real-time basis. Berger and Gottorna (2001, p. 186) see these companies operating command centres that are not unlike those of a military operations room. Their challenge will be to optimize complex supply chains, increasingly in real time, to help companies synchronize operations.

It is almost certainly true that the world of tomorrow will belong to those who are brave enough to move early and decisively. Inspirational leadership will be an essential ingredient for success. New emerging technologies in e-business will strengthen the supply chain of the auto-industry as we move into value chain competition. The auto-industry will explore a range of waves of change, mostly driven by e-business technologies, that are having an impact on the ways in which companies compete with each other. The intensity of these waves is high, posing significant challenges for business. However, even as business leaders respond to today's challenges, they must also keep an eye on the horizon for the first signs of the waves to come. Beyond such monitoring, those companies that can influence the future of their industry will surely dominate.

THE SURVEY

In order to study the power and challenges of e-business in enhancing competitive advantage for the auto-industry, an electronic survey has been conducted in the automotive companies in Asia. The survey developed through the web which had the advantage of reduced cost and reduced response time compared with mail-out surveys or interview (Benjamin, 1995). At the first stage research objectives and research scope were clearly defined. The conceptual framework for the survey was built around four stages of e-business illustrated by Arthur D. Little's Michael Taylor as follows (Varney and McCarthy, 1996):

Stage 1: Companies digitize internal data. It is a publishing model without a significant impact on business processes.

Stage 2: Companies start thinking about re-engineering a part of the business process. Integration with back-end systems begins.

Stage 3: Companies move into original content, which may be highly interactive. With the goal of one-to-one marketing, a company seeks to develop profiles of users accessing its sites so they can be treated uniquely.

Stage 4: Companies that are fully enabled, seek to achieve dynamic segmentation, in addition to developing basic user profiles. Specifically, segmentation of site visitors is done in real time, based on user activity. The internet's ability to function as a micromarketing channel is also questioned during the survey (Raisinghani, 2000).

The survey covered 10 countries across Asia Pacific and was conducted in four different languages—English, Japanese, Korean and Chinese—over a 16-week period. In total, 112 responses were received from major OEMs, component suppliers, dealers and portals. Designing the research questions and their measurement scales were the next step. Key questions on automotive e-business development survey in Asia were as follows:

- What are the key drivers of Asian automotive e-business strategies?
- How far along is e-business infrastucture in Asian automotive companies?
- How much e-business investment is being planned in the next five years?
- What are the e-business challenges foreseen for implementation in Asia?
- Will e-business scale in Asia reach Western levels in the next five years?
- How will the e-business roles change in the auto B2B/B2C space in Asia?

After pre-testing the questionnaire to confirm that the questions and their measurements are appropriate, correct and understandable, a web form was designed to contain the research questions. A web server was developed to collect and process the research data electronically. As an extention to the web server, server scripts were also programmed in order to process and analyse the research data. The result of the survey shed some important insights to the above key questions.

SURVEY RESULTS

The survey confirms that increased customer interaction is the top reason driving internet strategy for Asian auto companies. For the OEMs and suppliers, closer customer contact and supply chain and e-procurement cost savings are the main drivers. For the dealers, getting closer to existing customers and providing greater reach are the focal points for e-strategy. However, given the disparity among Asian auto markets, e-business value savings will differ from market to market. For example in Japan, supply chains are generally more effective than in the US, marginalizing e-business gains. The savings in Japan would come in its expensive distribution channel, where the many layers of middlemen could be bypassed using e-business. Throughout Asia, e-business is predicted to lower costs by one third in procurement, supply chain and average transaction costs.

The surveys revealed a questionable commitment to e-business in the Asian auto industry. Currently, most auto manufacturers use e-business only for internal administration (see Figure 1), and devote less than 0.5% of their total revenues to e-business infrastructure and processes. For suppliers in the industry, this figure is even lower. Despite all the talks of e-business, the development has been slow, with only 5-15% of IT budgets devoted to e-business. The current infrastructure in the industry is largely internally focused, incongruent to customer-orientation of e-business.

The survey shows that the e-business market in Asia is different. In Asia the proportion of car sales influenced by the internet is much lower than those of the US and the EU (15% vs 40%). There is a large gap in affordability, with the number of months' salary to buy a car in Asia often 10 times higher than the same figure in the West. While the US market has been purchasing goods on the internet for a couple of years, Asian web users have yet to perform many consumer and business transactions on the web. Culturally, Asians prefer to base consumer and business decisions on personal relationships. The region suffers from a shortage of skilled human resources, as well as a lack of economic scale. Middleman remain dominant in Asian commerce, and hinder the development of e-business in the region. All of these factors have led to an internet immaturity in the region, and demand for multinationals to develop a proprietary business model for the region.

According to the survey results, Internal conflict of interest was cited as a key obstacle to implementing e-business strategy . At the regional level, challenges to the expansion of e-business in Asia can be summarized as follows:

Figure 1. Current share of OEMs indicating level of e-enablement and its future

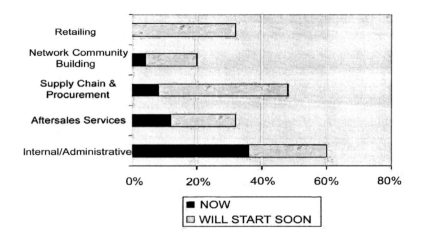

- There is shortage of human resources, especially in non-Japanese markets.
- Connectivity is still low due to the high proportion of poverty in the region.
- There are obstacles crossing the many cultural boundaries in the region to achieve a sufficient level of transparency.
- There is little standardization across markets.
- Intellectual property protection measures are still lacking in most of the countries in the region.

At the industry level, there are also major e-business implementation bottlenecks across Asia:
- Manufacturers risk alienating dealers as they replace elements of their function with portal sites.
- How to pass savings on to customers.
- E-procurement is not easy for engineered materials.
- Organizational maturity of many suppliers is lacking.
- The integration of several differing legacy systems is a difficult and expensive process.
- There is conflict of interest with existing infrastructure.
- Organizing sales around infrastructure threatens to up-end the current system.
- The Internet only provides the means to communicate; some companies are not necessarily willing to share information.

CONCLUSION

Not all companies are ready to board the e-train. While the technology is changing every six months, and with the future of that technology still uncertain, companies in Asia find it futile to try and grasp the mercurial e-business. They propose to wait for a few years to see what actually works, rather than start the IT projects that require constant capital investments to maintain. These companies are now starting to feel the crunch from their lack of judgment. An internet year is equivalent to around two weeks, such that waiting for an extended period to join the trend can be fatal. The internet wave is moving into its second phase after the first euphoric explosion. The new e-business companies come armed with solid business plans, proven industry professionals, and pose a real threat to the industry's established companies. As these new competitors develop their e-business processes, customers are being trained away from traditional business practices, essentially phasing laggards out of their markets. While many of these companies fail, they are pushing technological thresholds, antiquating traditional companies' business models in the process. Benefits of e-business are rarely in the form of additional revenues. The capacity for originality on the internet should be exercised. Without developing something new, companies risk copying existing material, thereby limiting the appeal of their effort. Expectations are difficult to quantify, and are often too impatient. Seeking immediate benefits, companies adopt e-business in areas outside of core competencies, hoping either to boost revenues or to sell off the successful entity for millions of dollars. E-business is not a silver bullet; it takes time to realize the benefits, just like any new business practice.

The challenges the automotive industry in Asia faces with regard to the e-business age are enormous. Adequate moves have not been made in the right direction in Asian auto-industry. The industry's characteristic lack of flexibility makes implementing the fast decision-making processes needed for e-business difficult. The trial and error approaches are in stark contrast to the long-term strategic planning to which car makers are accustomed. It seems that the apparent answer is not to build the e-business from within, but from outside the organization. Those companies that become stuck in internal politics and develop risk-minimization strategies will miss the e-train entirely. Therefore, car manufacturers are being forced to form flexible decision-making structures as quickly as possible.

The reality is that there are many challenges and obstacles for e-business in the Asian auto industry and many losers in this trend are still to come. The biggest winner in the Asian auto industry's eventual transition to e-business practices will be the customer, who will enjoy greater convenience, less sales pressure, more choices, increased visibility, more information and lower prices.

REFERENCES

Applegate, L.M., McFarlan, F.W. & McKenney, J.L. (1996). *Corporate Information Systems Management: Text and Cases*. Homewood, IL: Richard D. Irwin.

Bakos, J. Y. (1998). Reducing buyer search costs: implications for electronic marketplaces. *Management Science, 43*(12).

Bakos, J. Y. & Brynjolfsson, E. (1999). Bundling information goods. *Management Science, 45*(11).

Benjamin, R.I. (1995). Electronic markets and virtual chains on the information super highway. *Sloan Management Review, 36*(2), 62-72.

Berger, A.J. & Gattorna, J.L. (2001). *Supply Chain Cybermastery: Building High Performance Supply Chain of the Future*. England: Grower Publishing Limited.

Colberg, T.P. (1990). The compelling case for EDI. *The Financial Manager, 3*(1), 20-26.

Cunningham, C. & Tynan, C. (1993). Electronic trading, inter-organizational systems and the nature of buyer-seller relationships: the need for a network perspective. *International Journal of Information Management, 6*(3), 73-77.

Dearing, B. E. (1990). The strategic benefits of EDI. *The Journal of Business Strategy, 11*(1), 4-6.

Funk, J. (2001). *Automotive Industry: Automotive Giants Get Ready for the e-Business Age*. In A. Landmann, H. Wolters, W. Bernhart & H. Harsten (Eds.), *The Future of the Automotive Industry: Challenges and Concepts for the 21st Century*. Warrendale, PA: Society of Automotive Engineers, Inc.

Hotelling, H. (1929, March). Stability in competition. *The Economic Journal,* 41-57.

Johnston, R.B. (1998). *Trading Systems and Electronic Commerce*. Melbourne: Eruditions Publishing.

Johnston, R.B. (2000). Principles of digitally mediated replenishment of goods: Electronic commerce and supply chain reform. In S.M. Rahman & M.S. Raisinghani (Eds.), *Electronic Commerce: Opportunity and Challenges*. Hershey, PA: Idea Group Publishing.

Lee, Ronald M. (2000). Electronic trade scenario for global supply chains. In S.M. Rahman & M.S. Raisinghani (Eds.), *Electronic Commerce: Opportunity and Challenges*. Hershey, PA: Idea Group Publishing.

Lowy, A., Ticoll, D. & Tapscott (eds.) (1998). *Blue Print to the Digital Economy*. New York: McGraw Hill.

Palmer, J.W. & Griffith, D.A. (1998). An emerging model of web site design for marketing. *Communications of ACM, 41*(3), 44-51.

Raisinghani, M.S. (2000). Electronic commerce at the dawn of the third millennium. In S.M. Rahman & M.S. Raisinghani (Eds.), Electronic commerce: Opportunity and challenges. Hershey, PA: Idea Group Publishing.

Rochester, J.B. (1989). The strategic value of EDI. *I/S Analyser, 27*(8), 1-14.

Salop, S. (1979). Monopolistic competition with outside goods. *Bell Journal of Economics, 10*, 141-156.

Varney, S.E. & McCarthy, V. (1996). E-commerce: Wired for profits. *Datamation, 42*(16), 43-50.

Zwass, V. (1999). *Foundations of Information Systems*. NY: Harcourt Brace Publishing Co.

Chapter XVI

Job Satisfaction in the Information and Communication Sector: The Case of Egypt

Marwa El-Ayouti
Maastricht School of Management, The Netherlands

Sherif Kamel
The American University in Cairo, Egypt

ABSTRACT

The information and communication technology industry is growing worldwide, penetrating all sectors and services. Therefore, organizations are formulating different formulas and mechanisms to provide a competitive and challenging working environment to attract the best human resources around the globe to join their infrastructure build-up in terms of humanware. Egypt, as a developing country, has been investing heavily in building its information and communication technology infrastructure with a focus on human resources. However, many organizations are continually faced with various challenges to keep their key human resources due to the emerging offerings and opportunities at various levels locally, regionally and internationally. This chapter presents the findings of a research that was conducted in Egypt in 2001 with a primary objective to understand the overall level of job satisfaction among employees in the ICT sector in Egypt. The research aimed at identifying the major factors that affect their satisfaction and highlighting the driving forces leading to the "brain drain" of skilled ICT professionals to jobs overseas.
The research assesses the major aspects affecting job satisfaction and ranks them by importance. Moreover, the empirical evidence illustrates the willingness of ICT professionals to seek job opportunities abroad, and the major forces leading to brain drain. Within the

scope of the research, job satisfaction is studied as a function of four groups of job aspects, namely, economic, social, training and development, and psychological aspects. Economic aspects cover variables such as pay, rewards and benefits. Social aspects include relationships with colleagues, teamwork and working conditions. Training and development covers the amount of training received by employees and their access to technologies. Psychological aspects include factors such as interest and scope of work, challenges and disciplinary procedures. The survey was conducted among ICT professionals employed in key ICT companies operating in Egypt, as well as companies in other sectors including financial institutions including organizations from the private sector, governmental organizations and multinational firms. The research is important to assess the problems faced by many organizations in Egypt due to the brain drain of its skilled ICT professionals to jobs overseas due to clearer career paths and advancement opportunities, better access to new technologies and higher pay. Respectively, the findings of the research represent important guidelines for various organizations to be able to retain its ICT skilled professionals in Egypt and similar environments.

OVERVIEW

The past few years were marked with explosive growth in the information technology sector. The phenomenon of rapid integration of technologies by massive businesses and the increasing importance of information and communication technology[1] for economic development and advancement has created a globally significant increase in demand for highly skilled information technology expertise. ICT workers are needed in nearly every industry, whereby many computer scientists, computer engineers, systems analysts and computer programmers work for governmental institutions, insurance companies, academic and financial institutions. In order to maintain competitive edges and cost-efficient operations, high tech and non-technology companies and institutions are competing for the same workers. On the other hand, the supply of such employees grew at a slower pace, thus further raising global competition among companies and employers. This shortage in ICT professionals has plagued the sector by enormous levels of employee turnover, and job-hopping from one company to another and from one country to another.

The fierce and global competitive market has created high escalations in salaries paid to ICT professionals, whereby labor employed in the ICT sector has become relatively paid better off than others in similar positions in different industries. Natarjan (2000) asserts that the ICT sector has clearly different measures than other sectors. For example, a fresh graduate with minimal ICT knowledge is paid more than an executive in other fields. Respectively, the concept of rewards has undergone a sea change in the information age (Natarjan, 2000).

It is important to note that employers in this tight labor market have been suffering from high turnover rates and difficulties in employee recruitment, retention, and retraining. Furthermore, the global competition has led to a case of "brain drain," whereby countries are losing their most skilled professionals to other countries. In that context, the brain drain scenario has been significant in the IT sector in Egypt, whereby the majority of skilled employees have been seeking jobs abroad aiming for higher pay and more opportunities for training and development. With the increasing importance of the industry in Egypt, failure to meet demand for IT professionals could have severe consequences for the economy's competitiveness and growth, thus creating urging needs to retain skilled professionals and meet their needs. Battey (2000) states that there is a need to find out what people want and try to give it to them. The significant growth of the ICT industry in Egypt over the past few years has created a rising need and demand for highly skilled ICT professionals. The fact that this enormous level of demand is eminent at a worldwide scale creates a critical importance of acquiring and retaining these skills. Additionally, the growing importance of ICT to economic growth and development makes it necessary to maintain local ICT specialists within the country.

Respectively, motivating employees and creating a high level of job satisfaction can achieve retaining ICT professional skills. In accomplishing this target, it is necessary to study the current level of employee job satisfaction in the ICT sector in Egypt, and identify the key job aspects that affect their satisfaction. Furthermore, it is essential to understand the key factors that drive skilled labor to seek job opportunities abroad. Understanding underlying job satisfaction factors and drivers in this research will help ICT companies better meet employee needs so as to retain company staff.

The main objective of this research is to use theoretical and empirical evidence to understand the overall level of job satisfaction among ICT professionals in Egypt, identifying the major factors that affect their satisfaction, and highlight the key driving forces leading to the brain drain of skilled ICT professionals to jobs abroad. The research focuses on ICT sector in Egypt, which has not been an issue previously considered. The research attempts to study whether Egyptian ICT employees are satisfied or not with their jobs; and, whether that encourages them to look for job opportunities abroad or not. The research was developed through the conduct of a case study that includes a set of surveys and interviews covering a sample size of 110 respondents in addition to secondary data that was not comprehensive in the case of covering the market in Egypt due to lack of documentation. In that respect, the conduct of the research had a number of limitations that included lack of resources and statistics available on the ICT sector in Egypt such as number of companies and number of employees in the sector. There were only a few publications about the sector however the content was not comprehensive[2]. Moreover, limitations included lack of publications about the issue of job satisfaction in the ICT sector in particular. Additionally, certain multinational firms had restrictions on conducting employee surveys inside their companies. Finally, the number of people willing to answer an online questionnaire was very limited, thus creating a high fallout rate for questionnaires distributed online.

JOB SATISFACTION IN THE ICT SECTOR— A GLOBAL PERSPECTIVE

Job satisfaction is among the most difficult concepts to define in the field of organizational behavior. Various definitions and means of measurement have been developed; however, there is no one specific definition that has been used to directly describe the concept. Job satisfaction has been defined as:

- An affective state resulting from fulfillment of a need or removal of a tension that is caused by a need in the job context (Dunnettee, 1976).
- The collection of attitudes that employees have about their jobs (Johns, 1988).
- A collection of related job attitudes that can be related to various job aspects (Hellriegel, 1998).

Job satisfaction can be defined as the feeling a worker has about his job. Johns classifies job satisfaction into two major aspects: facet and overall satisfaction. With respect to facet satisfaction[3], it relates to employees tendency to be more or less satisfied with various facets of the job (Johns, 1988). Facet satisfaction affects a person's attitude towards his job. Research suggests that the most relevant attitudes toward jobs are contained in a small group of facets including the work itself, pay, promotions, recognition, and benefits, working conditions, supervisions, co-workers and organizational policy (Johns, 1988). As for overall satisfaction, it is the overall combined indicator of a person's attitude towards his or her job, weighing out the various facets (Johns, 1998). It is an average of the attitudes held towards various facets of the job. Johns (1998) states that two workers may express the same level of overall satisfaction. However, they may have different attitudes towards separate facets that offset each other overall.

Various theories have been developed to explain job satisfaction. These studied include Maslow's need hierarchy theory, Alderfer's need theory (existence-relatedness-growth theory, reinforcement theory, expectancy theory, goal setting theory and the equity theory. Each of these theories follows a different model in understanding motivation and job satisfaction, relating to job aspects from different perspectives. Job satisfaction differs across industries and sectors. Such a concept also applies in the world of information and communication technology. Battey (2000) states that ICT employees must feel satisfied with their jobs or they are out the door. Additionally, in today's environment, where demand for network professionals far outstrips supply, resulting in an escalation of salaries, there is sometimes no substitute for adequate and competitive monetary rewards (Blum, 2000). Job satisfaction in the technology field is generally linked to the establishment's stake in keeping on the forefront of technological development, thus a stake in exposing its employees to the same. Without such interest, organizations will quickly lose grip on new happenings and drag its employees into obsolescence, which will result in lower compensation for employees and thus, dissatisfaction (Blum, 2000).

JOB SATISFACTION IN THE ICT MARKET

A survey of 1,500 chief information officers (CIOs) in 21 countries, conducted by Deloitte and Touche Consulting Group, showed that ICT managers throughout the world are experiencing a difficult combination of unprecedented demand for ICT workers and high turnover rates (Mitchell et al., 1997). The US Department of Commerce – Office of Technology Policy has also stated in a published report that the shortage of ICT workers is not only within the borders of the United States. Various other studies document a worldwide shortage of ICT workers. According to a survey conducted by the Indianapolis Business Journal, almost all ICT professionals ranked the shortage of skilled technical talent as the top problem facing the industry (Pletz, 1998). Due to the tight labor market, Battey (2000) emphasizes that high-tech talent in the information and communication fields should be retained. With the increasing importance of ICT professionals, failure to meet demand for ICT professionals could have severe consequences for the economy's competitiveness, growth and job creation. Evidence used to prove the emerging shortage first focuses on the upward pressure on salaries. There has been a recognized substantial salary increase in ICT professions rising with the competition for skilled labor. Based on a compensation survey conducted for the Information Technology Association of America (ITAA), by William M. Mercer, the average hourly compensation for computer network professionals rose by approximately 20 percent from 1995 to 1996, while Deloitte and Touche Consulting Group revealed a 7.4 percent increase in salaries from 1996 to 1997 (Mitchell et al., 1997).

In an online survey (with 941 respondents) conducted by Computerworld, the majority proved to be happy and loyal to their companies. However, they felt undervalued by their employers, receive little communication on how they can contribute and are overworked (Ouellette, 2000). Besides a positive perception of jobs, job satisfaction involves several factors that directly and indirectly influence it; such factors include tangible and moral motivators, perception of supervisors, and working conditions. There is no one theory that examines all the different factors affecting job satisfaction. Locke's (1976) extensive review of the literature indicates that the most important factors affecting job satisfaction are: mentally challenging work, equitable rewards, supportive working conditions and supportive colleagues (Robbins, 1989).

Mentally challenging work implies that employees prefer jobs where they can use their skills and abilities offer a variety of tasks, freedom and received feedback on how well they are performing. Little challenge at work creates boredom while too much challenge creates frustration and feelings of failure; however, moderate challenge creates maximum satisfaction (Robbins, 1989). Hellriegel (1998) refers to these job aspects as Growth-Need Strength, which is the degree to which an individual desires the opportunity for self-direction, learning and personal accomplishments at work. In a report published by IT World (2001), pay (within the ICT industry) is not a key motivating factor as long as it compares to industry standards, the important issue is how challenging their job is and how much room there is to grow and learn, which was indicated by 718 respondents representing 48 percent of the total response.

Equitable rewards and fair pay relative to work performed are necessary for satisfaction. When individuals perceive the fair pay systems and promotion policies in line with their expectations and worth, the job demands, and individual skill levels, satisfaction is likely to result. Pay is not necessarily measured by the absolute amount one is paid; instead, it is the perception of fairness (Robbins, 1989). It should also be noted that not all people demand high pay. Some workers are certainly willing to accept less physically demanding work, fewer working hours, or less responsibility for lower pay (Johns, 1988). In a Computer World's Survey, respondents linked recognition to performance (Ouellette, 1999). Blum (2000) reports that more than 50 percent of the respondents are satisfied with their salaries however 33 percent are dissatisfied. When looking at equitable rewards, less than 50 percent of the respondents stated that they are satisfied with the relation between their salaries and their performance. In an article published by Info World (1999), the author mentioned that compensation could be used as a benchmark for value; however, it remains as one piece of the puzzle when it comes to job satisfaction and staff motivation. The literature indicates that compensation is ranked as the top priority by only 29 percent of the respondents (Info World, 1999). Natarjan (2000) argues that many ICT employees join jobs even at low salaries, considering it an opportunity to update their knowledge and to be used to their own advantage. Respectively, job satisfaction has different connotations for people in the ICT sector adding some parameters such as salary, perks, stock options, profit-sharing, work atmosphere, promotions, supervision, nature of work have different rankings for ICT employees.

Supportive working conditions exist when individuals have a work environment that creates personal comfort and facilitates doing a good job (Robbins, 1989). Supportive colleagues are more of an intangible achievement whereby individuals fill their need for social interaction at work. Having friendly and supportive co-workers leads to increased job satisfaction. In addition, the supervisor's behavior is an essential part of a worker's satisfaction (Robbins, 1989). Results of Lucent NetworkCare survey show that 88 percent of respondents are satisfied with their relationship with co-workers and 77 percent are satisfied with the relationships with their supervisors. Respondents claimed that the most important element in their job satisfaction is the degree to which management shows its interests in the opinions and well being of their employees (Blum, 2000).

Table 1 shows the results of a number of ICT professionals' job satisfaction surveys including Computer World 2000 Job Satisfaction Survey; 2000 InfoWorld Compensation Survey; 2001 ITPRC Poll and Lucent NetworkCare' network professionals 2000 job satisfaction survey. The outcome shows that respondents ranked job aspects by importance including training, advancement and growth opportunities as critical factors in the satisfaction of ICT professionals. Additionally, equitable rewards such as salaries and bonuses are also essential job aspects.

There is strong evidence that high job satisfaction is associated with lower turnover, reduced absenteeism, and more positive work-related acts, whereas dissatisfaction often leads to various negative attitudes such as absenteeism, turnover and lower job performance, which negatively affect organizations (Lincoln and Kalleberg, 1990). The Harvard Business Review reports that a 5 percent increase in retention results in a 10 percent decrease in cost and an increase in productivity ranging from 25 percent to 65 percent (Albuquerque, 1999). Robbins (1989) states that employees' dissatisfaction can be expressed in a number of ways including employees can quit, complain, be insubordinate, steal organizational property or shirk a part of their job responsibilities. These expressions are grouped into four responses that differ from one another along two dimensions: constructiveness or destructiveness and activity or passivity. The literature demonstrates that employee turnover in the ICT sector varies. For example, the 2000 Lucent NetworkCare survey shows that 59 percent of the respondents have been with their current employer for less than two years, thus showing a high turnover rate and reflecting the high level of demand (Blum, 2000). Moreover, based on the results of Computer World's Survey, approximately 89 percent of respondents indicated that they were not willing to leave their jobs (Ouellette, 2000).

Table 1. Ranking of job aspects by importance

Ranking of Job Aspect by Highest Importance	Computer World (Ouellette, 2000) n = 941	InfoWorld (Battey, 2000)	ITPRC (The ITPRC Poll , 2001)	Lucent NetworkCare (Blum, 2000) n = 271
1	Salaries	Telecommuting	Salaries	Training and opportunity to learn new skills
2	Bonuses	Opportunity for advancement	Learning opportunities	Type of work
3	Training	Formal ICT training	Type of work	Job success
4	Access to new technologies	Defined career path	People	Growth opportunities
5	Opportunity for advancement	Flexible work schedules	Advancement opportunities	Monetary Recognition

Blum (2000) stated that by providing training and non-monetary awards, firms could spell the difference between losing talented people and maintaining a stable workforce. The best weapon against rapid turnover is to increase job satisfaction using strategies that can mollify the need to compete for network professionals solely on monetary terms (Blum, 2000). In further explaining the high turnover rates, as a general trend, Maister (1997) states that it is no longer unethical, or even unusual, for young professionals to move between firms to advance their careers: in all professions, the mobility of individuals is on the rise.

In the case of Egypt, Elamrani (2000) states that despite high demand for ICT employees, ICT companies still need to deal with a human resources issue. Recruitment experts argue that the international shortage of human resources in the ICT sector should force local salaries to become more competitive. In Egypt, human resources managers of ICT companies are already struggling to maintain ICT professionals on their payrolls and the level of employee turnover in most companies' ranges from one and a half to two years (Elamrani, 2000). The information technology revolution in the West is growing at a very high pace, and demand is too high, further encouraging the migration of Egyptian employees. According to an article published in the *Financial Times* in August 2000, Western Europe and Japan are short of 60,000 and 200,000 ICT professionals respectively (Elamrani, 2000). In the case of the US, the shortage is 175,0000 ICT professionals. In the case of Egypt, it is believed that the high ICT turnover should not be difficult to settle down, and enticing ICT specialists to stay at home should not be difficult because the cost of creating ICT jobs in Egypt is relatively low (costing US$20,000, versus US$250,000 in the US). By creating the jobs, ICT specialists in Egypt would have more job security, and thus would not seek opportunities abroad (Elamrani, 2000).

During the last 20 years, Egypt has experienced rapid improvements in its ICT sector, with vast developments and investments taking place in its communications and information infrastructure. The government of Egypt has become a major user of ICT, and intends to further expand public sector demand and use of ICT services. Moreover, the growth of the private sector has been characterized by the establishment of a significant number of start-ups as well as the entry of several multinational high tech companies, either as representative offices, branches or even through project participations with both the public and private sectors. Statistics published by the US-Egypt Presidents' Council in 2000 indicate a 32 percent growth in the ICT market in Egypt over the past five years (www.us-egypt.org, 2000). The sector's growing importance has driven up demand for ICT professionals. Currently, the ICT labor market employs a total workforce of around 5000 professionals (www.mcit.gov.eg, 2001). The distribution of these employees is assumed to be 2000 professionals employed in multinational firms such as Microsoft, IBM, and Oracle among others, 2000 in the local software development firms and 1000 in supporting firms that provide training and consulting in the sector (Information Technology Landscape, 2000). Market requirements forecast that an additional 5,000 ICT professionals are needed every year for at least 10 years to be able to sustain the growing local demand.

Numerous efforts have been allocated to develop the human capital required to meet growing industry needs. Kamel (1997) stated that the increasing role of human resources in ICT received focal attention in 1985, with nation-wide efforts adopted through establishments of several training and professional development institutions governed by the Cabinet of Egypt, Information and Decision Support Center (IDSC). Kamel further indicated that these development efforts have resulted in training over 50,000 individuals during the period 1986-1989 and that more was expected in the years to follow. In addition to these national developments, multinational firms have also highly invested in human capital during the past couple of years (Hamroush and El Sineity, 2000). Despite the increasing competitiveness of the ICT labor market in Egypt, the market has been witnessing the global brain drain phenomenon, whereby ICT employees have been seeking better job opportunities abroad for various reasons such as higher pay, better career paths and better chances to further develop their skills. Countries including the US, Canada and Germany have recently facilitated and encouraged the immigration of ICT professionals through newly introduced immigration policies. Moreover, employee turnover has been significant among local employers, whereby attractive and competitive job offerings have been moving employees around from one company to another. In order to reduce the loss of highly skilled labor and minimize the risks and costs associated with high employee turnover, it is essential to understand the elements contributing to the employees' satisfaction and identify the forces that drive them to seek opportunities abroad. This would enable ICT organizations to better meet their staffing requirements and retain their most valuable assets.

CASE STUDY: SATISFACTION IN THE ICT MARKET IN EGYPT

The objective of the study was to test the level of job satisfaction among ICT professionals in Egypt through identifying their key motivational factors, as well as further understanding their willingness to seek job opportunities abroad. An empirical investigation was carried out attempting to answer the research question and test the formulated research hypotheses. The study is best described as an exploratory quantitative case study, aiming at understanding and gaining insights on the level of job satisfaction in the ICT sector in Egypt. Primary data needed were mainly collected through an employee survey conducted using self-administered questionnaires and personal interviews. Additionally, secondary data was used to explain the theoretical concepts of job satisfaction, as well as benchmarking with other surveys previously conducted in the field. In order to collect sufficient information to cover various segments of the ICT sector, it was necessary to select a relatively large and diverse random sample representing private, public and multinational companies operating in Egypt. Furthermore, because ICT professionals are employed in various industries, it was necessary to additionally include a diverse sample, employed in different industries, such as financial institutions, telecommunications, retail and service providers. In obtaining a representative sample, it was necessary to further classify the sample by job titles, years of experience, gender and age. Therefore, both organizational sampling (based on the nature of company) as well as employee sampling (based on employee demographics) were used for this survey.

The total sample size used in the analysis was 110 ICT professionals, including 100 questionnaires and 10 interviews. The self-administered questionnaire was circulated among 75 ICT professionals, whereas the online questionnaire was mailed to a mailing list of 180 employees. The response rate for the self-administered questionnaire was 87 percent, as for the online questionnaire; the response rate was 19 percent. Survey respondents represent a cross-section of industries, primarily led by IT and telecommunication companies. In this case, it was difficult to select a stratified sample, due to the nature of the sample. Organizations also included multinational service providers, government agencies, information centers, financial institutions and retailers. It is important to note that the sampling considered a number of elements including gender, age, years of experience in ICT as well as in managerial and technical capacities and expertise. Interviews were conducted with 10 senior level ICT executives and professionals. With respect to the questionnaire, they mainly included structured close-ended questions; as for open-ended questions, they were mainly addressed in personal interviews. The questionnaire was divided into three sections; the first covered personal information, the second section addressed the aspects related to the level of satisfaction or dissatisfaction and the third section covered the level of importance of job aspects. All rating scales for close-ended questions were based on the Likert rating having five scale categories.

Figure 1 demonstrates the conceptual framework, developed based on the literature covered, and used in the study analyzing job satisfaction in the ICT sector in Egypt and further understanding the willingness and key motivational factors driving the employees to seek work opportunities abroad. The model groups the various job factors (pay, rewards, promotion, motivational schemes, mentally challenging work, training and development, keeping up with new technologies, people - management, colleagues and work teams, equality, working conditions and work environment) into four major groups, namely economic, social, psychological, and training/development: Job Satisfaction = f (economic, social, psychological, training).

The questionnaire used in the survey was constructed based on the four groups of variables, whereby data collected would indicate respondents' levels of satisfaction with job

Figure 1. Conceptual framework

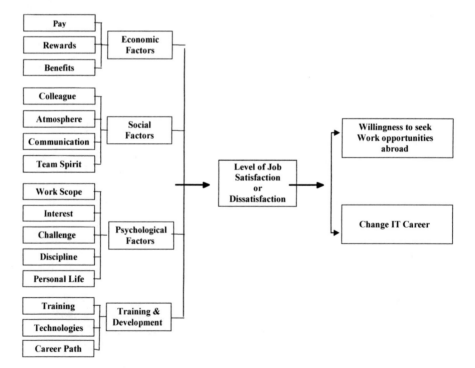

aspects as well as their ranking for each. The questionnaire used was successful in gathering the sufficient information needed, covering:

- the satisfaction and the importance of economic aspects (pay, rewards, benefits)
- social aspects (relations with colleagues, team work and support, working conditions and interdepartmental communications)
- psychological aspects (interest and scope of work, challenges, disciplinary procedures, working hours)
- personal versus professional life balance
- scope for own input for decision making
- aspects related to training and development (amount of training received, access to new technologies, career path) as shown in Table 2.

The data collected was analyzed using statistical models. The job facets were analyzed, both, separately and as combined groups of aspects with an objective to identify the importance of each factor to individuals, and understanding the level of satisfaction held by individuals for each factor. Job aspect ranking by importance and by degree of satisfaction was also undergone based on separate factors as well as on groups of related aspects. Ranking the four groups of aspects by importance and by degree of satisfaction allowed for performing a gap analysis aiming at identifying the factors with highest disparity between importance and satisfaction. Further analysis was undergone, comparing the importance and degree of satisfaction of job aspects among the different sample classes. Correlations were done based on age, gender, title and years of experience. Percentages of the respondents willing to seek job opportunities abroad were also calculated and the key driving forces for traveling were ranked based on the most frequently occurring reasons ranked by respondents. Furthermore, the most preferred countries were reached by analyzing the most frequently named countries.

Job satisfaction is studied in terms of four groups of job aspects, (economic, social, psychological, and training). Both, the importance of and satisfaction with job aspects were analyzed in addition to a gap analysis that was undergone to indicate the extent to which employee needs were met. Following are some analysis illustrating the overall satisfaction

Table 2. Groups of job aspects

Economic Aspects	Psychological Aspects
❑ Pay ❑ Rewards ❑ Benefits	❑ Interest and scope of work itself ❑ Challenges ❑ Disciplinary procedures ❑ Working hours ❑ Personal versus professional life balance ❑ Scope for own input for decision making
Social Aspects	**Training and Development Aspects**
❑ Relationships with colleagues ❑ Team work and support ❑ Working conditions ❑ Interdepartmental communication	❑ Amount of training received ❑ Access to technologies ❑ Career path

ratings as well as the detailed ratings of each of the job variables and further providing analysis and comparisons of each group of aspect based on age, gender, years of industry experience and job position. Importance and satisfaction ratings for all job variables listed within the four groups of aspects, were measured on a five-point scale, where the number one corresponds to very unimportant or very dissatisfied and number five corresponds to very important and very satisfied. Furthermore, data analyzed also indicated the levels of turnover and employee willingness to seek jobs abroad. Through statistically modeling the research findings and the data collected from the sample size of 110, the following empirical evidences regarding levels of job satisfaction among ICT employees in Egypt were obtained.

Overall Job Satisfaction

By analyzing job satisfaction as a function of the four groups of job aspects, (economic, psychological, training and development and social), and by calculating the weighted average of overall satisfaction of the job facets, research findings showed that, overall, more than 50 percent of all respondents were satisfied with their current jobs as illustrated in Figure 2.

General Satisfaction for Working in the ICT Sector

Respondents were also surveyed to determine their general level of satisfaction working in the field of ICT in general, as well as their satisfaction working in the ICT sector in Egypt in specific. In that respect, 90 percent of the respondents stated that they were satisfied; however the ratio dropped to 58 percent when asked about their satisfaction working in Egypt indicating that 32 percent of the respondents were dissatisfied working in the market in Egypt even though they were satisfied with an ICT career.

Importance of Various Job Aspects

During the survey, 15 job factors that impact employee satisfaction were listed and respondents were asked to rate each factor based on its importance to their satisfaction. Figure 3 indicates the ranking of these factors by importance, number five being very important and one being very unimportant. The results show that the majority of respondents ranked recognition on work they do and access to new technologies as the two most important

Figure 2. Overall job satisfaction

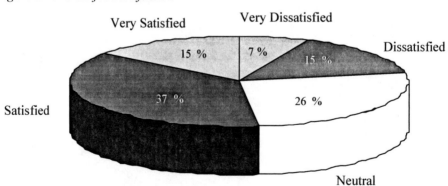

factors contributing to their job satisfaction. Good working environment and training and development were equally ranked as the next most important factors. Monetary rewards were listed further down the list, with salary ranked as the fifth most important factor. Psychological aspects such as regular feedback on performance and opportunity to contribute to business goals, and job security were rated as the least important factors. Clearly, ICT professionals demand more from work recognition, access to new technologies and high training than they demand from monetary rewards. By grouping these factors, it was clear that the most important group of factors that affects employees' satisfaction was the group of economic aspects which clearly meets Maslow's need hierarchy whereby physiological and basic needs come first.

Training and development aspects were rated as the second most important, followed by social aspects and lastly psychological aspects. Ranking job security as the least important contradicts with Maslow's where safety needs come second after physiological needs. However, this may be explained by the job stability available in companies in Egypt due to local labor laws. These ranking results are very similar to those obtained in other ICT surveys, where aspects like training, opportunity for advancement, pay and rewards were ranked as top priority, followed by social and psychological aspects.

Figure 3. Ranking of various job aspects by importance

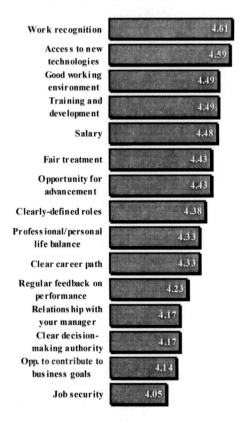

Figure 4. Job aspects with highest disparity between importance and satisfaction

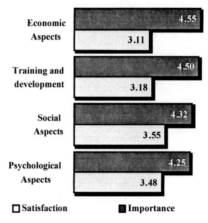

Gap Analysis - Overall Disparity Between Importance and Satisfaction

Respondents were asked to indicate their satisfaction levels on each of the job aspects. When comparing the results of satisfaction and importance, it was clear that, although economic factors and training and development have been ranked as the most important aspects, however, they feature the highest level of disparity between importance and satisfaction, and are rated at the lowest satisfaction levels. Figure 4 illustrates that the importance rating is slightly higher than the satisfaction rating for economic and training aspects. Satisfaction was lowest for the most important job aspects and highest for the least important job aspects, indicating that employees' needs were not being met, as they desired.

Social Aspects Ratings

Overall satisfaction with social aspects was the highest among the other groups of job aspects. Respondents were most satisfied with their working relations with their direct managers. However, their view of the level of cooperation among the different departments in their organization was less favorable with only 34 percent indicating positive interdepartmental cooperation. When comparing social aspects based on different age groups, it was clear that individuals' age and importance of social aspects were directly related. The survey results indicated that the level of satisfaction with respect to social aspects was slightly higher for those above 30 years of age; it also indicated that social aspects were more important to female professionals than they are to males. However, males were more satisfied with these aspects than females, despite their lower importance to the former. The results indicated that males had lower social job expectations than females, thus were easily satisfied. ICT professionals with five to ten years of industry experience were more satisfied with all social aspects relative to those with less than five years and those above ten years. Furthermore, this class of respondents showed the highest importance ranking for all social job aspects. When looking at respondents with different job positions, it was clear that the importance of social aspects was the same for managerial and technical employees and higher for juniors. Surprisingly, managers were those least satisfied with this group of aspects and

Figure 5. Social aspects ratings

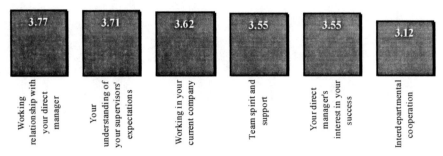

| 3.77 | 3.71 | 3.62 | 3.55 | 3.55 | 3.12 |

Working relationship with your direct manager | Your understanding of your supervisors' expectations | Working in your current company | Team spirit and support | Your direct manager's interest in your success | Interdepartmental cooperation

the results further indicates that managers were very dissatisfied with the level of cooperation between different departments within the company, and showed disappointment towards team spirit and support. Figure 5 shows the ratings of the social aspects.

Psychological Aspects Ratings

On average, 66 percent of the respondents were satisfied with all psychological job aspects. The exception was with satisfaction with the time they had away from work for their personal lives. Only 25 percent of respondents were satisfied with this aspect, and most of those satisfied were employed in governmental organizations. Employees, however, seem to feel that their work contributes high value and importance to their organizations, especially that they show high satisfaction in the way they understand their job fit within the company. Satisfaction with psychological job aspects followed the same pattern among the age groups as with social aspects. It was indicated that the importance of psychological aspects was higher among females than males who also showed higher satisfaction for psychological aspects. Psychological aspects were most important to employees with five to 10 years of industry experience. Similarly, the level of satisfaction among this segment was highest. Although managers rank psychological aspects more important than junior and technical employees, however, the level of satisfaction of managers was lowest. Figure 6 demonstrates the psychological aspect ratings.

Training and Development Aspects Ratings

Although respondents ranked training and development as the second most important group of aspects, unfortunately, overall average showed that employees were dissatisfied with the amount of training they receive. Furthermore, they had a negative perception on the opportunity they had for improvement and having a clear career path. Empirical evidence indicates that ICT professionals in Egypt barely feel that they have a clear career path and that there is no further career development available for them. Although some employees stated that they were satisfied with the technologies they use emphasizing that the growth of Internet has facilitated their access to updated technologies and information, it remains that in many other companies, high tech is not provided unless it is badly needed. Individuals upgrade themselves through personal efforts and not company efforts. Interview results further prove that multinationals are more concerned, to an extent, with training and developing their employees than local companies. Public sector institutions have the highest dissatisfaction with all training and development aspects, especially, their access to updated

Figure 6. Psychological aspects ratings

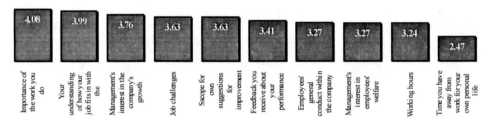

technologies. The major factors mentioned that are deterring the level of training provided were costs and high risk of training.

The survey results showed that there was no significant difference among the age groups with respect to the importance of satisfaction with the training and development aspects. The importance of both aspects had no significant difference between females and males. Unlike the previous groups of aspects, the importance of training and development was highest among those who have less than five years of industry experience. However, the level of satisfaction was highest among employees who have five to 10 years of experience, although its importance to them was lowest. Managers were dissatisfied with all aspects related to training and development indicating that companies need to provide more training to their employees as well as stress more on ICT professionals career path and future within the organization. Figure 7 demonstrates the training and development aspect ratings.

Economic Aspects Ratings

Economic variables have received the lowest satisfaction rating among the four groups of aspects, although the majority of non-public sector respondents had clearly indicated that the level of salaries among ICT professionals had rapidly increased over the past couple of years. Salary increases were caused by the aggressive competition caused by multinationals who were aggressively penetrating the market with high salaries and better packages. In fact, they believe that they are paid relatively higher when compared to other sectors but they were still convinced that their salaries did not fully pay off their skills and efforts when compared to other markets rendering them extremely underpaid. The dissatisfaction with economic variables was highest among ICT professionals employed in public sector and governmental institutions with a satisfaction average for those above 30 being relatively higher as well as among female respondents. It is important to note that although the economic aspects were the most important group of aspects across all segments. Unfortunately, people who had

Figure 7. Training and development aspects ratings

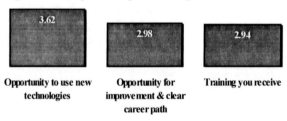

Figure 8. Economic aspects ratings

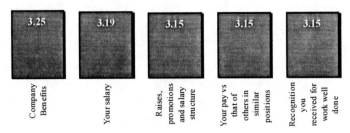

more than 10 years of experience were dissatisfied and the remaining respondents were slightly satisfied. In general, managers were dissatisfied with the economic aspects of their jobs, the pay raises, and promotions and salary structures as well as the pay they received when compared to others in similar managerial positions in the company. Figure 8 demonstrates the economic aspect ratings.

Overall Satisfaction Levels

Overall satisfaction was slightly higher among respondents above those 30 years of age. This relates to Cranny's (1992) emphasis on individual demographics as a factor affecting job satisfaction. On average, female ICT professionals were slightly more satisfied than males with regard to economic, training and development and psychological job aspects. Male respondents, on the other hand showed higher satisfaction with social job aspects, especially with those related to team spirit and support. One of the significant results was that the most satisfied ICT professionals were those who have been in the industry for a period between 5 to 10 years. Those with less than five years come next and were still satisfied with all job aspects. However, respondents who have been in the industry for more than 10 years were least satisfied and were actually dissatisfied with the two most important job aspects, namely training and development and economic aspects. These results show that employees in the ICT sector in Egypt reach maximum satisfaction between five to 10 years of industry experience but after 10 years, the level of satisfaction with all job aspects deteriorates. Moreover, the results have clearly shown that managers were the least satisfied group of employees whereas juniors were the most satisfied with all job aspects representing high risk to organizations due to the presence of de-motivated managers as well as facing high turnover rates of skilled professionals. For example, 75 percent of surveyed managers expected to be employed in new organizations within five years showing low stability ratios.

Turnover Ratios and Brain Drain Implications

The survey results showed that 46 percent had less than five years of overall work experience and over 75 percent have been employed in their current company for a period less than five years, which indicates a high level of turnover in the ICT sector. Additionally, 60 percent of the employees surveyed expected to be employed in other companies within the next five years and 38 percent expect to be promoted by their current employer. The high turnover is caused by the scarcity of ICT skills, lack of stability and corporate loyalty and turning their focus primarily to monetary aspects. Some of the employees entertained the idea of moving to more challenging sectors where they can improve and be able to define clearer career paths and also have the chance to hold higher posts in other sectors than in ICT. Strauss (1999) indicates that culture and user trends towards technology need to be studied to be able to determine the market capacity and penetration. In Egypt, the public sector employees of ICT companies that were employed for more than five years have shown the highest company loyalty level and were the least willing to change their current employers at least for the coming five-year period. In other segments, 60 percent stated that they expected to move to new companies in five years' time.

Overall job satisfaction results indicated that 71 percent of respondents were willing to seek job opportunities abroad. The primary three forces urging them to search for overseas opportunities were their desire for having a clear and promising career path, which they lack in Egypt; the possible access and exposure to high levels of technology; and better pay. In addition to a number of other factors including more training, better work experience and work environments. Such opportunities they feel could present itself in a number of countries including the US, Canada, the UK, UAE, Germany, Australia and France.

CHALLENGES AND OPPORTUNITIES

This study attempted to identify the degrees of importance of various job facets, map them to the levels of current satisfaction, as well as pinpoint and evaluate the key driving forces that were leading to brain drain of ICT professionals in Egypt. There were a number of challenges and opportunities identified from the findings of the study as follows:

- There exists a gap between the levels of satisfaction of respondents working in the ICT sector versus those working in the ICT sector in Egypt where 90 percent were satisfied working in the ICT sector with only 58 percent satisfied working in the ICT sector in Egypt due to poor financial arrangements and lack of proper training and development with 43 percent and 45 percent of the respondents respectively satisfied with these two vital job facets.
- ICT companies associate salaries of ICT employees directly with sales quotations that have indirectly impacted other ICT professionals who were more technical and did not receive any credibility and were not compensated on sales volumes.
- Seventy-five percent of managers expected to be employed in new organizations within in five years showing low stability and high risk to organizations with minimal communication and collaboration within different organizations leading to higher turnover rates.
- High dissatisfaction among employees with their working hours that is directly creating lower job productivity and performance and leading to the availability of inefficient systems or labor shortages.
- There is a major difference between privileges, training and development and pay structures provided by multinationals versus local companies. The gap gets even wider when getting the public sector into the picture, representing the segment that has the highest level of dissatisfaction with the opportunities they have in accessing new technologies. Public sector employees are very dissatisfied with economic aspects, compared to other respondents.
- Egyptian ICT companies are facing the problem of high turnover and are suffering from the brain drain of its ICT professionals seeking opportunities abroad.

- There exists a shortage in labor with only 5,000 ICT professionals while the market needs up to 150,000 ICT professionals.
- Overall, the majority of the respondents stated that they were satisfied with their current jobs, with 52 percent of the sample satisfied, 26 percent neutral about their jobs and 22 percent stating that they are dissatisfied.
- Results have clearly indicated that 71 percent of the respondents are willing to seek job opportunities abroad where they will receive higher training levels, and have a clear and challenging career path. Furthermore, it is evident that IT professionals holding managerial levels seem to be those most likely to leave.
- Results prove that the key driving forces for the brain drain, ranked by priority, are having a clear career path, broader scope for development, better access to higher levels of technology, better pay, and finally having more challenging work environments.
- Most respondents felt that to an extent, the Egyptian culture hinders the sector's growth. The domestic illiteracy and ignorance levels act as major disincentives for employees to progress.

CONCLUSION

The survey findings indicated that companies should do more efforts in understanding the needs of their employees and better meet their job expectations and consequently reducing the gap between needs and satisfaction. This could be achieved through internal employee surveys aiming at understanding employee needs. However, more attention should be given to economic factors and training and development, as they have the highest need-satisfaction gap. Moreover, Top management should work on improving the levels of interdepartmental cooperation and further encourage teamwork by reorganize work groups into more efficient structures. The problem of long working hours faced by most of the respondents should be handled by employers by determining the reasons behind the late hours, to provide employees with better balances between personal and professional lives. Additionally, employers should set more ambitious career paths for their employees; they should have clearer pictures for their development paths in their companies in specific and the market in general. In reducing the brain drain and turnover rates, companies should increase restrictions on ICT employment contracts in order to guarantee retaining employees in the Egyptian ICT market for a certain period of time. In return, however, employees must be motivated and encouraged to remain in their jobs.

As indicated earlier, the two most important factors to retain individuals within the Egyptian market were providing clear career paths and providing better access to technologies. Therefore, it is necessary for companies to have more interest in managers. Since they are the least satisfied segment, companies must understand and meet managers' needs , because high dissatisfaction levels among this group is risky to corporations. The focus in motivating this segment should be via meeting their economic and training and development needs. Moreover, the high importance of ICT to the public sector should be a key element when considering the high dissatisfaction among public sector employees by providing more incentives to them as well as training to boost their morale and maintain their high level of loyalty.

It is necessary to mention that the findings of the study regarding the overall level of job satisfaction among ICT professionals in Egypt were surprising and interesting. The level of satisfaction was expected to be lower than what was actually indicated through the results. However, there still remains the problem of skilled ICT brains being drained to job opportunities abroad, where they get the opportunity of advancement and career development. Their overall job satisfaction does not fully compensate for all their needs. The reason they travel is not that they are generally dissatisfied, instead, it is that they need to find the job that provides them with a clear career path, provides a chance to grow, and exposes them to advanced technologies. Therefore, these job aspects are the key motivational factors for retaining ICT professionals in Egypt.

ENDNOTES

[1]   For simplicity purposes, the acronym IT will be used for information technology and ICT will be used for information and communication technology throughout the chapter.

[2]   Publications used included documents published by the Cabinet of Egypt Information and Decision Support Center, The American University in Cairo Library and the American Chamber of Commerce.

[3]   An example of facet satisfaction could be reflected in loving the work, although hating the working conditions or being interested in the job but feeling that the pay is bad.

REFERENCES

Albuquerque, N.M. (1999). Increasing employee satisfaction, performance unlimited. Retrieved in January 2001 from the World Wide Web: www.performance-unlimited.com/satisfy.htm

Battey, J. (2000). Retaining your most valuable assets. Retrieved in January 2001 from the World Wide Web: www.infoworld.com

Blum, R. (2000). Lucent Technologies Network Professionals Job Satisfaction. Retrieved in January 2001 from the World Wide Web: www.lucentnps.com

Cranny, C.J., Smith, P. C. and Stone, E. F. (1992). *Job Satisfaction: How people feel about their jobs and how it affects their performance.* New York: Lexington Books.

Dunnettee, M.D. (1976). *Handbook of industrial and organizational psychology.* New York: McGraw Hill.

Egypt Information and Communications Technologies Dashboard (2000). US-Egypt Presidents' Council. Retrieved in June 2001 from the World Wide Web: www.us-egypt.org

Elamrani, I. (2000) Wanted high tech help: Are Egypt's IT human resources up to snuff? *Business Monthly.* Retrieved in June 2001 from the World Wide Web: www.us-egypt.org/uptosnuff.html

Hamroush, H. and El Sineity, H. (2000). Info tech sector – Status and opportunities. LEADIM US and FCS International Marketing Insights.

Hellriegel, D., Slocum, J.W. and Woodman, R.W. (1998). *Organizational Behavior.* Ohio: South-Western College Publishing.

InfoWorld (1999). Motivation: Many factors at play. June.

The Information Technology Landscape in Egypt (2000). Retrieved in May 2001 from the World Wide Web: www.american.edu/carmel

IT World. (2001). Survey: 66% of ITers are job hunting. March.

The ITPRC Poll (2001). The Information Technology Professional's Resource Center. Retrieved in April 2001 from the World Wide Web: www.itprc .com/poll.htm

Johns, G. (1988). *Organizational Behavior: Understanding Life at Work*. Scott Foreman and Company, 2nd edition.

Kamel, S. (1997, September-December). The birth of Egypt's information society. *International Journal of Computer and Engineering Management, 5*(3).

Lincoln, J.R. and Kalleberg, A.L. (1990). *Culture, Control and Commitment*. Cambridge University Press.

Locke, E.A. (1976). Job satisfaction and the secondary head teacher: the creation of a model of job satisfaction. University of New Castle Upon Tyne. Retrieved in May 2001 from the World Wide Web: www.ncl.ac.uk

Maister, D. H. (1997). Managing the Professional Service Firm. First Free Press Paperbacks Edition.

Ministry of Communication and Information Technology (2001). Retrieved in May 2001 from the World Wide Web: www.mcit.gov.eg

Mitchell, G., Carnes, K.H. and Mendnsa, C. (1997). *America's New Deficit: The Shortage of Information Technology Workers*. Office of Technology Policy, Department of Commerce, United States of America.

Natarjan, H. (2000) Job satisfaction in information technology era. *The Hindu.* Retrieved in May 2000 from the World Wide Web: www.indoaserver.com/the hindu/2000/05/24/ stories

Ouellette, T. (1999). Job satisfaction survey: Living with the pain. Retrieved in March 2001 from the World Wide Web: www.computerworld.com

Pletz, J. (1998, July). High-tech firms struggling to find workers. *Indianapolis Business Journal, 19*(17).

Robbins, S.P. (1989). *Organizational Behavior*. Prentice Hall Inc., 8th ed.

Strauss, J. and Frost, R. (1999). *Marketing on the Internet: Principles of Online Marketing*. New Jersey: Prentice Hall.

US-Egypt Presidents' Council (2001). Retrieved in April 2001 from the World Wide Web: www.us-egypt.org

Chapter XVII

Evaluating the Factors Affecting Decision Support System Usage by Strategic Decision Makers in Egypt: Using a Structural Equation Modelling Approach

Ibrahim Elbeltagi
De Monteford University, UK

ABSTRACT

This chapter draws on a survey of CEO and IT managers in local authorities in Egypt to explain the key factors affecting their use of DSS in making strategic decisions. This chapter proposes and tests a Structural Equation Model (SEM) that extends the generally accepted Technology Acceptance Model to assess relationships between an extensive range of constructs and their relation with DSS usage via Perceived Ease of Use and Perceived Usefulness. The SEM approach has enabled the development of a framework that will support a sustainable approach towards the adoption and use of DSS in developing Middle Eastern countries.

INTRODUCTION

This chapter draws on a survey of CEO and IT managers in local authorities in Egypt to explain the key factors affecting their use of DSS in making strategic decisions. A Structural Equation Model (SEM) that extends the generally accepted Technology Acceptance Model is proposed and tested to assess the relationships between an extensive range of constructs and their relation with DSS usage via Perceived Ease of Use (PEU) and Perceived Usefulness (PU). The SEM approach has enabled the development of a framework that will support a sustainable approach towards the adoption and use of DSS in developing Middle East countries. This framework in particular highlights the need for a far greater understanding of cultural diversity at both a national and organizational level in implementing strategic computer-based systems.

BACKGROUND

The unprecedented growth of Information Technology (IT) has inspired IT practitioners, researchers, developers, and innovators to seek new, more sophisticated, and more effective acceptance and usage methods (Agarwal and Prasad, 1998a; Moore and Benbasat, 1991; Taylor and Todd, 1995). Interest in the subject has been manifested in the abundance of R&D based projects undertaken to identify the factors that lead to successful adoption and use of IT in general and Decision Support Systems in particular (DSS) (Agarwal and Prasad, 1998a; Agarwal and Prasad, 1998b; Davis, 1989; Rose and Straub, 1998; Thompson and Rose, 1994). The last two decades have generated a multi-disciplinary research body that expands over the field of technology, Human Computer Interaction (HCI) and social psychology to shed light on user acceptance of technology (Agarwal and Prasad, 1998a; Agarwal and Prasad, 1998b; Davis, 1989; Rogers, 1995). Resulting from the research findings, many models have been developed to predict the relationship between user perception and technology acceptance and use. The Technology Acceptance Model (TAM), initially developed in 1986 by Fred Davis, has been used extensively and is respected in the industry (Davis, 1989; Moore and Benbasat, 1991; Taylor and Todd, 1995; Thompson, Higgins, and Howell, 1991).

Computing technology and information systems represent substantial investments for organizations; investments on which they hope to realize a return in areas such as making effective Strategic Decision Making (SDM) and improving efficiency. Simply acquiring the technology is insufficient. In order to obtain the anticipated benefits, it must be used in context of its end users. The most expensive shortcoming of DSS is that it is not typically used in making effective strategic decisions. However, if all the different variables that could affect this usage were considered in their specific environment, then CEO and other users would be more likely to apply the technology in all the different stages of SDM. There are many factors affecting the utilization of IT in supporting effective SDM. These factors range from the systems themselves, the organizations that use the systems, the decision-makers and the overall environment. Yet, recent studies of technology acceptance and usage have only been concentrated in the technologically developed world. Certainly, of the large number of IT acceptance and usage studies covered in recent literature reviews, few if any took place in the developing world (Rose and Straub, 1998; Thompson and Rose, 1994). The developing countries clearly have their own unique characteristics; research in these countries is indeed required to enhance our understanding of DSS acceptance and usage and this will enable us to identify the steps required for a more sustainable approach to the implementation and use of this technology.

This research study examines and defines the factors that influence DSS usage in making strategic decisions in local governments in Egypt. By understanding these factors, managers can develop strategies to increase the utilization of the DSS. The research is of value to local authorities in Egypt for four main reasons:

- **Understanding the factors affecting user acceptance of DSS**: knowledge of the factors affecting user acceptance of DSS, how they can be measured, and how they relate to each other is crucial in the development, implementation, and successful management of DSS. With this knowledge, interventions during implementation (such as training or involving user in development) can be used to increase user acceptance and usage.
- **Prediction of user acceptance of DSS**: before investing a large amount of money in technology, an organization must be able to predict whether the investment will be accepted and used.
- **Selection of alternatives**: relative measures of user acceptance can be used to choose between alternative technologies.
- **Guiding development**: measurement of specific aspects or elements of a technology which affect user acceptance can be used to provide guidance to system/software developers as to which of these aspects or elements are important to the decision maker or need to be improved to use the system effectively. This knowledge can also be used in the early stages of software development to identify potential problems before they occur or sort them out easily.

DSS IMPLEMENTATION AND USAGE

Research into information technology adoption and use has been motivated by the desire to predict the factors that lead to IT use (Thompson and Rose, 1994). For the purpose of this study DSS technology is defined broadly to include a wide range of applications, because participants used different packages as well as different applications for different levels of decision-making in local authorities in Egypt this includes various software applications including: database application and more specialized applications branded under terms such as DSS, MIS, and EIS.

Under a general assumption of a positive relationship between IS/IT utilization and performance, numerous individual, organizational, and technological variables have been investigated in efforts to identify key factors affecting IS/IT behaviour. (Saga and Zmud, 1994) identified 20 empirical studies aimed at investigating the nature and determining factors of IT acceptance. Also a literature review by Prescott and Conger (1995), for instance, include 70 IT adoptions and use articles based on the diffusion of innovation paradigm alone.

The overwhelming majority of information technology adoption and usage research projects have been carried out in the technologically developed world. In fact, of the one hundred IT adoption and use studies covered in two recent literature reviews (Prescott and Conger, 1995; Thompson and Rose, 1994), none took place in developing countries or were conducted on DSS usage on SDM. Perhaps this is understandable given that the majority of academic institutions and IT users are located in the industrialised world. The consequence, however, is that the study of such phenomenon in the developing world has not established why IT has thus failed to transfer effectively (Goodman and Press, 1995; Knight, 1993; Mahmood, Gemoets, and Gosler, 1995; Odedra, Lawrie, Bennett, and Goodman, 1993) and this is a severely limiting factor. Mutual understanding between decision-makers from different parts of the world and cultural backgrounds is essential to mutually beneficial relationships. Currently, the developing countries invest a lot of money in IT related enterprises but the return on this investment is still lower than expected. We need to understand how and why DSS has or has not been used by decision makers in developing countries in order to improve this return. Many students from developing countries attend Western universities and then go back to their home countries. Egyptian researchers undertake projects to offer their technical and business knowledge but also to bring back some understanding of Western. A transfer of cultural knowledge in the opposite direction is only partly realised and is viewed as an inhibiting factor in technology acceptance and usage (Rose and Straub, 1998).

While information technology-specific adoption and use has not been evaluated across cultures of varying technological development levels, diffusion of non-IT innovations has been tested successfully (Rogers, 1995). Although these studies do suggest that information technology adoption and use models tested in developed nations may be applicable to less developed countries, no hard evidence presently exists. Of the 70 IT-based studies which either confirmed or extended the Roger's Diffusion of Innovation (DOI) model evaluated by Prescott and Conger (1995), none were conducted within developing nations (Rose and Straub, 1998).

A suitable first model for testing in developing world would be one that has shown robustness across the spectrum of IT application. This robust model should have the highest probability of success in future transfers across economic and cultural boundaries (Rose and Straub, 1998). Davis' Technology Acceptance Model (TAM) is a model closely related to Rogers' DOI model which has demonstrated this robustness. For this reason, TAM was selected as an appropriate model for studying DSS usage in making strategic decisions in local authorities in Egypt.

ADAPTED TECHNOLOGY ACCEPTANCE MODEL (TAM)

MIS research provided a wealth of research streams in which to gather information relevant to the factors influencing DSS implementation and use. The streams included IT infrastructure, database, IS success and IS planning. All of these areas identified factors that could potentially affect DSS implementation and use in making decisions. The literature review identified ten factors that affect IS implementation (see Table 1).

Figure 1 depicts the research model employed in the study. It is a reduced TAM model, excluding attitude and intention to use, because this research targeted only the local authorities that had already adapted DSS systems in their organizations. The basic idea for the model is predicting DSS usage in making strategic decisions as a dependent variable, by using both perceived ease of use and perceived usefulness with the different contextual variables. In this context, the model hypothesises that DSS usage, and the attitudes of decision makers towards this usage, can be accurately predicted by means of a host of relevant contextual factors.

Table 1. Key factors identified in IS implementation literature

No.	Factor
1	Management support
2	Having the right resources
3	Planning for the DSS implementation
4	Having the right skills
5	User expectation
6	Having the right development tools
7	Quality of the data resources
8	Champion
9	User participation
10	Prototyping

The perceived ease of use is instrumental in driving DSS usage. The perception of the user friendliness of software applications (ease of use) is viewed as a major intermediary latent variable, along with context specific variables that consider a wide range of issues that are clearly country specific. The adapted TAM model provides the necessary conceptual underpinning to ascertain the factors of importance in facilitating DSS usage. The constructs composing the research model were operationalized using a combination of items extracted from previous relevant research.

System Usage

It is now self-evident that computer technology is being increasingly utilized in the workplace. The extent to which decision makers use information systems or engage in other computer-related activities is most economically determined by asking them directly. This method is frequently used (Deane, Podd, and Henderson, 1998). Based on previous research

Figure 1. Towards a conceptual DSS adoption model for SDM

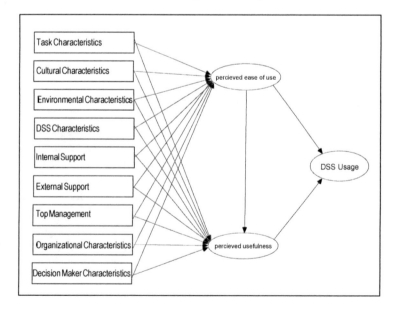

examining the usage of IT in the workplace, which relied very heavily on defining usage based on self-reported estimates (Birdi, Pennington, and Zapf, 1997; DeLone and McLean, 1992; Igbaria, Pavri, and Huff, 1989), three dimensions of DSS usage were included in this study:

- *Actual usage of DSS:* This dimension is widely used in MIS studies. For the purpose of this study, it is indicated by the self-reported percentage of use of DSS in SDM compared to the whole SD made during a period.

- *Frequency of use:* Many researchers suggest this measure, for example, DeLone (1988), Raymond (1985), and Sirnivasan (1985). Frequency of use was measured on a five-point scale ranging from "several times a month" to "once a year."

- *Level of use:* This serves to measure proficiency of use of the DSS. The respondents were asked to indicate their level of DSS usage in SDM on a five-point scale ranging from "no use" to "extensive use." Many researchers have used this measure, for example, Igbaria et al. (1989) and Maish (1979). The ranges of use have been changed from days to months and from months to years because the nature of SDM makes the frequency of its use more sporadic.

Perceived Ease of Use (PEU) and Perceived Usefulness (PU)

These two constructs, originally proposed by Davis, define the PU as the degree to which a person believes that using a particular system would enhance his or her job performance. The PEU is the degree to which a person believes that using a particular system would be free of effort (Davis, 1989). The validity of these two in Davis's model was re-examined in a number of other studies. Adams et al. (1992) replicated Davis's study with a focus on evaluating the psychometric properties of the two scales, while they examined the relationship between ease of use, usefulness, and system usage. The results showed that the reliability and validity of the two scales were very high. Another test of the reliability of the PEU and PU scales using two software packages showed that the instrument exhibited a high degree of test-re-test reliability (Hendrickson, Massey, and Cronan, 1993). As Davis (1989) pointed out, psychometricians emphasise that the validity of the measurement scale is built from the outset. To ensure the content validity of the scales, the items selected must represent the concept about which generalizations are to be made (Bohmstedt, 1970). Statements used in this research to operationalize the PEU and PU were basically adapted from Davis's study (1989), with minor changes in wording and the addition of one item to PU: "lower cost," which reflects the developing world's environment, where cost is an important factor in using DSS.

Task Characteristics

Several studies have attempted to develop conceptual models of the strategic decision-making process based on studies of multiple decision situations (Fahey, 1981; Mazzolini, 1981; Mintzberg, 1976). They have broadly viewed the process in three steps: problem formulation and objective setting, identification and generation of alternative solutions, and the analysis and choice of a feasible alternative. These models appear to be variations or extensions of the intelligence-design-choice phases discussed by Simon (1965). Most strategic decisions are characterised by uncertainty and complexity. Complexity means the existence of multiple and conflicting interpretations of the problem definition, which is particularly troublesome for the decision maker in using DSS. With highly complex decision situations, "...the answers are obtained through subjective opinions rather than from objective data" (Daft and Lengel, 1986). Thus, characteristics of the task (i.e., strategic decision) are generally seen to be an important element likely to affect DSS usage in making effective strategic decisions. To operationalize the concept of task characteristics, the researcher combined the complexity of the task as one of the most important characteristics of strategic decisions and the different stages of this process. The respondents were requested to indicate, on a five-point scale, their degree of agreement or disagreement with each item (number five being strongly agree and one strongly disagree). Although researchers expected that information technology would increase the amount of information available for strategic decision-making, the soft, personal information often used by management (El Sawy, 1985; Mintzberg, 1975) is not easily captured by a computer-based system (Karten, 1987). To measure what the CEO in local authorities think about the possibility of computerizing SDM, the respondents were asked to indicate, on a five-point scale, their degree of agreement or disagreement (5 being strongly agree and 1 strongly disagree) with the following two statements: "strategic decision process is too complex to be computerized" and "strategic decision making tasks are too person-centred to be computerized."

Cultural Characteristics

This construct investigates how the psychological context on both the individual and organizational level affects the perception and use of DSS in SDM. Hofstede's dimensions of cultures, power distance, individualism and uncertainty avoidance were adopted in general to measure this construct. Power Distance (PD) is the extent to which the less powerful members of organizations within a country expect and accept that power is distributed unequally. In large PD situations, superiors and subordinates consider themselves unequal; hierarchy is important. Centralization and structure are also important. Subordinates expect to be told what to do or directed. In small power distance countries, there is limited dependence of subordinates on their bosses. Malaysia, Guatemala, Panama, the Philippines and Mexico are, according to Hofstede's work, the strongest in PD, while the Scandinavian nations, New Zealand, Israel and Austria are the weakest. The Arab countries ranked seventh.

Individualism (IDV) pertains to societies in which the ties between individuals are loose; everyone looks after himself or herself and his or her immediate family. Collectivism as its opposite pertains to societies in which people from birth onwards are integrated into strong, cohesive groups, which throughout people's lifetime continue to protect them in exchange for unquestioning loyalty. In highly individualistic cultures, speaking one's mind is a virtue. In the collectivist or low IDV culture, on the other hand, harmony is more important. High IDV nations include the USA, Australia, UK, Canada and Netherlands. The lowest IDV nations are the nations of the Pacific Rim and several Central American countries. The Arab countries ranked 27th.

Nations high in masculinity (MAS) index attach the most importance to earnings, recognition for doing a job well, the opportunity for advancement, and challenging work. A low MAS index reflects the importance of a good working relationship with the direct supervisor, co-operation with fellow employees, an acceptable family space, and employment security. High MAS countries include Japan, Austria, Venezuela and Italy. Low MAS nations are Denmark, Netherlands, Norway and Sweden. The Arab countries ranked 23rd.

Uncertainty Avoidance (UA) is defined as the extent to which the members of a culture feel threatened by uncertain or unknown situations. A need for predictability and a predisposition for written and unwritten rules express this dimension. UA leads to a reduction of ambiguity. According to Hofstede, the emotional need for rules in strong UA nations can result in a talent for precision and punctuality, especially where the PD is relatively small. Strategic planning demands a greater tolerance for ambiguity. Weak UA cultures are more likely to stimulate innovation and to tolerate deviant ideas. Greece, Portugal, Guatemala, Uruguay and Belgium are the strongest in UA, while Hong Kong, Sweden, Denmark, Jamaica and Singapore score the lowest. The Arab countries ranked 27th.

The literature indicates that the gap between the DSS professional and CEO may play an important role in DSS usage in SDM (Hatten and Hatten, 1997), and therefore the researcher has added this to the cultural dimensions of Hofestede. Although other dimensions may also be important, these were chosen as most obvious to the CEO in both the two countries. The respondents were asked to indicate, on a five-point scale, their degree of agreement or disagreement (number one being "strongly disagree" and five being "strongly agree") as to the effect of these items on DSS usage in SDM.

DSS Characteristic

Previous studies have found that certain DSS characteristics seem to have an important influence on the effectiveness of the systems: user-friendliness; ease of use; size (cost) of DSS; range of alternatives; timeliness, accuracy and relevancy of output (Igbaria et al., 1989; Udo and Davis, 1992a; Udo and Davis, 1992b). Executives' access to computerised information systems has arisen as an issue in the strategic use of these systems (Hasan and Lampitsi, 1995). Some researchers attempting to measure IS success have put forward factors related to DSS characteristics like system quality, information quality, information use and user satisfaction with the information (DeLone and McLean, 1992; Li, 1997). Based on the literature, the research instrument asked the respondents to indicate their agreement or disagreement with 12 statements reflecting the different DSS characteristics that might affect DSS usage in SDM. The response options are anchored on a five-point Likert-type scale, ranging from number one (strongly disagree) to five (strongly agree).

Environmental Characteristics

The government plays a major role in local authorities in both developed and developing countries, as regulator and/or investor (Blanning, Bui and Tan, 1997). Government policies on human resources development could include developing technical skills for building a computer literate society, which in turn will create favourable market conditions for using DSS strategically (Blanning et al., 1997). Both "favourable government policies" and "uncertainty in environment" were mentioned as one of the key facilitators of the strategic use of IT (King and Teo, 1996). In addition to the previous items, pressure from competition was mentioned in many studies as one of the factors for using IT strategically (Blanning et al., 1997), for example (Benjamin, Rockart, Morton, and Wyman, 1984; Johnston and Carrico, 1988; Neo, 1988). Based on this literature, the instrument asked the respondents to indicate their agreement or disagreement with four statements reflecting the different environmental characteristics that might affect DSS usage in SDM. The response options are anchored onto a five-point Likert-type scale, ranging from number one (strongly disagree) to five (strongly agree).

Organizational Characteristics

Many studies have investigated the influence of organizational attributes on the effectiveness of information systems in general (Cheney, Mann, and Amoroso, 1986; Lind,

Zmud, and Fischer, 1989) and DSS in particular (Guimaraes, Igbaria, and Lu, 1992; Sanders and Courtney, 1985). Based on previous literature, the instrument asked the respondents to indicate their agreement or disagreement with seven statements reflecting the different organizational characteristics that might affect DSS usage in SDM. The response options are anchored on a five-point Likert-type scale, ranging from number one (strongly disagree) to five (strongly agree).

Internal Support Characteristics

Internal support given to decision makers within the organization either through training within the organization or other sources of support is critical, especially in developing countries where there is lack of resources. As a result, some decision makers rely on help from unspecialised persons (i.e., their colleagues), manuals, books, and help screens. Based on previous literature, the instrument asked the respondents to indicate their agreement or disagreement with five statements reflecting the different internal support characteristics that might affect DSS usage in SDM. The response options are anchored on a five-point Likert-type scale, ranging from number one (strongly disagree) to five (strongly agree).

External Support Characteristics

Due to insufficient internal technical expertise, especially in developing countries, the availability and quality of external support could be considered as an important determinant of DSS effectiveness in SDM. Recommendations from outside consultants were found to be an important variable in using IT strategically (Neo, 1988). In addition, the support that decision makers get from government agencies is important and varies from one country to another. For example, some governments may wish to maintain tighter control over their information infrastructure, as is the case in most developing countries, while others may prefer to take the market approach (Blanning et al., 1997). In addition, a good relationship with external vendors was one of the facilitators of success of end user computing (Shayo, Guthrie and Igbaria, 1999). Based on this literature, the instrument asked the respondents to indicate their agreement or disagreement with three statements reflecting the different external support characteristics that might affect DSS usage in SDM. The response options are anchored on a five-point Likert-type scale ranging from number one (strongly disagree) to five (strongly agree).

Decision Maker Characteristics

The importance of decision maker characteristics as determinants of information systems success has been emphasized by several authors (Guimaraes et al., 1992; Igbaria et al., 1989; Sanders and Courtney, 1985). Computer experience and user training have been found to have strong effects on microcomputer usage (Cheney et al., 1986). The importance of user training has long been proposed as a critical component of MIS success, in general, and for microcomputer usage in particular (Igbaria, 1992). Cognitive style as a decision maker characteristic has probably received the most attention. Huber (1983) reviews these studies and concludes that cognitive style is not a sufficient basis for driving DSS design guidelines because cognitive style is only one of many individual differences (Huber and Robey, 1983). Computer anxiety was found to have an effect on IS usage (Igbaria et al., 1989). In addition to that, some studies regard motivation as the key to MIS success (DeSanctis, 1982). Others find a positive relationship between user attitude and the successful use of information systems (Toubkin and Simis, 1980). In addition, some managers will have a more positive attitude toward change and a greater willingness to implement new ways of doing things. Innovative decision-makers are more eager to try new ideas, have more favorable attitudes toward change, are less dogmatic, and are more able to cope with uncertainty and ambiguity (Brancheau and Wetherbe, 1990; Rogers, 1995). Decision makers' characteristics were measured by asking managers to indicate their agreement or disagreement with 12 statements reflecting the previously mentioned different dimensions of these characteristics in DSS usage in SDM. The response options are anchored on a five-point Likert-type scale ranging from number one (strongly disagree) to five (strongly agree).

Top Management Support Characteristics

It is important that top management participation be active and not merely symbolic. Simply giving the go-ahead for the DSS implementation in the organization is not sufficient (Ang and Teo, 1997). Some ways that top management can demonstrate its support could be by providing necessary resources and leadership, by setting goals and policies for DSS and showing interest by participating in DSS design and development (Ang and Teo, 1997; King, 1996). Based on previous studies responses to six statements on a five-point scale format, ranging from number one (strongly disagree) to five (strongly agree) were used to determine top management support.

RESEARCH METHOD

The unit of analysis for this research is CEO or delegate in local government in Egypt. The sampling frame included the directory of DSS units in the Egyptian local governments issued by the Information and Decision Support Centre (IDSC). A package that was mailed to senior executive officers contained two items: a cover letter explaining the importance of the study, and the questionnaire with a stamped return address on the back. The covering letter requested the respondent to return the completed questionnaire within two weeks. The respondents were assured of the confidentiality of their responses.

Of the 309 questionnaires that were returned from sample, 294 (about 73.5 percent) were valid, 12 incomplete and three returned by the post-office due to incorrect addresses. To ensure that the valid responses were representatives of the larger population, a non-response bias test was used to compare the early and late respondents. χ^2 tests show no significant difference between the two groups of respondents at the 5 percent significance level, implying that non-response bias is not a concern.

Cronbah's coefficient ± was used to assess the reliability of all multi-item scales. All scales showed reasonable reliability (Ramaprasad, 1987) as indicated in Table 2.

Following Taylor and Todd (1995), because of sample size limitations, multi-item constructs for the external variables were measured using a summated scale derived as the average value of all items pertaining to these constructs.

SEM techniques are a second-generation multivariate technique and have gained increasing popularity in management sciences, notably marketing and organizational behaviour, in the last decade (Chau, 1997). AMOS 4.0 program (Arbuckle and Wothke, 1999) was used to test the hypothesized linear effect of each group of variables on PEU, PU and

Table 2. Cronbah's coefficient ± for constructs

Factors	α
DSS usage (3 items)	0.70
PEU (6 items)	0.69
PU (7 items)	0.72
Task characteristics (5items)	0.65
Cultural characteristics (4 items)	0.78
DSS characteristics (12 items)	0.68
Environmental characteristics (4 items)	0.71
Organizational characteristics (7 items)	0.78
Internal support characteristics (5 items)	0.74
External support characteristics (3 items)	0.81
Decision maker characteristics (12 items)	0.68
Top management support (6 items)	0.79

DSS usage. There are a number of measures generated by AMOS to evaluate the goodness of fit of the model, as with other commercial statistical software packages that adopt the structural equation modelling approach.

The most popular index is perhaps the chi-square statistic. This statistic tests the proposed model against the general alternative in which all observed variables are correlated. It measures the distance (difference, discrepancy, deviance) between the sample covariance or correlation matrix and the fitted covariance or correlation matrix (Joreskog and Sorbom, 1993). With this index, significant values indicate poor model fit while insignificant values indicate good fit. This is why it is also called a "badness-of-fit" measure. Hartwick and Barki (1994) pointed out a major shortcoming of this index. They noted "in large samples, the chi-square statistic will almost always be significant, since chi-square is a direct function of a sample size. In small samples, the statistic may not be chi-square distributed, leading to inaccurate probability values." In their study, Hartwick and Barki used four other measures of overall model goodness of fit: chi-square/degree of freedom, Non-Normed Fit Index (NNFI), Comparative Fit Index (CFI), and Average Absolute Standardised Residual (AASR). In another study, Segars Grover (1993) included several other measures of model fit: goodness-of-fit Index (GFI), Adjusted Goodness-of-fit Index (AGFI), fit criterion, and Root Mean Square Residual. Table 3 lists the recommended values of various measures of model fit as suggested by these authors. Many researchers recommend that multiple fit criteria be used (Bollen and Long, 1993; Breckler, 1990; Tanaka, 1993) in order to attenuate any measuring biases inherent in different measures.

Table 3. Recommended values of goodness-of-fit measures

Goodness of fit measure	Recommended Value
Chi-square	$p \geq .05$
Chi-square/degree of freedom	≤ 3.0
Goodness-of-fit Index (GFI)	$\geq .90$
Adjusted Goodness-of-fit Index (AGFI)	$\geq .80$
Normed Fit Index (NFI)	$\geq .90$
Non-Normed Fit Index (NNFI)	$\geq .90$
Comparative Fit Index (CFI)	$\geq .90$
Root Mean Square Residual (RMSR)	$\leq .10$
Incremental Fit Index (IFI)	≥ 0.90

Adapted with modifications from Hartwick and Barki (1994) and Segars and Grover (1993)

The hypothesized research model is shown in Figure 2. The goodness of fit measures for this model are summarized in Table 4 indicating a significant $\chi^2 = 246.58, df = 225, p = .154$. This result indicated a good fit, as the probability level was above the generally accepted critical value p = .05, which supported the research hypotheses.

The methodological problems in cross-cultural research (Ercan et al., 1991) were noted, and mindful of the ongoing debate (Boyd, 1993) in the field, the authors acknowledged and attempted to integrate current developments into their research design. As with the major part of cross-cultural research (Leung and Bond, 1989), this was a cross-sectional static study. In particular, it is important to note that the number of cultures generally included in cross-cultural research needs to be low (Nath, 1968; Sekaran, 1983), and that much of the research as yet should be viewed as being primarily developmental in nature (Adler, 1983). Moreover, it is necessary to appreciate that language is not a neutral vehicle, and that our thinking is affected by the words, phrases and categories available in our language (Hofstede, 1980). Consequently, equivalence of meaning is more important than direct translation, and research study needs to be designed, executed and interpreted from each participating culture's perspective and not from a single culture. Such points were borne in mind in the process of questionnaire design and analysis of results.

The discussion and analysis that follows examines and defines the relevance of the factors that influence DSS usage in making strategic decisions in local governments in Egypt.

Table 4. Fit measures for task characteristics model

Fit Measure	Task Characteristics model
Discrepancy (CMIN)	246.58
Degrees of freedom	225
P	0.15
Number of parameters (NPAR)	100
Discrepancy / df (CMINDF)	1.10
RMR	0.06
GFI	0.94
Adjusted GFI	0.91
Parsimony-adjusted GFI	0.65
Normed fit index (NFI)	0.68
Relative fit index (RFI)	0.57
Incremental fit index (IFI)	0.96
Tucker-Lewis index (TLI)	0.94
Comparative fit index (CFI)	0.95
Parsimony ratio (PRATIO)	0.75
Parsimony-adjusted NFI (PNFI)	0.51
Parsimony-adjusted CFI (PCFI)	0.72
RMSEA (PCLOSE)	0.02
P for test of close fit	1.00

ANALYSIS AND DISCUSSION

This study provides an understanding of the factors that affect CEO DSS usage in supporting managers in developing strategies to increase the utilization of the DSS.

STRUCTURAL EQUATION ANALYSIS

This study integrated the theoretical approaches and empirical findings of research on DSS usage in local authorities in Egypt, and tested a structural equation model examining TAM and other organizational and human factors that supposedly increase DSS usage by CEO in local authorities in particular and other organizations in general. PU and PEU showed significant direct effect on DSS usage at 0.001 and 0.10 levels and in consequence confirmed all earlier cited studies about TAM (Davis, 1989; Igbaria, Zinatelli, Cragg, and Cavaye, 1997). As TAM proposes, both PU and PEU are important in technology acceptance and usage. However, their relative importance in the acceptance process has been shown to be different in previous studies. For instance, (Davis, 1993) found that usefulness dominated ease of use, whereas (Adams, Nelson, and Todd, 1992) found ease of use to be more influential than usefulness.

In understanding the main relationships in the creation of the overall model, consideration has been given to the dynamics of the relationship between the independent and latent variables, and their overall impact on usage as the chosen performance indicator. It is important to better identify what the latent variables are in the context of the underlying issues that were researched. PEU in particular considers what the user viewed to be the central issues in creating user friendliness of software, and whether the current DSS was causing a barrier to entry or facilitating further use.

PU is based on DSS users' key business performance measures for success and consequently, has direct implications on the independent variables that identify the overall usage.

Finally, DSS usage provides a performance indicator specific to software applications supporting the strategic decision-making process.

We will first consider SEM in terms of the effects of the latent variables on independent variables. The latent variables have emerged through many other variables in the context of perceived ease of use (PEU) and perceived usefulness (PU), as outlined above. Further analysis of the data (see Figure 2) in the study have shown that the top management characteristics, i.e., understanding of DSS and involvement in the process of design and development, influence the PEU while none of the other research constructs have any significant effect on PU. The results showed a strong direct and positive relationship between perceived usefulness from one side and DSS characteristics and PEU from the other. In addition, there was an inverse relationship between PU and both top management and external support characteristics. These results for PU are somewhat surprising because this author expected that top management characteristics and support would have a positive direct effect on PU. This expectation was supported by an earlier result of this research, showing a positive relationship between PEU and top management. One plausible explanation for this result might be that decision makers think that central government creates a barrier to any benefits of functionality that DSS could offer to them by centralizing most of the strategic decision-making, as was obvious from the interviews with CEO and IT managers.

Figure 2. DSS adoption model for SDM

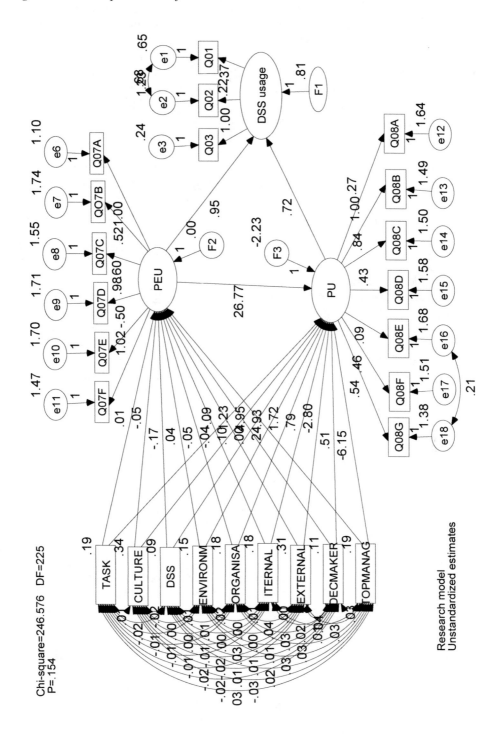

Chi-square=246.576   DF=225
P=.154

Research model
Unstandardized estimates

Evidence for the assumption of mediation of PEU and PU between DSS usage and new external constructs raises some important implications for the construction of research models of information technology adoption phenomena. These new constructs need to be re-examined in different contexts to confirm their validity. It appears that the relative importance of PEU is higher than PU, although both were found to be important, suggesting that the usability of DSS is crucial for its actual use in SDM in local authorities in developing countries, particularly in Egypt. Consequently, it is assumed that DSS needs to be driven by business processes, and where possible, the ability to customize applications will support the need for ease of use. This is of relevance to other researchers in evaluating these two constructs and in considering other related issues such as the stage and environment of DSS implementation.

Implications for Practice: Perhaps the most significant implication of the findings of this research is the necessity of moving toward decentralization regarding strategic decision-making where top management were found to have a negative relationship with PU. Clearly as indicated in many studies DSS implementation needs to be user-led and consequently, strategic decision makers need to be directly involved in the process of evaluating and implementing DSS. The integration of technical improvements and functionality of DSS in terms of (1) usability and (2) decision maker support is also an imperative if success of DSS in SDM in local authorities is to be ensured. The results also showed a negative relationship between external support and PU, suggesting dependence on internal support to guarantee productive usage of DSS. Next generation groupware and user-centric software tools enable users to overcome some issues such as lack of internal support and software that specifically meets individual needs. In the future, moves towards adaptive software applications through profiling solutions which capture behavioral patterns, has the potential for radical technology-led change in perceived ease of use and use of DSS in the strategic decision-making process.

REFERENCES

Adams, D.A., Nelson, R.R. and Todd, P.A. (1992). Perceived usefulness, ease of use, and usage of information. *MIS Quarterly, 16*(2), 227-248.

Agarwal, R. and Prasad, J. (1998a). A conceptual and operational definition of personal innovativeness in the domain of information technology. *Information Systems Research, 9*(3), 204-215.

Agarwal, R. and Prasad, J. (1998b). The antecedents and consequents of user perceptions in information technology adoption. *Decision Support Systems, 22*(11), 15-29.

Agarwal, R. and Prasad, J. (1999). Are individual differences germane to the acceptance of new information technologies? *Decision Sciences, 30*(2), 361-391.

Ang, J. and Teo, T. (1997). CSFs and sources of assistance and expertise in strategic IS planning: a Singapore perspective. *European Journal of Information Systems, 6,* 164-171.

Arbuckle, J.L. and Wothke, W. (1999). *AMOS 4.0 user's guide.* Chicago, IL: Smallwaters Corporation.

Benjamin, R.I., Rockart, J.F., Morton, M.S.S. and Wyman, J. (1984). Information technology: a strategic opportunity. *Sloan Management Review, 25*(3), 3-10.

Birdi, K., Pennington, J. and Zapf, D. (1997). Aging and errors in computer-based work: An observational field study. *Journal of Occupational and Organizational Psychology, 70*(1), 35-47.

Blanning, R.W., Bui, T.X. and Tan, M. (1997). National information infrastructure in Pacific Asia. *Decision Support Systems, 21*(3), 215-227.

Bohmstedt, G.W. (1970). Reliability and validity assessment in attitude measurement. In G.F. Summers (Ed.), *Attitude Measurement* (pp. 80-99). Chicago: Rand-McNally.

Brancheau, J.C. and Wetherbe, J. C. (1990). The adoption of spreadsheet software: testing innovation diffusion theory in the context of end user computing. *Information Systems Research, 1*(2), 115-143.

Chau, P.Y.K. (1997). Re-examining a model for evaluating information center success using a structural equation modeling approach. *Decision Sciences, 28*(2), 309-334.

Cheney, P.H., Mann, R.I. and Amoroso, D.L. (1986). Organizational factors affecting the success of end-user computing. *Journal of Management Information Systems, 3*(1), 65-80.

Daft, R. L. and Lengel., R. H. (1986). Organizational information requirements, media richness and structural design. *MIS Quarterly, 32*(5), 554-572.

Davis, F. D. (1989). Perceived usefulness, perceived ease of use, and user acceptance of information technology. *MIS Quarterly, 13*(3), 319-340.

Davis, F. D. (1993). User acceptance of information technology: systems characteristics, user perceptions and behavioral impacts. *International Journal of Man-Machine Studies, 38*(3), 475-487.

Deane, F. P., Podd, J. and D. Henderson, R. (1998). Relationship between self-report and log data estimates of information system usage. *Computers in Human Behavior, 14*(4), 621-636.

DeLone, W.H. (1988). Determinants of success for computer usage in small business. *MIS Quarterly, 12*(1), 51-61.

DeLone, W.H. and McLean, E.R. (1992). Information systems success: the quest for the dependent variable. *Information Systems Research, 3*(1), 60-95.

DeSanctis, G. (1982). *An Examination of an Expectancy Theory Model of Decision Support System Usage.* Unpublished PhD dissertation, Texas Tech University, Texas.

El Sawy, O.A. (1985). Personal information systems for strategic scanning in turbulent environments: can the CEO go on-line? *MIS Quarterly, 9*(1), 53-59.

Fahey, L. (1981). On strategic management decision process. *Strategic Management Journal, 2*, 43-60.

Goodman, S.E. and Press, L.I. (1995). Computing in Vietnam: an Asian tiger in the rough. *Communications of the ACM, 38*(1), 11-16.

Guimaraes, T., Igbaria, M. and Lu, M. (1992). The determinants of DSS success: an integrated model. *Decision Sciences, 23*(2), 409-431.

Hartwick, J. and Barki, H. (1994). Explaining the role of user participation in information system use. *Management Science, 40*(4), 440-466.

Hasan, H. and Lampitsi, S. (1995). Executive access to information systems in Australian public organizations. *Journal of Strategic Information Systems, 4*(3), 213-223.

Hatten, M.L. and Hatten, K.J. (1997). Information systems strategy: Long overdue—and still not here. *Long Range Planning, 30*(2), 254-266.

Hendrickson, A.R., Massey, P.D. and Cronan, T.P. (1993). On the test-retest reliability of perceived usefulness and perceived ease of use scales. *MIS Quarterly, 17*(2), 227-231.

Huber, G.P. and Robey, D. (1983). Cognitive style as a basis for MIS and DSS designs: much ado about nothing?. *Management Science, 29*(5), 567-583.

Igbaria, M. (1992). An examination of microcomputer usage in Taiwan. *Information and Management, 22,* 19-28.

Igbaria, M., Pavri, F.N. and Huff, S.L. (1989). Microcomputer applications: an empirical look at usage. *Information and Management, 16*(4), 187-197.

Igbaria, M., Zinatelli, N., Cragg, P. and Cavaye, A.L.M. (1997). Personal computing acceptance factors in small firms: a structural equation model. *MIS Quarterly, 21*(3), 279-305.

Johnston, H.R. and Carrico, S.R. (1988). Developing capabilities to use information strategy. *MIS Quarterly, 12*(1), 37-50.

Joreskog, K.G. and Sorbom, D. (1993). *LISREL 8: Structural equation modelling with the SIMPLIS command language.* Chicago, IL: Scientific Software International.

Karten, N.(1987). Why executives don't compute. *Information Strategy, 4*(1), 38-40.

King, W.R. (1996). Strategic issues in groupware. *Information Systems Management, 13,* 73-76.

King, W.R. and Teo, T.S.H. (1996). Key dimensions of facilitators and inhibitors for the strategic use of information technology. *Journal of Management Information Systems, 12*(4), 35-53.

Knight, J. (1993). Contumacious computer. In W.W. Cotterman and M.B. Malik (Eds.), *Information Technology in Support of Economic Development.* Atlanta, GA: Georgia State University Business Press.

Li, E.Y. (1997). Perceived importance of information system success factors: A meta analysis of group differences. *Information and Management, 32*(1), 15-28.

Lind, M.R., Zmud, R.W. and Fischer, W.A. (1989). Microcomputer adoption: The impact of organizational size and structure. *Information and Management, 16*(3), 157-163.

Mahmood, M.A., Gemoets, L.A. and Gosler, M.D. (1995). Information technology transfer and diffusion to mexico: A preliminary analysis. *Journal of Global Information Management, 3*(4), 5-15.

Maish, A.M. (1979). A user's behaviour toward his MIS. *MIS Quarterly, 3*(1), 39-52.

Mazzolini, R. (1981). How strategic decisions are made. *Long Range Planning, 14*(3), 85-96.

Mintzberg, H. (1975). The manager's job: Folkore and fact. *Harvard Business Review, 53*(4), 49-61.

Mintzberg, H.R.D. and Theoret, A. (1976). The structure of the 'unstructured' decision processes. *Administrative Science Quarterly, 21,* 246-275.

Moore, G.C. and Benbasat, I. (1991). Development of instrument to measure the perceptions of adopting an information technology innovation. *Information Systems Research, 2*(3), 192-222.

Neo, B.S. (1988). Factors facilitating the use of information technology for competitive advantage: an exploratory study. *Information and Management, 15,* 191-201.

Odedra, M., Lawrie, M., Bennett, M. and Goodman, S. (1993). Sub-Saharan Africa: a technological desert. *Communications of the ACM, 36*(2), 22-29.

Prescott, M.B. and Conger, S.A. (1995). Information technology innovations: a classification by IT locus of impact and research approach. *Database, 26*(2and3).

Ramaprasad, A. (1987). Cognitive process as a basis for MIS and DSS design. *Management Science, 33*(2139-148).

Raymond, L. (1985). Organizational characteristics and MIS success in the context of the small business. *MIS Quarterly, 9*(1), 37-52.

Rogers, E.M. (1995). *Diffusion of Innovations.* New York: The Free Press.

Rose, G. and Straub, D. (1998). Predicting general IT use: applying TAM to the Arabic world. *Journal of Global Information Management, 6*(3), 39-46.

Saga, V. and Zmud, R. (1994). The nature and determinants of IT acceptance, routinization, and infusion. *IFIP Transactions A Computer Science and Technology, A*(45), 67-86.

Sanders, G.L. and Courtney, J.F. (1985). A field study of organizational factors influencing DSS success. *MIS Quarterly, 9*(1), 77-94.

Segars, A.H. and Grover, V. (1993). Re-examining perceived ease of use and usefulness: a confirmatory factor analysis. *MIS Quarterly, 17*(4), 517-526.

Shayo, C., Guthrie, R. and Igbaria, M. (1999). Exploring the measurement of end user computing success. *End User Computing, 11*(1), 5-14.

Simon, H.A. (1965). *The shape of automation.* New York: Harper and Row.

Sirnivasan, A. (1985). Alternative measures of systems effectiveness: associations and implications. *MIS Quarterly, 9*(3), 243-253.

Taylor, S. and Todd, P. (1995). Assessing IT usage: The role of prior experience. *MIS Quarterly, 19*(4), 561-570.

Thompson, R. and Rose, D. (1994). *Information Technology Adoption and Use.* Paper presented at the Administrative Sciences Association of Canada, Canada.

Thompson, R.L., Higgins, C.A. and Howell, J.M. (1991). Personal computing: toward a conceptual model of utilization. *MIS Quarterly, 15*(1), 125-144.

Toubkin, A. and Simis., P. (1980). *User Expectation of Attitudes in the Design of Productive Information Systems.* Paper presented at the 13th Hawaii International Conference on Systems Sciences, Honolulu.

Udo, G.J. and Davis, J.S. (1992a). Factors affecting decision support system benefits. *Information and Management, 23*, 359-371.

Udo, G.J. and Davis, J. S. (1992b). A comparative analysis of DSS user-friendliness and effectiveness. *International Journal of Information Management, 12*(3), 209-224.

Chapter XVIII

The Perception of Managers on the Impacts of the Internet in Brazilian Hotels: An Exploratory Study

Luiz Augusto Machado Mendes Filho
FARN, Brazil

Anatália Saraiva Martins Ramos
UFRN, Brazil

ABSTRACT

The present study has an exploratory nature and aims to analyze the perception of managers on the efficiency, access importance, use as a communication tool, benefits and difficulties of Internet use in Brazilian hotels and also its effects according to the facilities rank and property size plus managers' age and experience time. It has been used as a questionnaire to collect data from the managers of 35 hotels in the city of Natal, RN, Brazil. By using analysis of variance (ANOVA) and the Tukey test, results showed that there is almost no significant difference on the perception of managers on the impact of Internet use in hotels. However, those variables that were different show that for younger and less experienced managers and luxurious hotels with more than 50 rooms, there is a more favorable perception on the impacts of the Internet.

INTRODUCTION

Business and leisure are being increasingly linked in countries, societies, people and companies that are being connected in most diverse ways. Such links are constantly being reinforced by two of the most growing and biggest industries in the world: Tourism and IT (Information Technology).

Note the importance of Information Technology and its significance for the Tourism Industry, as organizations use the WWW for interactivity and competitiveness. The key factor for successful organizations is their willingness to do business in this new way.

Technology has been increasingly developing a major role in the Tourism area, particularly in hotel operations and, must be a relevant part of hotel activities. According to studies and data, the use of technological tools will allow more competition for hotels.

Technology will be the catalyst of change, a source of growing connectivity and one of the most important factors in distinguishing success among hotel companies. Few issues have greater importance to the hospitality business than the technology decisions that will be made in the coming years (Van Hoof et al., 1995; Buhalis, 1999; Cline, 1999).

The tourism area, from which hotels are a segment, has an outstanding performance in global businesses, for it moves US$3.5, which is equivalent to 11.7 percent of the world's Gross Domestic Product and also has a 4.1 percent growth prospects a year, according to the World Travel and Tourism Council (WTTC, 2001).

In tourism, the use of information technologies for basic functions is becoming usual (Lage, 2000) – conferences, business meetings in distant places, training, designed routes and airlines, reservations and tickets purchased through computer systems, tourist shops, restaurants – all these services have led tourist companies to adopt more updated methods in order to increase competition. Consumers are already becoming familiar with new technologies; they demand more flexible, interactive and specialized products and services, which will bring new management techniques from the intelligent use of IT used to accomplish tour companies business processes (Buhalis, 1998).

Though many experts and businessmen agreed that the Internet is probably the most important technological tool, it is still relatively new and misused in hotel industry (Van Hoof & Verbeeten, 1997).

Viewing this scenario of Internet use in hotels, most precisely in the city of Natal, estate of Rio Grande do Norte (Brazil), we had posed a research question- *which factors affect the perception of hotel managers on the impacts of the Internet in their facilities?*

In order to answer that question, field research was conducted to identify the factors that contribute to the perception of hotel managers relating to Internet use in their hotels. The following specific aims were defined:

- Describing the hotel and manager profiles and their organizational and individual features of Internet use, respectively.
- Determining which aspects of Internet use are considered important to hotel managers, identifying their individual perceptions in terms of efficiency, access importance, use as a tool of communication, benefits and difficulties of Internet use in hotels.
- Identifying which organizational and individual factors contribute to the perception of managers as to the use of the Internet in hotels, particularly according to the number of rooms, rate, the manager's age and their experience in the hotel business.

This article is divided in five parts – the first one in the introduction itself. On the second part, we present basic concepts and a theoretical background. The third part deals with methodological resources used on the research. In the fourth part, results are presented and discussed through descriptive and inferential analysis. In the end, a few statements are presented on the Internet's role in the hotel industry, according to the results and main problems of the research.

THE INTERNET IN THE TOURISM AND HOTEL INDUSTRY

Tourism and the hotel industry depend progressively on the resource of new information technology to follow and update the tools which allow an efficient development of activities in each section of the hotel leading to better results for its management (Matoso, 1996). According to Phillips and Moutinho (1998) and Sheldon (1997), IT is one of the critical factors of success in the hotel industry.

During the 80's and 90's, several authors from companies and universities had foreseen that as new technologies were increasingly used, hotels would benefit in a great range of situations. For example, better qualified services for customers, increased sales and profits, efficiency in operation and integration of hotel sectors, quick communication and cost reduction (Van Hoof et al., 1995; Laudon & Laudon, 1999).

Technological applications enable information and knowledge to bring competitive advantage to the future profile of the hotel. The "Age of Information" idea is that the most modern companies will build their success upon the amount of knowledge they have about their clients as well as give information on their products and services and how they will profit in this new environment (Olsen & Connoly, 2000).

The Internet as a mean of communication gives several advantages or benefits comparing to other vehicles. According to Lage (2000), when it comes to the tourist area, the main points are: the new relationship between consumers and companies, marketing for actively participating consumers, the importance of detailed information, self-service application, credibility and agility of communication.

In a specific way, the Internet provides an expansion on hotel services changing this industry and giving new opportunities to clients thus being a new channel to be developed. Besides on-line reservation services, the Internet allows hotel to sell their services and charge them electronically and to offer new products through the World Wide Web (Laudon & Laudon, 1999; Blank, 2000).

Through the Web, the user can check a hotel's location, compare rates, see pictures and watch videos, get tourist destination information and about other facilities, check room availability, book and confirm their booking for the amount of time they want to stay, among other services. Hence, the interactivity of the Web provides an ideal medium for distributing accommodations online, consolidating itself as a very adequate platform for bringing information and services to the client in a very straightforward, efficient and quick way (Flecha & Damiani, 2000; Hotels, 2001).

Tourism is among the largest on-line industries and is one of the most important kinds of commerce through the Web. It corresponds to almost 40 percent of all global electronic commerce transactions (Werthner & Klein, 1999; Scottish Executive, 2000). Therefore, the data shows that all major companies linked to the tourism industry (hotels, agencies, air companies, rentals) do possess some kind of e-commerce activity through the Web

(O'Connor, 1999). The Internet is probably the newest star on communication and it is extremely valuable on tourism industry. The use of the Internet and the World Wide Web is spreading quickly on most developments of the consumer's access area to travel databases. There are hundreds of thousands of suppliers' homepages, associations, e-news, newsgroups and chats for the travel and tourism community. This bunch of technologies provides many opportunities for the industry to interact with its consumers and suppliers. It is also possible that, through information technology, products and services may be personalized according to the tourist needs, and thus, becoming a differential feature for those who adopt it (Sheldon, 1997; Buhalis, 1998).

The purchase of products and services through the Internet is revolutionizing the world of business and people's lives as well. For some clients, it is more comfortable to book an air ticket through the company homepage than going to the travel agency (Franco Jr., 2001).

No technology had ever had such full acceptance to allow that to happen. As the Internet began and grew, the use of such technologies at home or work and the new opportunities that arose from the lower costs in telecommunication equipment made it possible for suppliers to distribute information to their clients and process reservations directly with the clients (O'Connor, 2001). So, it became easy for IT to link clients to suppliers and thus, many new ways of doing business were created, reshaping the industry and creating new intermediates in tourism industry. According to Jeong and Lambert (2001), the Internet has already modified the competitive strategy of some hotels. It is through the Internet that the client can have a "self-understanding" in a service that is being offered to him in a more efficient way. In hotels, check-in processes can already be completely automatic, from the Internet booking until the moment the client takes his keys in an automatic dispenser. The result is that clients can become more informed and willing to have quick answers from the orders on-line.

From the theoretical fundaments and similar studies briefly presented above, a frame been developed for the research aiming at three targets to be explored through the five dimensions of analysis that build the construct "The perception of the importance of Internet use": efficiency, access, mean of communication, benefits and difficulties.

On the other hand, to relate these dimensions of Internet use to conditioning factors, the model suggests a group of four variables: two on organizational level (Hotel Rate and Number of Rooms) and two on an individual level (Managers' Age and Hotel Experience).

RESEARCH METHODOLOGY

According to its aims, the research was defined as descriptive since it describes the features of a certain population as well as establishes relationships between variables through a standardized data collection technique. Its approach is quantitative, once the research used quantification not only in the data collection process, but also in their treatment through statistical methods. The technical procedures used to gather the data enable us to identify this research as a fieldwork - for empirically investigating the place where the event took place and for questioning people whose behavior it intended to know. The field research was applied to an entire universe of medium and big hotels. The data collection tool was a questionnaire with closed questions, organized in two parts. The first one had profile questions for manager/respondent, hotel and Internet use. The second part had perception questions using a non-metric scale for measuring the importance from one to five (on a five-point Likert-type scale), which tried to measure different levels of individual manager importance on the following aspects of Internet use: Efficiency, Access to Internet, Means of Communication, Internet Benefits and Internet Difficulties, containing 44 perception evaluation items. This questionnaire was adapted from Van Hoof and Combrink (1998) and validated for Brazilian reality enabling to confirm the variables that belong to the questionnaire's blocks.

The field research was developed in the city of Natal, capital of Rio Grande do Norte estate in Brazil. The organizational unity chosen was hotel enterprise with more than 40 rooms (for in the researched area they are considered as medium to big-sized) rated on the "Guia Quatro Rodas Brazil." The subjects of the research were the managers who were more involved with Internet use in his hotel.

The "Guia Quatro Rodas Brazil" was used as a reference for rating the categorized researched hotels for two reasons: first for that is the guide which has been currently used by tourists, tour agencies and tour operators for over 36 years in Brazil; secondly because EMBRATUR

(Brazilian Tourism Institute) official organ from the Ministry of Sport and Tourism is still evaluating the hotels according to its new Brazilian Rating System for Hosting Means; once its old system had low credibility for rating (Duarte, 1996), it was not possible to use that new system.

Small properties are out of the study for these sort of facility have less awareness on the importance of adopting technological solutions and also have less financial conditions to invest in IT (Cooper et al., 1998). It is also believed that could interfere in the perception of managers on the impacts of the Internet.

Nine out of the 44 hotels selected were not given the questionnaire application, for these reasons: three of them had already taken the pre-test; four were not rated in the "Guia Quatro Rodas Brazil," one is not working and another one where it was not possible to contact its manager to answer the questions, though it was visited three times. Thirty-five hotels were studied and the managers spent 25 minutes to answer the questionnaire.

This study is considered of unique transversal type, because it extracted only one sample from the interviewees of the target-population and the information was collected only once. The first phase of collecting data refers to pre-test application period developed on the first week of August 2001, in three hotels. After that phase, some due changes were made and the questionnaires were then applied from August 14 to September 13, 2001.

With respect to statistical treatment of data, Microsoft's STATISTICA software for Windows was used to have the descriptive analysis of data, and for inferential results, analysis of variance (ANOVA) and HSD Tukey test were carried out.

In the descriptive analysis, software calculated the frequency table in each one of the variables used in the study and distributed in five parts of the questionnaire. On the first and second parts (Interview/hotel profile and Internet use) it was calculated only the percentages of each of the variables involved. On the remaining parts (Manager Perceptions, Benefits and Difficulties), the variables *percentages* and *averages* were calculated.

The analysis of variance was used to check if there was any significant difference on the opinions of hotel managers according to their individual profile (age and experience) and the organizational profile (rate and number of rooms). The ANOVA allows the researcher to compare averages of several different samples (three or more) with data from the ordinal level to determine if population averages from these samples have any significant differences (Montgomery, 1996).

It was also used Tukey's HSD test ("honestly significant difference") to locate where significant differences were located between the averages. Turkey's HSD test is specific for different sized samples, which is the case of this research. Tukey's HSD test is one of the most useful tests for multiple comparisons.

RESULTS

The results of the research were divided in two parts: The first one consists on a descriptive analysis where hotels and managers are profiled and also the perception of managers to the use of the Internet in hotels; the second part presents the analysis based on Tukey's variance statistical tests.

Descriptive Results of the Research

Sampled Hotels and Managers Demographic Profiles—In Table 1, note that most respondents were women (65.7 percent), hotel reservation managers (60 percent), up to 35 years old (68.6 percent). In respect to their hotel experience, results were concentrated on six to 15 years of experience (42.9 percent), but it is important to say that there is also a considerable percentage of five-year-old experience (40 percent).

Table 2 shows that the 35 researched hotels are rated as "simple" or "medium-comfortable" (74.3%), a little more than a half of them have less than a hundred rooms.

Aspects of Internet Use in Hotels—When questioned about the use of the Internet in the hotels, most of the managers answered that they did have Internet of any kind in their facilities (97.1 percent). Another data shows that 97.1 percent of the hotels have their own e-mail address.

Table 1. Managers' profile

Position	N	%
General Manager	3	8.6
Guest Manager	2	5.7
Commercial Manager	4	11.4
Administrative Manager	2	5.7
Reception Manager	3	8.6
Reservation Manager	21	60.0
Total	35	100.0
Age	N	%
Less than 25 years old	8	22.9
26 to 35 years old	16	45.7
Over 36 years old	11	31.4
Total	35	100.0
Hotel Experience	N	%
Less than 5 years	14	40.0
6 to 15 years	15	42.9
Over 16 years	6	17.1
Total	35	100.0

Table 2. Hotels profile

Hotel Rate	N	%
Simple	14	40.0
Medium Comfort	12	34.3
Comfortable/ Very Comfortable/ Luxury	9	25.7
Total	35	100.0
Number of hotel rooms	N	%
Less than 50 rooms	7	20.0
51 to 100 rooms	11	31.4
101 to 150 rooms	10	28.6
Over 151 rooms	7	20.0
Total	35	100.0

When it was asked if the hotel used the Internet to build up any kind of relationship with its clients, 85.7 percent of managers answered "yes" which seems to demonstrate their interest in using the Web as an electronic marketing tool aiming their customers' faithfulness. Another relevant information is that only four (11.4 percent) out of the 35 managers said they used an intranet in their work. This indicates that hotels do not seem to consider the importance of using the Internet as a communication and cooperation tool for their employees. A possible reason for this data is that some of these hotels do not use an Internet platform as a way of corporate communication and cooperation.

Relating to hotel-supplier integration, only 20 percent of the hotels use the Internet to purchase goods from the supplier. Mendes, Filho and Ramos (2001) stated that administration and food and beverage managers do research their product prices, but do not buy them through the Web; therefore, the Web is used only for price investigation.

Slightly more than 90 percent of hotels already have their homepages; 54.3 percent of such pages have existed for over two years which resembles the research carried by Lituchy and Rail (2000) in the U.S. and Canada, where 89.2 percent of these facilities already have a web site on the Internet. The vast majority (55.9 percent) has already been on the Web for over two years.

Most of these hotels are also using their homepages to offer Web-based room reservation services, for 85 percent of them do have that service.

The Perception of Managers Concerning Internet Use in Hotels—As to the managers' perception of the importance of using the Internet in hotels, they gave their opinions about: efficiency, Internet access, mean of communication, benefits and difficulties, as follows.

Internet Efficiency

Companies in general use the Internet as a marketing tool and specifically in hotels, as the research has demonstrated. When asked about the efficiency, managers reported that the Internet was more efficient when used as a marketing tool and advertising tool for 82 percent considered it very important and the remaining (17.1 percent) said it was important. The use of the Internet on room reservations had also reached an excellent level of importance, 71.4

percent of the managers said it was very important. The use of the Internet for reservations has reached a considerably important level, 71.4 percent of managers consider it very important. On the other hand, the use of the Internet for personal training had the smallest average (3.8 percent) from the options mentioned; only 31.4 percent of the managers consider it important for that aim.

The Importance of Internet Access

When asked how important Internet access was for them and their employees, managers identified their own access as much more important than their employees'. According to the data obtained, 88.6 percent of the managers consider their own access very important while only 5.8 percent for the employees. Interviewees also said that it was important for them to provide Internet services to the guests; the average of answers was 4.7 percent.

Internet as a Mean of Communication

Managers answered that Internet use, as a mean of communication with clients and guests is the most important for them and gave it an average score of 4.6. The use of the Internet to communicate with the central office/headquarters had also a very good 4.5 average. On the other hand, the use of the Internet to communicate with employees had a 2.4 average in the managers' opinion.

Internet Benefits

On the managers' opinion, the most expressive benefit reached was the increase of hotel advertising and marketing in the local and worldwide media, considering the most important by 85.7 percent of the interviewees (Table 3). Another benefit that also had a great result was the increase of sales and reservations through the Web, 80 percent of the managers said it is very important for their facilities. The result is coherent to Abreu and Costa study (2000) in which it was demonstrated that the increase in the sales was the main aim expected by hotels when using the Internet.

Table 3. Biggest benefit that the Internet can bring to a hotel

Benefits	Not important	Little important	Neutral	Important	Very Important	Average
Increasing hotel advertising and marketing	2.9%	0.0%	0.0%	11.4%	85.7%	4.8
Increasing Sales and reservations	0.0%	2.9%	0.0%	17.1%	80.0%	4.7
Improving client service by providing hotel information	0.0%	0.0%	0.0%	37.1%	62.9%	4.6
Reducing hotel costs	0.0%	0.0%	5.7%	31.4%	62.9%	4.6
Improving hotel image	0.0%	2.9%	5.7%	45.7%	45.7%	4.3
Facilitating the relationship with clients through messages and direct mail.	0.0%	5.7%	2.9%	45.7%	45.7%	4.3
Increasing competition (by competing with other hotels)	0.0%	2.9%	2.9%	51.4%	42.9%	4.3
Allowing bigger knowledge on the client	0.0%	5.7%	2.9%	60.0%	31.4%	4.2

Table 4. Biggest difficulty for the hotel to use the Internet

Difficulties	Not difficult	Little difficult	Neutral	Difficult	Very difficult	Average
Cost and time involved on Internet installation process	17.2%	17.2%	14.2%	5.7%	45.7%	3.5
Clients and employees are not used to using the Internet	14.3%	14.3%	5.7%	34.3%	31.4%	3.5
Developing training courses for employees who have no knowledge about Internet.	20.0%	31.4%	5.7%	22.9%	20.0%	2.9
Client becomes suspicious about using the Internet	28.5%	25.7%	14.3%	22.9%	8.6%	2.6
Safety and trust of hotel data to be exposed on the Web	40.0%	11.4%	17.2%	17.2%	14.2%	2.5
Employees waste time by using Internet for personal purposes	31.4%	17.2%	11.4%	20.0%	20.0%	2.4
Specialized labor cost for homepage maintenance and update	20.0%	51.4%	5.7%	14.3%	8.6	2.4
Complex Internet management	48.6%	22.8%	8.6%	8.6%	11.4%	2.1

However, there were two benefits that were mentioned by 5.7 percent of the managers as less important for their hotels: to facilitate the relationship with the client through messages, forwarded messages and birthday cards and to allow a greater knowledge on the client through homepage register forms.

Internet Difficulties

According to Table 4, for 45.7 percent of the managers interviewed, cost and time involved in the setting of the Internet makes its use very difficult in a hotel. A reason that may justify this statement is that most hotels are quite simple, with less than a hundred rooms. This may mean less financial power to invest time and money for Internet access. The variable "clients and employees are not used to using the Internet and/or a computer" reached 31.4 percent of managers' opinions as an item that makes it difficult for their facilities to use the Internet.

According to managers' opinion, the complexity of Internet management (48.6 percent) and also the safety and trust of hotel data that can be exposed on the Web (40 percent) do not seem to be difficult elements to be dealt with when it comes to Internet presence in the hotel.

Inferential Results of Internet Use in Hotels

It was used the one-way average comparison technique (ANOVA) with a 0.05 significance level to check if there were differences in the opinions of managers followed by a Tukey test to determine the bias of such differences.

The results of the research are intended to identify which factors contributed to the perception of managers relating to Internet use in hotels. The analysis was developed for four variables: according to the number of rooms and rate – both related to the organizational profile; age of managers and experience in the hotel industry – both related to individual profile. Inside each profile, the perception of the importance of Internet use was analyzed the following variables: communication use, access importance, benefits and difficulties of using the Internet.

Effect of Managers' Age on Perception on the Use of Internet

The analyses of variance did not detect any significant variable for the effect of managers' age on their perceptions according to the following variables: Internet efficiency and access. However, there is significance in the difference of perception in the following variables: use for communication, benefits and difficulties.

According to the ANOVA test, (Table 5) a significant variable was found relating to the use of the Internet as a mean of communication: the importance of the Internet to communicate with the central office.

The analysis of variance has identified significance in two benefits given by the use of the Internet in hotels: to allow a greater knowledge on the client and to reduce the costs of the hotel. In the area of difficulties related to the installation of the Internet, only one variable had a significance level lower than 0.05: the development of training for employees who do not know how to use the Internet.

Table 5. Effect of managers' age on the perception of the importance of Internet use

IMPORTANCE OF INTERNET USE *Mean*	Less than 25 years old	26 to 35 years old	Over 36 years old	F-value	P
Efficiency					
Improving hotel marketing and advertising	4.75	4.94	4.73	1.220	0.309
Making reservations	4.75	4.81	4.36	1.798	0.182
Assessing competition	4.13	4.19	4.36	0.168	0.846
Training employees	4.13	3.75	3.55	0.563	0.575
Internet Access					
Enabling Internet access for the Manager	5.00	4.75	4.82	0.504	0.609
Enabling Internet access for the Guests	4.75	4.75	4.55	0.699	0.505
Enabling Internet access for the Employees	3.63	2.94	2.73	1.299	0.287
Mean of Communication*					
Communicating with guests	4.88	4.63	4.36	2.744	0.079
Communicating with central office	4.75	4.75	4.18	3.844	**0.032***
Communicating with suppliers	4.25	3.88	3.82	0.766	0.473
Communicating with employees	3.00	2.38	1.91	1.614	0.215
Benefits*					
Increasing hotel advertising and marketing on local and global media.	4.88	4.63	4.91	0.582	0.565
Increasing hotel reservations and sales	5.00	4.75	4.55	1.308	0.285
Improving client service by providing hotel information	4.88	4.56	4.55	1.340	0.276
Reducing hotel costs	4.63	4.81	4.18	4.218	**0.024***
Improving hotel image and facilitating the consolidation of its name/brand	4.38	4.25	4.45	0.258	0.774
Increase competition (Competition with hotels from other places)	4.63	4.25	4.27	0.881	0.424
Facilitating relationship with the client	4.75	4.06	4.36	2.158	0.132
Allowing greater knowledge on the client	4.63	4.31	3.64	5.904	**0.007***
Difficulties*					
Cost and time required for installing Internet in the hotel	3.88	3.81	2.64	2.225	0.125
Clients and employees are not used to using IT	3.25	3.94	3.18	1.117	0.340
Need of Training for employees who do not know the Web	2.50	3.75	2.00	6.564	**0.004***
Client suspicious of using the Internet	2.63	2.38	2.82	0.342	0.713
Safety and trust of data in Internet ambient	2.38	2.50	2.73	0.129	0.880
Waste of time due to the use of Internet by employees for personal purposes	2.75	2.81	2.82	0.005	0.995
Specialized labor cost	2.63	2.38	2.27	0.191	0.827
Complex Internet management	2.13	2.31	1.82	0.387	0.682

* Variable with significance p<0.05

According to the Tukey test, younger managers (up to 35 years old) considered more important the use of the Internet to communicate with the central office rather than those over 35 years old.

Through the Tukey test, it was possible to conclude that managers up to 25 years old agreed that the Internet allows a bigger knowledge of the client than the managers older. Managers who were from 26 to 35 years old consider the Internet more important to reduce costs than the ones who are over 35 years old.

By using the Tukey test, the conclusion is that from 26 to 35 year old managers agree that training for employees who do not have any knowledge on the Web makes the use of IT more difficult than the ones who are over 35.

The Effect of Managers' Experience Time in Hotel Industry on the Perception on the Use of Internet Use

When it comes to the effect of managers' experience in hotel industry in their perceptions, it was not identified significant variables related to the efficiency of the Internet, access to the Internet and difficulties in its use. The effect of managers' hotel experience on the use of the Internet for communication had the following significant variables using ANOVA: the importance of the Internet to communicate with employees, guests and

Table 6. Effect of managers experience time on their perception

IMPORTANCE OF INTERNET USE	Less than 5 years	6 to 15 years	Over 16 years	F-value	P
Mean					
Efficiency					
Improving hotel marketing and advertising	4.79	4.87	4.83	0,155	0,857
Making reservations	4.71	4.80	4.17	2,376	0,109
Assessing competition	4.29	4.27	4.00	0,205	0,816
Training employees	3.79	4.00	3.17	1,104	0,344
Internet Access					
Enabling Internet access for the Manager	5.00	4.67	4.83	1,267	0,296
Enabling Internet access for the Guests	4.79	4.60	4.67	0,554	0,580
Enabling Internet access for the Employees	3.50	2.93	2.17	2,723	0,081
Mean of Communication*					
Communicating with guests	4.79	4.60	4.17	3,792	**0,033***
Communicating with central office	4.79	4.53	4.17	2,413	0.106
Communicating with suppliers	4.36	3.73	3.50	3.842	**0.032***
Communicating with employees	2.64	2.60	1.17	3.392	**0.046***
Benefits*					
Increasing hotel advertising and marketing on local and global media.	4.64	4.87	4.83	0.351	0.706
Increasing hotel reservations and sales	4.64	4.80	4.83	0.306	0.738
Improving client service by providing hotel information	4.79	4.40	4.83	3.254	0.052
Reducing hotel costs	4.64	4.60	4.33	0.558	0.578
Improving hotel image and facilitating the consolidation of its name/brand	4.14	4.47	4.50	0.886	0.422
Increase competition (Competition with hotels from other places)	4.50	4.27	4.17	0.649	0.529
Facilitating relationship with the client	4.71	4.20	3.67	4.776	**0.015***
Allowing greater knowledge on the client	4.43	4.00	4.00	1.416	0.257
Difficulties					
Cost and time required for installing Internet in the hotel	3.07	3.73	3.67	0.656	0.526
Clients and employees are not used to using IT	3.86	3.33	3.33	0.539	0.588
Need of Training for employees who do not know the web	2.93	3.13	2.33	0.611	0.549
Client suspicious of using the Internet	2.64	2.67	2.17	0.310	0.735
Safety and trust of data in Internet ambient	2.93	2.13	2.67	1.014	0.374
Waste of time due to the use of Internet by employees for personal purposes	3.00	2.67	2.67	0.181	0.836
Specialized labor cost	2.36	2.67	1.83	1.019	0.372
Complex Internet management	1.93	2.13	2.50	0.334	0.719

* Variable with significance p<0.05

suppliers. From Table 6, it was observed that the ANOVA test also found a variable with a significance level below 0.05: the Internet facilitates the relationship with the client in terms of its benefits.

The Tukey test also indicated that managers with less than five years experience in hotel industry consider the use more important to use the Web to communicate with employees, guests and suppliers, rather than their colleagues who have over five years of experienced in the area. Through the Tukey test, it was also concluded that managers who have less than five years of hotel experience think the use of the Internet facilitates the relationship with the client far more than the more experienced managers.

Effect of Hotel Rate on the Perception of Internet Use

The ANOVA test has found no significant result relating the effect of hotel rating to the efficiency of, access to , and difficulties of the Internet. However, as it shown on Table 7, the ANOVA test applied to the benefits of the Internet to the hotel has found a variable with a significance level below 0.05: Internet use does improve the service to clients by providing information of the hotel through its web page and e-mail. From the Tukey test, managers of luxurious hotels consider it more important to use the Internet to improve service to the client rather than economy-class hotel managers.

Besides the variables mentioned above, three variables showed significant results in the study on the use of the Internet for communication: the importance of the Internet to communicate with employees, guests and suppliers. Through the Tukey test, luxurious hotel managers (comfortable, very comfortable and luxurious) consider it more important to use the Web to communicate with employees rather than medium-comfort and simple hotel managers. The test also determined that medium-comfortable hotel managers consider the Internet as a more important tool to communicate with guests than simple hotels. On the other hand, medium- comfort hotel managers consider the Internet less important to communicate with suppliers than luxurious hotel managers.

Effect on the Number of Rooms in the Perception of Internet Use

The effect of the number of hotel rooms in the perception of the managers showed no significant variable related to efficiency, communication, benefits and difficulties. According to Table 8, the ANOVA test identified only one variable that has a significance level below 0.05 in relation to the number of hotel rooms: the importance of Internet access for the managers themselves.

Through the Tukey analysis, it was validated that managers in hotels with more than 100 rooms consider their access to the Internet more important than in a smaller hotel (less than 100 rooms).

CONCLUSION

The Internet does enable tourist companies to increase their competitiveness. IT can improve the efficiency of suppliers and provide tools for the development and delivery of different tourist products. One of the benefits reached is the reducing the dependence from the intermediates on the distribution of tourist products. Hotel owners should invest more money in technology besides concentrating more time and attention to subjects on that area.

Table 7. Effect of hotel rate on the perception of managers

IMPORTANCE OF INTERNET USE	Simple	Medium comfort	Luxury	F-value	P
Mean					
Efficiency					
Improving hotel marketing and advertising	4.79	4.92	4.78	0.471	0.629
Making reservations	4.79	4.50	4.67	0.633	0.537
Assessing competition	4.29	4.33	4.00	0.351	0.707
Training employees	3.93	3.25	4.22	2.136	0.135
Internet Access					
Enabling Internet access for the Manager	4.64	4.92	5.00	1.327	0.279
Enabling Internet access for the Guests	4.50	4.75	4.89	2.179	0.130
Enabling Internet access for the Employees	2.86	3.33	2.89	0.531	0.593
Mean of Communication*					
Communicating with guests	4.29	4.83	4.78	6.108	**0.006***
Communicating with central office	4.36	4.83	4.56	2.116	0.137
Communicating with suppliers	3.93	3.58	4.44	3.381	**0.047***
Communicating with employees	1.57	2.67	3.22	6.056	**0.006***
Benefits*					
Increasing hotel advertising and marketing on local and global media.	4.86	4.58	4.89	0.595	0.558
Increasing hotel reservations and sales	4.71	4.67	4.89	0.352	0.706
Improving client service by providing hotel information	4.36	4.67	5.00	6.232	**0.005***
Reducing hotel costs	4.64	4.50	4.56	0.174	0.841
Improving hotel image and facilitating the consolidation of its name/brand	4.36	4.25	4.44	0.180	0.836
Increase competition (Competition with hotels from other places)	4.14	4.50	4.44	1.017	0.373
Facilitating relationship with the client	4.29	4.50	4.11	0.615	0.547
Allowing greater knowledge on the client	4.00	4.42	4.11	1.048	0.362
Difficulties					
Cost and time required for installing Internet in the hotel	3.21	3.33	4.00	0.689	0.509
Clients and employees are not used to using IT	3.14	3.50	4.22	1.597	0.218
Need of Training for employees who do not know the web	2.50	2.67	3.89	2.966	0.066
Client suspicious of using the Internet	2.71	2.08	3.00	1.329	0.279
Safety and trust of data in Internet ambient	2.36	3.08	2.11	1.241	0.302
Waste of time due to the use of Internet by employees for personal purposes	2.57	2.92	3.00	0.244	0.785
Specialized labor cost	2.00	2.92	2.33	1.953	0.158
Complex Internet management	1.86	2.33	2.22	0.390	0.680

* Variable with significance p<0.05

IT affects all aspects of hotel value chain; going far beyond sectors and departments. As technology will be intrinsically linked to hotel business, its executives will insert technology in all their strategic decisions for the facility. That implies all the employees (including managers and directors) to have enough knowledge to extract the potential technology provides.

Using the Internet in the hotel industry in Natal has good prospects of growth, though in many hotels the use of such technology is still crawling. On the other hand, there are some hotels using and steadily setting the trend. It will be an important and strategic issue for businessmen to stimulate such Internet use policies inside the tourist trade, so they become "wired" to this new reality that can work in even terms with their competitors.

In this research, it was possible to portray the situation of mid and big-sized hotels in Natal, RN, Brazil, and contribute by offering a panoramic view on the use of the Internet and some impacts perceived by managers in the hotel industry. It has been demonstrated that

Table 8. Effect of the number of rooms in the perception of managers

IMPORTANCE OF INTERNET USE Mean	Less than 50 rooms	51 to 100	101 to 150	Over 151 rooms	F-value	P
Efficiency						
Improving hotel marketing and advertising	4.86	4.82	4.80	4.86	0.043	0.988
Making reservations	4.86	4.55	4.60	4.71	0.364	0.779
Assessing competition	4.14	4.64	4.30	3.57	2.030	0.130
Training employees	3.43	4.00	3.90	3.57	0.430	0.733
Internet Access*						
Enabling Internet access for the Manager	4.29	4.91	5.00	5.00	3.264	**0.030***
Enabling Internet access for the Guests	4.43	4.73	4.80	4.71	0.922	0.441
Enabling Internet access for the Employees	2.86	3.27	2.80	3.14	0.296	0.828
Mean of Communication						
Communicating with guests	4.57	4.73	4.40	4.71	0.903	0.451
Communicating with central office	4.57	4.73	4.50	4.43	0.393	0.759
Communicating with suppliers	3.86	4.09	3.80	4.00	0.251	0.860
Communicating with employees	2.43	2.36	2.20	2.57	0.104	0.957
Benefits						
Increasing hotel advertising and marketing on local and global media.	4.86	5.00	4.50	4.71	0.853	0.476
Increasing hotel reservations and sales	5.00	4.45	4.80	4.86	1.387	0.265
Improving client service by providing hotel information	4.43	4.64	4.70	4.71	0.508	0.679
Reducing hotel costs	4.57	4.64	4.40	4.71	0.413	0.745
Improving hotel image and facilitating the consolidation of its name/brand	4.57	4.27	4.20	4.43	0.405	0.750
Increase competition (Competition with hotels from other places)	3.86	4.64	4.30	4.43	2.087	0.122
Facilitating relationship with the client	4.29	4.64	4.10	4.14	0.949	0.429
Allowing greater knowledge on the client	4.29	4.27	4.00	4.14	0.282	0.838
Difficulties						
Cost and time required for installing Internet in the hotel	3.57	2.73	3.60	4.29	1.457	0.245
Clients and employees are not used to using IT	3.14	3.27	3.90	3.86	0.602	0.619
Need of Training for employees who do not know the web	2.57	2.82	3.10	3.14	0.231	0.874
Client suspicious of using the Internet	2.29	2.55	2.90	2.43	0.306	0.821
Safety and trust of data in Internet ambient	2.57	3.09	2.40	1.86	0.978	0.416
Waste of time due to the use of Internet by employees for personal purposes	3.14	2.73	2.30	3.29	0.662	0.582
Specialized labor cost	2.71	2.36	2.10	2.57	0.385	0.764
Complex Internet management	2.29	1.45	2.80	2.00	1.751	0.177

* Variable with significance p<0.05

there are few differences of opinion as to the use of the Internet in hotels. That leads to an important conclusion: nowadays, the Internet has become a highly relevant instrument, notwithstanding any demographic variables that may occur (e.g., age, experience, size and rate).

However, for its transversal and temporal character as well as its restraint to Brazilian hotels with more than 40 rooms in a specific city, it is not possible to generalize all hotel universes. Hence, there is an expectancy that other researches on academic level may complete and broaden this basis of knowledge on the impacts of IT applications, remarkably the ones developed for the Web platform and therefore, help the production sector to better understand them and adopt them effectively in their businesses.

For that purpose to be fulfilled, other research should be developed by incorporating other variables, using other analysis techniques and observing different cities, bigger hotel samples or even comparative studies with the results obtained.

REFERENCES

Blank, D. (2000). Internet will shape revenue-management role. *Hotel and Motel Management, 215*(11), 54-55.

Buhalis, D. (1998). Strategic use of information technologies in the tourism industry. *Tourism Management, 19*(5), 409-421.

Cline, R. (1999). Hospitality 2000 - The technology. *Lodging Hospitality, 55*(7), 18-26.

Cooper, C. et al. (1998). *Tourism - Principles and Practice.* 2nd edition. Boston, MA: Addison Wesley.

Flecha, A. C. & Damiani, W. B. (2000). Avanços da tecnologia da informação: resultados comparados de sites da indústria hoteleria. *Conference Proceedings of the 20th National Meeting of Production Engineering*, São Paulo, Brazil.

Franco Jr., C. F. (2001). E-business: Tecnologia de informação e negócios na Internet. São Paulo: Atlas.

Guia Quatro Rodas Brazil. (2001). São Paulo: Abril.

Hamel, G. (2001). Is this all you can build with the Net? Think bigger. *Fortune, 143*(9), 134-138.

Hotels. (2001). Hotels'2001 worldwide technology survey - part.1. *Hotels, 35*(2), 75-85.

Lage, B. H. (2000). Comunicação de massa e turismo. In B.H. Lage & P.C. Milone, Turismo: teoria e prática. São Paulo: Atlas.

Jeong, M., & Lambert, C. (2001). Adaptation of an information quality framework to measure customers' behavioral intentions to use lodging Web sites. *International Journal of Hospitality Management, 20*(2), 129-146.

Laudon, K. C., & Laudon, J. P. (1999). Sistemas de informação com Internet. 4th ed. Rio de Janeiro: LTC.

Matoso, J. M.G. (1996). A Informática na Hotelaria e Turismo. (1st ed.), Lisboa: Plátano Edições Técnicas.

Mendes Filho, L. A. M., & Ramos, A. S. M. (2001). The impact of Internet adoption in the hotel industry: The opinion of hotel managers in Bangor-Maine (USA). *Conference Proceedings of the 7th International Congress on Industrial Engineering and Operations Management*, Salvador, BA, Brazil.

Monteiro, P. (1999). Automação 5 estrelas: Sistemas de administração hoteleira invadem o mercado, facilitam a troca interna de informações e tornam o atendimento mais ágil e eficaz. *Automação*, 30-33.

Montgomery, D. (1996). *Design and Analysis of Experiments.* (4th ed). New York: John Wiley & Sons.

O'Connor, P. (2001). *Distribuição da informação eletrônica em turismo e hotelaria.* Porto Alegre: Bookman.

Olsen, M. D. & Connoly, D. J. (2000). Experience-based travel. *Cornell Hotel and Restaurant Administration Quarterly, 41*(1), 30-40.

Phillips, P. A. & Moutinho, L. (1998). *Strategic Planning Systems in Hospitality and Tourism.* CAB International, Wallingford, UK.

Scottish Executive (2000). A new strategy for Scottish tourism. Edinburg. Retrieved from the World Wide Web on July 21: http://www.scotland.gov.uk/library2/doc11/sfst.pdf.

Sheldon, P. (1997). *Tourism Information Technology.* CAB International, Wallingford, UK.

Van Hoof, H. B. et al. (1995). Technology needs and perceptions: an assessment of the U.S.

lodging industry. *Cornell Hotel and Restaurant Administration Quarterly, 36*(5), 64-69.

Van Hoof, H. B. & Combrink, T. E. (1998). U.S. Lodging managers and the Internet: perceptions from the industry. *Cornell Hotel and Restaurant Administration Quarterly, 39*(2), 46-54.

Van Hoof, H. B. & Verbeeten, M. J. (1997). Vendors receive mixed reviews. *Hotel and Motel Management, 212*(11), 42.

Werthener, H. & Klein, S. (1999). *Information Technology and Tourism: A Challenging Relationship* (Springer Computer Science). New York: Springer Verlag.

WTTC. (2001). World Travel & Tourism Council. Retrieved from the World Wide Web on May 6, 2001: http://www.wttc.org.

Chapter XIX

Information Technology Project Management to Achieve Efficiency in Brazilian Companies

Marly Monteiro de Carvalho
University of São Paulo, Brazil

Fernando José Barbin Laurindo
University of São Paulo, Brazil

Marcelo Schneck de Paula Pessôa
University of São Paulo, Brazil

ABSTRACT

This chapter focuses on applying the best practices in Information Technology (IT) project management in Brazil. The theoretical models adopted to discuss this issue are the Capability Maturity Model - CMM (Humphrey, 1989; Paulk et al., 1995), Project Management Maturity Model – PMMM (Kerzner, 2000 and 2001); the Project Management Body of Knowledge - PMBoK (PMI, 2000), and Quality Systems for software - ISO9000-3 (2001) and ISO 12207 (1995).

Several problems have been discussed regarding the efficiency of IT projects. Evaluation of efficiency is a controversial issue, and meeting project efficiency goals involves balancing scope expectations and the available resources.

This chapter presents IT project cases in Brazilian companies and a comparative analysis of their IT projects management models. The study is based on multiple cases: financial services, telecommunications and building materials companies. Interviews with the main actors from different levels of the organisational hierarchy have been done.

INTRODUCTION

Information Technology (IT) has an important role in the strategic function of the leading companies in the competitive markets (Porter, 2001). On the other hand, there is still an important discussion about the difficulties of finding evidence of returns over the investments in IT, called the "productivity paradox," (Willcocks & Lester, 1997; Brynjolfsson, 1993; Strassman, 1990).

The evaluation of project efficiency is a rather controversial issue. The uncertainty and the complexity inherent to IT projects pose a hindrance to the evaluation of their efficiency, both regarding cost and time frames, and in terms of quality. Meeting project efficiency goals involves balancing scope expectations and the available resources (Rabechini Jr. & Carvalho, 1999). Thus, IT project management addresses the full range of concepts, tools and techniques to improve project performance and organizational effectiveness and efficiency (Carvalho et al., 2002; Laurindo et al., 2002).

This chapter presents the results of studying the adoption of efficiency models in Information Technology area in the selected Brazilian companies. A comparative analysis among project management models adopted is done. The study is based on multiple cases, financial, telecommunications and building materials companies.

METHODOLOGICAL ASPECTS

In order to investigate the application of efficiency models to Information Technology area of Brazilian companies, the adopted methodological approach was multiple cases (Yin, 1991; Claver et al., 2000). The cases selection criteria was the following: the role that IT plays in the company; IT management model and organizational structure; local dispersion; and IT application complexity. Based on these criteria, three cases were selected: a financial company, a telecommunication and a building materials company. Interviews were performed with executives from the IT area and others from different hierarchical levels and areas. The characteristics of the cases analyzed are as follows:

- Case "A" is a Brazilian manufacturing company that belongs to the agribusiness and building materials industries; in 2000 it had revenue of US$ 400 millions and hired 6,000 employees, but our focus was restricted to a business unit hereafter called AN1; that achieved 60% of company total revenue.
- Case "B" is a Brazilian multiple bank with revenue of US$4,500 millions and 17,000 employees in 2000.
- Case "C" is a global manufacturing company that belongs to the electronics industry which, in 2000, achieved revenue of US$2,000 million from its Latin American branch with 2,700 employees.

EFFICIENCY MODELS IN IT FIELD

In spite of different approaches regarding the best practices in the IT area, there is a general consensus about the importance of three, widely used efficiency models: the Capability Maturity Model - CMM (Humphrey, 1989; Paulk et al, 1995), the Project Management Maturity Model – PMMM (Kerzner, 2000, 2001); the Project Management Body of Knowledge - PMBoK (PMI, 2000), and Quality Systems for software - ISO9000-3 (2001) and

ISO 12207 (1995). In order to verify managerial IT practices in the studied companies, the analysis was performed based on these models. All of them are empirical and were developed based on best practices used in real projects. Although they have different approaches in their conception, they are rather more complementary than conflictive.

Capability Maturity Model (CMM)

The implementation of formal efficiency procedures is quite new in IT projects. Pressman (1987) describes quality assurance activities in software. Humphrey (1989) identifies maturity levels in the IT project development process, based on the managerial behavior found in companies. The fundamental concepts of the process maturity derive from the belief that the development management process is evolutionary. Paulk et al. (1995) identify the distinguishing characteristics between immature and mature organizations, as shown in Table 1.

The CMM – Capability Maturity Model (Humphrey, 1989; Paulk et al., 1995; Pessôa & Spinola, 1997) was developed by SEI – the Software Engineering Institute, of Carnegie Mellon University, and presents five maturity levels, each corresponding to a set of structural requirements for key process areas (Figure 1).

Although each project is unique, it could be organized in a process to be applied in other projects. IT projects managers used to apply a "methodology", i.e. they establish the steps to be followed in order to develop a system. Another singular characteristic is the dynamic technologies breakthrough that demands continuous improvements in the development methods and management of changing process, as described in CMM model, at level 5, the highest level of maturity.

The analysis through CMM requirements shows that all cases denote improvement possibilities. *Cases "A"* and *"B"* do not use CMM as a referential model, but an internal developed "methodology." According to CMM requirements, *Cases "A"* and *"B"* are at the first maturity level. However, this does not mean that they are equally efficient, which can be explained by the difficulty of passing to higher stages. *Case "B"* presents more structured

Table 1. Immature organization x mature organization (adapted from Paulk et al., 1995)

IMMATURE ORGANIZATION	MATURE ORGANIZATION
• *Ad hoc*; improvised process by practitioners and managers	• Coherent with action plans; the work is effectively achieved
• Not rigorously followed and not controlled	• Processes are documented and continuously improved
• Highly dependent on personal knowledge	• Perceptible top and middle management commitment
• Little understanding of progress and quality	• Well controlled assessment of the process
• Compromising product functionality and quality to meet schedule	• Product and process measures are used
• High risk when new technology is applied	• Disciplined use of technology
• High maintenance costs and unpredictable quality	

Figure 1. Maturity levels (adapted from Paulk et al., 1995)

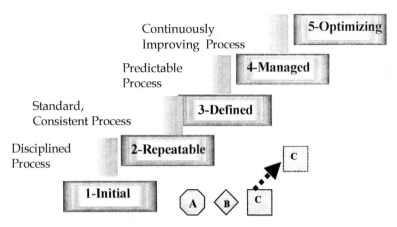

project evaluation and control procedures, discussing effectiveness aspects (formal meetings among IT and users) and efficiency (cost and benefit analysis). *Case "C"* adopted CMM and has just moved to the second level.

The CMM second level has a consistent project management structure and the goal of this level is to deliver projects on time. To perform this, the model have several points that must be achieved, like effort and size estimation, strong process control (such as periodic meetings between technical people and managers), and several measures to show project status more clearly.

CMM is not an adequate reference for the assessment of internal methodologies, since it was not conceived to perform this kind of analysis. ISO 15504 (1998) proposed the standard project SPICE as a more appropriated model to evaluate maturity level of specific processes. While CMM level of maturity specifies a set of processes that have to be performed, ISO 15504 establishes maturity levels for each individual process: level 0-incomplete; level 1-performed; level 2-managed; level 3-established; level 4-predictable; level 5-optimizing. This is a different approach of CMM, since an organization does not perform a maturity level, but have a maturity profile: a maturity level is measured for each specific process. This new approach is a very useful to the organization perspective because one can easily measure strong and weak points of their process and plan improvement activities. Furthermore, from the companies' point of view, it is easier to understand staged levels as the performed processes are already predefined.

The SPICE approach defined in standard ISO 15504 (1998) had firstly influenced *CMM for Systems Engineering,* published in 1995 and more recently influenced CMM I (CMM-I1; CMM-I2), just published in 2002. CMM-I, the integration model, was enhanced in two dimensions: *scope dimension* and *evaluation dimension.*

In the *scope dimension*, this new model incorporated other published models and cover all project activities, not only software, as the original software CMM did, but also other engineering fields. In the *evaluation dimension,* CMM-Il incorporated both approaches: the traditional (called staged CMM) and the maturity profile (called continuous CMM). Figure 2 shows the continuous CMM-I representation to be compatible with ISO/IEC 15504 standard.

Figure 2. Continuous maturity process representation in CMM-I (adapted from CMM-I1, 2002)

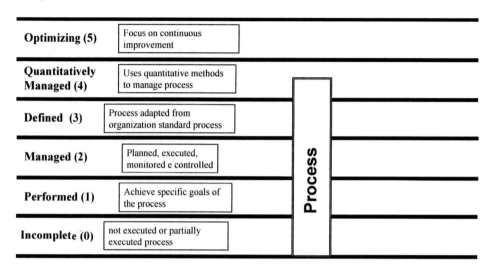

CMM-I (and software CMM) considers that maturity level is an organizational characteristic and it is independent of the professionals involved.

Project Management Model

Project Management plays an important role in the competitive scenario, and achieves in 90's the status of methodology. The model proposed by Project Management Institute - PMI (2000), called Project Management Body of Knowledge (PMBoK), provides a framework to manage project efficiency, balancing scope expectations and the available resources (Rabechini Jr & Carvalho, 1999). This model proposes the following nine key areas: (i) integration; (ii) scope; (iii) time; (iv) cost; (v) quality; (vi) human resource; (vii) communication; (viii) risk; (ix) procurement.

Nevertheless, the PMBoK framework cannot provide a standard benchmark for project management capability as CMM to software engineering capabilities. In order to extend the capability maturity model (CMM) to project management, Kerzner (2000) and (2001) proposes a Project Management Maturity Model (PMMM).

The PMMM differs in many aspects from the CMM, but this framework also introduces benchmarking instruments for measuring an organization's progress along the maturity model, detailing five levels of development for achieving maturity: level 1 - common language, level 2 - common processes, level 3 - singular methodology, level 4 - benchmarking, and level 5 - continuous improvement, as shown in Figure 3.

It is important to highlight the differences in terminology between the CMM and PMMM, (compare Figures 2 and 3) which could lead to misunderstanding when both models are being implemented in the IT domain of the same organization.

PMMM addresses the key knowledge areas across the project management process, in compliance with PMBoK, and integrates them with the Project Management Office – PMO in the strategic level.

Figure 3. Project management maturity model – PMMM (adapted from Kerzner, 2001)

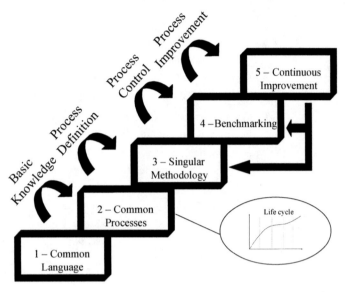

Kerzner (2000) identifies a life cycle in PMMM level 2, common processes, which could be broken into five phases: embryonic; executive management acceptance; line management acceptance; growth and maturity, as shown in Figure 4. It is important to note that some simultaneity among the phases can occur.

The embryonic phase means that the organization starts to recognize the benefits of project management - PM, usually by lower and middle levels of management. The two next phases are achieved when the PM concepts are accepted and have visible support and commitment by executive and line management.

Kerzner (2001) emphasizes the growth phase as the most critical, because it is the beginning of the creation of the PM process, and warns that different methodologies for each project should be avoided.

The last life cycle phase –maturity – is difficult to achieve due to several factors such as organizational resistance to project cost control and horizontal accounting.

The main characteristics of these life cycle phases emphasized by Kerzner (2001) are described in Table 2.

Analysis through the PMMM life cycle analysis requirements states that all cases do not achieve the maturity phase. According to this model, *Case "A"* is in the first life cycle phase, embryonic. In *Case "B"*, it could be identified a strong commitment with PM programs by executive management board, but there is a lack of support by the line management. *Case "B"* develops different projects evaluation and control procedures for each type of project, which affect the PM efficiency. *Case "C"* presents the higher maturity level, it could be classified in the beginning of growth phase. The support of executive and line management to PM programs is visible and there are effective planning procedures (see Figure 4).

Table 2. Life cycle phases characteristics (Kezner, 2001)

Phase	Characteristics
embryonic	• recognizing the need for PM; • recognizing PM's potential benefits; • applications of PM to the business; • recognizing the changes necessary to implement PM.
executive management acceptance	• visible executive support; • executive understanding of PM; • project sponsorship; • willingness to change the way the company does business.
line management acceptance	• visible line management support; • line management commitment to PM; • line management education; • release of functional employees for PM training programs.
growth	• development of company PM life cycles; • development of a PM methodology; • a commitment to effective planning; • minimization of scope; • selection of PM software to support methodology.
maturity	• development of a management cost/schedule control system; • integration of schedule and cost control; • development of an educational curriculum to support PM.

Figure 4. Life cycle phases (Kerzner, 2000)

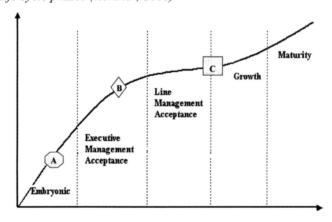

Quality Systems

It is important to note that the adoption of systems models, such as ISO 9000, focuses on the creation and maintenance of a quality system, applied to any process. The ISO 9001:2000 new version, published in the year 2000, was fully restructured to have a more clear process focused approach. Other ISO standards offer an overview of these standards to the software field and contribute to deploying this approach to specific processes, such as: software products (ISO 9126-NBR 13596), quality requirements for software packages (ISO 12119), and the software life cycle process (ISO 12207).

ISO 9000-3 (2001) is a guide to help with ISO 9001 interpretation for the software field, i.e., the development, supply, acquisition and maintenance of software (Pessôa & Spinola, 1997). The previous versions of this guide were developed by the ISO/TC/SC2 committee, the quality branch of ISO. Nowadays this ISO 9000-3 guide is being revised by ISO/IEC JTC1/SC7, the information technology branch, and a new version is planned to be published in 2002. The ISO9001:2000 new structure made this task easier than previous versions and it is incorporating a map of the relationship between IT standards (ISO/IEC JTC1/SC7) and its respective quality systems described in ISO 9001 to this standard. For example, ISO 9001 specifies that the organizations have to identify their processes and ISO 12207 (ISO12207) proposes a set of processes involving software development, supply, acquisition and maintenance. In addition to ISO 12207, other standards are referenced, such as ISO 9126 for software products, ISO 12119 for quality requirements for software packages and ISO 15504 for software evaluation. This was considered an improvement of the standards structure that matches quality system standards with technical and specific standards.

ISO 9001:2000 standards have the purpose of certifying organizations whose Quality Systems comply with the standards and provides a structure to manage quality independent of the organizational activity. This is not enough for specific fields of application and, for this reason there are complementary sets of standards in some areas, like QS-9000 for the automobile industry and TL-9000 for the telecommunications industry.

The standards from ISO/IEC/ JTC1/SC7 have the purpose of complementing the quality system for the IT specific area, not focusing on applications as with the automobile or telecommunications industry, but considering the specificities of software and systems development.

In general, ISO 9000 can be a good starting point for implementing a quality system. This system allows the organizations to disseminate quality culture and create the initial structure to implement more specific quality systems. This can be observed in the studied cases.

In general, the Quality System (ISO 9000), processes (CMM) and project (PMI) models have the possibility of mutual and complementary synergy, maintaining consistency with their fundamental points. On the other hand, there are important differences among these models, especially concerning the degree of abstraction. (Pessôa et al., 1997b; Tingey, 1997).

CASE ANALYSIS

In order to identify the distinctive characteristics between *Cases "A," "B" and "C"* a comparative analysis was performed, as shown in Table 3.

In the 1990's, *Case "A"* had undergone changes in guidelines and the top management body. The new leadership starts a centralization process due to a cost reduction policy in management areas, with a dramatic reduction in the number of employees in the corporate IT area (from 200 employees in 1990 to 40 in 2000). The range of attributions of the IT teams of the business units was reduced to user support and follows patterns and priorities defined by corporate IT. The culture of the company favors internal development, but this behavior

Table 3. Comparative analysis

IT ANALYSIS	CASE "A"	CASE "B"	CASE "C"
IT STRUCTURE	By systems	Client	Product line
IT OPERATION	Decentralized	Centralized	Decentralized
SYSTEM DEVELOPMENT	Centralized; Internal	Centralized; Internal	Centralized; Outsourcing
REASONS FOR IT DECENTRALIZATION	Local Dispersion; Business Units; Wish for Control	Local Dispersion	Local Dispersion; Business Units; Wish for Control
EFFICIENCY MODELS	No formal model	ISO 9000	ISO 9000; CMM; PMI
IT PROJECTS CONTROL	Ad hoc	Structured	Partially Structured

is slowly changing. The corporate IT does not have systematic approaches to plan and control costs and resource requirements, nor to evaluate applications performance.

Case "B," certified by ISO 9000, shows great concern about IT efficiency, especially in cost and quality aspects. IT flexibility is important, due to the dynamic aspect of the financial sector, with a very short life cycle for product development.

The steps of the adopted IT evaluation process are: internal discussion in each business unit; analysis by both IT and business units; analysis of the whole set of proposed IT applications; grouping similar application proposals; economic and financial analysis; analysis by the Steering Committee, and control of planned expenses. Economic and financial evaluation of the projects is based on time and investment estimates. Project benefits are estimated in terms of the reduction of the work force and other operational expenses, and also in quality improvement expectations.

Case "C" presents a decentralization culture, with business unit autonomy, both in global and local operations. However, some functions were centralized, like human resources, financial and IT. This corporate IT area represents a trade off between efficiency and effectiveness approaches. There are IT teams for each business unit, but subordinated to a global centralized area. So, this structure demands management of conflicts among global and local interests.

Due to this corporate IT area, the company is standardizing IT applications, especially through the implementation of one ERP system throughout all the company. This process faces resistances and the IT area is one of its main drivers. Some specific applications are supplied by outsourcing.

Each business unit defines its specific set of Critical Success Factors – CSF (Rockart, 1979) that must be aligned with corporate CSF, they are: quality emphasis, excelling in performance and technical assistance. These CSF show the vision of IT as an enabler of efficiency improvement. This company implemented ISO 9000 in the manufacturing area, but activities related to IT had very few processes. For this reason, the IT area implemented CMM (level 2) in order to achieve efficiency and quality.

IT effectiveness evaluation, although not systematic, is done by cost vs. benefits analysis, payback and through comparison with strategic goals. Priorities are discussed twice a month in meetings among business unit and the respective IT team.

However, efficiency process are not in the same level, since it is possible to find important differences in costs, times and quality management in IT projects according to two other models, PMBOK (PMI, 2000) and PMMM (Kerzner, 2001).

CONCLUSIONS

In spite of the Capability Maturity Model (CMM) and Project Management Models (PMMM and PMBoK) being widely used in developed countries, in Brazil, only *Case "C"* (a global company) adopted these methods.

The studied cases suggested that these managerial IT practices are not in widespread use in Brazilian companies. On the other hand, the ISO standards are well known and adopted.

In *Case "B,"* IT is a source of competitive advantage, and in the other cases, IT does not present the same strategic relevance. *Case "B"* efficiency and effectiveness of IT projects represents the possibility of gains in competitiveness, and so, this company would benefit with formal efficiency models. Thus, *Case "B"* should substitute ad hoc procedures by project management models like PMBoK and PMMM, in order to improve efficiency.

Case "A" presents a poor relationship between corporate IT and the business unit; and there is an important possibility of increasing IT outsourcing. Furthermore, there is a lack of alignment between IT and the business unit strategies. IT project management is still in a embryonic phase and it should be fostering a commitment by executive and line management.

Case "C" tends to drive the adoption of more detailed effectiveness evaluation systems, since this company has already demonstrated initiatives in using IT project efficiency procedures based on CMM and PMBoK.

REFERENCES

Brynjolfsson, E. (1993). The productivity paradox of Information Technology: Review and assessment. *Communications of the ACM*, 36(12), 67-77.

Carvalho, M. M., Laurindo, F. J. B. & Pessôa, M. S. P. (2002). Applying efficiency models in information technology area of Brazilian companies. In the *Proceedings of IRMA 2002 Information Resources Management Association International Conference, Issues and Trends of Information Technology Management in Contemporary Organizations, May 19-22,* Seattle, WA, pp. 109-110.

Claver, E., Gonzalez, R., & Llopis, J. (2000, April). An analysis of research in information systems (1981-1997). Information & Management, 37(4), 181-195.

CMM-I-1 (2002). Capability Maturity Model Integration – version 1.1 – for Systems Engineering and Software Engineering – continuous representation CMU/SEI/SW, V1.1 – CMU/SEI –2002-TR01– downloaded from www.sei.cmu.edu (02-02-2002).

CMM-I-2 (2002). Capability Maturity Model Integration – version 1.1 – for Systems Engineering and Software Engineering – staged representation CMU/SEI/SW, V1.1 – CMU/SEI –2002-TR02 downloaded from www.sei.cmu.edu (02-02-2002).

ISO 12207 (1995) – ISO/IEC12207:1995 – Information Technology – Software Life Cycle Processes – ISO.

ISO 9000-3 (2001, May). Software Engineering-guidelines for the application of ISO 9001:2000 to software – working draft WD4 ISO/IEC JTC-1 /SC7/WG18 N48.

ISO/IEC/TR15505-2 - SPICE (1998) – Technical Report Information Technology – Software Process Assessment- Part 2: a reference model for processes and process capability. First edition 1998.

Frame, J. D. (1994) The New Project Management – Tools for an Age of Rapid Change, Corporate Reengineering, and Other Business Realities. São Francisco: Jossey-Bass Publishers.

Humphrey, W. S. (1989). Managing the software process. Reading, MA: Addison-Wesley (SEI series in software engineering).

Kerzner, H. (2000). Applied Project Management Best Practices on Implementation. John Wiley & Sons.

Kerzner, H. (2001). Project Management – A Systems Approach to Planning, Scheduling, and Controlling. New York: John Wiley & Sons.

Kerzner, H. (2001). Strategic Planning for Project Management – Using a project management maturity model. New York: John Wiley & Sons.

Laurindo, F.J.B., Carvalho, M.M., & Shimizu, T. (2002) Management of Information Technology Effectiveness in Brazilian Companies. In IRMA 2002 - Information Resources Management Association International Conference: Issues and Trends of Information Technology Management in Contemporary Organizations, Proceedings, (May 19-22, pp. 412-414), Seattle, WA.

Meredith, J. R., & Mantel Jr., S. J. (1995). *Project Management: A managerial approach*. New York: John Wiley & Sons.

Paulk, M. C., Weber, C. V., Curtis, B., & Chrissis, M. B. (1995). *The capability maturity model: Guidelines for improving the software process*/CMU/SEI. Reading, MA: Addison-Wesley.

Pessôa, M., Spinola, M., & Volpe, R. L. D. (1997). Uma experiência na implantação do modelo CMM. In: Simpósio Brasileiro De Engenharia De Software, 11., WQS´97 - Workshop Qualidade De Software, Fortaleza, 14/10/1997. *Anais.* Fortaleza, UFC, 49-57.

Pessôa, M.S.P., & Spinola, M. M. (1997). Qualidade de Processo de Software: um novo paradigma. In: IV Inftel – Congresso Petrobrás De Informática and Telecomunicações, São Paulo, 1 a 5/12/1997. *Anais.* São Paulo.

Porter, M.E. (2001). Strategy and the Internet. *Harvard Business Review*, 63-78, March.

Pressman, R.S. (1987). *Software Engineering, a practitioner's Approach* 2a. edição McGraw Hill Book Co. (2nd ed.).

Project Management Institute (2001). A Guide to the Project Management Body of Knowledge (PMBoK). MD: Project Management Institute Inc.

Rabechini Jr., R., & Carvalho, M.M. (1999). Concepção de um programa de gerência de projetos em instituição de pesquisa. *Revista Valenciana Dèstudis Autonòmics*. Espanha: Valência.

Rockart, J.F. (1979). Chief Executives Define Their Own Data Needs. *Harvard Business Review*, 57(2), 81-92, Mar./Apr.

Strassman, P. A. (1990). The Business Value of Computers. New Canaan. *The information Economic Press.*

Tingey, M. O. (1997). *Comparing ISO 9000, Malcolm Baldrige, and the SEI CMM for software: a reference and selection guide.* Englewood Cliffs, NJ, Prentice Hall.

Willcocks, L.P., & Lester, S. (1997). In search of information technology productivity: Assessment issues. *Journal of the Operational Research Society,* 48, 1082-1094.

Yin, R.K. (1991). *Case Study Research: Design and Methods.* Newbury Park. Rev. ed. Sage Publications.

Chapter XX

Adoption of Enterprise Resource Planning Software by Organizations in India: A Managerial Framework

Monideepa Tarafdar
University of St. Thomas, USA

Rahul K. Roy
Indian Institute of Management Calcutta, India

ABSTRACT

Enterprise Resource Planning (ERP) systems are designed to integrate various functions and processes, and are used by organizations as the first-level transaction processing systems in their information architecture. Although many studies have been conducted and reported on ERP implementation cases in the developed countries, there is not much literature on the experiences of companies in Asia and other parts of the developing world. These organizations confront issues that are significantly different from those faced by companies in the developed world, because of differences in the sophistication of IT use, and cultural and social contexts. This chapter describes a three-stage model for analyzing the deployment of ERP in developing countries, based on an empirical study of ERP implementation exercises in Indian organizations. Each stage describes a specific aspect of the implementation process. The specific characteristics of each stage and their implications for managers have also been discussed.

INTRODUCTION

Enterprise Resource Planning systems are designed to integrate various functions and processes in organizations. ERP software is developed in the form of different modules, each of which helps to perform distinct functions within the company. The various modules are integrated such that they interface with the same organization database and workflows can be designed across different modules. The software helps ensure availability of information and standardize business processes. ERP software evolved from earlier Manufacturing Resource Planning (MRP) systems, which included inventory management, procurement and production planning functions (Sandoe et al., 2001). The implementation of ERP software started in the early 1990's and during the late 1990's, the growth rate of the ERP market was between 30 and 40 percent. As of 2001, 30,000 companies worldwide had implemented ERP and the total value of the ERP market was at \$25 bn. Although many studies have been conducted and reported on ERP implementation cases in the developed countries (Davenport, 1993; Parr et al., 1999; Lee et al., 2000, for example), there is very little literature and information on the experiences of companies in Asia and other parts of the developing world (Liyang, 2002; Tarafdar et al., 2002). At the same time, the rate of adoption of ERP in these regions has been quite high. There is a need to study and analyze issues and problems associated with ERP adoption in these companies. This is because their problems are significantly different than issues faced by organizations in the developed world, because of differences in the sophistication of IT use, and in cultural and social contexts. We describe, in this chapter, some of the experiences that companies in India have gone through, in the implementation of ERP. We develop a framework for analyzing the critical factors and issues that influence the ERP adoption process, and highlight the areas of opportunity and risk. The framework is based on empirical research. It agrees well with existing theoretical concepts in this domain, and is sufficiently general so as to be extended to other developing countries.

BACKGROUND

The deployment and use of ERP software is quite different from traditional software development. ERP software is a single program that serves the needs of all the different functions in the organization. It is bought off the shelf and then configured to include the specific characteristics of processes of individual companies. Parts of the software have also to be customized such that it can correctly represent the workflow and processes of the particular company. Although similar packaged software, like Supply Chain Management and Customer Relationship Management packages is now available, ERP systems were the first of such software to be developed, sold, implemented and used. The study of ERP implementation experiences in Indian companies is an interesting case of new technology adoption because many Indian companies go from very rudimentary IT based systems to sophisticated ERP systems in one quantum jump (Sharma, 2001). This gives rise to some crucial issues that need to be addressed during ERP implementation, and the subsequent use of the software (Markus et al., 1999). The documentation of the ERP experience in India has been mostly in the nature of journalistic articles in professional/business publications, which either describe the current state of affairs in the ERP industry or report on implementation strategies of individual companies (Connor, 1999; Sadagopan, 1999; Dasgupta, 2001; Sharma, 2001). There is an absence of systematic research, which analyzes and generalizes the characteristics and problems of the ERP implementation experience, on the basis of a systematic empirical study.

Existing research on ERP adoption is based on studies conducted on organizations in the developed countries. The literature can be divided into three tracks. The first track has developed some descriptions of the phenomenon of the adoption of ERP. These studies suggest that the ERP implementation process consists of distinct stages. The first stage comprises review and selection of the right package, selection of consultants and clarifying the business related factors that make ERP a necessity. This stage has been variously referred to as the Chartering phase (Markus et al., 1999) and Design phase (Ross et al., 1999). The second stage describes different aspects of the actual implementation process and consists of project management, software customization and process re-engineering. This is the Project phase (Markus et al., 1999) or Implementation phase (Ross et al., 1999). During the third phase, managers familiarize themselves with the software. System bugs are reported and fixed and the operational effects on the business are felt. This is referred to as the Shakeout (Markus et al., 1999 et al) or the Stabilization Phase (Ross et al., 2000). Finally, an organization enters a fourth phase, referred to as the Upward and Onward phase (Markus et al., 1999) or Transformation phase (Ross et al., 2000). In this phase, strategic business benefits from ERP occur, additional technical skills are built and upgrades are planned for.

The second literature track analyses the ERP implementation process in terms of changes that take place in the organization. One such study conducted by Scott et al. (2000) suggests that ERP adoption results in four distinct change components. **Technical Change Processes** imply changes in the IS architecture (hardware and software). **Business Process Changes** result in process re-engineering. The **Organizational Learning Process** incorpo-

Figure 1. Literature on enterprise resource planning-conceptual foundations

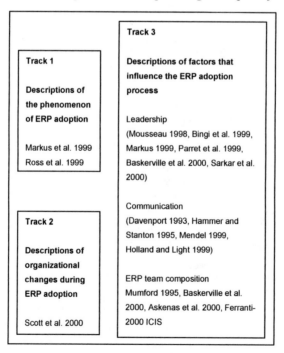

rates increased competence with new technology and acceptance of technology in business processes. The ***ERP Use Process*** helps managers learn from the successes and failures of working with the ERP software and carry out related incremental technical and process improvements.

A third category of studies analyzes and points out a number of factors that influence the ERP adoption process. First, leadership support has been an important factor in facilitating the adoption process (Mousseau, 1998; Bingi et al. 1999; Markus, 1999; Parret et al., 1999; Baskerville et al., 2000; Sarkar et al., 2000). These studies report that strong leadership support is important for ensuring the availability of resources and manpower. It is also important for signaling to the employees the importance and criticality of the application. Second, open and honest communication on the part of the leaders of the ERP initiative helps employees to understand the rationale for ERP implementation and enables them to appreciate problems in existing systems. It has been found that communication with employees, results in greater understanding of the organizational needs and hence quicker acceptance of the software (Davenport, 1993; Hammer et al., 1995; Mendel, 1999; Holland et al., 1999). A third influencing factor is the skills and competencies of the implementation team. It has been suggested that implementation teams which have good technical knowledge, are empowered to take decisions, are politically close to important people in the organization and have a good understanding of end user needs, enable the organization to minimize implementation difficulties and time and cost overruns (Mumford, 1995; Ferranti, 1998; Baskerville et al., 2000; Askenas et al., 2000). Although most organizations expect that ERP would lead to a reduction in internal and external co-ordination costs (Gurbaxani et al., 1991), they have been primarily concerned about issues relating to data conversion, organizational politics, and the extent of fit of the software with the existing processes (Chang et al., 2000). Existing studies about ERP have been summarized in Figure 1.

THE ADOPTION OF ERP SOFTWARE IN INDIA: A BRIEF OVERVIEW

Issues and Problems

The first ERP systems were adopted in India in the mid 1990's. According to figures published by the National Association for Software Companies, which is a body that analyzes and directs the growth and competence areas of the Indian software industry, the Indian ERP market grew at an average rate of 70 percent over the years 1995 to 2001. As of 2001, about 800 companies had implemented ERP software. The key ERP vendors in the Indian industry include SAP, Peoplesoft, Oracle and Baan. The ERP growth trend, and the market shares of the different vendors have been described in Tables 1 and 2.

The growth was fuelled by a variety of factors. The dominant one was to standardize and simplify the IT architecture, and replace the patchwork of incompatible legacy systems that most Indian companies had, with integrated software. Another reason was to enhance the efficiency of data acquisition and make accurate and timely information available to everyone in the organization. A third was to achieve Y2K consistency. Many companies had planned to overhaul existing mainframe based systems and replace them with Y2K compatible systems, and ERP had emerged as a state of art client/server-based solution that could address this problem as well.

Table 1. The growth of the ERP market in India

Year	Size of the RP market in India ($ million)						
	1995-1996	1996-1997	1997-1998	1998-1999	1999-2000	2000-2001	2001-2002
Size	25	56	129	279	521	958	1324

Table 2. Market share of ERP vendors in India for the year 1998-1999

	Size of the market ($billion)	Percentage Share
SAP	2.95	16.9
People soft	1	5.7
Oracle	.92	5.3
McKesson	.85	4.9
J D Edwards	.62	3.5
Baan	.48	2.7
Others	10.2	58.9
Total	17	100

The implementation process of ERP in many Indian organizations has been fraught with problems. These relate to time and money overruns and inadequate planning (Connor, 1999). Organizations have been particularly frustrated with the time and effort involved in the customization of the package (Natarajan, 1998). A study conducted by the Gartner Group reveals that there is a 230 percent cost overrun and a 178 percent schedule overrun for ERP projects in India. In some cases, organizations have gained considerable benefits from enterprise systems. This has been by way of better internal co-ordination, automated processes, reduced transaction time, and better data storage and retrieval capabilities. However in many other cases the results have been, endless implementation cycles, futile re-engineering efforts not accepted by line managers, and rejection of the software as just another technological innovation and not very useful for the business. Many CIO's believe that "these packages cost the earth, take ages to implement and deliver nothing" (Chattopadhyay, 2000). The move towards ERP is a project of huge scope and managers have found it very difficult to estimate budgets with regard to the infrastructure and the human expertise. Another major concern has been to get employees and managers to accept the process changes and re-engineering entailed in ERP implementation. Additionally there are hidden costs of training, customization, integration and testing, data conversion, and consulting. Indeed, many Indian companies have abandoned ERP projects midway when they realized that some critical processes that they could not change could not be supported by the ERP software.

Research Problem and Research Design

Existing reports of ERP adoption by Indian companies, mostly journalistic literature, broadly describe the experiences of individual companies. The reports do not draw upon each other: they mention the different aspects of ERP adoption in a fragmented and isolated manner. Clearly, a systematic approach is required for managing different issues that are associated with the adoption of ERP software by Indian companies. Managers need to plan for, and address the requirements of different aspects of the implementation process. In order to do this, they require having access to research findings that analyze ERP adoption in a holistic manner, that can provide the big picture, and that are based on empirical studies.

In this research, we have used empirical studies, to understand in an integrated manner, the factors that characterize the ERP adoption process in Indian companies. We first use the literature to develop the different tracks along which ERP adoption has been studied. We then attempt to understand the process in the Indian context, in the light of these tracks. Finally, we present our research findings in the form of an overarching framework that draws together the different concepts and tracks from literature, and integrates them with the empirical results from our study. Our investigation has four aspects to it. First, we attempted to analyze the characteristics of the company's business such as the industry, the number of facilities and products, the critical success factors for the business, and the kind of information processing tools required or used by the company. Second, we tried to understand why the use of ERP was considered, what goals it was expected to achieve, and what role it was expected to play. Third, we studied the characteristic features of the implementation process, such as the sequence in which the different modules were implemented, the allocation of manpower for the purpose, and the role of the consultants involved. Finally, we analyzed the operational and strategic impact of the ERP software, and the changes instituted because of implementation of the software.

We studied the ERP adoption processes of 25 companies from 10 different industries in the manufacturing and service sectors, which had implemented ERP software. We adopted an exploratory survey method (Kerlinger, 1994) in order to generate process descriptions of the phenomenon.

RESEARCH FINDINGS: A FRAMEWORK FOR ANALYZING THE ADOPTION OF ERP IN INDIAN ORGANIZATIONS

The ERP implementation process in Indian companies can be modeled as a three-stage process, as shown in Figure 2. These stages describe different aspects of the implementation and subsequent use of the software. The Planning Stage refers to the activities that are performed before the ERP software is actually implemented. These activities address various requirements of business and IS strategy planning as well as project planning. The Implementation Stage describes different issues and activities that must be addressed once the implementation process is under way. The Post Implementation Review Stage is concerned with analysis of benefits and changes accruing from the ERP system. It also includes an analysis of key knowledge and skills acquired from the implementation process, and their application to subsequent rounds of implementation of the software.

Figure 2. Model for adoption of ERP in Indian organizations

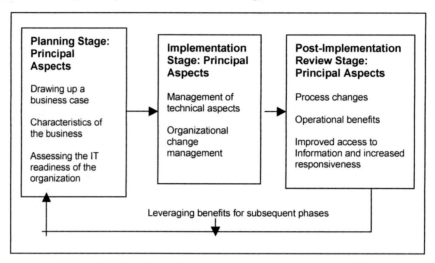

This framework also has implications for managers who are involved in planning and executing the ERP implementation process. Various aspects characterize each stage of the model. A study of these aspects reveals specific strategies for managing and controlling each stage, which can have a significant impact on the ERP adoption process. Managers need to address issues such as vendor selection, process re-engineering, personnel training, change management and benefits analysis. We describe below, the different stages of the framework, and the management implications for addressing the requirements of each stage.

Stage 1: Planning Stage

The decision to adopt ERP software is usually a part of the strategic information systems plan. The planning process is carried out within the framework of four factors.

Drawing up a Business Case for ERP

ERP was implemented for three reasons. For most of the companies that we studied, the decision to implement ERP was part of a larger attempt towards reducing costs and increasing market share and profitability. They expected that the software would improve their critical processes and help achieve the critical success factors for the business. For example, two companies were low cost producers in their industries and wanted to use ERP for better information management regarding their inventory, which would help reduce their inventory levels. It is essential that there be a clear idea of the deliverables from the ERP software. For example, there should be a detailed plan for the processes that would need a redesign and the elements that would be changed. In this context, we observed that there was reluctance on part of the companies to re-engineer their processes using the *"best practices"* feature of the software. Most companies planned to customize the software to their needs, and did not want to change their processes. A second reason for implementing ERP was the presence of plenty of slack resources, adopted ERP as a result of similar actions on part of their competitors. They were not very clear as to the deliverables they wanted from the use of the software. A third reason was that some organizations were looking for Y2K compatibility and to upgrade their IT infrastructure. They were primarily concerned with the technical design of the software, its utility as an integrated transaction processing system and its value in streamlining the data storage and retrieval process in the organization. Awareness of the latest ERP technologies and application to the business is desirable in such cases.

Characteristics of the Business

More than 90 percent of the companies we studied were categorized as large companies, and had a turnover greater than 5,000 million Indian Rupees (INR). They operated out of many different locations, were regarded as innovative, and were among the first in their industries to introduce the ERP software. For many of the companies, the product or service was not tangible, but based on information. In most organizations, *Financial Accounting & Control* was the first module to be implemented, followed by the *Materials Management, Sales & Distribution* and *Production Planning.* Very few companies implemented the *Human Resource Management* module in the first phase but many of them planned to do so in the next phase.

A prominent characteristic of the organizations was that the majority of them needed extensive information interchange among processes. This implied the requirement for process integration across different functions. Therefore, the internally focused modules such as materials management and production planning modules were among the first to be implemented in these companies. This finding was in support of the oft-quoted reason for ERP implementation, namely, the attempt to integrate information flows across of islands of information within the organization (Davenport 1998, Wagle 1998; Markus et al., 1999). In such cases, it is essential to have information about problems with existing processes and the nature of existing information flows such that the rationale and plan for re-engineering can be developed. A few organizations were such that informal (word of mouth, for example) communication was common; in these companies, ERP was one of the means to formalize the communication processes.

Assessing the IT Readiness of the Organization

Most of the companies had a separate MIS department prior to the start of the implementation of the ERP software. The department performed routine maintenance jobs, in addition to developing software for different functions and departments. In most of the companies, only the basic accounting processes were automated before the introduction of ERP. In some of them, inventory-recording functions were also computerized. A few of them had some decision support applications for forecasting, prior to ERP adoption.

However, the MIS function was not considered to be a very important one, prior to the implementation of the ERP software. Consequently, the head of the MIS department was not a member of the top management team and did not participate in strategic planning exercises. Since ERP is a highly visible and technically very complex software, it is essential to radically change the status of the IS function as part of the manpower planning operations. Hence, restructuring and new recruitment for the IS sometimes becomes necessary. These companies instituted new CIO positions. These positions were powerful and visible, and took charge of the implementation process. IS professionals, trained in both technology and business were recruited. In some organizations, the existing IS head was given greater powers and made responsible for heading the implementation process. In a few companies, a senior functional executive was delegated to manage the implementation process, to whom the existing IS head reported.

Eighty percent of the companies that we studied had different PC-based FoxBase or dBase applications for different departments, rather than client/server systems. Consequently there were significant changes in the IT strategy and architecture as a result of ERP implementation. These changes involved migration of data from legacy systems into an integrated platform, integration of application programs into the enterprise system, and connection of separate servers and terminals into a single networked configuration. There was a need for training and technical skill acquisition such that the new systems could be maintained.

Project Planning

There are three aspects to project planning. The first relates to project size. For all the companies, the ERP project was much larger than any previous IS project in terms of the scale of resource commitment, range of operations affected, and the number of people involved in development and technical support. Therefore, the risk of failure was perceived to be high. Therefore, there was a need for planning for resources such that increases in the IT budget could take place. A second aspect was the recruitment of external consultants to help with software configuration, customization and expertise transfer. In this context, it is necessary that consultants be reviewed and selected such that costs and requirements can be accurately estimated. The third aspect has to do with the formation of the ERP implementation project team, and allocation of executives from the functional areas to the project team. The best functional executives were allocated to the ERP project team. A quarter of the organizations felt that this left the other functional areas inadequately staffed. There is a need to plan for the temporary transfer of employees so understaffing does not occur in the functional areas.

Stage 2: Implementation Stage

The second stage of the ERP process is the ***Implementation Stage***. Two major aspects are found to describe this stage.

Management of Technical Aspects

For more than 80 percent of the organizations, the ERP system was significantly different from their existing systems, and required new and advanced technical skills. Only a quarter of the companies felt that their present crop of IT people were qualified to handle the sophisticated technology. Hence the implementation process was at all times a joint exercise between external consultants and company employees in almost all of the organizations that we studied. These consultants also trained the IS professionals, who carried out the post implementation maintenance of the system. This was a double-edged sword, because ERP skills are highly marketable and many organizations were worried about increased dependence on employees whose potential rate of attrition could be very high. Such instances have been reported in several studies conducted by SAP. In this regard, there is a need for managing the expectations of employees who are involved in the ERP project, such that they stay on during the subsequent activities of system use and maintenance. Moreover, those IS professionals who were not directly involved in the ERP project or had not trained on the software, were often cynical of the possible benefits of the projects. In almost half of the cases they refused to co-operate. Sometimes they actively tried to derail the implementation process. This was attributed to a lack of motivation and a feeling of alienation on part of these employees. Hence, there is a need for making sure that these employees indirectly support the project requirements and help in the overall effort.

Organizational Change Management

ERP resulted in significant changes at various levels in all the organizations. Task definitions changed and new skills were required for many employees, as different tasks were combined together. About half of the people we interviewed, felt that their responsibilities had increased. Reorganization of tasks resulted in changes in the reporting structure in more than half of the companies. In most cases, there was greater transparency as a result of changes in financial reporting practices. Such changes have some implications for managers. It is essential to communicate the rationale for adopting ERP and the accompanying changes. Most companies experienced that technical changes were relatively easier to institute because they required hard skills that could be developed or acquired. Employees found it more difficult to accept the new reporting structures, re-organized processes and new ways of working. These transformations were even more difficult to accept quickly because of the magnitude of change involved. Almost every important function was altered in some way. Senior managers were apprehensive that they were not able to communicate clearly enough to the rest of the organization, the nature and rationale behind the changes that were necessitated by the new software. This increased the chances of the changes being rejected. Hence, the primary risk of failure of the ERP system stemmed from human change acceptance issues, and not technical problems.

Stage 3: Post Implementation Review Stage

The final stage in the ERP implementation process is the *Post Implementation Review Stage*. This stage consists of activities of the following broad themes.

Process Changes

For half the organizations, there were significant changes in business processes. The remaining companies customized the ERP software to the requirements of their existing processes. In a third of the cases, there was greater understanding of task requirements because of multi-tasking and the combination of different stages of tasks into single steps. In addition, there were enhancements in the overall technical capacities of employees and IS professionals. A major concern in this stage is that the new processes do not stick and employees tend to go back to the previous processes. Hence, there is a need to put in place strategies for formalizing new processes and preventing backsliding to the old ones. Organizations need to monitor and articulate the benefits of the ERP system to their employees such that the new processes are maintained.

Operational Benefits

A little more than half the organizations we studied experienced tangible, operational benefits as a result of ERP implementation. These benefits were in terms of improved customer service, reduced costs, better inventory management, and the facilitation of real time processing and availability of financial and other information. The most significant change in many organizations was that they had moved from being individual function- driven to process-driven. This was because consequent to task reorganization and multi-skilling, employees could visualize the entire process, rather than just a small part. In supporting findings, respondents felt that there was improved integration between different processes, and that there was improved job design as a result of the use of the ERP software. Most of the companies also felt that the software helped reduce the number of overlapping activities and enhanced managers' understanding of their tasks and roles. These companies expected that the operational benefits would translate into financial benefits also. However, there were no attempts to analyze the direct impact of these benefits on the company's financial performance. In such cases, the implications for managers is that the organization should make attempts to analyze the financial implications of these benefits in order to justify continued investments in ERP. This is especially important because 90 percent of the companies in our study were found to have carried out a phased implementation of the software.

The remaining companies did not perceive any operational benefits after the ERP implementation. The only perceived changes were increased structure and method in their processes. They felt that the software was difficult to navigate, there were too many complex screens and it took a long time to complete the tasks.

Access to Information and Increased Responsiveness

Almost all the organizations we studied, felt that there was better access to information at the point of origin, and better flow of information across different departments after the ERP software was implemented. Employees felt empowered because they could conveniently access information that was required for decision-making. This led to better decision-making and greater accountability. The management implication here is that managers should carry out continued analysis of information requirements, such that existing information availability mechanisms can be monitored for effectiveness and new information requirements can be addressed, through the ERP software.

Leveraging Experience for Subsequent Phases

One of the major purposes of ERP adoption in the developed countries has been the integration of the majority of the internal processes of companies to create a systematic structure for storing and retrieving information seamlessly across functions (Davenport, 1998). Therefore, most companies have followed the "Big Bang" method of implementation, where all the modules of the software are implemented simultaneously. In the case of Indian companies, however, it was interesting to note that 90 percent of the companies we studied, carried out phased implementation, instead of a "Big Bang" implementation. Initially, companies choose to implement only those modules, which addressed functions that they consider absolutely critical for their operations. This is done because of two reasons. First, most organizations do not want to commit the vast resources required for a big bang implementation, especially because these are significantly greater than their previous annual IT budgets. Second, ERP software requires advanced technology and is very different from the existing systems. It affects many more functions in the organization than had previous IT systems. Therefore, organizations prefer to change gradually and minimize the risks of failure. These issues have not been addressed in the literature so far.

It is interesting to note that about a third of the companies surveyed, had a well-developed IT function and first implemented ERP in their most successful and high-profile divisions. They wanted the pilot implementation to be a model for the other divisions to follow. Other organizations where the IT function was not well developed, implemented ERP in their

Table 3. Planning stage

Principal Aspects of the Stage	Description of Principal Aspects	Implications for Managers
Business Imperatives for ERP	Planned as part of a larger attempt towards reducing costs and increasing market share and profitability Expected change of processes to suite the ERP software Response to competitor's actions Technical upgradation of IS architecture	Clear idea of the deliverables from the process is desired Detailed plan for process re-engineering is required Awareness of the latest ERP technologies and application to the business
Business Characteristics	Innovators and pioneers in the industry Multiple products and facilities all over India Extensive information interchange along processes Islands of computerization and information availability	Study of problems with existing processes and the nature of information flow is required. Rationalization of information hand-offs is required.
Manpower Planning	Working with external consultants Formation of ERP project teams	Review and selection of consultants based on experience and estimated cost is necessary. Planning for the temporary transfer of employees from functional areas to the project team is essential
Impact on IT Strategy	Acquisition of radically new technologies Development of advanced technical and project management skills Change in the status of the IS function	Planning for increases in IT budget Training and technical skill acquisition plan is required Restructuring and new recruitment for the IS function is necessary

least busy and least important division to begin with. They preferred to minimize the visibility of implementation problems and potential failure.

Organizations which adopted the phased approach, perceived themselves to be well prepared for subsequent rounds of implementation both in terms of technical preparedness and ability to articulate and communicate the rational behind the change processes. We also observed the feedback loop from the final stage to the first two stages, which indicates that learnings during the first phase are fed back such that the organization can be better prepared for subsequent phases. In this context, it is important to remember that many of the key factors of an ERP project, like manpower and resource planning and change management, are applicable to other IS projects as well. An important management implications in this regard is that organizations should develop strategies to internalize the knowledge gained from the ERP implementation process and use it for the subsequent stages and for other IS projects.

The framework been summarized in Tables 3, 4 and 5.

Table 4. Implementation stage

Principal Aspects of the Stage	Description of Principal Aspects	Implications for Managers
Change Management	Change in processes Change in reporting structure Change in task job definition Change in financial reporting practices	Management of Change: Communication of the rationale behind the ERP implementation process and the accompanying changes
Technical Skills	Training of existing IT personnel and recruitment of new IT personnel	Management of expectations of IS professionals not involved in the project: Motivation problems Management of expectations of IS professionals involved in the project: Attrition problems of trained IS professionals

FUTURE TRENDS

Future developments in ERP software need to be analyzed in the light of two contexts. The first relates to the enhancement of technical and functional capabilities of the ERP software. Many ERP vendors are positioning themselves as one-stop vendors for all the different functional requirements, and are adding Customer Relationship Management and Supply Chain Management functionalities into their software. This is in response to integration problems that organizations have had, when they have tried to interface different best of breed solutions. A Forrester Report study states that 50 percent of all IT investment is spent in interfacing and ensuring compatibility between different applications. Moreover, ERP packages are now providing web-enabled functionalities and e-business suites for use in B2B and B2C transactions. SAP has launched mySap.com, Baan has a similar product called iBaan, and Oracle has incorporated e-business functionalities into the new generation ERP software called Oracle 11i. Basic ERP packages are expected to serve as the back end database part, to which e-business modules incorporating functions relating to e-procurement, CRM and SCM would be added. Organizations would be challenged to ensure that back end information could be seamlessly accessed by the e-business applications.

The second context that would shape the future of the ERP industry in India is the decreasing cost of ERP solutions. Between 1995 and 2000, most customers have been large companies who are market leaders and with considerable slack resources. As our study has shown, most of the large companies have already implemented ERP. The future market is represented by companies in the in the Small and Medium Enterprise (SME) segment. Between 1998 and 2000, a few Indian software companies started providing indigenous ERP solutions, which are less expensive that those of the bigger and more well known companies. One such product, Marshall, designed by a company called Ramco, is popular among the smaller companies.

Table 5. Post implementation review stage

Principal Aspects of the Stage	Description of Principal Aspects	Implications for Managers
Process Changes	Greater understanding of task requirements Multiple tasking and task-stage integration	Strategies for formalizing new processes and prevention of slipping back to the old ones: Monitoring and articulating the benefits
Improved Performance Along Operational Parameters	Improvement in service levels Decrease in costs	Attempts to analyze and study the effect of operational results to the financial results
Increased Responsiveness	Improved Information availability Integration across functions	Continued analysis of information requirements Strategies to increase the effectiveness of decisions
Feedback Learning for Subsequent Stages	Technical skills More effective management of the change process	Strategies to internalize the knowledge gained from the ERP implementation process and use it for other IS projects

These two contexts suggest opportunities for future research in the ERP domain. Future research efforts would need to be directed at analyzing ERP adoption as part of an overall framework for adoption of E-business, along with the implementation of other packaged software such as CRM and SCM. Study of ERP adoption by SMEs, and the accompanying specific problems and issues is another area of potential investigation.

CONCLUSIONS

This study is one of the first attempts at empirical research, in the domain of ERP implementation in India. Therefore the emphasis of this study has been on enhancing the quality and level of understanding of the phenomenon at a conceptual level. The major theoretical contribution of the study is that it presents a general conceptual framework through which issues related to ERP implementation in Indian organizations can be analyzed and the relevant aspects addressed, by individual companies. The generality of the framework has been further enhanced because of the number of industries covered in the study. The framework can hence be used for organizations in other developing societies, too. The model also has practical implications for managers planning and implementing the software. These implications have been derived from specific aspects of the different stages. Relevant management strategies for controlling the ERP adoption process have been described, based on these implications.

Although the findings are based on exploratory research on a limited data set, this study has generated considerable scope for further research. First, these findings could be validated in a second confirmatory study on a larger data set. Second, an investigation of the applicability of the model to similar developing economies would help increase the ability to generalize and increase its external validity (Yin, 1984). Third, it would be interesting to analyze the differences in this model, with similar models developed by Markus et al. (1999) and Ross et al. (2000). Finally, the framework can be used a basis for analyzing the adoption of ERP in companies in the SME segment.

Over the last few years, many organizations in India have implemented ERP solutions and have consequently benefited from improved processes and better information availability. For many others (Natarajan, 1999; Rajshekhar et al., 2000), the adoption of ERP has resulted in a very painful transition and adaptation period, while the benefits have not been immediate or tangible. In fact, in some cases the benefits have been perceived to be much less when compared to the massive costs. The model serves as a useful starting point from where the ERP experience of Indian companies can be analyzed. It also presents some practical implications for managers, for managing and controlling relevant aspects of the implementation process.

REFERENCES

Appleton, E.L. (1997, March). How to survive ERP. *Datamation,* 51-52.

Askenas, L. & Westelius, A. (2000). Five roles of an information system: A social constructionist approach to analyzing the use of ERP systems. In W. Orlikowski et al. (Eds.), *Proceedings of the 21st International Conference on Information Systems.* W.

Baskerville, R., Pawlowski, S. & McLean, E. (2000). Enterprise resource planning and organizational knowledge: patterns of convergence and divergence. In W. Orlikowski et al. (Eds.), *Proceedings of the 21st International Conference on Information Systems..*

Bingi, P., Sharma, M. K. & Godla, J. K. (1999). Critical issues affecting an ERP implementation. *Information Systems Management, 16*(3), 7-14.

Boudreau, M. & Robey, D. (1996). Coping with contradictions in business process re-engineering. *Information Technology and People, 9,* 40-57.

Chang, S., Gable, G., Smythe, E. & Timbrell, G. (2000). A delphi examination of public sector ERP implementation issues. In W. Orlikowski et al. (Eds.), *Proceedings of the 21st International Conference on Information Systems.*

Connor, S. J. (1999). The ERP dilemma. *Dataquest—India,* September 15.

Dasgupta, S. (2000). The technology behind the Colgate smile. *Network Computing,* December 18.

Davenport, T. H. (1993). *Process Innovation: Reengineering Work Through Information Technology.* Boston, MA: Harvard Business School Press.

Davenport, T. H. (1998, July-August). Putting the Enterprise into the Enterprise System. *Harvard Business Review.*

Davenport, T. H. (2000). *Realizing the Promise of Enterprise Systems.* Boston, MA: Harvard Business School Press.

De, R. (2001, October). ERP is back with a bang. *Express Computers: The IT Business Weekly.*

Ferranti, M. (1998). Debunking ERP misconceptions. *Info World, 20*(33).

Gautam, V. (1996, April). ERP: The new mantra for competitive edge. *Dataquest—India,* 62.

Guba, E. G. & Lincoln, Y. S. (1994). Competitive paradigms in qualitative research. In N.K.

Denzin & Y.S. Lincoln (Eds.), *Handbook of Qualitative Research*. California: Sage Publications.

Gurbaxani, V. & Whang, S. (1991). The impact of information systems on organizations and markets. *Communications of the ACM, 34*(1), 59-73.

Hammer, M. & Stanton, S. (1995). *The Reengineering Revolution*. New York: Harper Collins.

Holland, C. & Light, B. (1999, May-June). A critical success factors model for ERP model for ERP implementation. *IEEE Software*, 30-36.

Kerlinger, F. N. (1986). *Foundations of Behavioral Research*. 3rd Edition. New York: CBS Publications.

Koh, C., Soh, C. & Markus, M. L. (2000). A Process Theory Approach to Analyzing ERP Implementation and Impacts: The Case of Revel Asia. *Journal of Information Technology Cases and Applications*, 2(1), 4-23.

Liang, Z. & Maosheng, L. (2002). The integration of material flow, cash flow and information flow in e-commerce. Issues and Trends of Information Technology Management in Contemporary Organizations. In M. Khosrowpour (Ed.), *Proceedings of Information Resource Management Association (IRMA) Conference*.

Markus, M. L. & Tanis, C. (1999). The enterprise systems experience- from adoption to success. In R.W. Zmud (Ed.), *Framing the domains of IT research: Glimpsing the future through the past*. Cincinnati, OH: Pinnaflex Educational Resources.

Mendel, B. (1999). Overcoming ERP project hurdles. *InfoWorld, 21*(29).

Mousseau, P. (1998). ERP projects call for multi-talented managers. *Computing Canada, 24*(42).

Mumford, E. (1995). Creating chaos or constructive change: business process re-engineering versus socio-technical design. In G. Burke & J. Peppard (Eds.), *Examining Business Process Re-engineering: Current Perspectives and Research Directions*. London: Kogan Page, (pp. 192-216).

Natarajan, G. (1998). Implementing ERP: A process-centric approach. *Dataquest –India*. November 11.

Parr, A. N., Shanks, G. & Darke, P. (1999). Identification of necessary factors for successful implementation of ERP systems. In O. Ngwenyama, L. D. Introna, M. D. Myers & J. I. DeGross, (Eds.) *New Information Technologies in Organizational Processes: Field Studies and Theoretical Reflections on the Future of Work* . Boston, MA: Kluwer Academic Publishers, (pp. 99-119).

Pender L. (2000). The missing link. *CIO Magazine,* June 15.

Rajshekhar, M. & Singh, I. (2000). Can ERP work. *Business Standard – The Strategist,* June 6.

Ross, J. W. & Vitale, M. R. (2000). The ERP revolution: Surviving vs. thriving. *Information Systems Frontiers, 12*(2), 233-241.

Sadagopan, S. (1999). ERP honeymoon is over. *Computers Today*. July 1-15.

Sandoe, K., Corbitt, G. & Boykin, R. (2001). *Enterprise Integration*. New York: John Wiley and Sons.

Sarkar, S. & Lee, A. S.(2000). Using a case study to test the role of three key social enablers in ERP implementation. In W. Orlikowski et al. (Eds.), Proceedings of the 21st International Conference on Information Systems.

Scott, J. E. & Vessey, I. (2000). Implementing Enterprise Resource Planning Systems: the Role of Learning From Failure. *Information Systems Frontiers, 2*(2), 213-232.

Shankar, M. K, Banerjee, G. & Srilatha, D. (1998, August). Onto the ERP Bandwagon. *Computers Today*.

Sharma, M. (1999). Avon cycles: From munims to ERP. *Dataquest – India*. March 21.

Slater, D. (1998). The Hidden Costs of Enterprise Software. *CIO Magazine*. January 15.

Tarafdar, M. & Roy, R. (2002). A framework for analyzing the adoption of enterprise resource planning systems in Indian organizations. issues and trends of information technology management. In M. Khosrowpour (Ed.), *Contemporary Organizations, Proceedings of Information Resource Management Association (IRMA) Conference*.

Wagle, D. (1998). The case for ERP systems. *The McKinsey Quarterly, 2*, 130-138.

Willcocks, L. & Sykes, R. (2000). The role of the CIO and IT function in ERP. *Communications of the ACM, 43*(4).

Yin, R. K. (1984). Case Study Research: Design and Methods. California: Sage Publications.

WEB SITES

Retrieved May 17, 2002 from the World Wide Web: http://www.indiainfoline.com/cyva/erp/ar01.html, *ERP*

Retrieved May 14, 2002, from the World Wide Web: http://www.iiitb.ac.in/ThinkTank/ThinkTank_ERP.htm, *ERP in India*

Chattopadhyay, R. Three in one, *Business Standard*. May 14, 2002. Retrieved May 17, 2002 from the World Wide Web: http://www.business-standard.com/strategist

White paper. Retrieved July 20, 2001 from the World Wide Web: http://www.sun.com/datacenter/applications/erp/

About the Authors

Sherif Kamel is an Assistant Professor of Management Information Systems at the School of Business, Economics and Communication of The American University in Cairo, Egypt, and is currently the Associate Director of the Management Center of the university. He was the Director of the Regional IT Institute during the period 1992-2001. From 1987 to 1992, he worked at the Cabinet of Egypt Information and Decision Support Center where he co-established and managed its training department. In 1996, he was one of the co-founding members of the Internet Society of Egypt. Dr. Kamel has published over 60 articles in IT transfer to developing countries, electronic commerce, human resources development decision support applications and knowledge management. He serves on the editorial and review boards of a number of information systems and management journals and is the associate editor of the *Annals of Cases on Information Technology Applications and Management in Organizations*. Dr. Kamel is currently the VP for Communications for the Information Resources Management Association (IRMA). He is a graduate of the London School of Economics and Political Science (UK) and The American University in Cairo (Egypt).

* * *

Amir Albadvi holds joint appointment as Assistant Professor of IT and Systems in the Industrial Engineering Department, Tarbiat Modarres University, Iran, and as Lecturer in E-strategy in Management and Economy Department, Sharif University of Technology. He graduated from London School of Economics (LSE), UK, in 1997 with a PhD in Information Systems. He is recognized as the Information Resource Management Association's (IRMA) World Representative for Iran. He has more than 11 years experience in strategy formation for auto-industry. Dr. Albadvi has conducted extensive research work in the area of e-strategy for the automotive industry in emerging markets and has published a number of award-winning case studies and articles in international conference proceedings. His research concentrates on electronic commerce and the strategic use of IT. His latest publication is in the area of national information technology strategy.

Nabeel A. Y. Al-Qirim is a Lecturer at the School of Information Technology, Auckland University of Technology, New Zealand. He has a bachelor's degree in Electrical Engineering, MBA (UK), InfoSys. (Honors with distinction), Cert. (Education), and PhD (Current). His research interests and publications are in IT & e-commerce, small business, education and telemedicine. He worked in the IT industry for 12 years as a consultant and in managing total IT solutions (cabling, networking, internetworking, LAN/WAN, imaging systems, and printing solutions) with international companies: IBM, COMPAQ, Data General, Group Bull and Siemens Nixdorf.

Stewart Bishop is a Senior Lecturer in the Department of Computer Science, Mathematics and Physics, University of the West Indies, Barbados, where he lectures in Mathematics and Information Systems. His area of research is Information Technology for development and he has presented papers at regional and international conferences and published on IT utilisation in Caribbean countries. Currently he is assisting the government of Barbados in the formulation of its National Information Technology Strategic Plan. He is a member of IFIP Working Group 9.4, IRMA and a former President of the Information Society of Barbados.

Brian Dobing is an Assistant Professor in Information Systems at the University of Lethbridge, Canada. He received his MBA and MSc in Computational Science from the University of Saskatchewan and his PhD from the University of Minnesota, USA. His research focuses on issues in user-analyst relationships and object-oriented analysis. He has recently published articles in the *Journal of Database Management, Internet Research* and *Journal of Computing Information Systems*.

Minyue Dong holds a master's diploma of International Management at HEC, University of Lausanne, Switzerland, with an exchange MBA program at Richard Ivey Business School, University of Western Ontario and a bachelor's degree of economics obtained in China. Ms. Dong conducts PhD research in the field of international financial accounting at HEC and is a Teaching Assistant for the master's program of international management. Her research focus is on the determinants and economic consequences of voluntary information disclosure of non-US firms from developing countries. She also has several years of entrepreneurial experience in international trading.

Ibrahim Elbeltagi is a Senior Lecturer in Information Management at the School of Computing at De Montfort University, UK. He published many papers in refereed national and international conferences. His research interests and publication are in the areas of strategic use of information systems, IS Diffusion in developing countries and trust in electronic commerce. Ibrahim recently received his PhD in strategic use of DSS in local authorities in the UK and Egypt. He is also teaching professional context of ICT and management support systems in the School of Computing, De Montfort University. He is also a member of the Centre for IT Service Management Research at De Montfort University.

Marwa El-Ayouti is a Decision Support Business Partner in Vodafone, Egypt, specializing in financial modeling, planning and forecasting, financial analysis and reporting. Before joining Vodafone Egypt in June 2000, she worked for the International Division of the United Bank of Egypt, handling bank-to-bank relations, trade, money market and forex relations. Ms. El-Ayouti holds a master of business administration with a specialization in globalization from Maastricht School of Management in The Netherlands. She is also a graduate of the American University in Cairo with a bachelor of arts in Economics and a minor in Business Administration.

Luiz Augusto Machado Mendes Filho received an MS in Production Engineering in 2002 and a BS in Computer Science in 1995 from Federal University of Rio Grande do Norte, Brazil. Currently, Mr. Filho has been teaching Information Systems and Business Administration at FARN, (Faculdade Natalense para o Desenvolvimento do Rio Grande do Norte), Brazil. He has already published 13 articles in national and international congresses and is member of the Program Committee of the IRMA. His current research interests include strategic use of information technology and impact of Internet in organizations.

Stewart T. Fleming received the Bachelor of Engineering Degree in Information Engineering from the University of Strathclyde, Glasgow, in 1990. He studied under the supervision of Professor Alistair Kilgour at the Department of Computing and Electrical Engineering, Heriot-Watt University, Edinburgh, graduating with a PhD in 1996. Between 1993 and 1996, he worked in industry, developing systems for digital mapping and sales and marketing consultancies. From 1996 to 1998, he was Head of Information Systems in the Department of Business Studies at the Papua New Guinea University of Technology. He is currently a Lecturer within the Department of Computer Science at the University of Otago, on the South island of New Zealand. His current research interests include Software Engineering, Computer Security and the Information needs of Developing Countries.

M. Gordon Hunter is an Associate Professor in Information Systems in the Faculty of Management at the University of Lethbridge, Canada. Dr. Hunter has previously held academic positions in Canada, Hong Kong, and Singapore, and visiting positions in Germany, USA and New Zealand. He has a Bachelor of Commerce degree from the University of Saskatchewan in Canada. He received his doctorate from Strathclyde Business School, University of Strathclyde in Glasgow, Scotland. Dr. Hunter is an Associate Editor of the *Journal of Global Information Management*. He serves on the editorial board of the *Journal of Global Information Management*, and the *Journal of Information Technology Cases and Application*. Dr. Hunter has conducted seminar presentations in Canada, USA, Asia, New Zealand, Australia, and Europe. His current research interests relate to the productivity of systems analysts with emphasis upon the personnel component, including cross-cultural aspects, and the effective use of information systems by small business.

Suttisak Jantavongso currently is an Assistant Lecturer at the School of Business Systems at Monash University, Australia. He graduated from Monash University with a Business Systems degree in 1999 and a Master of Digital Communications in 2000. During his study, he worked with JiJi Press (Japan) in the 13th Asian Games in Bangkok in 1998 and as a Kanban Systems project with Wilson Transformer Company in Melbourne in 1999. He is currently undertaking a Doctorate degree in the school of Multimedia Systems. His main research interests are in e-business and international business, especially in social and cultural issues and mobile communications.

Kevin Johnston was born in Umtata, Transkei, South Africa in 1953. He obtained a BSc from Rhodes University, a BSc (Honors) from the University of South Africa (UNISA), and an MCom from the University of Cape Town (UCT). Kevin is married with two daughters. Kevin has over 20 years of experience in the IT industry in Southern Africa, working for companies such as De Beers, Liberty Life and BoE. Kevin has spoken at IT conferences in Africa, Europe and the USA. He is currently a Senior Lecturer in Information Systems at UCT.

Jaroslav Král graduated in 1959 from the Faculty of Mathematics and Physics of the Charles University, Prague, Czech Republic. Since 1959, he has been working in computer science at the Czech Academy of Sciences, Czech Technical University, Masaryk U. Brno, and Charles University, Prague. His research interests were: random number generators and simulations, and hash methods, combinatorial problems connected with the problem of optimal program segmentation, formal language theory, parsing and compiler construction, and the development of process control systems. His present interests are the development of large information systems, software confederations, education of software experts and computational linguists. Jaroslav Král published more than 100 publications in international journals and at international conferences. Jaroslav Král took part (mainly as Project Leader) in several successful projects including macroprocessors, compilers, flexible manufacturing systems, and automated warehouse systems. Jaroslav Král is now a Full Professor at the Faculty of Mathematical Physics of Charles University Prague, and a Visiting Professor at the Faculty of Informatics of Masaryk University Brno, Czech Republic.

Yi-chen Lan is a Lecturer at the School of Computing and IT, the University of Western Sydney, Australia. He teaches Information Systems and Management courses in both undergraduate and graduate levels. Prior to that he worked in industries for five years, holding management responsibilities in the areas of information systems and quality assurance program in a multinational manufacturing company. His main areas of research are global transition process, global information systems management issues, and globalization framework development. He received his undergraduate and postgraduate degrees from the University of Western Sydney. His PhD research is enterprise transition to globalization.

Fernando José Barbin Laurindo holds graduate, MSc and PhD degrees in Production Engineering from the Polytechnic School of University of São Paulo, Brazil. He is also a graduate in law (University of São Paulo) and made Extension Course in Business Administration from Fundação Getúlio Vargas. His researches focus on Information Technology and Business Strategies, Information Technology Planning and Project Management. For 15 years he worked for companies in the manufacturing, financial and service sectors. He is Assistant Professor in the Department of Production Engineering, Polytechnic School - University of São Paulo - EPUSP (since 1997).

Wai K. Law is an Associate Professor of Management at the University of Guam. He earned a master's degree in Computer Science before more than ten years of teaching and research in integrated disciplines of Management Science, Operations Management and Logistics Management. His recent interests are in Information Resources Management and Business Strategy. He served many years on a university committee on Information Technology, and has successfully led the completion of various information projects.

Raymond Koon-Ying Li is a Senior Lecturer at Monash University, Australia. His current research interests include mobile agents, automatic essay scoring using LSA, virtual project office, and web-based project evaluation using AHP and Culture issues of e-business/v-business. His aim is to develop cost-effective business solutions using emerging technologies. For the last few years, Mr. Li has initiated a number of industrial collaborative research programs. Some of the successful multimedia intranet-based developments are: an induction program for Bristol Myers Squibb, competency testing for detective Training at the Victoria

Police; and a Just-in-Time training program for nurses at South Health Network in Melbourne. Besides teaching and research, Raymond also consults.

Marly Monteiro de Carvalho holds a Production Engineering degree (Engineering School of São Carlos - University of São Paulo). She holds an MSc and a PhD in Production Engineering from the Federal University of Santa Catarina. Her researches are focused on Project and Technology Management, Quality and Business Strategies. For several years, she was a Researcher at the Technological Research Institute of São Paulo State, Brazil (1992-2000). She is Assistant Professor in the Department of Production Engineering, Polytechnic School - University of São Paulo – EPUSP (since 1992).

Adekunle Okunoye is a doctoral Student at the Turku Center for Computer Science and University of Turku, Department of Information Technology, Finland. He holds BSc and MSc degrees in Computer Science. He is a member of the British Computer Society with about 10 years of practical experience. His research focuses on knowledge management, new information and communication technologies, globalization, and national development. To date, he has published in various conference proceedings and journals.

Alexander Osterwalder holds a master's degree in political science and business information systems. Currently he works as a Research and Teaching Assistant at the Business School of the University of Lausanne in Switzerland. He has published several papers on ICT-related business strategy and business models and ICT opportunities in developing countries. After co-founding Netfinance, a company active in education for online investors, Alexander has worked as a journalist for the Swiss business journal BILANZ. He is a managing editor of *Virtual Organization Net*. Furthermore, he works for the Summer University on Human Rights based in Geneva, Switzerland.

Anatália Saraiva Martins Ramos received her PhD in Production Engineering from Federal University of Rio de Janeiro, Brazil. She is currently Professor at Federal University of Rio Grande do Norte and a Researcher at CNPq (Brazilian National Science Foundation). Dr. Anatália Ramos has worked in scientific work evaluation committees for congresses and journals and has published over 30 articles in national and international congresses. She has already been awarded the Best Article award by the Information Systems area, given by the National Association of Graduate in Business Administration. Her current research interests include strategic use of information technology and impacts of Internet in organizations.

Mathias Rossi is PhD candidate at the Information Systems Department of the business school of the University of Lausanne (HEC), Switzerland, and holds a master's degree in political science and business information systems. He has teaching and research experience in the field of enterprise competency management. Before joining HEC, Mathias Rossi was Director of a firm active in human resources for the watch industry, has conducted research at the University of Lausanne, at the Ecole d'Etudes Sociales et Pédagogiques and has studied economics and statistics at the University of Economic Science in Budapest and at the University of Colchester. His research interests include theory and practice of competence-based organization and management, knowledge based architectures and systems, knowledge management, Internet, new technologies and developing countries. He has written journal articles on competence-based management and tools. He is co-editor of the

Revue Economique et Sociale, bulletin de la société d'études économiques et sociales. Mathias Rossi is the proud father of an adorable one-year-old daughter named Jessica.

Rahul Roy, PhD, is an Associate Professor with the Management Information Systems group of Indian Institute of Management Calcutta, India. He is currently visiting the Department of Management of University of Northern Iowa. Prof. Roy's teaching interest is in the areas of Systems Thinking & Business Simulation, Management Information Systems, Systems Analysis and Design and Software Project Management. His current research centers around modeling global diffusion of Internet and modeling organizational adoption of Information Technology, with particular emphasis on developing countries. His research has been published in *Communications of the ACM, European Journal of Operations Research, System Dynamics: An International Journal of Policy Modeling* and in a collected volume published by Kluwer Academic Publishers. Prof. Roy has also presented papers at the International Conference on Information Systems 01, International System Dynamics Conference. He is a member of the System Dynamics Society and serves on the editorial board of *System Dynamics: A Journal of Policy Modeling.*

Marcelo Schneck de Paula Pessôa holds graduate, MSc and PhD degrees in Electronic Engineering from the Polytechnic School of University of São Paulo, Brazil. His research focuses on Information Technology, Software Quality and Software Process Development. For several years, he has been a consultant in the IT arena and also is an Assistant Professor and the current Head of the Department of Production Engineering, Polytechnic School - University of São Paulo - EPUSP.

Ian M. Sims holds MAcc (UWA), BBus (Cowan), CPA, and FAIPMM degrees. Mr. Sims has considerable experience at a senior level in logistics, supply management and financial information systems in the public sector (civil and military), the mining industry and manufacturing and has lectured for many years in Accounting Information Systems at universities in Australia and Asia. His experience has been gained in a variety of line management, consulting and academic roles and has managed complex information systems in both private sector and university environments. This combination of skills, together with his formal qualifications as a Certified Practicing Accountant, gives him a strong background in implementation of change in logistics and financial information systems environments and provides the foundation for his current role as IT coach and trainer to senior executives, management teams and professional accountants.

Adrie Stander is currently a Senior Lecturer in Information Systems at the University of Cape Town, South Africa. He obtained BSc degrees in Information Systems and Psychology from the University of South Africa and an MTech from Cape Technikon. Adrie has over 20 years experience in the South IT industry. He has a keen interest in the human side of IT and has done research in many related areas such as mobile usability, cultural aspects of user interfaces and gender issues in the IT industry. Adrie has spoken at conferences in Africa, Europe and the USA.

Craig Standing has an international reputation in the field of Management Information Systems. He has published widely in leading journals and presented his work at conferences worldwide. He is a Consultant to local and international companies in the private and public sector, specializing in electronic commerce and knowledge management. Dr. Standing completed a Master of Science in Computation at the University of Manchester Institute of Science and Technology, and a Doctor of Philosophy at the University of Western Australia. He is a member of the British Computer Society and the Australian Computer Society. He is currently an Associate Professor in the School of Management Information Systems at Edith Cowan University in Western Australia.

Monideepa Tarafdar, PhD, is Assistant Professor at the Graduate Programs in IT and IS at the University of St. Thomas, St. Paul, Minnesota, USA. Her current research and teaching interests lie in the areas of Strategic Information Systems Management, Management of IT, Enterprise Systems and Organizational Aspects of IS. Her teaching has been in the areas of Data Management, MIS, and E-Commerce. Her research has appeared or is forthcoming in *Journal of Information Technology Cases* and *Applications and System Dynamics: An International Journal of Policy Modeling*.

During the 1990's, **Benedict Tootell** completed a Bachelor of Arts (Honors) and a Master of Business Administration (International Business) at Monash University, Iran. He spent five years working in marketing and market research positions with a number of multinational companies, before returning to study in 2001. In mid 2001, he completed a Graduate Certificate in Information Management and Systems and has recently completed a master's in Information Technology at Monash University. He has spent the past year developing interactive training applications for the Victoria Police Force. He is the Founder of Desktop Multimedia, a company specializing in the design and development of multimedia training applications.

Nata van der Merwe is currently a Lecturer in the Department of Information Systems at the University of Cape Town, South Africa. She has qualifications in Linguistics, Education and Information Technology, with her highest qualification being an MA from the University of Stellenbosch, South Africa. Nata has 15 years experience in the IT Industry and IT-related academic environments. She is currently leading a study of the issues surrounding the retention of women in the IT industry.

Michal Žemlička is an Assistant Professor at the Faculty of Mathematics and Physics of Charles University, Prague. He graduated in 1996. His current research interests are extensible compilers, theory of parsing, the design of large software systems, data structures, and computational linguistics.

Sajjad Zahir is a Professor of Management in the area of Decision Sciences and Information Systems at the University of Lethbridge, Canada. He received his doctorate degree from the University of Oregon, Eugene, USA. His current research interests are in Multicriteria Decision Models, Decision Support Systems and Intelligent Systems and the Internet technologies. He has published in the *European Journal of Operational Research, Canadian Journal of Administrative Sciences, Journal of the Operational Research Society, Journal of American Society for Information Science, International Journal of Information Technology and Decision Making, Internet Research: Electronic Networking Applications and Policy, Journal of Computer and Information Systems, International Journal of Operations and Quantitative Management, INFOR*, and also in several physics journals.

Index

International Journal of IT Standards & Standardization Research(JITSR)

NEW!   **NEW!**

The International Source for Advances in IT Standards and Standardization Research

ISSN:	1539-3062
eISSN:	1539-3054

Subscription: Annual fee per volume (2 issues):
Individual US $85
Institutional US $145

Editor: Kai Jakobs
Technical University
of Aachen, Germany

Mission

The primary mission of the *International Journal of IT Standards & Standardization Research* is to publish research findings to advance knowledge and research in all aspects of IT standards and standardization in modern organizations. Furthermore, the *International Journal of IT Standards & Standardization Research* will be considered as an authoritative source and information outlet for the diverse community of IT standards researchers. JITSR is targeted towards researchers, scholars, policymakers, IT managers, and IT standards associations and organizations.

Coverage

JITSR will include contributions from disciplines in computer science, information systems, management, business, social sciences, economics, engineering, political science, and communications. Potential topics include: technological innovation and standardization; standards for information infrastructures; standardization and economic development; open source and standardization; intellectual property rights; economics of standardization; emerging roles of standards organizations and consortia; conformity assessment; standards strategies; standardization and regulation; standardization in the public sphere; standardization in public policy; tools and services related to standardiztion; and other relevant issues related to standards and standardization.

For subscription information, contact:

Idea Group Publishing
701 E Chocolate Ave., Ste 200
Hershey PA 17033-1240, USA
cust@idea-group.com
www.idea-group.com

For paper submission information:

Dr. Kai Jakobs
Technical University of Aachen, Germany
Kai.Jakobs@i4mail.informatik.rwth-aachen.de